D1070386

New Developments and Techniques
in Structural Equation Modeling

NEW DEVELOPMENTS AND TECHNIQUES IN STRUCTURAL EQUATION MODELING

By

George A. Marcoulides
California State University at Fullerton

and

Randall E. Schumacker
University of North Texas

Lawrence Erlbaum Associates, Publishers
Mahwah, New Jersey   London

Lawrence Erlbaum Associates, Inc., Publishers
10 Industrial Avenue
Mahwah, NJ 07430

Cover design by Kathryn Houghtaling Lacey

Library of Congress Cataloging-in-Publication Data

Marcoulides, George A.
  New developments and techniques in structural equation modeling / by George A.
Marcoulides and Randall E. Schumacker.
    p. cm.
  Includes bibliographical references and index.
  ISBN 0-8058-3593-8 (acid-free paper)
    1. Multivariate analysis.   2. Social sciences—Statistical methods.   I. Schumacker,
Randall E. II. Title.

QA278.M359 2001
519.5'35—dc21   00-054359

Printed in the United States of America
10 9 8 7 6 5 4 3 2 1

Contents

Preface

A number of years ago we published an edited volume that introduced the latest issues and techniques within the field of structural equation modeling (SEM). The volume received widespread attention as "a wonderful addition to the literature on SEM" and "a state-of-the-art communication from the frontiers of structural modeling." But since new developments in the field of SEM continue to propagate at an incredible rate, we felt the need to collaborate on another edition that would reflect the progress that has been made in the past few years.

The purpose of this new edited volume is to introduce the latest developments and techniques in the SEM field. The goal is to provide an understandable working knowledge of the latest developments in SEM with a minimum of mathematical proofs. By focusing primarily on the application of each SEM technique with example cases and situations, we hope that the chapters are both enlightening and instructional. Each chapter assumes that the reader has already mastered the equivalent of a multivariate statistics course that included coverage of most basic SEM techniques. Anyone with a limited background in SEM can consult several other introductory books on SEM (e.g., Byrne, 1998; Schumacker & Lomax, 1996; Raykov & Marcoulides, 2000) to familiarize themselves with the various issues in the application of these modeling techniques.

Each chapter in this volume contains an up-to-date description of a new development or technique in SEM and is often written by the author(s) who originally proposed the model or contributed substantially to its development. Each chapter also provides complete references to the pertinent literature on the topic. The decision regarding the selection and the organization of the chapters for this volume was quite challenging. Obviously, within a single edited volume, only a limited number of topics could be addressed. In the end, the choice of the material was governed by our own beliefs (and often heated discussions) concerning what are currently the most important new developments and techniques within the SEM field. The final topics selected for this volume include latent variable mixture modeling, models for dealing with nonstandard and noncompliance samples, multilevel modeling, interaction modeling, new developments in the analysis of growth curve and longitudinal data, specification searches, item parceling, and equivalent models.

Muthén in Chapter 1 provides an overview of latent variable mixture modeling. Latent variable mixture modeling includes models with both categorical and continuous latent variables. Models that include a categorical latent variable are used to represent latent classes or mixtures in which group membership is not known but inferred from observed data. Conventional latent class, structural equation, and growth models are also extended and integrated into a general modeling framework. Model specifications and output using the Mplus program are provided throughout the chapter. In addition, Mplus input specifications for the analyses considered in the chapter are made available through a World Wide Web browser from http://www.statmodel.com/.

In Chapter 2, Yuan and Bentler examine multi-sample SEM modeling in what they refer to as nonstandard samples. The use of the term nonstandard samples is meant to include realistic data collection situations in which samples with missing data, nonnormal data and data with outliers are usually obtained. Since the current literature on multi-sample models of sample means and covariance matrices is based on either normal theory maximum likelihood or generalized least squares, there are some obvious limitations to the use of these approaches with nonstandard samples. This chapter attempts to offer a unified treatment of methods for estimating models of means and covariances in situations where nonstandard samples are encountered. Software examples for handling missing data, outliers, and nonnormal data are available through a World Wide Web browser from http://www.mvsoft.com/.

In Chapter 3, Jo and Muthén examine the problem of estimating treatment effects in design situations where participants do not always comply with a given treatment assignment. By looking at compliance status as a categorical latent variable, Jo and Muthén demonstrate how to deal with the problem from a broader SEM framework. Using data from three different studies (a) the Job Search Intervention study for unemployed workers, (b) the Study of Vitamin Supplement Effect on Survival Rates in young children, and (c) The Johns Hopkins Public School Preventive Intervention Study, Jo and Muthén demonstrate how the categorical latent variable approach can tackle compliance information in realistic situations. Generalizations of the approach to other modeling situations are also discussed and sample Mplus programs are provided in an appendix.

Multilevel modeling is an approach that can be used to analyze hierarchical (or clustered) data. In Chapter 4, Heck provides an introduction to multilevel modeling techniques using a SEM approach. Conceptual and methodological issues related to multilevel models are examined and general overviews of the mathematical details are provided. Step-by-step illustrations are also provided for examining several models such as multilevel confirmatory factor analysis, multilevel path analysis, and multilevel models with latent variables. Model specifications and output using the Mplus program are provided throughout the chapter.

In Chapter 5, Jedidi and Ansari extend the discussion of multilevel modeling in the previous chapter and describe procedures for hierarchical Bayesian inference of multilevel structural equation models. In particular, they illustrate how Markov Chain Monte Carlo procedures like Gibbs sampling and Metropolis-Hastings methods can be used to perform Bayesian inference, model checking, and model comparison without the need for multidimensional numerical integration. Using a customer satisfaction data set involving measurements on satisfaction, expectation disconfirmation, and performance variable, Jedidi and Ansari demonstrate the proposed estimation method and compare it to traditional multilevel methods.

Models with interaction and nonlinear effects are often encountered in the social and behavioral sciences. Kenny and Judd (1984) formulated the first nonlinear SEM model using a multiple indicant product approach. Several extensions for estimating and testing such models have been proposed in the literature (for a complete exposition on interaction and nonlinear effects in SEM, see the edited volume by Schumacker & Marcoulides, 1998). An important extension provided by Jöreskog and Yang in 1996 pointed out problems and issues related to modeling interaction effects with multiple indicant products and showed that only one product variable is needed to identify all the parameters of the model. Because one of the implications of using product variables turns out to be nonnormality, Yang-Jonsson (1997) examined the estimation of the Kenny and Judd model with three estimation methods: (i) maximum likelihood, (ii) weighted least squares, and (iii) weighted least squares on the augmented moment matrix. Yang-Jonsson found that maximum likelihood works well for samples with 400 to 3200 observations. However, her results revealed that asymptotic standard errors and chi-squares of the estimates are incorrectly computed. Using the Satorra-Bentler type scaling corrections, Yang-Wallentin and Jöreskog in Chapter 6 illustrate how both asymptotic standard error and chi-squares of estimates in interaction models can be corrected for nonnormality. Interaction examples in the LISREL8.3 release are available through a World Wide Web browser at http://www.ssicentral.com/.

In Chapter 7, Duncan, Li, Duncan, Yang-Wallentin, Acock, and Hops consider the analysis of interaction effects in the context of latent growth curve modeling. Latent growth curve models (also referred to as latent change analysis models) allow researchers to investigate individual (intraindividual) development across time as well as between individual (interindividual) differences and similarities in change patterns (growth or decline) across time. However, to date, latent growth curve models have predominantly been used to examine linear effects. But researchers in the social and behavioral must often deal with complex models that involve interaction effects. As such, methods that permit one to consider interaction between dynamic, longitudinal change variables are essential to ensuring a better understanding of patterns of change over time. Using the Jöreskog and Yang SEM interaction approach as a basis, Duncan et al extend the method to latent growth curve models.

In Chapter 8, Hamagami and McArdle examine how missing patterns of observations influence results obtained from longitudinal data analyses and examine whether the bivariate dual change score model can accurately recover characteristics of the data. Using SEM methodology, Hamagami and McArdle illustrate that characteristics of linear dynamic systems can be accurately evaluated. Generalizations of the approach to various incomplete data situations are examined via simulation and a pseudo-code for generating a system of time series based on the model is provided in an appendix.

The modification of an initially specified SEM model in order to improve data-to-model fit has been termed a specification search. Despite the fact that the SEM literature has demonstrated that specification errors "can have serious consequences" and that one should "attempt to correct these errors," no optimal procedure or single strategy for conducting specification searches has been defined. Marcoulides and Drezner in Chapter 9 introduce a genetic algorithm as an alternative specification search approach for use in SEM. Using simple examples, an overview of genetic algorithms is provided along with a demonstration of an actual SEM specification search.

Item parcels are quite common in SEM models. The practice of item parceling generally involves summing or averaging together two or more items and using the result as the basic unit of analysis in the SEM model. Although the practice appears to have originated more than 30 years ago, there is still considerable controversy surrounding the use of item parcels; perhaps the use of item parcels depends on the unidimensionality of the items being summed or averaged together. In Chapter 10, Bandalos and Finney provide an extensive coverage of the topic of item parceling in SEM models and warn how uninformed use of item parcels may actually result in a poorer understanding of the relationships among sets of items.

The problem of equivalent models has been a concern since the earliest developmental stages of SEM. Equivalent models are those that provide identical statistical fit to the data as a hypothesized model but may imply very different substantive interpretations of the data. In the final chapter, Raykov and Penev provide an overview of problems associated with testing equivalent models and examine how individual case residuals may be useful for selecting between some equivalent models. Using examples in which individual case residuals are defined in terms of projections of subject raw data upon a model-generated space and provide additional fit indices, Raykov and Penev conclude that individual residuals are worthy adjuncts to substantive theories and offer considerations for ruling out some equivalent models. Model specifications using the SAS system and proof of the various propositions are provided in an appendix.

This volume could not have been completed without the assistance and support provided by many individuals. First, we would like to thank all the contributors for their time and effort in preparing chapters for this volume. They all provided excellent chapters and worked diligently through the various publication stages. Our association with the *Structural Equation Modeling* journal has been invaluable in helping us to keep informed about new developments in theory and mathematical procedures relevant to SEM, and for this we wish to thank the Editorial Board, the ad hoc reviewers, and the many contributors to the journal. We are also greatly indebted to Larry Erlbaum for the encouragement and support that facilitated this work and other similar works. Thanks are also due to all the wonderful people on the editorial staff at Lawrence Erlbaum Associates for their assistance and support in putting together this volume. Finally, we thank our families for their love and for continually enduring a seemingly endless list of projects.

George A. Marcoulides
Randall E. Schumacker

About the Authors

Alan C. Acock is Professor and Chair of Human Development and Family Studies at Oregon State University. He received his Ph.D. in Sociology from Washington State University. Structural equation modeling is his primary area of statistical research. His publications have appeared in the *American Sociological Review, Structural Equation Modeling, Multivariate Behavioral Research,* and *Quantity and Quality.* His substantive research focuses on intergenerational influence as well as the effects of family structure. He has received the Rueben Hill Award for Outstanding Contribution to Family Theory and Research. (Email: alan.acock@orst.edu)

Asim Ansari is an associate professor at the Columbia Business School, Columbia University. He received his Ph.D. from New York University. His research focuses on applying Bayesian methods for customer relationship management, cross-selling, mass customization and personalization over the Internet. He is also interested in the analytical modeling of optimal product positioning and pricing decisions. His publications have appeared in such journals as the *Journal of Marketing Research, Marketing Science, Journal of Consumer Research, Psychometrika,* and *Marketing Letters.* (Email: maa48@columbia.edu)

Deborah L. Bandalos is an associate professor and director of the program in Quantitative and Qualitative Methods in Education at the University of Nebraska, Lincoln where she teaches courses in structural equation modeling, multiple regression, and educational and psychological measurement. Her main research interests are in the applications of structural equation modeling to scale development and in understanding and assessing how students learn statistical material. (Email: dbandalos@unl.edu)

Peter M. Bentler has published widely in personality, attitudes, drug abuse, health, sexuality, and related psychological topics, but in recent years he has concentrated primarily on methodology, psychometrics, and statistics. He is Professor and Chair of the Department of Psychology, and Professor of Statistics, at the University of California, Los Angeles, and is a past president of the Society of Multivariate Experimental Psychology, the Psychometric Society, and the Division of Evaluation, Measurement, and Statistics of the American Psychological Association. (Email: bentler@psych.ucla.edu)

Zvi Drezner is Professor of Management Science at California State University, Fullerton. He received his B.Sc. in Mathematics and Ph.D. in Computer Science from the Technion, Israel Institute of Technology. His research interests are in location theory and computational statistics. He has published over 150 articles in such journals as *Operations Research, Management Science, IIE Transactions,* and *Naval Research Logistics.* (Email: zdrezner@fullerton.edu)

Susan C. Duncan received a doctorate in physical education in 1992 from the University of Oregon. She is currently a research scientist at Oregon Research Institute and at the Oregon Center for Applied Science in Eugene, Oregon. Duncan is a productive scientist and author, known for her work focusing on substantive, statistical, and methodological issues related to substance use, problem behaviors, and health promoting behaviors among adolescents. (Email: susand@ori.org)

Terry E. Duncan earned a Ph.D. in physical education and measurement and statistics in 1989 from the University of Oregon. He is currently a research scientist at Oregon Research Institute and at the Oregon Center for Applied Science in Eugene, Oregon. Duncan is an active and distinguished researcher, author, reviewer, and consultant with expertise in statistical methods for longitudinal designs, structural equation modeling, approaches for the analysis of missing data, generalized linear model, the etiology of substance use and development, and exercise and health behavior. (Email: terryd@ori.org)

Sara J. Finney is a doctoral candidate in the Quantitative and Qualitative Methods in Education Program at the University of Nebraska, Lincoln. She will begin work as an assistant professor at James Madison University in the spring semester of 2001 where she will teach structural equation modeling and multivariate statistics. Her main interests are in the application of structural equation models to assess validity and in the development of statistics self-efficacy measures. (Email: sfinney@unl.edu)

Fumiaki Hamagami is a research associate with the Department of Psychology at the University of Virginia. His research interests are in combining mathematical modeling to longitudinal data analysis, especially linear and nonlinear dynamic system approaches to describing change phenomena. He also serves as a co-principal investigator in the National Growth and Change Study funded by the National Institute of Aging. Together with Dr. McArdle he is developing a World Wide Web site for longitudinal studies on the Wechsler Adult Intelligence Scale and other psycho-cognitive batteries. (Email: fh3s@cms.mail.virginia.edu)

Ronald H. Heck is Professor of Educational Administration and Policy at the University of Hawaii at Manoa. His professional interests include the application of modeling techniques to studying organizations and educational policy. Recent publications include (with Scott L. Thomas) *An Introduction to Multilevel Modeling Techniques.* Mahwah, NJ: Lawrence Erlbaum. (Email: rheck@hawaii.edu)

Hyman Hops is a senior research scientist at the Oregon Research Institute. He has been conducting research on children, adolescents and families for over 30 years in various settings including schools, homes, and laboratories. His studies have included both treatment and descriptive-epidemiologic varieties. He is currently involved in several longitudinal studies examining factors related to competent functioning as well as problem behaviors from elementary school to young adulthood. A special focus has been on the intergenerational transmission of these behaviors across two and soon to be three generations. (Email: hymanh@ori.org)

Kamel Jedidi is Professor of Marketing at the Graduate School of Business, Columbia University. He holds a bachelor's degree in Economics from the Faculte' des Sciences Economiques de Tunis, Tunisia and Masters and Ph.D. degrees in Marketing from the Wharton School, University of Pennsylvania. His most recent publications have appeared in the *Journal of Marketing Research, Marketing Science,* the *International Journal of Research in Marketing, Psychometrika,* and the *Journal of Classification.* His methodological interests lie in multidimensional scaling, classification, structural equation modeling, and Bayesian and finite-mixture models. His substantive research interests include product design and positioning, diffusion of innovations, market segmentation, and the long-term impact of advertising and promotions. He was awarded the 1998 *IJRM* Best Article Award and the Marketing Science Institute 2000 Best Paper Award. (Email: kj7@columbia.edu)

Booil Jo completed her Ph.D. in Applied Statistics and Psychometrics at the Graduate School of Education and Information Studies at the University of California, Los Angeles. Her primary area of research is latent variable modeling and causal modeling. After she finished her dissertation in 1998, she has continued her research as a postdoctoral researcher at UCLA. Her current research is focused on developing statistical models that can provide practical guidelines in dealing with complications in randomized intervention studies. Such topics include noncompliance, program implementation, attrition, and clustering. (Email: booil@ucla.edu)

Fan Yang-Wallentin received her Ph.D. in Statistics at Uppsala University in 1997. She is currently a research associate in the Department of Information Science, Division of Statistics at Uppsala University and senior lecturer in Statistics at the University of Gävle. Her research interests are in the areas of measurement, factor analysis, and structural equation modeling, especially nonlinear structural equation modeling. (Email: fan.yang@dis.uu.se)

Karl G. Jöreskog is Professor of Multivariate Statistical Analysis at Uppsala University, Sweden. His main interests are in the theory and applications of structural equation models and other types of multivariate analysis, particularly their applications in the social and behavioral sciences. He is co-author of *LISREL 7—A Guide to the Program and Applications* published by SPSS in 1989, and *LISREL 8—Structural Equation Modeling With the SIMPLIS Command Language,* published by SSI in 1993. (Email: karl.joreskog@dis.uu.se)

Fuzhong Li received a Ph.D. in exercise and sport science from Oregon State University and is currently a research scientist at Oregon Research Institute in Eugene, Oregon. His main research interests are in older adult health behaviors, with a particular focus on issues of disease prevention, self-perceptions, and various aspects of physical activity intervention and prevention. His methodological research interests include structural equation modeling. (Email: fuzhongl@ori.org)

George A. Marcoulides is Professor of Statistics at California State University at Fullerton and Adjunct Professor at the University of California at Irvine. He is currently Editor of the Quantitative Methodology Book Series, Editor of the *Structural Equation Modeling* journal, and on the editorial board of several other measurement and statistics journals. His contributions have received Best Paper Awards from the Academy of Management and the Decision Sciences Institute. He is the recipient of the 1991 UCEA William J. Davis Memorial Award for outstanding scholarship. His research interests include generalizability theory and structural equation modeling. (Email: gmarcoulides@fullerton.edu)

John J. McArdle is Professor of Psychology at the University of Virginia. He is a principal investigator of the National Growth and Change Study funded by the National Institute of Aging, investigating growth and change in human cognitive aging. His research interests center around the development of longitudinal designs, methodology, and modeling. He is a past president of the Society of Multivariate Experimental Psychology and of the Federation of Behavioral, Psychological, & Cognitive Science. (Email: jjm@virginia.edu)

Bengt O. Muthén is Professor in the Graduate School of Education and Information Studies at the University of California, Los Angeles. He received his Ph.D. in Statistics from Uppsala University, Sweden. He was the 1988–89 President of the Psychometric Society. He currently has an Independent Scientist

Award from the National Institute of Health for methodology development in the alcohol field. He is one of the developers of the Mplus computer program, which implements many of his statistical procedures. His research interests focus on the development of applied statistical methodology in education and public health. Education applications concern achievement development while public health applications involve developmental studies in epidemiology and psychology. Methodological areas include latent variable modeling, analysis of individual differences in longitudinal data, preventive intervention studies, analysis of categorical data, multilevel modeling, and the development of statistical software. (Email: bmuthen@ucla.edu)

Spiridon Penev is Senior Lecturer of Statistics with the Department of Statistics at the University of New South Wales, in Sydney, Australia. He obtained his Ph.D. from the Department of Mathematics, at Humbolt University in Berlin, Germany. His research and teaching interests are in statistical modeling, specifically in wavelet methods in statistics, structural equation models, and asymptotic methods of statistical inferences. (Email: spiro@maths.unsw.edu.au)

Tenko Raykov is a Professor of Quantitative Psychology and Psychometrics at the Department of Psychology of Fordham University, New York. His research interests are in the area of structural equation modeling, measurement, and multivariate statistics. Recent publications include (with George A. Marcoulides) *A First Course in Structural Equation Modeling,* Mahwah, NJ: Lawrence Erlbaum. (Email: raykov@murray.fordham.edu)

Randall E. Schumaker is Professor of Educational Research at the University of North Texas and Professor of Medical Education at the University of North Texas Health Science Center. He was founder and past editor of the *Structural Equation Modeling* journal (1994–1998), co-author of *A Beginner's Guide to Structural Equation Modeling* (with Richard G. Lomax), and coeditor of *Advanced Structural Equation Modeling: Issues and Techniques* and *Interaction and Nonlinear Effects in Structural Equation Modeling* (both with George A. Marcoulides). In 1996 he received an outstanding scholar award at UNT. He currently serves on the editorial board of several journals and pursues his research interests in structural equation modeling, Rasch measurement, and medical education. (Email:rschumaker@unt.edu)

Ke-Hai Yuan is Assistant Professor of Psychology at the University of North Texas. His current research on covariance structure analysis focuses on nonnormal data, missing data, and data with outliers. His other research interests include bootstrap and cross-validation, estimating equations, item response theory, meta-analysis and multilevel modeling. (Email: kyuan@unt.edu)

New Developments and Techniques
in Structural Equation Modeling

1

Latent Variable Mixture Modeling

Bengt O. Muthén
University of California, Los Angeles

This chapter discusses models with latent variables that are continuous and/or categorical. It also gives an overview of modeling issues related to cross-sectional analysis using latent class models, modeling of longitudinal data using latent class models, and modeling of longitudinal data using a combination of continuous and categorical latent variables (growth mixture models). A series of examples are presented. The analyses are carried out within a general latent variable modeling framework shown in the appendix using the Mplus program (Muthén & Muthén, 1998). Mplus input specifications for these analyses can be obtained from www.statmodel.com. To introduce the analyses, a brief overview of modeling ideas is presented in Figs. 1.1 to 1.3.

The top left part of Fig. 1.1 shows three distributions for a continuous outcome variable y. The idea is that the data consist of different groups of individuals, but the group membership is not observed. The two broken curves represent the distribution

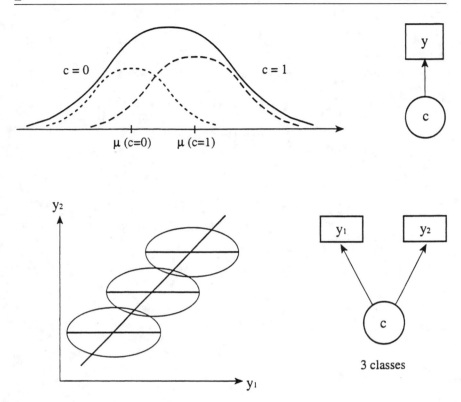

FIG. 1.1.   Mixture modeling.

of y for two latent classes, $c = 0$ and $c = 1$, which have different means. These two distributions are not observed, but only the mixture of the two, shown by the solid curve. There are many examples of such unobserved heterogeneity. An example often used in the statistic literature considers the length of fish in a stream. The analysis task is to find out how many cohorts of fish there are in the stream. In Fig. 1.1, there are two cohorts of fish, where the older fishes are longer. Alcohol researchers may consider brain wave responses to stimuli, measuring a P300 wave amplitude that is assumed to differ between individuals susceptible to alcohol dependence versus those who are not, with the interest in classifying individuals. Reading researchers may consider a latent class corresponding to reading disability and a class of normal readers with the interest in estimating the mean difference and classifying individuals as early as possible. The top right part shows the corresponding path diagram, using c to denote the latent categorical variable with two classes.

The bottom left part of Fig. 1.1 shows unobserved heterogeneity with respect to two continuous outcomes, y_1 and y_2. The line indicates a strong relationship between the outcomes, but this relationship is due to mixing three different classes of individuals, each having unrelated outcomes. The corresponding path diagram is shown to the right, viewing y_1 and y_2 as indicators of the latent categorical variable c. This type of modeling is referred to as *latent profile analysis* or *latent class analysis* when the outcomes are categorical. The modeling has features similar to factor analysis in that it is assumed that a latent variable accounts for the association between the outcomes. This is also referred to as a conditional independence assumption, with the idea that if a sufficient number of classes is introduced, the independence is more and more likely to hold.

There is, however, a more profound aspect of the latent profile/class model that has interesting possibilities for model generalizations. This is that each latent class has different parameter values and possibly a different model. In latent profile/class analysis, the model is the same across classes—namely, an independence model. The parameter values differ across classes. For latent profile analysis, the mean for each outcome variable changes over classes, and in latent class analysis with binary outcomes, the probability of each outcome variable changes over classes. More complex class-specific models and changes in parameter values across classes are, however, possible. This realization leads to a huge set of new modeling opportunities indicated in Figs. 1.2 and 1.3.

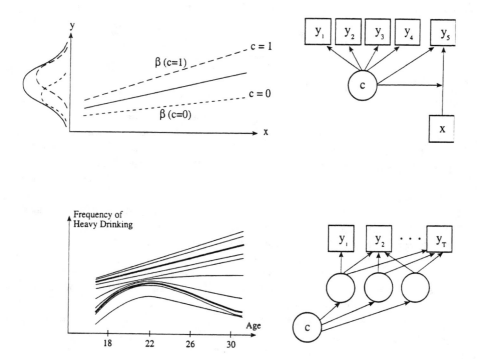

FIG. 1.2.   Mixture modeling.

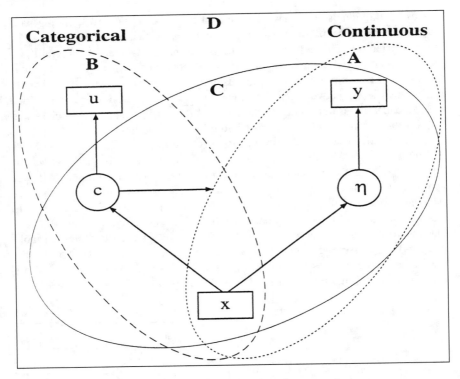

FIG. 1.3.   General modeling framework.

The top part of Fig. 1.2 shows a regression analysis with unobserved hetero-geneity. The solid line gives the regression for the mixture, which is not correct for either class. The right part of the picture shows a generalization of the latent profile/class modeling, where y_1-y_4 are class indicators, but where the key inter-est is in capturing the variation across class in the regression of y_5 on x. Here the arrow from c to y_5 indicates that the intercept in y_5 differs across classes, where-as the arrow from c to the arrow from x to y_5 indicates that the slope in the regres-sion differs across classes. In this way, the most important class variation in parameter values is for the regression model, and the latent profile part is merely a vehicle for making it easier to identify the classes.

The bottom part of Fig. 1.2 shows latent variable modeling where different classes have different growth models. An example is development of the fre-quency of heavy drinking, ages 18 to 30. The general population is likely to be quite heterogeneous with respect to this development. The left part of the figure shows two average growth curves as solid curves. A normative class shows a typ-ical increase in this behavior in the early 20s, with a subsequent decline.

However, less prevalent classes are present, such as the class of individuals whose heavy drinking does not decline in their late 20s. Within each class, there is further heterogeneity as indicated by the thinner curves. The path diagram on the right shows three continuous latent variables corresponding to the three growth factors of quadratic growth influencing the repeated measures on y. The arrows from the categorical latent variable c to these growth factors indicate that their means vary across the latent classes as seen in the graph on the left.

The modeling ideas in Figs. 1.1 and 1.2 may be summarized as in Fig. 1.3. Here, the modeling framework labeled D is the Mplus framework given in the appendix. A fuller discussion of this framework with references is given in Muthén (in press). Three different ellipses represent various special cases of the general framework.

On the right, an ellipse labeled A represents a framework where the latent variables η are continuous, including exploratory and confirmatory factor analysis, structural equation modeling (SEM), and latent growth curve modeling. This is the framework of conventional SEM as it has been practiced for the last couple of decades, using software such as AMOS, EQS, and LISREL.

On the left, an ellipse labeled B represents a framework where the latent variables c are categorical, including latent class analysis with or without covariates. Typically in the past, modeling using Framework B has been separate from modeling in Framework A.

The ellipse labeled C represents a framework where a combination of categorical and continuous latent variables is used. This includes latent profile analysis and mixture cluster analysis, both excluding continuous latent variables. Complier-average causal effect estimation in randomized trials is another application, discussed by Jo

TABLE 1.1
Summary of Techniques Using Latent Classes

Class	Outcome/ Indicator Scale	Number of Time Points	Number of Outcomes/ Time Points	Within-Class Variation
LCA	Categorical (u)	Single	Multiple	No
LPA	Continuous (y)	Single	Multiple	No
LCGA	Categorical (u) Continuous (y)	Multiple	Single	No
LTA	Categorical (u)	Multiple	Multiple	No
GMM	Continuous (y)	Multiple	Single Multiple	Yes
GGMM	Categorical (u) Continuous (y)	Multiple	Single Multiple	Yes

LCA – latent class analysis, LPA – latent profile analysis, LCGA – latent class growth analysis, LTA – latent transition analysis, GMM – growth mixture modeling, GGMM – general growth mixture modeling.

and Muthén (chap. 3, this volume). Growth mixture modeling is an example where both categorical and continuous latent variables are used.

The square labeled D represents the general framework, adding direct indicators u for the categorical latent variables.

Because latent variable modeling with categorical latent variables is an emerging methodology, the summary of techniques using latent classes given in Table 1.1 may be useful. The techniques are defined by the characteristics given in the three columns. Here, LCA and LTA fall into Framework B, LPA falls into Framework C, LCGA falls into Framework B or C, GMM falls into Framework C, and GGMM falls into Framework D.

LATENT CLASS ANALYSIS

Latent class analysis (LCA) was introduced by Lazarsfeld and Henry (1968), Goodman (1974), Clogg (1995), and others. The setting is cross-sectional data with multiple items measuring a construct represented as a latent class variable. The aims are to identify items that indicate classes well, estimate class probabilities, relate class probabilities to covariates, and classify individuals into classes.

Consider the LCA model for the special case of binary outcomes u. Letting the categorical latent variable c have K classes ($c = k$; $k = 1, 2, \ldots, K$), the marginal probability for item $u_j = 1$ is

$$P(u_j = 1) = \sum_{k=1}^{K} P(c = k)\, P(u_j = 1 \mid c = k), \tag{1}$$

while the joint probability of all us, assuming conditional independence, is

$$P(u_1, u_2, \ldots, u_r) = \sum_{k=1}^{K} P(c = k)\, P(u_1 \mid c = k) P(u_2 = 1 \mid c = k) \ldots P(u_r = 1 \mid c = k). \tag{2}$$

There are two types of parameters—the conditional item probabilities for each class and the class probabilities. In the Mplus framework, LCA parameters are expressed in logit form, where

$$P = \frac{1}{1 + e^{-L}}, \tag{3}$$

$$L = \text{logit}[P] = \ln[P/(1 - P)], \tag{4}$$

for example, $L = 0$ gives $P = 0.50$, $L = -1$ gives $P = 0.27$, $L = 1$ gives $P = 0.73$, $L = -3$ gives $P = 0.05$, and $L = -10$ gives $P = 0.00005$.

LCA Estimation and Testing

A by-product of LCA is estimated class probabilities for each individual, analogous to factor scores in factor analysis. These are estimates of

$$P(c = k \mid u_1, u_2, \ldots, u_r) = \frac{P(c = k)P(u_1 \mid c = k)P(u_2 \mid c = k)\ldots P(u_r \mid c = k)}{P(u_1, u_2, \ldots, u_r)}. \quad (5)$$

Note that each individual is allowed fractional class membership and may have nonzero values for several classes.

In Mplus, parameters are estimated by maximum-likelihood estimation via the EM algorithm, where c is seen as missing data. The EM algorithm maximizes the expected complete-data log likelihood conditional on $(u_{i1}, u_{i2}, \ldots, u_{ir})$ with respect to the parameters. The E step computes $E(c_i \mid u_{i1}, u_{i2}, \ldots, u_{ir})$ as the posterior probability for each class and $E(c_i\, u_{ij} \mid u_{i1}, u_{i2}, \ldots, u_{ir})$ for each class and u_j. The M step estimates $P(u_j \mid c_k)$ and $P(c_k)$ parameters by regression and summation over individual posterior probabilities, respectively. Multiple starting values are strongly recommended because the likelihood may have several different local maxima.

As an overall test, the likelihood-ratio χ^2 with H_1 as the unrestricted multinomial may be used, although with many items the chi-square approximation is poor due to small cell sizes. Models with different number of classes can be compared using the Bayesian information criterion (Schwartz, 1978)

$$BIC = -2 \log L + r \ln n, \quad (6)$$

where r is the number of free parameters in the model. A low BIC value indicates a better fitting model.

LCA of Alcohol Dependence

Consider the example in Table 1.2, where in the National Longitudinal Survey of Youth (NLSY), nine diagnostic criteria for alcoholism were analyzed in a sample of 8,313 young adults (Muthén & Muthén, 1995). A three-class solution fit well as measured by the chi-square test against the unrestricted multinomial. In this solution, Class 1 is the most prevalent, with 75% showing low probabilities of endorsing the criteria. Class 2 has 21% of the individuals and has high probabilities for Larger and Major Role-Hazard, having to do with drinking larger amounts than planned and drinking while driving. Class 3 has 3% and has high probabilities for most criteria. Loosely speaking, one may think of Class 3 as an alcohol dependence class, Class 2 as an alcohol abuse class, and Class 1 as a problem-free class.

In this application, the classes appear to be ordered in the sense that the item probabilities increase from Class 1 to Class 2 to Class 3. However, this is not always the case in LCA. (For an example with unordered classes for antisocial

TABLE 1.2
NLSY 1989: Latent Class Analysis of DSM–III–R Alcohol Dependence
Criteria ($n = 8,313$):

	Latent Classes				
	Two-Class Solution[1]		Three-Class Solution[2]		
	I	II	I	II	III
Prevalence	0.78	0.22	0.75	0.21	0.03
DSM–III–R Criterion	Conditional Probablities of Fulfilling a Criterion				
Withdrawal	0.00	0.14	0.00	0.07	0.49
Tolerance	0.01	0.45	0.01	0.35	0.81
Larger	0.15	0.96	0.12	0.94	0.99
Cut down	0.00	0.14	0.01	0.05	0.60
Time spent	0.00	0.19	0.00	0.09	0.65
Major role-hazard	0.03	0.83	0.02	0.73	0.96
Give up	0.00	0.10	0.00	0.03	0.43
Relief	0.00	0.08	0.00	0.02	0.40
Continue	0.00	0.24	0.02	0.11	0.83

Note. Source: Muthén and Muthén (1995).
[1]Likelihood ratio chi-square fit = 1,779, with 492 degrees of freedom.
[2]Likelihood ratio chi-square fit = 448, with 482 degrees of freedom.

behavior, see, Muthén & Muthén, 1999.) With ordered classes, one may ask what advantage LCA has versus doing regular factor analysis of binary outcomes using continuous latent variables (see e.g., Muthén, 1989). The answer is that LCA helps find clusters of individuals who are similar, whereas this is difficult in factor analysis. For these data, factor analysis suggested two factors. The estimated factor scores from the two-factor solution are plotted in Fig. 1.4.

Figure 1.4 shows that there is no natural cut points on the factors by which to divide individuals into having different levels of alcohol problems. However, the figure also includes the three classes found by the LCA. The three classes appear to be arranged along the principal axis of the two factors, the two factors being correlated around 0.7 in this example. This analysis shows that LCA is a vehicle for finding clusters of individuals, thereby complementing a regular factor analysis. A related observation is that data that fit well by a K-class model often fit well by a $K-1$-dimensional factor analysis model. For a related proof of an exact relationship for latent profile analysis, see Bartholomew (1987).

In terms of the alcohol problem diagnosis, discussions often center around how many criteria need to be fulfilled to give a certain diagnosis. Here, the LCA solution can be used as guidance as shown in Table 1.3 (see also Nestadt et al., 1994, for a similar analysis of schizophrenia criteria). Each individual can be classified into the class with largest posterior probability, and the classes can then

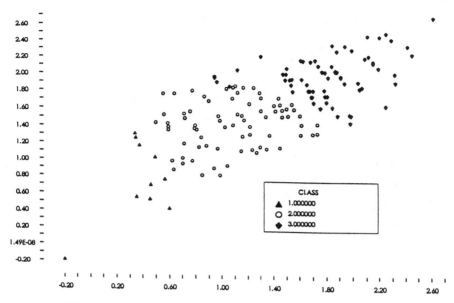

FIG. 1.4. Estimated factor scores from two-factor solution.

TABLE 1.3
Latent Class Membership by Number of DSM–III–R Alcohol Dependence
Criteria Met ($n = 8{,}313$)

		Latent Classes				
		Two-Class Solution		Three-Class Solution		
Number of Criteria Met	%	I	II	I	II	III
0	64.2	5335	0	5335	0	0
1	14.0	1161	1	1161	1	0
2	10.2	0	845	0	845	0
3	5.6	0	469	0	469	0
4	2.6	0	213	0	211	2
5	1.4	0	116	0	19	97
6	0.8	0	68	0	0	68
7	0.5	0	42	0	0	42
8	0.5	0	39	0	0	39
9	0.3	0	24	0	0	24
%	100.0	78.1	21.9	78.1	18.6	3.3

be cross-classified with the number of criteria met. Table 1.3 shows that Class 1 membership supports requiring $\leqslant 1$ criteria, Class 2 membership supports requiring 2–4 criteria, and Class 2 membership supports requiring $\geqslant 5$ criteria fulfilled.

LATENT CLASS ANALYSIS WITH COVARIATES

LCA with covariates (concomitant variables) has been considered by Bandeen-Roche, Miglioretti, Zeger, and Rathouz (1997), Dayton and Macready (1988), Formann, (1992), and Heijden, Dressens, and Bockenholt (1996). This modeling considers a covariate x, where the probability that individual i falls in Class k of the latent class variable c is expressed through multinomial logistic regression as

$$P(c_i = k \mid x_i) = \frac{e^{\alpha_k + \gamma_k x_i}}{\sum_{k=1}^{K} e^{\alpha_k + \gamma_k x_i}}, \tag{7}$$

where $\alpha_K = 0$, $\gamma_K = 0$ so that $e^{\alpha_K + \gamma_K x_i} = 1$, implying that the log odds of comparing Class k to the last Class K is

$$log[P(c_i = k \mid x_i)/P(c_i = K \mid x_i)] = \alpha_k + \gamma_k x_i. \tag{8}$$

In addition,

$$logit \; [P(u_{ij} = 1 \mid c_i = k, x_i)] = \alpha_{u_k} + \kappa_{jk} x_i, \tag{9}$$

where the α_{u_k} s are the logit counterparts to the conditional item probabilities discussed earlier and κ_j is a direct effect parameter for the influence of x on u_j. Muthén and Muthén (1999) gave an example of LCA with covariates applied to antisocial behavior classes related to age, gender, and ethnicity.

The model in Eqs. (7) and (9) relates to those considered in Clogg and Goodman (1985), studying invariance across groups of individuals similar to multiple-group analysis in SEM. A multiple-group analysis is not needed because the model in Eqs. (7) and (9) is sufficient for capturing across-group differences in parameters when the groups are represented by dummy x variables. For example, the direct effect of a group dummy variable x on a certain u implies that measurement invariance does not hold, but that the groups differ in their conditional item probabilities within class. The direct effect may vary across classes.

The LCA model with covariates also allows for direct dependencies among the us conditional on class (i.e., violations of the conditional independence assumption). A certain u variable may be changed into an x variable, which allows for a direct effect of this u on another u, conditional on class. The other u variables are still conditionally independent given class.

CONFIRMATORY LATENT CLASS ANALYSIS WITH SEVERAL LATENT CLASS VARIABLES

Confirmatory latent class analysis (CLCA) with several latent class variables was introduced in Goodman (1974), considering a panel study with two waves. Figure 1.5 shows an example based on the antisocial behavior analysis of Muthén and

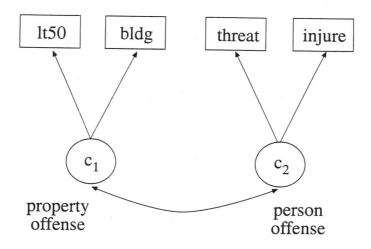

FIG. 1.5.   Confirmatory latent class analysis with several latent class variables.

		Class 1	Class 2	Class 3	Class 4
C1	Lt50	1	1	2	2
	Bldg	3	3	4	4
C2	Threat	5	6	5	6
	Injure	7	8	7	8

FIG. 1.6.   Restriction on the conditional probabilites for the items.

Muthén (1999). Among the three dimensions found in a factor analysis of 17 binary antisocial behavior items, items measuring two factors interpreted as property offense and person offense are considered. The property offense factor was well measured by the items *stole less than 50* and *broken into a building*, whereas the person offense factor was well measured by the items *seriously threaten* and *intent to injure.* The intent of the CLCA was to consider a dichotomized latent distribution for each of the two factors to capture non-normality of each factor and to divide individuals into classes based on each factor dimension. It is also possible to relate the corresponding two dichotomous latent class variables c_1 and c_2 to each other.

The way the CLCA model is drawn in Fig. 1.5 implies that the item probabilities for the threat and injure items should not vary across the c_1 classes, and the item probabilities for the lt50 and bldg items should not vary across the c_2 classes. In the Mplus framework, the analysis indicated by Fig. 1.5 is carried out by creating a latent class variable that combines the dichotomous c_1 and c_2 variables into one latent class variable with four classes. Using the numbering of classes shown at the bottom of Fig. 1.5, Fig. 1.6 shows the implied equality restrictions on the item probabilities, where each number corresponds to one parameter and repeated numbers indicate equalities.

LATENT CLASS GROWTH ANALYSIS

In longitudinal data, the multiple indicators of latent classes may correspond to repeated univariate outcomes at different time points. This is the situation considered in LCGA (see Nagin, 1999). Here the classes define different trends over time in the item probabilities. For example, using a linear trend with an intercept and a slope,

$$\Lambda_{u_k} = \begin{bmatrix} 1 & 0 \\ 1 & 1 \\ 1 & 2 \\ \vdots & \vdots \\ 1 & T-1 \end{bmatrix},$$ (11)

the logits for the u items may be expressed as

$$\Lambda_{u_k}\eta_{ui} + K_{u_k}x_i$$ (11)

where η_{ui} contains the intercept and slope growth factors expressed as

$$\eta_{ui} = \alpha_{u_k} + \Gamma_{u_k}x_i.$$ (12)

Here the K_{u_k} parameters capture effects on the us of time-varying covariates, varying across time but not across individuals, and the Γ_{u_k} parameters capture effects of time-invariant covariates on the growth factors. The growth factors have fixed values conditional on x (for the random counterpart, see next section).

As an example, data from Jackson, Sher, and Wood (1999) were reanalyzed. This analysis considers the co-occurrence of alcohol and tobacco use disorders—that is, the u variables correspond to two processes. In a college sample of 450 students, Jackson et al. found five classes as shown in Fig. 1.7. The classes are defined by five repeated measures of alcohol disorder and, concurrently, five repeated measures of tobacco disorder. For example, Class 4 shows tobacco use disorder (see bottom panel), but no alcohol use disorder (see top panel). However, the Jackson et al. analysis does not take into account the time ordering for the measures, but use a regular LCA.

As an alternative analysis, LCGA was carried out for the two processes as shown in the path diagram of Fig. 1.8. For each process, two growth factors are used corresponding to linear growth, I and S. Each of the growth factors is influenced by a latent class variable specific to the process, so that the means of the growth factors change over classes. Three classes are used for each process, and the two sets of three-class variables c_1 and c_2 are related to each other.

The trends for each process are shown in Fig. 1.9. For each process, there is a chronic class with high probabilities throughout and a low class with low probabilities throughout. For the alcohol use disorders, there is also a declining class, whereas for the tobacco use disorders, there is an increasing class. These trends are approximations of those seen in Fig. 1.8, although the class probability curves in Fig. 1.8 for each process have been combined into fewer trend classes in Fig. 1.9. Figure 1.8

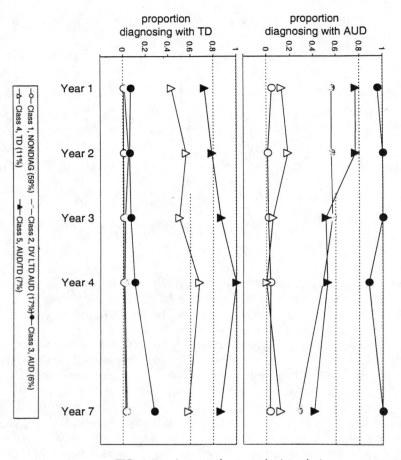

FIG. 1.7.   Latent class analysis solution.

also shows the estimates of the joint probability table for c_1 and c_2. The four classes with the smallest probabilities were not included in the Jackson et al. analysis.

GROWTH MIXTURE MODELING

The rest of this chapter considers growth mixture modeling of repeated measures data. In analyzing such data, individual differences in development are typically captured by random effects using mixed linear modeling or multilevel modeling. These random effects represent continuous variation across individuals in growth features such as initial status and rate of change. Often, however, more fundamental individual differences in development are present and need to be allowed for to make the

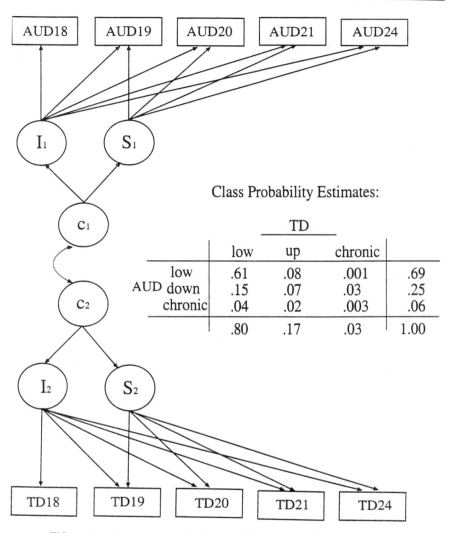

FIG. 1.8.   Co-occurrence of alcohol use and tobacco disorder.

modeling realistic. Such fundamental differences in development can be described by latent trajectory classes, where each class has a different random effect growth model. Random effects and trajectory classes are latent variables. Random effects are continuous latent variables, and trajectory classes are categorical latent variables. Growth mixture modeling (Muthén, in press; Muthén & Shedden, 1999; Muthén, Brown et al., 2000) uses both types of latent variables to represent individual differences in development, resulting in a very flexible repeated measures analysis.

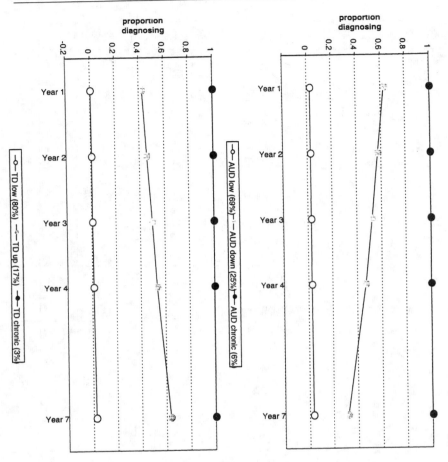

FIG. 1.9.   Latent class growth analysis solution.

Two examples clarify the ideas. Children in early school grades may be on a developmental path of reading disability, others may show mild forms of reading problems, whereas still others progress normally. Children in school may exhibit serious aggressive/disruptive behavior in the classroom, others may show more common forms of such behavior, whereas others show no such problems. The average trajectories of the three classes in these examples are different, and there is individual variation around the average trajectories. It is important to distinguish among individuals in the different classes because membership in different classes may have different antecedents and consequences. Growth mixture modeling provides estimates of the class probabilities, the average trajectory for each class, the trajectory variation in each class, and estimates of each individual's most likely class membership. The probabilities of class membership can be related to background variables, and class membership can be used to predict other outcomes.

Conventional Random Effects Modeling in a Latent Variable Framework

Consider a quadratic growth model for continuous outcomes $y_{it}(i = 1, 2, \ldots, n;$ $t = 1, 2, \ldots, T)$ that can be described by three random effects η_{0i}, η_{1i}, and η_{2i}, and time-specific residuals ϵ,

$$y_{it} = \eta_{0i} + \eta_{1i} x_{it} + \eta_{2i} x_{it}^2 + \kappa_t w_{it} + \epsilon_{it}. \tag{13}$$

In the latent variable framework, the random effects are referred to as growth factors (i.e., continuous latent variables). Here it is assumed that individuals are measured at the same time points so that the time scores $x_{it} = x_t$ (deviations from this can be handled via missing data techniques). Assume that for substantive reasons it is of interest to define η_0 as an initial status growth factor, setting the time score $x_1 = 0$. Also for identification purposes, $x_2 = 1$. With equidistant times of observation, the model would typically have $x_t = 0, 1, 2,\ldots, T-1$. The time-specific residuals have zero means and covariance matrix Θ, typically with different variances and often with some off-diagonal elements to represent residual correlation across time.

The variation in the three-growth factors is expressed as,

$$\eta_{0i} = \alpha_0 + \gamma_0 w_i + \zeta_{0i}, \tag{14}$$

$$\eta_{1i} = \alpha_1 + \gamma_1 w_i + \zeta_{1i}, \tag{15}$$

$$\eta_{2i} = \alpha_2 + \gamma_2 w_i + \zeta_{2i}, \tag{16}$$

where the αs are mean parameters and the ζs are residuals with zero means and covariance matrix Ψ and w is a time-variant covariate. Growth factors may be fixed or random. For example, with a fixed quadratic factor,

$$\Psi = \begin{pmatrix} \psi_{00} & & symm. \\ \psi_{10} & \psi_{11} & \\ 0 & 0 & 0 \end{pmatrix}, \tag{17}$$

so that, conditional on w, there is no variation in η_2.

Conventional Growth Modeling of Reading Data.

The reading data set is from the Early Assessment of Reading Skills (EARS) study a multiple-cohort study design repeatedly measuring children from kindergarten through third grade in a suburb of Houston. One key aim of the EARS study was to investigate if early identification of children at risk for poor academic outcomes could be made using longitudinal data. The outcome variable considered here is word-recognition skills repeatedly measured four times in Grade 1 and four times in Grade 2. In the current analyses, a subset of 411 children is considered. One cohort consisting of about half the children has data on all eight outcomes, whereas a second cohort has data on only the first four outcomes. The measurement occasions were October, December, February, and May of Grades 1 and 2. The children were also measured during kindergarten, and the current analyses use a measure of phonemic awareness at the end of kindergarten as a predictor of word-recognition development.

Initial exploration of the reading data suggests that a linear growth model is suitable for the eight time points. The growth model in Eqs. (13) to (16) without the η_2 term and without covariates is therefore used. The model allows the variances of the time-specific residuals ϵ to vary across time. The estimated model has a rather poor model fit [$n = 411$, number of parameters $= 13$, $\chi^2(31) = 470.767$ ($p = 0.0000$), log L $= -1145.785$, BIC $= 2369.812$, CFI $= 0.897$, RMSEA $= 0.186$ (CI: .171, .201)]. Modification indexes point to a covariance between the residuals for time point 3 and 4 as by far the most important source of misfit, but freeing this parameter does not improve the model fit in important ways. The estimated mean line for this model is shown in Fig. 1.10 as a solid dark line together with observed data for a random sample of children. The individual observations suggest a considerable amount of heterogeneity in the word-recognition development, possibly including a separate low-achieving group of children marked by darker lines.

Conventional Growth Modeling of Aggression Data.

The aggression data set is from a school-based preventive intervention study carried out by the Johns Hopkins Prevention Center in Baltimore public schools, Grades 1 to 7. Here only the control group is analyzed. The outcome variable of interest is teacher ratings of each child's aggressive behavior in the classroom from Grade 1 to Grade 7. Teacher ratings of a child's aggressive behavior were made from fall and spring for the first two grades and every spring in Grades 3 to 7. The ratings were made using the TOCA-R instrument, using an average of 10 items, each rated on a 6-point scale from *almost never* to *almost always*. Information was also collected on other concurrent and distal outcomes, including school removal and juvenile court records. The current analyses focus on 80 boys in the control group.

The quadratic growth model of Eqs. (13) to (16) without covariates is applied to the nine time points for Grades 1 to 7 of the aggression data. The estimated model shows a slightly negative variance for the quadratic growth factor. Restricting the covariance matrix as in Eq. (17) gave a rather poor model fit [$n = 80$, number of parameters $= 16$, $\chi^2(38) = 73.54$ ($p = 0.0005$), log L $= -627.28$, BIC $= 1324.67$, CFI $= 0.887$, RMSEA $= 0.108$ (CI: .070, .145)]. Modification indices point to correlations between time-specific residuals, but this does not improve the fit in important ways. A large modification index value is observed for the covariance between the intercept and quadratic growth factors, but this covariance cannot be included given the zero variance of the quadratic growth factor. It is not clear how to improve the fit of the model, although a suspicion is that the data contain more fundamental heterogeneity than can be cap-

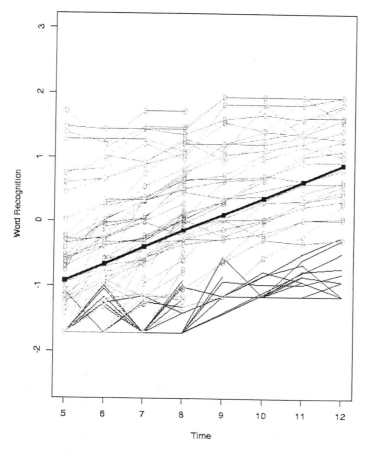

FIG. 1.10.   Word-recognition development.

tured by the conventional growth model used here. The estimated mean growth curve for the model with 16 parameters is shown in Fig. 1.11.

A Simple Growth Mixture Model

Model Specification.   The quadratic growth model of Eqs. (13) to (16) can be extended to a growth mixture model for K latent trajectory classes, where in Class k ($k = 1, 2, ..., K$),

$$\eta_{0i} = \alpha_{0k} + \gamma_{0k} w_i + \zeta_{0i}, \tag{18}$$

$$\eta_{1i} = \alpha_{1k} + \gamma_{1k} w_i + \zeta_{1i}, \tag{19}$$

$$\eta_{2i} = \alpha_{2k} + \gamma_{2k} w_i + \zeta_{2i}, \tag{20}$$

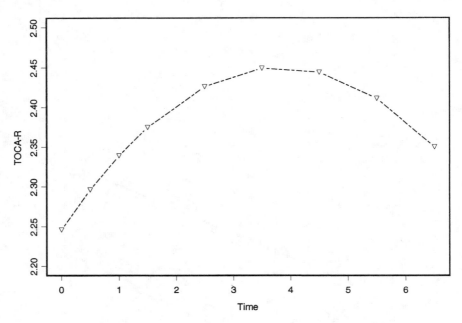

FIG. 1.11.   Estimated mean growth curve of aggression.

Here α_k parameters vary across classes to capture different types of trajectories. If there is no covariate w, the αs are the means of the growth factors. For example, a class with a trajectory that is low and flat has a low α_0 value, a zero α_1 value, and a zero α_2 value, whereas a class with a trajectory that accelerates from an early low level and then decelerates has a low low α_0 value, a positive α_1 value, and a negative α_2 value. The γ_k parameters allow variation across class in how a covariate influences the growth factors. Class-specific covariance matrices Ψ_k are allowed for ζ. Class-specific covariance matrices Θ_k for ε in Eq. (13) are also allowed for. The growth curve shape can also vary across classes through class-specific x_{it} values in Eq. (13).

Model Fit.   Tests of model fit require special attention in growth mixture modeling. It should be noted that a test against a completely unrestricted mean vector and covariance matrix, as in conventional structural equation modeling, is not used with mixture modeling. This is because the mixture modeling does not rely on normality assumptions where such summaries are natural. The set of sufficient statistics is nothing less than the raw data because the (mixture) distribution for the observed variables is not normal, but can be distinctly non-normal as a function of the mixture of normals.

However, the model can be evaluated based on the fit of first- and second-order moments in the following sense. For an estimated growth mixture model, estimated posterior probabilities of each individual's membership in each class are obtained as shown in the appendix. These probabilities can be used to classify an individual into the class that he or she most likely belongs to. For each class, the raw data can be multiplied by the individual probabilities of that class to compute weighted sample mean vectors and covariance matrices for each class that can be compared to the corresponding model-estimated quantities.

The quality of a growth mixture model can also be evaluated based on the precision of the classification. For individuals classified into a given class, the average posterior probability of belonging to this class should be high, and the average posterior probability of belonging to each of the other classes should be low.

A key issue in growth mixture modeling is to determine the number of classes. For comparison of fit of models that have the same number of classes and are nested, the usual likelihood-ratio chi-square difference test of twice the difference in log likelihood values can be used. Comparison of models with different numbers of classes, however, cannot be done by likelihood-ratio chi-square. Instead this is accomplished by a Bayesian information criterion (BIC; Schwartz, 1978) as mentioned in connection with LCA.

Growth Mixture Modeling of Reading Data

The next analysis step for the reading data is to try to account for heterogeneity in development using growth mixture modeling. The first task is to decide on the number of latent trajectory classes. A useful procedure for exploring the number of classes is to first fit a series of models that have zero growth factor covariance matrices Ψ (i.e., assuming that individuals are homogeneous with respect to their growth). Variation is still allowed for across individuals through time-specific variances in Θ. This type of modeling has been proposed by Nagin (1999) and was referred to as latent class growth mixture analysis (LCGA) earlier, given that the within-class homogeneity specification is analogous to LCA. Here LCGA is used to derive starting values for a growth mixture model. In particular, the estimated LCGA growth factor means are used as starting values, letting Ψ be free.

The analysis of the number of classes relies to a large degree on the BIC values. Plotting the BIC values against the number of classes, the lowest point in the BIC curve is sought. For this part of the analysis, it is important to make a special investigation of the degree of class-invariance of the covariance matrices Ψ_k and Θ_k. Different degrees of invariance give different sets of BIC curves with different minima. In the reading data, a class with problematic word-recognition development is found. This class can be seen as a class at risk for reading failure in that it has almost zero growth rate. This class needs a class-specific growth factor covariance matrix Ψ that shows larger intercept and slope variance than the other classes. Only in the two-class model is this not needed because the lowest class is less clearly a failing class.

Figure 1.12 shows a plot of the BIC values for the reading data, using 1 to 6 classes. BIC values are shown for both LCGA and growth mixture modeling. The

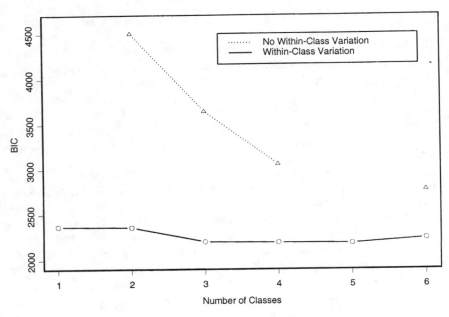

FIG. 1.12.   BIC values for reading data.

one-class BIC value is for the conventional growth model. It is seen that BIC is improved by using more than one class, and that five classes seems optimal in the growth mixture modeling. The LCGA BIC values are considerably worse for any given number of classes, showing that it is important to allow for within-class growth heterogeneity for this application.

For the five-class growth mixture model, the hypothesis of class-invariant growth factor covariance matrix Ψ is strongly rejected in favor of allowing Class 1 to have a different growth factor covariance matrix [$\chi^2(3)=80.13$, $p<.0000$]. The estimated mean curves for the five-class growth mixture model are shown in Fig. 1.13. Classes 1 to 5 have class probabilities 0.14, 0.34, 0.30, 0.13, and 0.10. This means that the problematic Class 1 contains 56 children.

Figure 1.14 shows the quality of the classification using average posterior probabilities from the five-class model.

The posterior-probability-weighted sample means and the estimated means for the outcomes are shown in Fig. 1.15.

Muthén, Francis, Khoo, and Boscardin (in press) investigated the question of how early it was possible to classify children into the problematic Class 1. As was done in their investigation, it is possible to take the estimated model parameters as a given and study the posterior probabilities for a certain individual, varying the number of repeated measures available. The Muthén et al. investigation indicated that a good classification was already possible at the end of first grade.

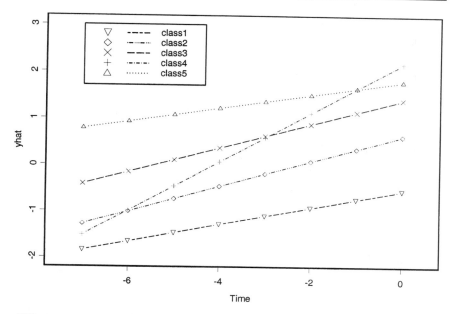

FIG. 1.13.　Estimated mean curves for the five-class growth mixture model for reading data.

	Class 1	Class 2	Class 3	Class 4	Class 5
Class 1	**0.872**	0.121	0.000	0.008	0.000
Class 2	0.026	**0.850**	0.075	0.049	0.000
Class 3	0.000	0.080	**0.850**	0.022	0.048
Class 4	0.001	0.147	0.058	**0.794**	0.000
Class 5	0.000	0.000	0.055	0.000	**0.945**

FIG. 1.14.　Average posterior probabilities from the five-class model.

Growth Mixture Modeling of Aggression Data

The BIC results for the aggression data using Classes 1 to 5 are shown in the top curve of Fig. 1.16. The BIC values indicate a better fit when allowing more than one class. It is seen that three classes is favored by BIC.

Inspection of the three-class growth mixture model shows that the likelihood could be significantly improved by allowing class-specific variances for the class with the lowest trajectory. This class shows considerably less fluctuation over

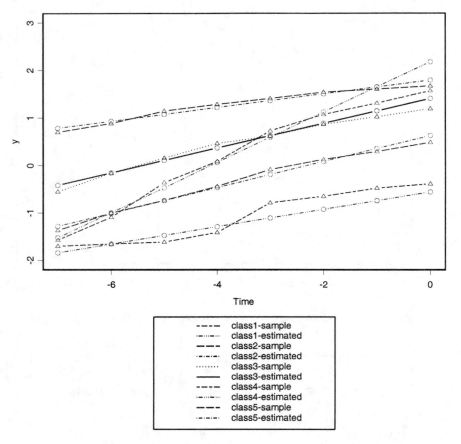

FIG. 1.15. Posterior-probability-weighted sample means and estimated
means for reading data.

time in aggression than the other two classes. In particular, the intercept variance
and the time-specific residual variances are lower for this class. The markedly
lower BIC values in the bottom curve of Fig. 1.16 show the superior fit when
allowing noninvariant variances for these models. With noninvariant variances,
the lowest values are at Classes 3 and 5. The five-class solution has class probabilities 0.08, 0.45, 0.06, 0.09, 0.32, while the three-class solution has class probabilities 0.09, 0.52, and 0.39. The first and last classes are very similar in the two
solutions.

For reasons of parsimony, and to have higher class counts, the three-class
model is chosen here. Fig. 1.17 shows the estimated mean growth curves for the
three-class model for Grades 1 to 7.

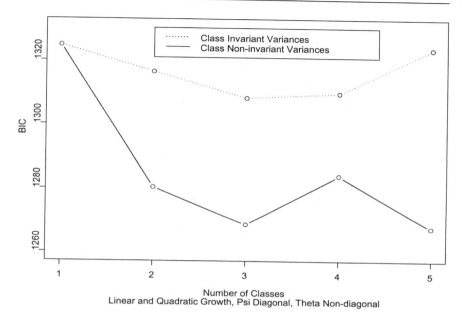

Number of Classes
Linear and Quadratic Growth, Psi Diagonal, Theta Non-diagonal

FIG. 1.16.   BIC plot for STD/GBG group.

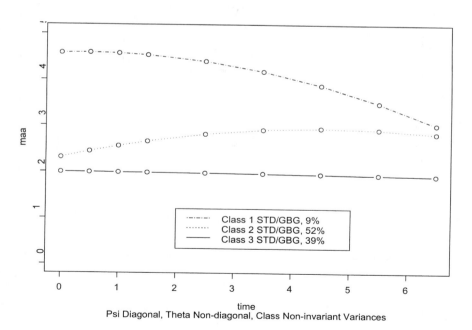

time
Psi Diagonal, Theta Non-diagonal, Class Non-invariant Variances

FIG. 1.17.   Three-class exploration for STD/GBG.

Class 1 has the lowest probability, showing a high aggression level in early grades that decreases over time. Class 2 has the highest probability and shows a slightly increasing aggression trajectory. Class 3 consists of children showing very low, flat, and stable aggression trajectories. Figure 1.18 shows the quality of the classification using average posterior probabilities from the three-class model. The posterior-probability-weighted sample means and the estimated means for the outcomes are shown in Fig. 1.19.

	Class 1	Class 2	Class 3
Class 1	**0.860**	0.140	0.000
Class 2	0.052	**0.926**	0.022
Class 3	0.000	0.076	**0.924**

FIG. 1.18.   Average posterior probabilites from the three-class model.

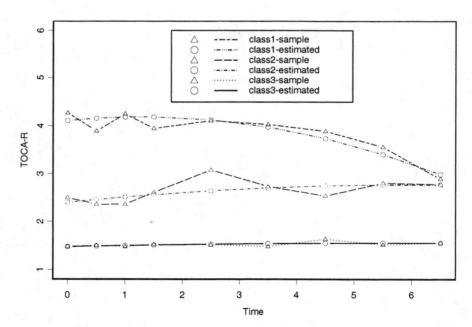

FIG. 1.19.   Posterior-probability-weighted sample means and estimated means for aggression.

Growth Mixture Modeling With Antecedents and Consequences

Growth mixture modeling allows for class variation in how covariates influence the growth factors and also in how the growth classes influence variables other than the repeated measures. The former aspect is illustrated by the reading data and the latter aspect by the aggression data.

A Growth Mixture Model for Reading With a Covariate Predicting Class Membership.

As discussed earlier, the growth mixture modeling produces posterior probabilities of class membership for each individual, and these can be used to classify individuals into their most likely class. Often the researcher wants to explore the profile of individuals in the different classes in terms of means of a set of background variables. This can be done using the individuals' classifications, but a more powerful analysis is to bring the background variables directly into the growth mixture analysis.

The five-class growth mixture model for word-recognition development is now expanded to include a predictor of class membership. A phonemic awareness measure taken at the end of kindergarten is used as a predictor. This variable is a proxy for some of the important prerequisites that a child needs to fully benefit from the instruction in Grade 1.

The modeling of the influence of phonemic awareness on class membership can be expressed as in multinomial logistic regression,

$$P(c_{ik} = 1 \mid A) = \frac{e^{\alpha_{c_i} + \gamma_{c_i} A_i}}{\sum_{k=1}^{K} e^{\alpha_{c_i} + \gamma_{c_i} A_i}}, \tag{21}$$

where $c_{ik} = 1$ if Individual i belongs to Class k, A stands for phonemic awareness, $\alpha_{c_K} = 0$, $\gamma_{c_K} = 0$. Here γ_{c_k} $(k = 1, 2, ..., K-1)$ express the effect of phonemic awareness on the log odds of being in Class k versus Class K. For a two-class model, this is a regular logistic regression except that the dependent variable is latent.

The estimates of the extended five-class growth mixture model showed a similar picture for the trajectory class shapes and the class probabilities, indicating a desirable stability in the five-class model. The estimates of the multinomial logistic regression show that the probability of being in a high class increases as a function of increasing phonemic awareness value. A plot of the class probabilities as a function of phonemic awareness is given in Fig. 1.20.

A Growth Mixture Model for Aggression With a Distal Outcome Predicted by Class Membership.

Many research questions related to growth mixtures concern the consequences of being in a certain trajectory class. For example, in the aggression data, it may be asked whether

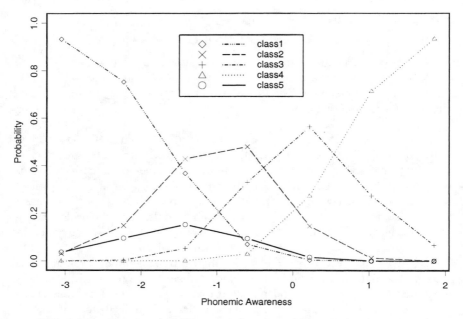

FIG. 1.20.   Class probabilities as a function of phonemic awareness.

members of the high class have a higher risk for obtaining a juvenile court record. The juvenile court record variable is scored as u=1 versus u=0 for having a record before age 18 or not.

With a binary distal outcome, the class influence is described as the logit regression

$$logit\ P(u_i = 1 \mid c_{ik} = 1) = log[P(u_i = 1 \mid c_{ik} = 1)/P(u_i = 0 \mid c_{ik} = 1)] = \alpha_{u_k}. \quad (22)$$

Here α_{u_k} is the log odds for $u_i=1$ versus $u_i=0$ for individual i in Class k. An odds estimate and a corresponding confidence interval are obtained by exponentiating the α_k estimate and confidence limits.

The estimated growth mixture model for aggression and juvenile court record shows the same three classes as found earlier (see Fig. 1.8). The estimated odds for having a juvenile court record are 4.81 for Class 1, 0.61 for Class 2, and 0.49 for Class 3. A likelihood-ratio test of no differential effect of class on the juvenile court record probability did not, however, give a strong rejection [$\chi^2(2)=5.22$, $.05<p<.10$] perhaps due to low power associated with the low sample size.

COMPUTATIONAL ISSUES

Modeling with categorical latent variables presents the same potential computational problems as finite mixture analysis. Finite mixture analysis sometimes presents convergence problems and results in multiple maxima (see e.g., Titterington, Smith, & Makov, 1985). The degree of such complications is related to the information about the latent classes available in the data and the particular model applied. For example, growth mixture modeling of repeated measures data with clear trajectory classes may be less prone to such complications than a latent profile model for cross-sectional data. Models that allow for a larger degree of across-class variation in parameters are more likely to show such complications. Particularly sensitive are models with a large degree of across-class variation in variance–covariance parameters. For example, a latent profile model with across-variation in within-class variance is typically more difficult to fit than a latent profile model that only allows the means to vary across classes. In some cases, class-specific variances can lead to a small class with a singular covariance matrix giving an infinite likelihood value. The possibility of multiple maxima is well known in LCA, where random starting points are often used. For all models, the analyst is urged to search for multiple maxima to find the solution with the highest log likelihood value. In some cases, multiple maxima may be an indication of the need for more classes, as was observed in Muthén and Shedden (1999).

The identification status of a finite mixture model is difficult to assess, and general rules do not seem to be available in the literature. There is also a possible difference between theoretical and empirical nonidentification. Goodman (1974) observed theoretical nonidentification for a latent class model with four binary outcomes and three classes. Although this model has one parameter less than the unrestricted multinomial model, there is one indeterminacy among the parameters of the model that holds for any parameter values. Other models may be empirically nonidentified (i.e., in a region of the parameter space, the information matrix used to compute the estimated standard errors may be singular). In some cases, saddle points are found with a Hessian that has both positive and negative diagonal elements. These problems can possibly be avoided by using other starting values. It is recommended that mixture models be built up from relatively simple models, adding parameters stepwise and checking to which extent the log likelihood value improves.

CONCLUSIONS

This chapter has presented a series of latent variable models that introduce categorical latent variables in the form of clusters of individuals and in the form of latent trajectory classes. The models are special cases of a general latent variable modeling framework offering a unified view of seemingly disparate models. Many other models not discussed here fit into this framework, including non-compliance modeling in randomized trials (see Jo & Muthén, chap. 3, this volume), mixture cluster analysis, mixture factor analysis, and mixture structural equation modeling. The general modeling framework offers a large set of new analysis opportunities going far beyond the conventional SEM of the last few decades. This chapter is offered as a stimulus for further methodological developments and applications using this general framework.

APPENDIX: A GENERAL LATENT VARIABLE FORMULATION

This section gives the statistical specification of the general latent variable mixture model used in Mplus, drawing on Muthén, Shedden, and Spisic (1999). Related technical descriptions are presented in Muthén and Muthén (1998; Appendix 8) and Muthén and Shedden (1999). Applications are given in Muthén (in press), Muthén and Muthén (1999), and Muthén, Francis, Khoo, and Boscardin (in press).

GENERAL MODEL FORMULATION

The observed variables are x, y, and u, where x denotes a $q \times 1$ vector of covariates, y denotes a $p \times 1$ vector of continuous outcome variables, and u denotes an $r \times 1$ vector of binary and ordered polytomous categorical outcome variables. The latent variables are η denoting an $m \times 1$ vector of continuous variables and c denoting a latent categorical variable with K classes, $c_i = (c_{i1}, c_{i2}, \ldots c_{iK})'$, where $c_{ik} = 1$ if Individual i belongs to Class k and zero otherwise.

The model relates c to x by multinomial logistic regression using the $K-1$-dimensional parameter vector of logit intercepts α_c and the $(K-1) \times q$ parameter matrix of logit slopes Γ_c, where for $k = 1, 2, \ldots, K$

$$P(c_{ik} = 1 \mid x_i) = \frac{e^{\alpha_{c_k} + \gamma'_{c_k} x_i}}{\sum_{k=1}^{k} e^{\alpha_{c_k} + \gamma'_{c_k} x_i}}, \tag{23}$$

where the last class is a reference class with coefficients standardized to zero, $\alpha_{c_k} = 0$, $\gamma_{c_k} = 0$.

The latent classes of c influence both y and u. Consider first the **y** part of the model. Conditional on Class k,

$$y_i = \nu_k + \Lambda_k \eta_i + K_k x_i + \epsilon_i, \tag{24}$$

$$\eta_i = \alpha_k + B_k \eta_i + \Gamma_k x_i + \zeta_i, \tag{25}$$

where the residual vector ε_i is $N(0, \Theta_k)$ and the residual vector ζ_i is $N(0, \Psi_k)$, both assumed to be uncorrelated with other variables. For u, conditional independence is assumed given c_i and x_i,

$$P(u_{i1}, u_{i2}, \ldots, u_{ir} \mid c_i, x_i) = P(u_{i1} \mid c_i, x_i) P(u_{i2} \mid c_i, x_i) \, P(u_{ir} \mid c_i, x_i). \quad (26)$$

The categorical variable $u_{ij}(j=1, 2, \ldots, r)$ with S_j-ordered categories follows an ordered polytomous logistic regression, where for Categories $s = 0, 1, 2, \ldots, S_j - 1$ and $\tau_{j,k,0} = -\infty, \tau_{j,k,S_j} = \infty$,

$$u_{ij} = s, \text{ if } \tau_{j,k,s} < u^*_{ij} < \tau_{j,k,s+1}, \quad (27)$$

$$P(u_{ij} = s \mid c_i, x_i) = F_{s+1}(u^*_{ij}) - F_s(u^*_{ij}), \quad (28)$$

$$F_s(u^*) = \frac{1}{1 + e^{-(\tau_s - u^*)}}, \quad (29)$$

where for $u^*_i = (u^*_{i1}, u^*_{i2}, \ldots, u^*_{ir})'$, $\eta_{ui} = (\eta_{u_{1i}}, \eta_{u_{2i}}, \ldots, \eta_{u_{fi}})'$, and conditional on Class k,

$$u^*_i = \Lambda_{uk}\eta_{ui} + K_{uk}x_i, \quad (30)$$

$$\eta_{ui} = \alpha_{uk} + \Gamma_{uk}x_i, \quad (31)$$

where Λ_{uk} is an $r \times f$ logit parameter matrix varying across the K classes, K_{uk} is an $r \times q$ logit parameter matrix varying across the K classes, α_{uk} is an $f \times 1$ vector logit parameter vector varying across the K classes, and Γ_{uk} is an $f \times q$ logit parameter matrix varying across the K classes. The thresholds may be stacked in the $(\Sigma^r_{j=1}(S_j - 1) \times 1)$ vectors τ_k varying across the K classes.

Mplus uses maximum-likelihood with the EM algorithm, viewing c_i as missing data. In the E step, the posterior probability of Individual i belonging to Class k is evaluated as

$$p_{ik} = P(c_{ik} = 1 \mid y_i, u_i, x_i) = P(c_{ik} = 1 \mid x_i)[y_i \mid c_i, x_i][u_i \mid c_{ik} = 1]/[y_i, u_i \mid x_i]. \quad (32)$$

For certain individuals, prior or auxiliary information may restrict the admissible class membership to a subset of all the classes. This includes having individuals with known class membership. In this case, the posterior probabilities in Eq. (32) are renormed for each individual to add to one over the admissible set of classes. In Mplus, this is referred to as having training data.

The M step consists of three separate optimizations: for the y, x part using quasi-Newton; for the u, c, x part using Newton–Raphson and quasi-Newton; and for the c, x part using Newton–Raphson and quasi-Newton. Each M step need not be reaching an optimum, but often a few steps are sufficient.

In Mplus, missing data assuming MAR (Little & Rubin, 1987) is allowed for with respect to y and u.

ACKNOWLEDGEMENT

The research was supported by grant K02 AA 00230–01 from NIAAA and by grant 40859 from NIMH. The work has benefited from discussions in Hendricks Brown's Prevention Science Methodology group and Muthén's Research Apprenticeship Course. The e-mail address is bmuthen@ucla.edu.

REFERENCES

Bandeen-Roche, K., Miglioretti, D. L., Zeger, S. L., & Rathouz, P. J. (1997). Latent variable regression for multiple discrete outcomes. *Journal of the American Statistical Association, 92,* 1375–1386.

Bartholomew, D. J. (1987). *Latent variable models and factor analysis.* New York: Oxford University Press.

Clogg, C. C. (1995). Latent class models. In G. Arminger, C. C. Clogg, & M. E. Sobel (Eds.), *Handbook of statistical modeling for the social and behavioral sciences* (pp. 311–359). New York: Plenum.

Clogg, C. C., & Goodman, L. A. (1985). Simultaneous latent structural analysis in several groups. In N. B. Tuma, (Ed.), *Sociological methodology, 1985* (pp. 81–110). San Francisco: Jossey-Bass.

Dayton, C. M., & Macready, G. B. (1988). Concomitant variable latent class models. *Journal of the American Statistical Association, 83,* 173–178.

Formann, A. K. (1992). Linear logistic latent class analysis for polytomous data. *Journal of the American Statistical Association, 87,* 476–486.

Goodman, L. A. (1974). Exploratory latent structure analysis using both identifiable and unidentifiable models. *Biometrika, 61,* 215–231.

Heijden, P. G. M., Dressens, J., & Bockenholt, U. (1996). Estimating the concomitant-variable latent-class model with the EM algorithm. *Journal of Educational and Behavioral Statistics, 21,* 215–229.

Jackson, K. M., Sher, K. J., & Wood, P. K. (1999). Trajectories of conjoint substance use disorders: A developmental, typological approach to comorbidity. Forthcoming in *Alcoholism: Clinical and Experimental Research.*

Lazarsfeld, P. F., & Henry. N. W. (1968). *Latent structure analysis.* New York: Houghton Mifflin.

Little, R. J., & Rubin, D. B. (1987). *Statistical analysis with missing data.* New York: Wiley.

Muthén, B. (1989). Dichotomous factor analysis of symptom data. In W. Eaton & G. Bohrnstedt (Eds.), *Latent variable models for dichotomous outcomes: Analysis of data from the epidemiological catchment area program* (pp. 19–65), A special issue of *Sociological Methods & Research, 18,* 19–65.

Muthén, B., & Muthén L. (1995). Tailoring Psychometric Techniques for Epidemiological and Clinical Applications. Technical report.

Muthén, B. (in press). Second-generation structural equation modeling with a combination of categorical and continuous latent variables: New opportunities for latent class/latent growth modeling. In L. M. Collins, & A. Sayer (Eds.), *New methods for the analysis of change.* Washington, DC: American Psychological Assoction.

Muthén, B., Brown, C. H., Masyn, K., Jo, B., Khoo, S., Yang, C., Wang, C. P., & Kellam, S. (2000). *General growth mixture modeling in randomized preventive interventions*. Unpublished manuscript, University of California, Los Angeles.

Muthén, B., Khoo, S. T., Francis, D., & Kim Boscardin, C. (in press). Analysis of reading skills development from kindergarten through first grade: An application of growth mixture modeling to sequential processes. *Multilevel modeling: Methodological advances, issues, and applications*. In S. R. Reise & N. Duan (Eds.), NJ: Lawrence Erlbaum Associates.

Muthén, B. & Muthén, L. (1998). *Mplus user's guide*. Los Angeles, CA: Muthén & Muthén.

Muthén, B., & Muthén, L. (1999). Integrating person-centered and variable-centered analysis: Growth mixture modeling with latent trajectory classes. *Alcoholism: Clinical and Experimental Research, 24*, 882–891.

Muthén, B., & Shedden, K. (1999). Finite mixture modeling with mixture outcomes using the EM algorithm. *Biometrics, 55*, 463–469.

Muthén B., Shedden, K., & Spisic, D. (1999). General latent variable mixture modeling. Technical report.

Nagin, D. S. (1999). Analyzing developmental trajectories: A semi-parametric, group-based approach. *Psychological Methods, 4*, 139–157.

Nestadt, G., Hanfelt, J., Liang, K. Y., Lamacz, M., Wolyniec, P., & Pulver., A. E. (1994). An evaluation of the structure of schizophrenia spectrum personality disorders. *Journal of Personality Disorders, 8*, 288–298.

Schwartz G. (1978). Estimating the dimension of a model. *The Annals of Statistics, 6*, 461–464.

Titterington, D. M., Smith, A. F. M., & Makov, U. E. (1985). *Statistical analysis of finite mixture distributions*. Chichester, England: Wiley.

2

A Unified Approach to Multigroup Structural Equation Modeling With Nonstandard Samples

Ke-Hai Yuan
University of North Texas

Peter M. Bentler
University of California, Los Angeles

It is well known that structural equation modeling (SEM) has become one of the most popular methods in multivariate analysis, especially in the social and behavioral sciences. In a SEM model with latent variables, the relationships among observed (manifest) variables is formulated through unobserved (latent) constructs. Because measurement errors are explicitly accounted for, coefficients in key parts of a model are uninfluenced by errors of measurement, implying greater theoretical meaningfulness and cross-population stability to the parameters than might be achieved with methods such as regression or analysis of variance, which do not correct for unreliability. This stability is a key goal of theory testing with SEM, where a substantive theory or hypothesized causal relationship among the latent constructs, facilitated by path diagrams, can be tested through SEM. With the help of popular software such as LISREL (Jöreskog & Sörbom, 1993) and EQS (Bentler, 2001), applications as well as new technical developments in SEM have increased dramatically in the past decade (e.g., Austin & Calderón, 1996; Austin & Wolfle, 1991; Bollen, 1989; Tremblay & Gardner, 1996). There exists a vast amount of recent introductory (Byrne, 1994; Dunn, Everitt, & Pickles, 1993; Kline, 1998; Mueller, 1996; Schumacker & Lomax, 1996) and overview material (Bentler & Dudgeon, 1996; Browne & Arminger, 1995; Hoyle, 1995; Marcoulides & Schumacker, 1996).

A commonly encountered situation is the existence of several samples. These may arise from one or several populations. If the samples are all from one population, their data can be combined for improved inference. However, if the samples are from several populations, it is important to understand how the populations might differ. For example, it might be interesting to know whether the factor structure of an established instrument, developed for a specific population, is also valid for other populations. In the context of SEM, it is natural to ask whether particular parameters, such as factor loadings, regression coefficients, or variances of factors, may be the same or different in various groups such as different ethnic, gender, or age groups. Motivated by such practical problems, Jöreskog (1971) developed a maximum likelihood approach to SEM with multiple groups. Sörbom (1974) studied differences in factor means across groups. Because practical data may not be normal, Bentler, Lee, and Weng (1987) and Muthén (1989) proposed a generalized least squares approach to parameter estimation and model test for multigroup structural models. Recently, Satorra (2000) and Satorra and Bentler (1999) proposed scaled tests in a multisample analysis of moment structures. The prior literature offers important guidance for multigroup modeling in practice. For example, standard software enables users to easily specify simultaneous estimation and evaluation of multigroup models.

With real data obtained under typical testing situations, nonstandard samples that contain missing data, nonnormal data and data with outliers are almost inevitable. As noted earlier, the literature on multigroup models of sample means and covariance matrices is based on either normal theory maximum likelihood or through generalized least squares. With nonstandard samples, however, there exist various limitations to the current methodologies for using sample moments for multigroup analysis. For example, the typical sample mean vector and sample covariance matrix are not defined when a sample contains missing data. For a complete sample with outliers, the sample mean and covariance matrix are biased estimates of their population counterparts. Even for a sample from a distribution with heavy tails, the sample moments may not converge at all or at least may not be efficient estimates of the corresponding population moments. These various drawbacks of the sample moments pass on to an analytical procedure that models these moments.

Certain problems with nonstandard samples for single group analysis have been studied and discussed extensively by various authors. Allison (1987), Lee (1986), Muthén, Kaplan, and Hollis (1987), Arbuckle (1996), and Jamshidian and Bentler (1999), for example, discussed approaches to dealing with normal missing data. Arminger and Sobel (1990) and Yuan and Bentler (2000a) developed approaches for dealing with non-normal missing data. Techniques for identifying outliers or influential cases can be found in Tanaka, Watadani, and Moon (1991), Cadigan (1995), Lee and Wang (1996), Bollen and Arminger (1991), and

Berkane and Bentler (1988). Approaches to robust inference for SEM can be found in Yuan and Bentler (1998a, 1998b, 2000b). Compared with classical methods, which are based on sample means and covariance matrices, these new developments offer various advantages in model estimation and evaluation. It is the aim of this chapter to develop parallel methods for multigroup analysis with nonstandard samples.

There are various ways to develop multigroup methods for nonstandard samples. Our purpose is to give a unified treatment for multiple groups, aiming to adopt the various developments in the statistical literature in estimating population means and covariance matrices. Suppose we have m groups and denote the mean vectors and covariance matrices in the population as μ_j and Σ_j, $j = 1, \dots, m$. Various methods have been developed for estimating μ_j and Σ_j with a nonstandard sample from the jth population. For example, the EM algorithm based on a normality assumption can be used to estimate μ_j and Σ_j for a normal sample with missing variables. There also exists an EM algorithm based on a multivariate t distribution that applies when a missing data sample possesses heavier tails as compared with the normal distribution. When a sample contains outliers or influential cases, there exist various robust methods for estimating μ_j and Σ_j. Our development is based on these new advances in estimating the population mean vectors μ_j and covariance matrices Σ_j.

Let $\bar{X}_{nj}$ and S_{nj} be working estimates for μ_j and Σ_j based on sample size n_j, for $j = 1, \dots, m$. Although it is anticipated that $\bar{X}_{nj}$ and S_{nj} might be better estimates than the sample mean vector $\bar{X}_j$ and covariance matrix S_j, we do not exclude the possibility of $\bar{X}_{nj} = \bar{X}_j$ and $S_{nj} = S_j$ in the case of normal sampling with no missing data. Actually, we may just regard $\bar{X}_{nj}$ as a data vector and S_{nj} as a symmetric data matrix, which approach μ_j and Σ_j, respectively, as our information about the jth group increases. It is typical that the μ_j in all the groups are of the same dimension, but here we do not need to assume this. Instead, we denote the dimension of μ_j as p_j. Let vech($\cdot$) be an operator that transforms a symmetric matrix into a vector by stacking the columns of the matrix leaving out the elements above the diagonal, $s_{nj} = \text{vech}(S_{nj})$ and $\sigma_j = \text{vech}(\Sigma_j)$. We use $t_{nj} = (\bar{X}'_{nj}, s'_{nj})'$ and $\delta_j = (\mu'_j, \sigma'_j)'$. We need to assume that each of our data vectors has an appropriate large sample property

$$\sqrt{n_j}(t_{nj} - \delta_{j_o}) \xrightarrow{\mathscr{L}} N(0, \Gamma_j), \quad j = 1, \dots, m, \tag{1}$$

where Γ_j is a $p_j^* \times p_j^*$ matrix with $p_j^* = p_j + p_j(p_j+1)/2$. When $t_{nj} = (X'_j, s_j)'$, the sample moments based on a sample from a normal distribution, then

$$\Gamma_j = \text{diag}[\Sigma_j, 2D_{P_j}^+(\Sigma_j \otimes \Sigma_j)D_{P_j}^{+'}],$$

where D_P^+ is the Moore–Penrose generalized inverse of the duplication matrix D_{pj} (Magnus & Neudecker, 1988). In such a case, a consistent $\hat{\Gamma}_j$ is easily obtained by replacing Σ_j by S_j. However, we need to obtain a better estimator for Γ_j when dealing with a general nonstandard sample. As we see in the next section, our proposed inference procedure just depends on Eq. (1), and we do not need to have the raw data once $t_{nj} = \hat{\delta}_j$ and a consistent $\hat{\Gamma}_j$ are available. Procedures for obtaining t_{nj} and $\hat{\Gamma}_j$ are given in a later section, based on our experience with current estimation methodologies in the statistical literature for nonstandard samples.

Suppose we are interested in the mean and covariance structures $\delta_j(\beta_j) = (\mu_j'(\beta), \sigma_j'(\beta_j))'$ for $j = 1, \ldots, m$. There are a variety of ways to use the information in Eq. (1) to estimate parameter $\theta = (\beta_1', \ldots, \beta_m')'$ and evaluate the structures $\delta_j(\beta_j)$. All involve minimizing some function of the distance between t_{nj} and $\delta_j(\beta_j)$. We choose the distance based on the normal theory likelihood function for the following reasons: (a) When data are normal, the estimator based on such a function is most efficient; (b) for data with influential cases or outliers, the robust mean vector and covariance matrix can be regarded as the sample mean vector and sample covariance matrix based on an approximately normal sample (Yuan, Chan &, Bentler, 2000); and (c) the estimation process of minimizing the maximum likelihood function is quite stable, which is very important when modeling several groups simultaneously.

With $N = n_1 + \cdots + n_m$, the maximum likelihood discrepancy function between t_{nj} and $\delta_j(\beta_j)$ is given by

$$F(\theta) = \frac{1}{N}\sum_{j=1}^{m} n_j F_j(\beta_j), \tag{2a}$$

where

$$F_j(\beta_j) = (\bar{X}_{nj} - \mu_j(\beta_j))'\Sigma_j^{-1}(\beta_j)(\bar{X}_{nj} - \mu_j(\beta_j)) \tag{2b}$$

$$+\mathrm{tr}\left[S_{nj}\Sigma_j^{-1}(\beta_j)\right] - \log\left|S_{nj}\Sigma_j^{-1}(\beta_j)\right| - p_j.$$

The analysis of multiple groups is interesting only when we put constraints on the separate β_js. In the most restricted case, when it is assumed that all samples come from the same population, parameters from each group may be constrained equal across groups. In a less restricted setting, only certain parameters such as factor means and loadings, or latent variable regression coefficients, may be constrained equal. Let the constraints be represented by a $r \times 1$ vector function

$$h(\theta) = 0. \tag{3}$$

Estimation of θ involves minimizing Eq. (2) under Constraint (3). We denote such an estimator as $\hat{\theta}$. The classical likelihood ratio test statistic is widely known to be of the form $T_{ML} = NF(\hat{\theta})$. Let $p^* = p_1^* + \cdots + p_m^*$ and q be the number of unknown parameters in $\hat{\theta}$. We also need to assume $\frac{n_j}{N} \to \gamma_j > 0$ to study the statistical properties of θ. When $t_{nj} = (\overline{X}_j', s_j')'$ are based on samples from normal distributions, both $\delta_j = \delta_j(\beta_j)$ and Constraint (3) hold in the populations, then

$$T_{ML} \xrightarrow{\mathcal{L}} \chi^2_{p^*-q+r}. \tag{4}$$

When data vectors t_{nj} are used in Eq. (2), Eq. (4) will not hold in general. There also exists a likelihood ratio statistic for testing Constraint (3). Let $\hat{\theta}^*$ be the estimate of θ without constraint (3). This $\hat{\theta}^*$ is just a collection of the $\hat{\beta}_j^*$ obtained by minimizing the function $F_j(\beta_j)$ in Eq. (2b). The commonly used likelihood ratio statistic in testing Constraint (3) is

$$T_{ML}^{(h)} = N[F(\hat{\theta}) - F(\hat{\theta}^*)],$$

which is also commonly referred to as the *chi-square difference test*. When all the samples follow multivariate normal distributions and $t_{nj} = (\overline{X}_j', s_j')'$, then

$$T_{ML}^{(h)} \xrightarrow{\mathcal{L}} \chi^2_r$$

under the null hypothesis of correct model structures and correct constraint. With a nonstandard sample, however, the behavior of $T_{ML}^{(h)}$ will not asymptotically follow a chi-square distribution even when the null hypothesis is correct.

Similarly, when data are normal and $t_{nj} = (\overline{X}_j', s_j')'$, it is easy to obtain standard error estimates for $\hat{\theta}$ based on

$$\sqrt{N}(\hat{\theta} - \theta_0) \xrightarrow{\mathcal{L}} N(0, \Omega).$$

The covariance matrix Ω is the inverse of the information or Hessian matrix associated with minimizing Eq. (2). For nonstandard samples, however, this matrix is inappropriate for obtaining standard errors. We need to find another Ω to replace the one based on inverting the information matrix.

The major purpose of this chapter is to give a unified treatment of multisample structural equation modeling based on minimizing Eq. (2) under Constraint (3). The most important results are appropriate standard errors for $\hat{\theta}$ and test statistics for evaluating the overall model structure and the constraint. These inferential procedures are developed in a later section. A further section gives brief guidelines for obtaining $t_{nj} = \hat{\delta}_j$ and $\hat{\Gamma}_j$ for several nonstandard samples. Some concluding remarks and discussions are offered at the end of the chapter.

MODEL INFERENCE

Under the null hypothesis of correct model structures about $\delta_j(\beta_j)$ and correct constraint $h(\theta)=0$, we first study the distribution of $\hat{\theta}$ before studying the properties of T_{ML} and $T_{ML}^{(h)}$. Rescaled statistics T_{RML} and $T_{RML}^{(h)}$ then follow from our study of T_{ML} and $T_{ML}^{(h)}$. Since standard ML theory cannot be applied without the normality assumption for observed data, to obtain the properties of $\hat{\theta}$ we use a generalized estimating equation approach instead (e.g., Liang & Zeger, 1986; Yuan & Jennrich, 1998). We use dot on top of a function to imply derivative [e.g., $\dot{h}(\theta)=\partial h(\theta)/\partial\theta'$, $\dot{F}(\theta)=\partial F(\theta)/\partial\theta$]. We may omit the argument of a function if evaluated at the population value [e.g., $\delta=\delta(\theta_0)$].

To obtain $\hat{\theta}$, one generally has to work with the Lagrangian function

$$L(\theta) = F(\theta)+h'(\theta)\lambda,$$

where λ is a $r\times 1$ vector of Lagrangian multipliers (e.g., Aitchison & Silvey, 1958; Bentler & Dijkstra, 1985). Because $\hat{\theta}$ minimizes $F(\theta)$ under the constraint in equation (3), it follows from the Lagrange multiplier theorem (e.g., Theorem 19.3 of Chong & Żak, 1996, p. 338) that $\hat{\theta}$ satisfies the generalized estimating equation

$$G(\hat{\theta}, \hat{\lambda}) = 0, \tag{5}$$

where

$$G(\theta, \lambda) = \begin{pmatrix} \dot{F}(\theta)+\dot{h}'(\theta)\lambda \\ h(\theta) \end{pmatrix}.$$

Notice that $G(\theta,\lambda)$ is just the derivative of L with respect to $(\theta',\lambda')'$. Since $\lambda_0=0$,

$$G(\theta_0, \lambda_0) = \begin{pmatrix} \dot{F}(\theta_0) \\ 0 \end{pmatrix}.$$

Using a first-order Taylor expansion on Eq. (5) at (θ_0,λ_0), or equivalently using the estimating equation approach as in Yuan and Jennrich (1998), we obtain

$$\sqrt{N}\begin{pmatrix} \hat{\theta} - \theta_0 \\ \hat{\lambda} - \lambda_0 \end{pmatrix} = -\dot{G}^{-1}(\theta_0, \lambda_0)\sqrt{N}G(\theta_0, \lambda_0)+o_p(1), \tag{6}$$

where

$$\dot{G}(\theta_0, \lambda_0) = \begin{pmatrix} \ddot{F}(\theta_0) & \dot{h}(\theta_0) \\ \dot{h}(\theta_0) & 0 \end{pmatrix}.$$

Denote

$$\dot{G}^{-1}(\theta_0, \lambda_0) = \begin{pmatrix} A^{11} & A^{12} \\ A^{21} & A^{22} \end{pmatrix},$$

then it follows from Eq. (6) that

$$\sqrt{N}(\hat{\theta} - \theta_0) = -A^{11}\sqrt{N}\dot{F}(\theta_0) + o_p(1). \tag{7}$$

Let $W_j = \mathrm{diag}\left[\Sigma_j^{-1}, \frac{1}{2}D'_{P_j}(\Sigma_j^{-1} \otimes \Sigma_j^{-1})D_{P_j}\right]$ and $e_j = t_{nj} - \delta_j$; then with Eq. (2b) we have

$$\dot{F}_j(\beta_{0j}) = -2\dot{\delta}'_j W_j e_j + O_p(1/n_j). \tag{8}$$

It follows from Eq. (8) that

$$\sqrt{n_j}\dot{F}_j(\beta_{0j}) \xrightarrow{\mathcal{L}} N(0, \Pi_j),$$

where $\Pi_j = 4\dot{\delta}'_j W_j \Gamma_j W_j \dot{\delta}_j$. Because $\dot{F}(\theta_0) = (n_1\dot{F}'_1(\beta_{01})/N, \ldots, n_m\dot{F}'_{1m}(\beta_{0m})/N)'$ and the various $\dot{F}_j(\beta_{0j})$ are independent,

$$\sqrt{N}\dot{F}(\theta_0) \xrightarrow{\mathcal{L}} N(0, \Pi_\gamma), \tag{9}$$

where $\Pi_\gamma = \mathrm{diag}(\gamma_1\Pi_1, \ldots, \gamma_m\Pi_m)$. It follows from Eqs. (7) and (9) that

$$\sqrt{N}(\hat{\theta} - \theta_0) \xrightarrow{\mathcal{L}} N(0, \Omega), \tag{10}$$

where $\Omega = A^{11}\Pi_\gamma A^{11}$. A consistent estimator $\hat{\Omega}$ of Ω can be obtained when θ is replaced by $\hat{\theta}$, γ_j by n_j/N, and Γ_j by $\hat{\Gamma}_j$. Standard errors of $\hat{\theta}$ follow from square roots of the diagonals of $\hat{\Omega}$.

When data are normal, $\Gamma_j = W_j^{-1}$, $\Pi_j = 4\dot{\delta}'_j W_j \dot{\delta}_j$, and

$$\Pi_\gamma = 4\mathrm{diag}(\gamma_1\dot{\delta}'_1 W_1 \dot{\delta}_1, \ldots, \gamma_m\dot{\delta}'_m W_m \dot{\delta}_m).$$

Because

$$\ddot{F}_j(\beta_{0j}) = 2\dot{\delta}'_j W_j \dot{\delta}_j + O_p(1/\sqrt{n_i}) \tag{11}$$

and A^{11} is a generalized inverse of $\ddot{F}(\theta_0)$, we have

$$\sqrt{N}(\hat{\theta} - \theta_0) \xrightarrow{\mathcal{L}} N(0, \Omega), \tag{12}$$

where $\Omega = A^{11}\Pi_\gamma A^{11} = A^{11}$. This corresponds to the standard results obtained when using the normality assumption for multiple samples.

Equation (10) characterizes the distribution of $\hat{\theta}$, the parameter estimator obtained by minimizing Eq. (2) under Constraint (3). Parallel results for $\hat{\theta}^*$ without the constraint are obtained when replacing A^{11} by A^{-1} in Eq. (7) to Eq. (12), where

$$A = 2\text{diag}(\gamma_1\dot{\delta}_1'W_1\dot{\delta}_1,\ldots, \gamma_m\dot{\delta}_m'W_m\dot{\delta}_m).$$

That is,

$$\sqrt{N}(\hat{\theta}^* - \theta_0)\xrightarrow{\mathcal{L}}N(0, \Omega^*),$$

where $\Omega^* = A^{-1}\Pi_\gamma A^{-1}$. Notice that the Π_γ matrix in Ω^* is the same as the one in Ω, which is block diagonal. Because A is also block diagonal, the β_j^* in θ^* are independent. The correlations between various $\hat{\beta}_j$ in Eq. (12), due to the Constraint (3), are totally characterized by A^{11}.

Parallel to the likelihood ratio test based on the sample moments under normality, we would like to have statistics that can be used for inference with nonstandard samples. For this purpose, we first study the statistic $T_{ML} = NF(\hat{\theta})$. Rescaled statistics for testing the structures $\delta_j = \delta_j(\beta_j)$ and Constraint (3) are given next. A parallel version is also obtained when interest centers on testing the Constraint (3).

Using the Taylor expansion on $F(\hat{\theta})$ at θ_0, we have

$$F(\hat{\theta}) = F(\theta_0)+\dot{F}'(\theta_0)(\hat{\theta} - \theta_0)+\frac{1}{2}(\hat{\theta} - \theta_0)'\ddot{F}(\bar{\theta})(\hat{\theta} - \theta_0), \tag{13}$$

where $\bar{\theta}$ lies between θ_0 and $\hat{\theta}$. Using Eq. (11) of Yuan and Bentler (1998b), we have

$$F_j(\beta_{0j}) = e_j'W_je_j+O_p(1/n_j^{3/2}). \tag{14}$$

Let

$$W = \text{diag}(W_1,\cdots,W_m),$$
$$W_\gamma = \text{diag}(\gamma_1W_1,\cdots, \gamma_mW_m),$$
$$\dot{\delta} = \text{diag}(\dot{\delta}_1, \cdots, \dot{\delta}_m)$$
$$e = (e_1',\cdots, e_m')',$$
$$e_s = (\sqrt{n_1}e_1',\cdots, \sqrt{n_m}e_m')'.$$

From Eq. (14), we have

$$NF(\theta_0) = e_s' W e_s + o_p(1). \tag{15}$$

Similarly, from Eqs. (8) and (7), respectively, we obtain

$$\sqrt{N}\dot{F}(\theta_0) = -2\sqrt{N}\dot{\delta}' W_\gamma e + o_p(1) = -2\dot{\delta}' W_\gamma^{\frac{1}{2}} W^{\frac{1}{2}} e_s + o_p(1)$$

and

$$\sqrt{N}(\hat{\theta} - \theta_0) = A^{11}\dot{\delta}' W_\gamma^{\frac{1}{2}} W^{\frac{1}{2}} e_s + o_p(1), \tag{16}$$

which further lead to

$$N\dot{F}'(\theta_0)(\hat{\theta} - \theta_0) = -2e_s' W^{\frac{1}{2}} W_\gamma^{\frac{1}{2}} \dot{\delta} A^{11}\dot{\delta}' W_\gamma^{\frac{1}{2}} W^{\frac{1}{2}} e_s + o_p(1). \tag{17}$$

Equation (11) implies

$$\ddot{F}(\theta_0) = 2\dot{\delta}' W_\gamma \dot{\delta} + O_p(1/\sqrt{N}). \tag{18}$$

It follows from Eqs. (16) and (18) that

$$N(\hat{\theta} - \theta_0)' \ddot{F}(\bar{\theta})(\hat{\theta} - \theta_0) = 2e_s' W^{\frac{1}{2}} W_\gamma^{\frac{1}{2}} \dot{\delta} A^{11}\dot{\delta}' W_\gamma \dot{\delta} A^{11}\dot{\delta}' W_\gamma^{\frac{1}{2}} W^{\frac{1}{2}} e_s + o_p(1)$$
$$= 2e_s' W^{\frac{1}{2}} W_\gamma^{\frac{1}{2}} \dot{\delta} A^{11}\dot{\delta}' W_\gamma^{\frac{1}{2}} W^{\frac{1}{2}} e_s + o_p(1). \tag{19}$$

Combining Eqs. (13), (15), (17), and (19) gives

$$NF(\hat{\theta}) = e_s' W e_s - 2e_s' W^{\frac{1}{2}} W_\gamma^{\frac{1}{2}} \dot{\delta} A^{11}\dot{\delta}' W_\gamma^{\frac{1}{2}} W^{\frac{1}{2}} e_s + e_s' W^{\frac{1}{2}} W_\gamma^{\frac{1}{2}} \dot{\delta} A^{11}\dot{\delta}' W_\gamma^{\frac{1}{2}} W^{\frac{1}{2}} e_s + o_p(1)$$
$$= e_s' U e_s + o_p(1), \tag{20}$$

where

$$U = W - W^{\frac{1}{2}} W_\gamma^{\frac{1}{2}} \dot{\delta} A^{11}\dot{\delta}' W_\gamma^{\frac{1}{2}} W^{\frac{1}{2}}.$$

Let

$$\Gamma = \text{diag}(\Gamma_1, \ldots, \Gamma_m),$$

then it follows from Eq. (1) that $z = \Gamma^{-\frac{1}{2}} e_s \xrightarrow{\mathscr{L}} N_{p*}(0, I)$. Now we have from Eq. (20)

$$NF(\hat{\theta}) = z'(\Gamma^{\frac{1}{2}} W^{\frac{1}{2}})\{I - W^{\frac{1}{2}}_\gamma \dot{\delta} A^{11} \dot{\delta}' W^{\frac{1}{2}}_\gamma\}(W^{\frac{1}{2}} \Gamma^{\frac{1}{2}})z + o_p(1). \tag{21}$$

The first term on the right-hand side of Eq. (21) is a quadratic form in z. Consequently, the asymptotic distribution of $T_{ML} = NF(\hat{\theta})$ can be characterized as the distribution of a quadratic form of normal variates (e.g., Muirhead, 1982). Let τ_j be the nonzero eigenvalues of $U\Gamma$ and $\chi^2_{j_1}$ be independent chi-square variates with degree of freedom 1. Then

$$T_{ML} \xrightarrow{\mathscr{L}} \sum_{j=1}^{p^*-q+r} \tau_j \chi^2_{j1}. \tag{22}$$

Unless all the τ_j are equal, there is no simple distribution to describe the randomness of the right-hand side of Eq. (22). However, a simple rescaling on T_{ML} can result in a statistic that is better approximated by the $\chi^2_{p^*-q+r}$ distribution. Let $c = \text{tr}(U\Gamma)/(p^*-q+r)$. Then the rescaled statistic

$$T_{RML} = T_{ML}/\hat{c}$$

approaches a distribution with mean equal to that of $\chi^2_{p^*-q+r}$. Similar statistics for inference based on sample covariance matrices have been proposed by Satorra and Bentler (1988) for single-sample analysis and by Satorra (2000) for multisample analysis. Simulation work in the single-sample case with the sample covariance matrix has shown that this type of correction works remarkably well under a variety of conditions (e.g., Curran, West, & Finch, 1996; Hu, Bentler, & Kano, 1992).

A special case results when data are normal and sample means and covariance matrices are used in Eq. (2). Then $\Gamma = W^{-1}$. Since $W^{\frac{1}{2}}_\gamma \dot{\delta} A^{11} \dot{\delta}' W^{\frac{1}{2}}_\gamma$ is an idempotent matrix with rank $(q-r)$, it follows from Eq. (21) that

$$T_{ML} \xrightarrow{\mathscr{L}} \chi^2_{p^*-q+r},$$

which is the basis for the likelihood ratio statistic.

To study the property of the test statistic $T^{(h)}_{ML} = N [F(\hat{\theta}) - F(\hat{\theta}^*)]$, we also need to characterize the distribution of $NF(\hat{\theta}^*)$. This can be obtained by replacing the A^{11} in (21) with A^{-1}. Specifically, let

$$U^* = W - W^{\frac{1}{2}} W^{\frac{1}{2}}_\gamma \dot{\delta} A^{-1} \dot{\delta}' W^{\frac{1}{2}}_\gamma W^{\frac{1}{2}},$$

then

$$NF(\hat{\theta}*) = e_s' U* e_s + o_p(1). \tag{23}$$

Because $W_\gamma^{\frac{1}{2}} \dot{\delta} A^{-1} \dot{\delta}' W_\gamma^{\frac{1}{2}}$ is an idempotent matrix with rank q, there are only $p*-q$ nonzero eigenvalues of $U*\Gamma$. Denote these as $\tau_j^*, j=1, \ldots, p*-q$, then

$$NF(\hat{\theta}*) \overset{\mathcal{L}}{\to} \sum_{j=1}^{p*-q} \tau_j^* \chi_{j1}^2.$$

Similarly, letting $c* = \text{tr}(U*\Gamma)/(p*-q)$, the rescaled statistic

$$T_{RML}^* = NF(\hat{\theta}*)/\hat{c}*$$

approaches a distribution with mean equal to that of χ_{p*-q}^2.

For testing Constraint $h(\theta)=0$, based on Eqs. (20) and (23), the statistic $T_{ML}^{(h)}$ can be expressed as

$$T_{ML}^{(h)} = e_s'(U - U*)e_s + o_p(1). \tag{24}$$

It can be verified that

$$U - U* = W^{\frac{1}{2}} W_\gamma^{\frac{1}{2}} \dot{\delta}(A^{-1} - A^{11})\dot{\delta}' W_\gamma^{\frac{1}{2}} W^{\frac{1}{2}} \tag{25}$$

and $W_\gamma^{\frac{1}{2}} \dot{\delta}(A^{-1} - A^{11})\dot{\delta}' W_\gamma^{\frac{1}{2}}$ is an idempotent matrix of rank r. It follows from Eqs. (24) and (25) that

$$T_{ML}^{(h)} \overset{\mathcal{L}}{\to} \sum_{j=1}^{r} \kappa_j \chi_{j1}^2,$$

where κ_j are the nonzero eigenvalues of $(U-U*)\Gamma$. Let $c_h=\text{tr}[(U-U*)\Gamma]/r$, then

$$T_{RML}^{(h)} = T_{ML}^{(h)}/\hat{c}_h$$

converges to a distribution with mean r. Satorra (2000) gave a rescaled version of the Wald-type statistic for testing a constraint like Eq. (3) when sample moment matrices are used in Eq. (2).

A more general version than testing $h(\theta)=0$ is to test one set of constraints nested within another set of constraints. Let the two sets of constraints be represented by $h(\theta)=0$ and $g(\theta)=0$, and

$$\mathcal{R}_h = \{\theta: h(\theta) = 0\} \subset \mathcal{R}_g = \{\theta : g(\theta) = 0\}. \tag{26}$$

A rescaled statistic for testing Eq. (26) can be derived similarly. Let U_h and U_g represent the U matrices corresponding to the constraints, then the likelihood ratio statistic $T_{ML}^{(h \subset g)} = T_{ML}^{(h)} - T_{ML}^{(g)}$ can be written as

$$T_{ML}^{(h \subset g)} = e_s'(U_h - U_g)e_s + o_p(1).$$

Let r_h and r_g be the numbers of independent constraints in $h(\theta)=0$ and $g(\theta)=0$, respectively, then

$$\text{tr}[(U_h - U_g)\Gamma] = \text{tr}(U_h\Gamma) - \text{tr}(U_g\Gamma) = (p^* - q + r_h)c_h - (p^* - q + r_g)c_g,$$

we have

$$c_{(h \subset g)} = [(p^* - q + r_h)c_h - (p^* - q + r_g)c_g]/(r_h - r_g). \qquad (27)$$

Suppose a software has already had the rescaling option for nonstandard samples with constraint built in, but rescaling for nested models is still not available. Then we can get $c_{(h \subset g)}$ using Eq. (27) in a straightforward way. Let $T_{ML}^{(g)}$ and $T_{RML}^{(g)}$ be the likelihood ratio statistic and the rescaled statistic, respectively. Then $\hat{c}_g = T_{ML}^{(g)}/T_{RML}^{(g)}$, and similarly to obtain $\hat{c}_h$. Because $p^* - q + r_h$ and $p^* - q + r_g$ are just the degrees of freedom in the two models, $\hat{c}_{(h \subset g)}$ immediately follows from Eq. (27). The above procedure was developed by Satorra and Bentler (1999), where the rescaled statistic for nested models is given for sample moments.

ESTIMATING δ_j AND Γ_j FOR NONSTANDARD SAMPLES

Estimation of covariance matrices for nonstandard samples can be accomplished by various procedures described in the statistical literature. Because the most commonly encountered nonstandard situations in the social and behavioral sciences are probably non-normal samples, samples with outliers, and samples with missing data, we deal with each of these situations in sequence. The following procedures for estimating δ_j and Γ_j are based on our experience with various practical nonstandard samples. A further discussion of these procedures applied to exploratory factor analysis can be found in Yuan, Marshall, and Bentler (1999).

Non-Normal Data

When samples come from distributions with heavy tails that are not due to outliers, sample mean vectors and covariance matrices may still be unbiased estimates of their population counterparts. For example, if a sample is from a multivariate t-distribution, the sample does not contain outliers, but is still non-normal. In such a case, using sample mean vectors and covariance matrices in Eq. (2) still leads to consistent parameter estimates when all of the population second-order moments exist. To obtain consistent standard errors, we need to have the population fourth-order moment matrices to exist. Let $X_{1j}, \ldots,$ X_{n_jj} be the sample from the jth group with sample mean $\bar{X}_j$, let $Y_{ij} = \{X'_{ij}, \text{vech}'[(X_{ij} - \bar{X}_j)(X_{ij} - \bar{X}_j)']\}'$ with sample mean vector $\bar{Y}_j$ and sample covariance matrix S_{Yj}. Then $t_{nj} = \bar{Y}_j$ and

$$\hat{\Gamma}_j = S_{Yj}$$

is a consistent estimator of Γ_j in Eq. (1). Using the sample fourth-order moment matrix to estimate its population counterpart was first used by Browne (1982, 1984) in the context of covariance structure analysis. Mooijaart and Bentler (1985) formulated an efficient way to compute S_{Yj}.

Data With Outliers

With non-normal data, sample moments are no longer the most efficient estimates of their population counterparts. If the non-normality is created by outliers, analysis based on sample moments can be misleading to a greater or lesser degree depending on the influence of the outliers. There are two ways to deal with outliers. One is to identify the influential cases through some analytical procedure and make a subjective decision whether to keep them. Another way is to use a robust approach. Regardless of whether any cases are outliers or just influential cases, their effect is automatically downweighted through this approach. Compared with an outlier-removal approach, the merit of a downweighting approach was discussed by Rousseeuw and van Zomeren (1990). We also use the downweighting approach here. We especially recommend the Huber-type weight because of its explicit control of the percentage of outliers when the majority of a data cloud follows a multivariate normal distribution.

For the sample $X_{1j}, \ldots, X_{n_jj}$ from the jth population, let

$$d_{ij} = d(X_{ij}, \mu_j, \Sigma_j) = [(X_{ij} - \mu_j)'\Sigma_j^{-1}(X_{ij} - \mu_j)]^{1/2}$$

be the Mahalanobis distance and $u_1(t)$ and $u_2(t)$ be some non-negative scalar functions. Maronna (1976) defined robust M estimators $(\hat{\mu}_j, \hat{\Sigma}_j)$ by solving the following equations:

$$\mu_j = \sum_{i=1}^{n_j} u_1(d_{ij})X_{ij} \Big/ \sum_{i=1}^{n_j} u_1(d_{ij}) \qquad (28a)$$

and

$$\Sigma_j = \sum_{i=1}^{n_j} u_2(d_{ij}^2)(X_{ij} - \mu_j)(X_{ij} - \mu_j)'/n_j. \tag{28b}$$

If $u_1(t)$ and $u_2(t)$ are decreasing functions, cases with larger d_{ij}s will get smaller weights than those with smaller d_{ij}s. If a case lies far away from the majority of the data cloud, its effect is downweighted. A solution to Eq. (28) can be obtained through iteratively reweighted least squares (e.g., Green, 1984). The Huber-type weight is given by

$$u_1(d) = \begin{cases} 1, & \text{if } d \leq r \\ r/d, & \text{if } d > r \end{cases} \tag{29}$$

and $u_2(d^2) = \{u_1(d)\}^2/\beta$ (e.g., Tyler, 1983). Here r^2 satisfies $P(\chi_{p_j}^2 > r^2) = \alpha$, α is the percentage of outliers one wants to control assuming the massive data cloud follows a multivariate normal distribution, and β is a constant such that $E\{\chi_p^2 u_2(\chi_p^2)\} = p_j$. The scaling factor β makes the estimator $\hat{\Sigma}_j$ unbiased for Σ_j if sampling is from a p_j-variate normal distribution. Notice that only the tuning parameter α needs to be decided in applying the Huber-type weight because r and β are just functions of α.

Let X_{ij}, $i=1, \ldots, n_j$ follow an elliptical distribution (e.g., Fang, Kotz, & Ng, 1990) and $S_{nj} = \hat{\Sigma}_j$ be a robust covariance matrix estimate. S_{nj} generally does not converge to the population covariance matrix. Instead, it converges to a constant times the population covariance matrix: $\kappa_j \Sigma_j$. The positive scalar κ_j depends on the weight function used in the estimation procedure, as well as the unknown underlying distribution of the data. Because of this issue, we recommend using the Huber-type weight with the same α for every sample of the m groups. Because multiple samples are commonly obtained by administering the same questionnaire to m groups, the massive data cloud in each sample should resemble the massive data clouds of other samples, although one may contain fewer or more influential cases than the others. Actually, robust covariance matrices from separate samples are much more similar than traditional sample counterparts when data have heavy tails (Yuan, Marshall, & Weston, 1999).

We resort to the estimating equation approach for getting a consistent estimator of Γ_j. Rewrite Eq. (28) as

$$\frac{1}{n_j} \sum_{i=1}^{n_j} G_j(X_{ij}, \delta_j) = 0, \tag{30a}$$

where

$$G_j(x, \delta_j) = \begin{pmatrix} u_1[d(x, \mu_j, \Sigma_j)](x - \mu_j) \\ u_2[d^2(x, \mu_j, \Sigma_j)]\text{vech}[(x - \mu_j)(x - \mu_j)'] - \sigma_j \end{pmatrix}. \tag{30b}$$

Then

$$\sqrt{n_j}\,(\hat{\delta}_j - \delta_{j0}) \xrightarrow{\mathscr{L}} N(0, \Gamma_j), \tag{31}$$

where $\Gamma_j = H_j^{-1} B_j H_j'^{-1}$ with

$$H_j = E\,[\dot{G}_j(X_{ij}, \delta_{j0})] \quad \text{and} \quad B_j = E\,[G_j(X_{ij}, \delta_{j0})G'(X_{ij}, \delta_{j0})].$$

A consistent estimator of Γ_j can be obtained by using consistent estimates for H_j and B_j. These are given by

$$\hat{H}_j = \frac{1}{n_j}\sum_{i=1}^{n_j} \dot{G}_j(X_{ij}, \hat{\delta}_j) \quad \text{and} \quad \hat{B}_j = \frac{1}{n_j}\sum_{i=1}^{n_j} G_j(X_{ij}, \hat{\delta}_j)G_j'(X_{ij}, \hat{\delta}_j).$$

Normal Missing Data

Data are said to be missing completely at random (MCAR) if their absence does not depend on the missing values nor on the observed values of the other variables. Data are said to be missing at random (MAR) if the missing data do not depend on the missing values, but may depend on the observed values of other variables. For the jth sample with missing data, denote X_{ij} as the vector of observed variables for the ith case with Dimension p_{ij}. Then $E(X_{ij}) = \mu_{ij}$ and $\text{Cov}(X_{ij}) = \Sigma_{ij}$ are, respectively, subvector of μ_j and submatrix of Σ_j. Under the assumption of normality, the log likelihood function based on X_{ij} is

$$l_{ij}(\delta_j) = \frac{p_{ij}}{2}\log(2\pi) - \frac{1}{2}[\log|\Sigma_{ij}| + (X_{ij} - \mu_{ij})'\Sigma_{ij}^{-1}(X_{ij} - \mu_{ij})]. \tag{32a}$$

The MLE of δ_j is actually obtained by maximizing

$$l_j(\delta_j) = \sum_{i=1}^{n_j} l_{ij}(\delta_j). \tag{32b}$$

Consequently, $\hat{\delta}_j$ satisfies the following generalized estimating equation

$$G_j(\hat{\delta}_j) = 0, \tag{33a}$$

where

$$G_j(\delta_j) = \frac{1}{n_j}\sum_{i=1}^{n_j} \dot{l}_{ij}(\delta_j). \tag{33b}$$

A solution to Eq. (33) is straightforward using the EM algorithm developed in Dempster, Laird, and Rubin (1977). Specific steps are also discussed in detail in

Little and Rubin (1987). Assuming the missing data mechanism is MAR, using the result for generalized estimating equations (e.g., Liang & Zeger, 1986; Yuan & Jennrich, 1998), we have

$$\sqrt{n_j}(\hat{\delta}_j - \delta_{j0}) \xrightarrow{\mathcal{L}} N(0, \Gamma_j), \tag{34a}$$

where $\Gamma_j = A_j^{-1} B_j A_j^{-1}$ with

$$A_j = -E[\dot{G}_j(\delta_{j0})], \quad B_j = E\Big[\frac{1}{n_j} \sum_{i=1}^{n_j} l_{ij}(\delta_{j0}) l'_{ij}(\delta_{j0})\Big]. \tag{34b}$$

A consistent estimate of Γ_j is given by

$$\hat{\Gamma}_j = \hat{A}_j^{-1} \hat{B}_j \hat{A}_j^{-1}$$

with

$$\hat{A}_j = -\dot{G}_j(\hat{\delta}_j), \quad \hat{B}_j = \frac{1}{n_j} \sum_{i=1}^{n_j} l_{ij}(\hat{\delta}_j) l'_{ij}(\hat{\delta}_j).$$

When $X_{ij} \sim N(\mu_{ij}, \Sigma_{ij})$, the corresponding observed information matrix is given by $\hat{A}_j$ (Kenward & Molenberghs, 1998; Little & Rubin, 1987) and $\hat{\Gamma}_j = \hat{A}_j^{-1}$ is consistent for Γ_j in Eq. (34). For a general non-normal distribution, the result in Eq. (34) is also correct as long as the missing data mechanism is MCAR. However, as discussed in Laird (1988), some bias may exist in using $\hat{\delta}_j$ to estimate δ_{j0} when data are not normal and missing data are MAR. Ideally, it would be desirable to model a data set through ML to avoid bias. However, because of complexity of the real world, there are always discrepancies between the underlying distribution of the data and a carefully specified modeling distribution. So we would consider the normal distribution assumption for missing data to offer only a working assumption in multivariate analysis. Fortunately, for estimating population mean vectors and covariance matrices, a recent simulation study by Yuan and Bentler (2000a) indicated that the bias is minimal for a variety of non-normal distributions. It is important to realize that once t_{nj} is used in Eq. (2), the parameter estimate $\hat{\theta}$ is the same whatever missing data mechanism is assumed. The important question is this: Which procedure leads to a more accurate evaluation of model structures? According to the results for single-group analysis in Yuan and Bentler (2000a), inference based on Eq. (34) is much more accurate than that based on the observed information matrix. We recommend using Eq. (34) for estimating Γ_j.

Non-normal Missing Data

When a sample contains both missing data and outliers, normal theory-based missing data procedures lead to inaccurate conclusions. As in the situation with complete data, appropriate downweighting procedures are needed for better inference. Little and Smith (1987) proposed several methods for such a purpose. Little (1988) further proposed the EM algorithm for modeling missing data by a multivariate t distribution as well as a multivariate contaminated normal distribution. Here we outline a procedure for using the multivariate t distribution to get $t_{nj} = \hat{\delta}_j$ and $\hat{\Gamma}_j$.

The density of the p-variate t distribution with degrees of freedom k is given by

$$f(x \mid \mu, \Sigma, k) = \frac{\Gamma[(p+k)/2]}{(k\pi)^{p/2}\Gamma(k/2)} |\Sigma|^{-1/2} \left(1 + \frac{(x-\mu)'\Sigma^{-1}(x-\mu)}{k}\right)^{-(p+k)/2}. \quad (35)$$

If X follows Eq. (35) with $k > 2$, then $E(X) = \mu$ and $\text{Cov}(X) = k\Sigma/(k-2)$. So the MLE of Σ converges to $\kappa \text{Cov}(X)$ with $\kappa = (k-2)/k$. As discussed previously, we recommend using t distributions with the same degrees of freedom for each of the m samples.

Denote Eq. (35) as $Mt_p(\mu, \Sigma, k)$. Because a marginal distribution of Eq. (35) is also a t distribution with the same degrees of freedom (e.g., Fang, Kotz, & Ng, 1990; Kano, 1994), if $X_{ij} \sim Mt_{p_{ij}}(\mu_{ij}, \Sigma_{ij}, k)$, its log likelihood function is

$$l_{ij}(\delta_j) = c_{ij} - \frac{1}{2}\log|\Sigma_{ij}| - \frac{(p_{ij}+k)}{2}\log\left[1 + \frac{(X_{ij}-\mu_{ij})'\Sigma_{ij}^{-1}(X_{ij}-\mu_{ij})}{k}\right], \quad (36a)$$

where $\delta_j = (\mu_j', \delta_j')'$. The MLE of δ_j can be obtained by maximizing

$$l_j(\delta_j) = \sum_{i=1}^{n_j} l_{ij}(\delta_j). \quad (36b)$$

Similarly, as in the last section, the $\hat{\delta}_j$ satisfies the following generalized estimating equation

$$G_j(\hat{\delta}_j) = 0, \quad (37a)$$

where

$$G_j(\delta_j) = \frac{1}{n_j} \sum_{i=1}^{n_j} \dot{l}_{ij}(\delta_j). \quad (37b)$$

We can maximize Eq. (36) for δ_j and k simultaneously. However, a data set may not exactly follow a t distribution, and the simultaneous ML procedure may not lead to the most efficient estimator of δ_j. In addition to requiring much more complicated computations, a nonadmissible MLE of k may occur with some practical data as discussed in Lange, Little, and Taylor (1989). Little (1988) recommended using several prefixed ks and then using the $\hat{\delta}_j$ corresponding to the largest $l_j(\hat{\delta}_j)$ as the final parameter estimator. Real data examples in Yuan and Bentler (1998a, 1998b) indicate that most of the smaller ks ($1 \leq k \leq 5$) can effectively control the influence of outliers in SEM. In practice, we suggest following Little's recommendation to try several prefixed k (e.g., $1 \leq k \leq 5$). With a fixed k, the solution to Eq. (37) is straightforward using the EM algorithm developed in Little (1988).

As discussed for the normal theory based likelihood function, the t distribution in Eq. (36) is only a working assumption for downweighting outliers. Real data may not exactly follow such an assumption. Consequently, computations to obtain good standard error estimators need to be modified. We use a sandwich-type covariance matrix to describe the distribution of $\hat{\delta}_j$. With a MAR assumption for the missing data mechanism, this is given by

$$\sqrt{n_j}\,(\hat{\delta}_j - \hat{\delta}_{j0}) \xrightarrow{\mathcal{L}} N(0, \Gamma_j), \tag{38a}$$

where $\Gamma_j = A_j^{-1} B_j A_j^{-1}$ with

$$A_j = -E[\dot{G}_j(\delta_{j0})], \quad B_j = E\left[\frac{1}{n_j}\sum_{i=1}^{n_j} \dot{l}_{ij}(\delta_{j0})\,\dot{l}_{ij}'(\delta_{j0})\right]. \tag{38b}$$

A consistent estimate of Γ_j is obtained from

$$\hat{\Gamma}_j = \hat{A}_j^{-1}\hat{B}_j\hat{A}_j^{-1} \tag{38c}$$

with

$$\hat{A}_j = -\dot{G}_j(\hat{\delta}_j), \quad \hat{B}_j = \frac{1}{n_j}\sum_{i=1}^{n_j} \dot{l}_{ij}(\hat{\delta}_j)\dot{l}_{ij}'(\hat{\delta}_j).$$

When evidence suggests that a data set does closely follow the t distribution used in obtaining $\hat{\delta}_j$, we may use the inverse of the observed information matrix $\hat{A}_j^{-1}$ instead of Eq. (38c) to describe the behavior of $\hat{\delta}_j$. However, the result in Eq. (38) is more accurate under violation of distributional assumptions. When the missing data mechanism is MAR, and the data set does not follow a multivariate t distribution, there may exist a bias for using $\hat{\delta}_j$ to estimate δ_{j0} (Laird, 1988). That is, the $\hat{\delta}_j$ may not approach δ_{j0} as the sample size increases. Based on results in Yuan and Bentler (2000a), we suspect that the bias would be minimal for most of the commonly encountered continuous distributions. Further studies on bias associated with the MLE from a misspecified t distribution and different missing data mechanisms would provide a valuable guide for future application of the method. For the same reason as discussed for the normality working assumption in the previous subsection, our interest is to obtain a better description of the variability in $t_{nj} = \hat{\delta}_j$.

DISCUSSION AND CONCLUSION

Motivated by the typical nonstandard samples for survey data in practice—that is, samples with nonnormal distributions, missing data, and outliers—we proposed replacing the sample mean vectors and sample covariance matrices by more appropriate quantities t_{nj} in the normal theory based likelihood function for multigroup SEM. Because the parameter estimator $\hat{\theta}$ depends on t_{nj}, possible merits of t_{nj} such as efficiency and robustness are inherited by $\hat{\theta}$. Standard errors of $\hat{\theta}$ are obtained through a generalized estimating equation approach. Two rescaled test statistics, one for the overall structural model with constraints, and one just for the constraints, are provided. Procedures for obtaining appropriate t_{nj} for each situation, and their large sample covariance matrices, are given for each of several nonstandard sampling setups. Our approach is so general that it can be applied to any types of nonstandard samples once a new method for estimating the population mean vector and covariance matrix together with the associated Γ matrix are available for such samples.

We have chosen to use the normal theory-based likelihood function as the discrepancy function to measure the distance between t_{nj} and $\delta_j(\beta)$ because of its relative advantage in reaching convergence. A generalized least squares approach using $\hat{\Gamma}_j^{-1}$ as weights is equally general, and development along this line is straightforward.

It would be ideal to demonstrate the earlier procedures with a practical example for each of the various types of nonstandard samples considered. Due to the unavailability of multiple samples that contain the various features, such a demonstration is not done at present. Future research clearly should be directed to evaluating our proposals. Based on our experience with the inference procedures for various one-group nonstandard samples, we would expect the proposed procedures to generally give much more reliable model and parameter evaluation than classical procedures based on sample moments. Our recommendation is to use the proper methods given herein to estimate (μ_j, Σ_j) and Γ_j when nonstandard samples occur in practice, and follow the discussed procedure for model evaluation.

ACKNOWLEDGEMENT

This project was supported by a University of North Texas Faculty Research Grant and Grants DA01070 and DA00017 from the National Institute on Drug Abuse.

REFERENCES

Aitchison, J., & Silvey, S. D. (1958). Maximum likelihood estimation of parameters subject to restraints. *Annals of Mathematical Statistics, 29*, 813–828.

Allison, P. D. (1987). Estimation of linear models with incomplete data. In C. C. Clogg (Ed.), *Sociological methodology 1987* (pp. 71–103). San Francisco: Jossey-Bass.

Arbuckle, J. L. (1996). Full information estimation in the presence of incomplete data. In G. A. Marcoulides & R. E. Schumacker (Eds.), *Advanced structural equation modeling: Issues and techniques* (pp. 243–277). Mahwak, NJ: Lawrence Erlbaum Associates.

Arminger, G., & Sobel, M. E. (1990). Pseudo-maximum likelihood estimation of mean and covariance structures with missing data. *Journal of the American Statistical Association, 85*, 195–203.

Austin, J. T., & Calderón, R. F. (1996). Theoretical and technical contributions to structural equation modeling: An updated annotated bibliography. *Structural Equation Modeling, 3*, 105–175.

Austin, J. T., & Wolfle, D. (1991). Annotated bibliography of structural equation modeling: Technical work. *British Journal of Mathematical and Statistical Psychology, 44*, 93–152.

Bentler, P. M. (2001). *EQS 6 structural equations program manual*. Encino, CA: Multivariate Software (www.mvsoft.com).

Bentler, P. M., & Dijkstra, T. (1985). Efficient estimation via linearization in structural models. In P. R. Krishnaiah (Ed.), *Multivariate analysis VI* (pp. 9–42). Amsterdam: North-Holland.

Bentler, P. M., & Dudgeon, P. (1996). Covariance structure analysis: Statistical practice, theory, and directions. *Annual Review of Psychology, 47*, 541–570.

Bentler, P. M., Lee, S.-Y., & Weng, L.-J. (1987). Multiple population covariance structure analysis under arbitrary distribution theory. *Communication in Statistics-Theory and Method, 16*, 1951–1964.

Berkane, M., & Bentler, P. M. (1988). Estimation of contamination parameters and identification of outliers in multivariate data. Sociological Methods and Research, *17*, 55–64.

Bollen, K. A. (1989). *Structural equations with latent variables*. New York: Wiley.

Bollen, K. A., & Arminger, G. (1991). Observational residuals in factor analysis and structural equation models. In P. V. Marsden (Ed.), *Sociological methodology 1991* (pp. 235–262). Oxford: Basil Blackwell.

Browne, M. W. (1982). Covariance structures. In D. M. Hawkins (Ed.), *Topics in applied multivariate analysis* (pp. 72–141). Cambridge: Cambridge University Press.

Browne, M. W. (1984). Asymptotic distribution-free methods for the analysis of covariance structures. *British Journal of Mathematical and Statistical Psychology, 37*, 62–83.

Browne, M. W., & Arminger, G. (1995). Specification and estimation of mean and covariance structure models. In G. Arminger, C. C. Clogg, & M. E. Sobel (Eds.), *Handbook of statistical modeling for the social and behavioral sciences* (pp. 185–249). New York: Plenum.

Byrne, B. M. (1994). *Structural equation modeling with EQS and EQS/Windows*. Thousand Oaks, CA: Sage.

Cadigan, N. G. (1995). Local influence in structural equation models. *Structural Equation Modeling, 2*, 13–30.

Chong, E. K. P., & Żak, S. H. (1996). An introduction to optimization. New York: Wiley.

Curran, P. J., West, S. G., & Finch, J. F. (1996). The robustness of test statistics to non-normality and specification error in confirmatory factor analysis. *Psychological Methods, 1*, 16–29.

Dempster, A. P., Laird, N. M., & Rubin, D. B. (1977). Maximum likelihood estimation from incomplete data via the EM algorithm (with discussion). *Journal of the Royal Statistical Society Series B, 39*, 1–38.

Dunn, G., Everitt, B., & Pickles, A. (1993). *Modeling covariances and latent variables using EQS*. London: Chapman & Hall.

Fang, K.-T., Kotz, S., & Ng, K. W. (1990). *Symmetric multivariate and related distributions*. London: Chapman & Hall.

Green, P. J. (1984). Iteratively reweighted least squares for maximum likelihood estimation, and some robust and resistent alternatives (with discussion). *Journal of the Royal Statistical Society, Series B*, 46, 149–192.

Hoyle, R. (Ed.), (1995). *Structural equation modeling: Concepts, issues, and applications.* Thousand Oaks, CA: Sage.

Hu, L.T., Bentler, P.M., & Kano, Y. (1992). Can test statistics in covariance structure analysis be trusted? *Psychological Bulletin, 112*, 351–362.

Jamshidian, M., & Bentler, P. M. (1999). Using complete data routines for ML estimation of mean and covariance structures with missing data. *Journal of Educational and Behavioral Statistics, 23*, 21–41.

Jöreskog, K. G. (1971). Simultaneous factor analysis in several populations. *Psychometrika, 36*, 409–426.

Jöreskog, K. G. & Sörbom, D. (1993). *LISREL 8 user's reference guide.* Chicago: Scientific Software International.

Kano, Y. (1994). Consistency property of elliptical probability density functions. *Journal of Multivariate Analysis, 51*, 139–147.

Kenward, M. G., & Molenberghs, G. (1998). Likelihood based frequentist inference when data are missing at random. *Statistical Science, 13*, 236–247.

Kline, R. B. (1998). *Principles and practice of structural equation modeling.* New York: Guilford.

Laird, N. M. (1988). Missing data in longitudinal studies. *Statistics in Medicine, 7*, 305–315.

Lange, K. L., Little, R. J. A., & Taylor, J. M. G. (1989). Robust statistical modeling using the *t* distribution. *Journal of the American Statistical Association, 84*, 881–896.

Lee, S.-Y. (1986). Estimation for structural equation models with missing data. *Psychometrika, 51*, 93–99.

Lee, S. Y., & Wang, S. J. (1996). Sensitivity analysis of structural equation models. *Psychometrika, 61*, 93–108.

Liang, K. Y., & Zeger, S. L. (1986). Longitudinal data analysis using generalized linear models. *Biometrika, 73*, 13–22.

Little, R. J. A. (1988). Robust estimation of the mean and covariance matrix from data with missing values. *Applied Statistics, 37*, 23–38.

Little, R. J. A., & Rubin, D. B. (1987). *Statistical analysis with missing data.* New York: Wiley.

Little, R. J. A., & Smith, P. J. (1987). Editing and imputation for quantitative survey data. *Journal of the American Statistical Association, 82*, 58–68.

Magnus, J. R., & Neudecker, H. (1988). *Matrix differential calculus with applications in statistics and econometrics.* New York: Wiley.

Marcoulides, G. A., & Schumacker, R. E. (Eds.), (1996). *Advanced structural equation modeling: Issues and techniques.* Mahwah, NJ: Lawrence Erlbaum Associates.

Maronna, R. A. (1976). Robust M-estimators of multivariate location and scatter. *Annals of Statistics, 4*, 51–67.

Mooijaart, A., & Bentler, P. M. (1985). The weight matrix in asymptotic distribution-free methods. *British Journal of Mathematical and Statistical Psychology, 38*, 190–196.

Mueller, R. O. (1996). Basic principles of structural equation modeling. New York: Springer Verlag.

Muirhead, R. J. (1982). Aspects of multivariate statistical theory. New York: Wiley.

Muthén, B. (1989). Multiple group structural modelling with nonnormal continuous variables. *British Journal of Mathematical and Statistical Psychology, 42*, 55–62.

Muthén, B., Kaplan, D., & Hollis, M. (1987). On structural equation modeling with data that are not missing completely at random. *Psychometrika, 52*, 431–462.

Rousseeuw, P. J., & van Zomeren, B. C. (1990). Unmasking multivariate outliers and leverage points. *Journal of the American Statistical Association, 85*, 633–639.

Satorra, A. (2000). Scaled and adjusted restricted tests in multi-sample analysis of moment structures. In D. D. H. Heijmans, D. S. G. Pollock, & A. Satorra (Eds.), *Innovations in multivariate statistical analysis: A Festschrift for Heinz Neudecker* (pp. 233–247). Dordrecht: Kluwer Academic.

Satorra, A., & Bentler, P. M. (1988). Scaling corrections for chi-square statistics in covariance structure analysis. *American Statistical Association 1988 proceedings of Business and Economics Sections* (pp. 308–313). Alexandria, VA: American Statistical Association.

Satorra, A., & Bentler, P. M. (1999). A scaled difference chi-square test statistic for moment structure analysis. University of California, Los Angeles: UCLA Statistics Series, No. 260 (www.stat.ucla.edu).

Schumacker, R. E., & Lomax, R. G. (1996). *A beginner's guide to structural equation modeling.* Mahwah, NJ: Lawrence Erlbaum Associates.

Sörbom, D. (1974). A general method for studying differences in factor means and factor structures between groups. *British Journal of Mathematical and Statistical Psychology, 27,* 229–239.

Tanaka, Y., Watadani, S., & Moon, S. H. (1991). Influence in covariance structure analysis: With an application to confirmatory factor analysis. *Communication in Statistics-Theory and Method, 20,* 3805–3821.

Tremblay, P. F., & Gardner, R. C. (1996). On the growth of structural equation modeling in psychological journals. *Structural Equation Modeling, 3,* 93–104.

Tyler, D. E. (1983). Robustness and efficiency properties of scatter matrices. *Biometrika, 70,* 411–420.

Yuan, K.-H., & Bentler, P. M. (1998a). Robust mean and covariance structure analysis. *British Journal of Mathematical and Statistical Psychology, 51,* 63–88.

Yuan, K.-H., & Bentler, P. M. (1998b). Structural equation modeling with robust covariances. *Sociological methodology, 28,* 363–396.

Yuan, K.-H., & Bentler, P. M. (2000a). Three likelihood-based methods for mean and covariance structure analysis with nonnormal missing data. *Sociological methodology, 30,* 165–200.

Yuan, K.-H., & Bentler, P. M. (2000b). Robust mean and covariance structure analysis through iteratively reweighted least squares. *Psychometrika, 65,* 43–58.

Yuan, K.-H., Chan, W., & Bentler, P. M. (2000). Robust transformation with applications to structural equation modeling. *British Journal of Mathematical and Statistical Psychology, 53,* 31–50.

Yuan, K.-H., & Jennrich, R. I. (1998). Asymptotics of estimating equations under natural conditions. *Journal of Multivariate Analysis, 65,* 245–260.

Yuan, K.-H., Marshall, L., & Bentler, P. M. (1999). A unified approach to exploratory factor analysis with missing data, nonnormal data, and in the presence of outliers. Under review.

Yuan, K.-H., Marshall, L., & Weston, R. (1999). Cross-validation through downweighting influential cases in structural equation modeling. Under review.

3

Modeling of Intervention Effects With Noncompliance: A Latent Variable Approach for Randomized Trials

Booil Jo
Bengt O. Muthén
University of California, Los Angeles

It is well known that experimental designs based on randomization are powerful in terms of statistical analysis and inference. However, the estimation of treatment effects can be biased even with successful randomization unless everyone complies with the given treatment. Noncompliance is not only an obstacle to fair statistical comparison between the treatment group and the control group, but also a major threat to obtaining power to detect intervention effects (Jo, 2000c). Depending on how noncompliance is dealt with in the estimation of treatment effects, different conclusions may be reached about the effect of the same intervention trial.

Figure 3.1 illustrates subgroups in the intervention trial based on treatment assignment and compliance. It is shown that belonging to the complier or non-complier category is not randomized but chosen by individuals, whereas the assignment to treatment or control condition is randomized. In the treatment condition, compliance behavior is actually observed and individuals can be categorized into either the *complier* or *noncomplier* category. In the control condition, compliance behavior cannot be observed because treatment is never offered. Therefore, individuals in the control condition are potentially either complier or noncomplier, but cannot be categorized based on observed compliance behavior. Potential compliers are individuals in the control condition who would comply

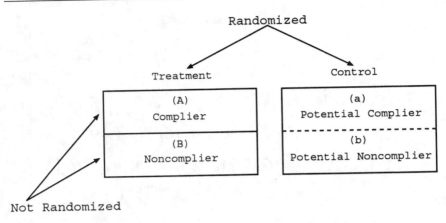

FIG. 3.1.   Randomization and compliance.

with the treatment if it had been offered. Potential noncompliers are individuals in the control condition who would not comply with the treatment even if it had been offered.

Intent to Treat (ITT) analysis is a standard way to estimate treatment effects in randomized experimental designs. In this method, average outcomes are compared by randomized groups ignoring compliance status information. In other words, the treatment effect is estimated assuming that every subject in the treatment condition actually received the treatment. It is shown in Fig. 3.1 that the treatment ($A + B$) and the control ($a + b$) groups are statistically comparable in this method because both groups consist of both compliers and noncompliers. However, if only compliers are the targeted subpopulation of interest, there is a possible bias in the estimation of treatment effects by including noncompliers in the analysis.

As-treated analysis is another commonly used method to estimate intervention effects in the presence of noncompliance. This method focuses on the receipt of the treatment, but ignores the fact that compliance behavior is not randomized but chosen by individuals, and the characteristics of compliers are often different from those of the rest. For example, people with higher motivation or a special interest in the treatment are more likely to participate in that treatment. This method presents an unfair statistical comparison between groups, by comparing recipients (A) in the treatment group with nonrecipients ($B + a + b$) both in the treatment and the control group.

When compliers are the targeted subpopulation of interest, there is a possible bias in the estimation of treatment effects in the presence of noncompliance both in ITT and as-treated analysis. To counter this unfair comparison, the possibility of estimating causal effects of the treatment only for the individuals who actually received the treatment has been explored under the label Complier Average Causal Effect (CACE; Angrist, Imbens, & Rubin, 1996; Bloom, 1984; Imbens & Rubin, 1997; Little & Yau, 1998) estimation. This method not only provides the estimation of treatment effects only for compliers, but also presents a fair statistical comparison by comparing the compliers (A) in the treatment group to the potential compliers (a) in the control group (see Fig. 3.1).

The CACE estimation method has been applied using several approaches. The major technical difficulty involved in CACE approaches is that the compliance status of the individuals in the control condition is unknown. The unknown compliance status in the control group makes it difficult to differentiate effects of the treatment based on compliance status. One way to solve this problem is to use the instrumental variable (IV) approach, where treatment effect estimates are adjusted by considering the proportion of noncompliers (Bloom, 1984). More recently, a refined form of the IV approach with clear underlying assumptions has been proposed (Angrist, Imbens, & Rubin, 1996). A more efficient way to solve this problem is to identify potential compliance status of the control group individuals so that average outcomes can be directly compared based on randomization. This method has been demonstrated through a Bayesian approach that combines the use of EM and data-augmentation algorithms (Imbens & Rubin, 1997) and the maximum-likelihood estimation method using the EM algorithm (Little & Yau, 1998). The idea of CACE made dramatic progress in the estimation of treatment effects in the presence of noncompliance. By introducing Bayesian inferential methods and missing data techniques, this approach opened the possibility for more flexible model-based estimation of treatment effects.

Structural equation modeling has potential for flexible CACE modeling. However, the exploration possibility of CACE modeling in this area is limited within the conventional framework. Although the unknown compliance status in the control group can be naturally seen as a missing data problem in general, subgroups of individuals based on compliance status can be better understood as a latent variable in the structural equation modeling framework. The systematic role of compliance categories distiguishes latent membership from missing data in outcome measures. That is, individuals in different compliance categories can be seen as finite mixtures (Titterington, Smith, & Makov, 1985) of subpopulations that might have separate distributions and different model parameters. If the compliance status is known for everybody, this problem can be solved using the multiple-group approach in conventional structural equation modeling. Because the group membership is unknown for individuals in the control group, this problem cannot be solved unless discrete latent variables can be included in the model.

The current study demonstrates that the problem of noncompliance can be dealt with in a broader framework of structural equation modeling by looking at compliance status as a categorical latent variable, and also demonstartes the flexibility of CACE modeling in this framework. To demonstrate how the latent variable approach works in dealing with compliance information in various situations, the Job Search Intervention Study for unemployed workers (Vinokur, Price, & Schul, 1995; Vinokur & Schul, 1997), the Study of Vitamin Supplement Effect on Survival Rates in young children (Imbens & Rubin, 1997; Sommer et al., 1986; Sommer & Zeger, 1991), and the Johns Hopkins Public School Preventive Intervention Study (Ialongo et al., 1999) are used as examples.

This chapter is organized as follows. First, it defines model assumptions and the estimation method using the ML-EM algorithm. Second, it demonstrates CACE estimation with a single continuous outcome, with results compared to those from the ITT approach. Third, it demonstrates CACE estimation with a single categorical outcome, with results compared to those from the ITT approach. Fourth, it demonstrates CACE estimation with multiple outcomes, with results compared to those from CACE estimation using a single outcome measure. Fifth, it demonstrates growth mixture CACE estimation using repeated outcome measures with a trend. Results are compared to those from CACE estimation using a single outcome measure. The chapter concludes with discussion.

CACE ESTIMATION IN THE LATENT VARIABLE MODELING FRAMEWORK

Model Assumptions

The common purpose of the models used in this study is to estimate the treatment effect for the compliers (CACE) and to draw causal inference about this treatment effect through experimental designs based on randomization. In line with Rubin's causal model, there are some general assumptions required to be able to make causal inference. In Rubin's causal model approach, the possibility of statistical causal inference is built based on the effect of treatment assignment at the individual level (Holland, 1986; Rubin, 1974, 1978, 1980). The assumption of potential exposability (Holland, 1988) implies that the nature of the treatment should be alterable so that individuals have the possibility of exposure to either condition, although they cannot be exposed to the treatment and the control condition at the same time. When this basic assumption is satisfied, Stable Unit Treatment Value (SUTVA) implies that potential outcomes for each person are unrelated to the treatment status of other individuals (Rubin, 1978, 1980, 1990). SUTVA and randomization in the study provide a statistical means of causal inference at the population level. The models used to analyze compliance in this study assume randomization and SUTVA in line with Rubin's causal model.

Assume the simplest experimental setting where there is only one outcome measure (y), the treatment assignment (T) is binary (1 = treatment, 0 = control), and the treatment received (D) has only two levels (1 = received, 0 = not received). By classifying the behavior types of the subjects based on combinations of T and D, four types of subpopulations can be defined. These definitions are based on the individual level, which is possible because of the assumption of potential exposability. An individual i cannot be exposed to the treatment ($T_i = 1$) and the control condition ($T_i = 0$) at the same time, but has the possibility of exposure to either condition.

Angrist et al. (1996) labeled the four categories as *complier, never-taker, defier,* and *always-taker*. Compliers are subjects who do what they are assigned to do ($D_i = 1 | T_i = 1$, and $D_i = 0 | T_i = 0$). Never-takers are subjects who do not receive the treatment even if they are assigned to the treatment condition ($D_i = 0 | T_i = 1$, and $D_i = 0 | T_i = 0$). Defiers are the subjects who do the opposite of what they are assigned to ($D_i = 0 | T_i = 1$, and $D_i = 1 | T_i = 0$). Always-takers are the subjects who always receive the treatment no matter which condition they are assigned to do ($D_i = 1 | T_i = 1$, and $D_i = 1 | T_i = 0$).

Among these four kinds of possible compliance behaviors, the current study focuses on compliers and never-takers. That is, it is assumed that there are neither defiers nor always-takers. This is a stronger assumption than monotonicity (Imbens & Angrist, 1994) in the instrumental variable approach, where it is assumed that there are no defiers. Although defiers and always-takers are also possible compliance behaviors, the existence of never-takers is a more commonly seen problem. In examples shown in this study, subjects were not allowed to choose a different treatment condition than the one to which they were assigned. For never-takers, it is assumed that the outcome is independent of the treatment assignment (the exclusion restriction; Angrist et al., 1996), implying no assignment effects of the treatment. Based on these assumptions (randomization, SUTVA, monotonicity, no always-takers, and the exclusion restriction), two kinds of subpopulations can be defined: never-takers and compliers. For simplicity, never-takers are labeled as noncompliers in this chapter.

CACE Estimation Using ML-EM

The randomization in the assignment of treatment condition provides the basis for identification in CACE models. In addition to the equality in the parameter values based on random assignment assumption, the observed compliance status among treatment group individuals (training data) also plays a key role in the estimation of the treatment effect for the compliers (CACE).

Consider a single outcome variable y_{ik} for individual i within latent class k,

$$y_{ik} = \alpha_k + \Gamma_{Tk}T_i + \varepsilon_{ik}, \tag{1}$$

where latent categorical variable c has K levels of compliance status ($k = 1, 2, ..., K$). c represents observed compliance status in the treatment group and latent compliance status in the control group. $c_i = (c_{i1}, c_{i2}, ..., c_{ik})$ has a multinomial distribution, where $c_{ik} = 1$ if individual i belongs to class k and zero otherwise. The categorical latent variable approach may also be referred to as finite mixture modeling, where sampling units consist of subpopulations that might have separate distributions and different model parameters (Muthén et al., 1997; Titterington, 1985). In finite mixture modeling, the number of mixture components is assumed to be known and fixed. For example, $K = 2$ in examples shown in this study ($k = 1$ for compliers, $k = 2$ for noncompliers). ε_{ik} represents the normally distributed residual with zero mean independent of treatment assignment T ($1 =$ treatment, $0 =$ control). Let $V(\varepsilon_{ik}) = \sigma_k^2$ be the residual variance within compliance class k. α_k is the mean for the control group within latent class k, and Γ_{Tk} is the intervention effect within latent class k. The parameters of interest in the CACE model are α_k, Γ_{Tk}, σ_k^2, and the proportion of the population from component k with $\Sigma_{k=1}^{K} \pi_k = 1$. The proportion of compliers is π_1, and the proportion of noncompliers is $1 - \pi_1 = \pi_2$.

The identifiability of the model can be shown by solving for these parameters in terms of the population quantities that have observable counterparts in the form of consistent estimates. As a first step, π_1 is directly identified as the observed proportion of compliers in the treatment condition $P(k = 1)$. The remaining parameters α_k and Γ_{Tk} are identified based on observed means and π_k.

Based on Eq. (1), the parameters that represent average treatment effects for compliers and noncompliers are defined as

$$\alpha_1 + \Gamma_{T1} - (\alpha_1 + 0) = \Gamma_{T1} = CACE \tag{2}$$

$$\alpha_2 + \Gamma_{T2} - (\alpha_2 + 0) = \Gamma_{T2}, \tag{3}$$

whereas the unknown control group means for compliers and noncompliers are

$$\mu_{C, k=1} = \alpha_1, \tag{4}$$

$$\mu_{C, k=2} = \alpha_2, \tag{5}$$

the treatment group means are

$$\mu_{T, k=1} = \alpha_1 + \Gamma_{T1}, \tag{6}$$

$$\mu_{T, k=2} = \alpha_2 + \Gamma_{T2}, \tag{7}$$

and the overall control group mean is

$$\mu_C = \pi_1 \mu_{C,k=1} + \pi_2 \mu_{C,k=2}. \tag{8}$$

Because $\Gamma_{T2} = 0$ under the exclusion restriction assumption, α_2 is directly identified from equation (7) as

$$\alpha_2 = \mu_{T,k=2}. \tag{9}$$

From Eqs. (4), (8), and (9), α_1 can then be expressed in terms of known quantities as

$$\alpha_1 = (\mu_C - \pi_2 \mu_{T,k=2})/\pi_1. \tag{10}$$

From Eqs. (6) and (10), the average treatment effect for compliers can be expressed in terms of known quantities:

$$CACE = \Gamma_{T1} = \mu_{T,k=1} - (\mu_C - \pi_2 \mu_{T,k=2})/\pi_1. \tag{11}$$

The parameters σ_1^2 and σ_2^2 can then be identified from the mixture distribution of y (Eq. [1]). Because variances are not involved in the identification of Γ_{T1} as shown earlier, CACE models can be identified in the same way (Eq. [2]–[11]) when the outcome measure is categorical.

A single binary outcome variable u_{ik} for individual i within latent class k can be defined in a logit form as

$$logit(\tau_{ik}) = \alpha_{uk} + \Gamma_{Tk} T_i, \tag{12}$$

where $\tau_{ik} = P(u_{ik} = 1 \mid c_{ik} = 1)$. α_{uk} represents the intercept in the logistic regression of u on T within compliance class k. Γ_{T1} can be defined as the treatment effect for compliers as in the CACE model with a continuous outcome measure.

This study also demonstrates CACE estimation in the random coefficient growth mixture modeling framework. The growth mixture CACE model can be expressed using a two-level formulation. Consider a single outcome variable y for individual i at time point h within compliance class k,

$$y_{ihk} = I_{ik} + S_{ik} h + \varepsilon_{ihk}, \tag{13}$$

where ε_{ihk} represents a vector of normally distributed residuals with zero mean independent of other variables in the model. Let $V(\varepsilon_{ihk}) = \sigma_{hk}^2$. I_{ik} and S_{ik} are individually varying continuous latent variables representing initial level of outcome and growth rate (slope), respectively. The time scores h are $0, 1, 2, \ldots, H$, representing linear growth over time, which may be fixed at different values depending on the distance between the measuring points. Individual variation in parameters I_{ik} and S_{ik} within compliance class k is specified in the second level as

$$I_{ik} = I_k + \zeta_{Iik}, \tag{14}$$

$$S_{ik} = S_k + \Gamma_{Tk}T_i + \zeta_{Sik}. \tag{15}$$

In Eqs. (14) and (15), I_k and S_k represent intercept parameters of initial status and slope for each compliance class k. ζ_{Iik} and ζ_{Sik} can differ at different levels of compliance status, but the common residual variances $V(\zeta_{Iik}) = \psi_I$ and $V(\zeta_{Sik}) = \psi_S$ are used across different compliance classes for simplicity of illustration in the examples shown for this study. Based on randomization, initial status is not regressed on T_i but growth rate (slope) is regressed on T_i. Γ_{Tk} represents a mean shift in the slope when subject i belongs to the treatment condition and is allowed to vary across different compliance status. Γ_{T1} can be identified in the same way as in the estimation of CACE using a single outcome measure. The difference is that the intervention effect is identified based on means of growth rate (latent variable) instead of observed outcome means. In a growth modeling framework, treatment effects can be defined either as the difference between treatment and control conditions in the growth rate or as the difference between treatment and control conditions in the oucome measure at the final time point (Muthén & Curran, 1997). The second definition is used in the study for easier comparison between an ANCOVA approach using univariate outcome and growth mixture CACE modeling. Based on Eqs. (13), (14), and (15), the average treatment effects for compliers (CACE) can be defined at the last time point as

$$CACE = \Gamma_{T1} \times H \tag{16}$$

When covariates are present, the information carried by the covariates influences the CACE model in two ways. First, the precision in the regression of y (or η) on T is affected by inclusion of covariates (e.g., ANCOVA). Second, the class probability π_i is allowed to vary as a function of covariates. The logistic regression model of c on a vector of covariates x is decribed in a logit form as

$$logit(\pi_{1i}) = \alpha_c + \beta_c x_i, \tag{17}$$

where π_{1i} denotes the probability of being a complier. Because it is assumed that the treatment assignment is random, π_1 is the same for the control and treatment groups. The logistic regression of compliance status also provides information about the characteristics of the compliers.

The maximum likelihood estimation method using the EM algorithm (Dempster, Laird, & Rubin, 1977; McLachlan & Krishnan, 1997; Tanner, 1996) is employed in the current study to estimate the unknown compliance status of each subject in the control condition and to estimate average treatment effects for compliers.

Consider the sampling distribution of y and x from the mixture of k components

$$g(y, x \mid \theta, \pi) = \sum_{k=1}^{K} \pi_k f(y, x \mid \theta_k), \tag{18}$$

where y and x represent observed data, θ represents model parameters, and π_k represents the proportion of the population from component k with $\Sigma_{k=1}^{K} \pi_k = 1$. The probability π is the parameter that determines the distribution of c. The observed data log likelihood is

$$Log\, L = \sum_{i=1}^{n} log[y_i \mid x_i]. \tag{19}$$

Given the proposed CACE model in the presence of both covariates (x) and continuous latent variables (η), the complete data log likelihood can be written as

$$Log\, L_c = \sum_{i=1}^{n} (log[c_i \mid x_i] + log[\eta_i \mid c_i, x_i] + log[y_i \mid c_i, \eta_i, x_i), \tag{20}$$

where

$$\sum_{i=1}^{n} log[c_i \mid x_i] = \sum_{i=1}^{n} \sum_{k=1}^{K} c_{ik} log\, \pi_{ik}. \tag{21}$$

In Eqs. (20) and (21), c represents categorical latent compliance class, and η represents continuous latent growth factors (e.g., I and S).

Maximum likelihood estimation using the EM algorithm maximizes the expected complete data log likelihood shown in Eq. (20). In maximizing the expected complete data log likelihood in Eq. (20), the E step computes the expected values of the complete data sufficient statistics given data and current parameter estimates. c is considered as missing data in this step. The conditional distribution of c given the observed data and the current value of model parameter estimates θ'' is given by

$$f(c \mid y, x, \theta) = \prod_{i=1}^{n} f(c_i \mid y_i, x_i, \theta). \tag{22}$$

The M step computes the complete data ML estimates with complete data sufficient statistics replaced by their estimates from the E step. This procedure continues until it reaches optimal status. The M step maximizes

$$\sum_{i=1}^{n} \sum_{k=1}^{K} p_{ik} log\, \pi_{ik} \tag{23}$$

with respect to model parameters. p_{ik} is the posterior class probability of individual i, conditioning on observed data and model parameters, where $\pi_{ik} = P(c_{ik}|x_i)$.

In the current study, ML-EM estimation of CACE was carried out by the Mplus program (Muthén & Muthén, 1998). Parametric standard errors are computed from the information matrix of the ML estimator using both the first- and second-order derivatives under the assumption of normally distributed outcomes. For more details about estimation procedures in general latent variable modeling, see Muthén and Shedden (1999) and the chapter authored by Muthén in this book. Aslo, check Mplus website (www.statmodel.com) for more examples.

ESTIMATION OF CACE WITH A SINGLE CONTINUOUS OUTCOME

This section demonstrates the estimation of CACE with a single continuous outcome using the Job Search Intervention Study for unemployed workers (JOBS II; Vinokur, Price, & Schul, 1995; Vinokur & Schul, 1997). The JOBS II Intervention Study is a randomized field experiment intended to prevent poor mental health and promote high-quality reemployment. The experimental condition consisted of five half-day training seminars, which included the application of problem-solving and decision-making group processes, inoculation against setbacks, provision of social support and positive regard from the trainers, and learning and practicing job search skills. The control condition consisted of a booklet briefly describing job search methods and tips.

TABLE 3.1
JOBS II: Sample Statistics ($N = 486$)

Variable	M	SD	Description
TX	0.67	0.47	Experimental condition (0 = control, 1 = treatment)
c	0.55	0.50	Compliance (0 = noncompliance, 1 = compliance) in TX group
Depress0	2.45	0.30	Depression level before TX
Depress6	2.01	0.73	Depression level 6 months after TX
Employ6	0.62	0.49	Employment status 6 months after TX (0 = unemployed, 1 = employed)
Age	36.61	10.04	Age in years
Motivation	0.32	0.47	Motivation level before TX (0 = low, 1 = high)
Education	13.37	2.01	School grade completed
Assertive	3.07	0.91	Assertiveness before TX
Nonmarried	0.62	0.49	Marital status (0 = married, 1 = other)
Econ-Hard	3.60	0.87	Economic hardship before TX
Non-White	0.19	0.39	Race (0 = white, 1 = other)
Female	0.58	0.49	Gender (0 = male, 1 = female)

The present study focused on the high-risk status group based on previous studies (Price, van Ryn, & Vinokur, 1992; Vinokur, Price, & Shul, 1995), which indicated that the job search intervention had its primary impact on high-risk respondents. Risk score was computed based on risk variables predicting depressive symptoms at follow-up (depression, financial strain, and assertiveness) in the screening data (Price et al., 1992). A total sample size of 486 was analyzed in this study after listwise deletion of cases that had missingness in covariates and outcome variables. The variables used in the current study are described in Table 3.1.

Depression and reemployment are the major outcome measures in the JOBS II intervention study. The level of depression 6 months after the intervention (Depress6) is used as a continuous outcome measure in this section. The effect of the intervention on reemployment is analyzed in a later section. Depression was measured with a subscale of 11 items based on the Hopkins Symptom Checklist (Derogatis, Lipman, Rickles, Uhlenuth, & Covi, 1974).

Table 3.2 shows the results from the JOBS II data analysis using the ITT approach. In this method, it is assumed that noncompliers receive the same effects from the intervention as compliers. Table 3.2 shows that there is a small and insignificant effect of the intervention on the level of depression (TX effect = -0.137, Effect size = 0.189). The effect size of the treatment is calculated by dividing the outcome difference in treatment and control condition means by the square root of the variance pooled across the control and treatment groups. In the ITT analysis, economic hardship was found to be a significant predictor of the level of depression. Individuals had a higher level of depression if they had economic hardship.

TABLE 3.2
Intervention Effects on Depression: ITT Analysis

Parameter	Estimate	SE
Average treatment effects on Depress6	-0.137	0.072
Depress6 Regressed on x		
Depress0	0.063	0.108
Age	0.000	0.003
Motivation	0.019	0.073
Education	-0.026	0.016
Assertive	-0.039	0.038
Nonmarried	-0.117	0.075
Econ-Hard	0.143	0.040
Non-White	0.057	0.092
Female	0.105	0.068
Intercept	1.895	0.389
σ_y^2	0.502	0.036

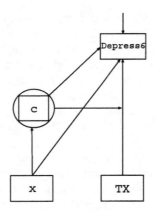

FIG. 3.2.   CACE estimation with a single continuous outcome.

Figure 3.2 illustrates the model to estimate differential treatment effects in the JOBS II Intervention Study using the CACE approach. This model has been previously analyzed by Little & Yau (1998) using the ML-EM, treating unknown compliance status as missing data (Little & Rubin, 1997). In this method, compliance status of control group individuals is estimated, and average causal effects of the treatment are estimated only for compliers. In this diagram, TX denotes treatment assignment (0 = control, 1 = treatment) and c denotes compliance status (0 = noncompliance, 1 = compliance). Individuals who completed at least one seminar were categorized as *compliers* (55% of treatment group individuals) and the rest were categorized as *noncompliers*. Here the compliance status of the control group is latent (unknown), and the compliance status of the treatment group is observed (known). The partly observed latent variable c is expressed as a square in a circle. In the path diagram in Fig. 3.2 and in the other path diagrams to appear later, squares represent observed variables and circles represent latent (missing) variables. The path from TX to y corresponds to the treatment effect. The arrow from c to this path indicates that the treatment effect is different depending on compliance status. The arrow from c to y means that the means are different between compliers and noncompliers in the control group. In this model, covariates (x) including baseline depression (Depress0) are used as predictors of not only the outcome measure (Depress6) but also the compliance status (c) to improve precision in the prediction of compliance status and the quality of the treatment effect estimates.

Table 3.3 shows the results from the CACE analysis of the JOBS II intervention. In the current study, effect sizes of CACE estimates were calculated in a conventional way by dividing the outcome difference in treatment and control condition means by the square root of the variance pooled across the control and treatment groups. A more correct way to calculate effect size is to use the pooled variance of each compliance class. However, this approach was not chosen

TABLE 3.3
Intervention Effects on Depression: CACE Analysis

Parameter	Estimate	SE
CACE	−0.351	0.139
Depress6 Regressed on x		
Depress0	0.065	0.107
Age	−0.001	0.004
Motivation	−0.002	0.076
Education	−0.030	0.017
Assertive	−0.040	0.038
Nonmarried	−0.120	0.076
Econ-Hard	0.151	0.041
Non-White	0.065	0.092
Female	0.099	0.069
Intercept (Complier)	2.133	0.425
Intercept (Noncomplier)	1.821	0.385
σ_y^2	0.490	0.036
c Regressed on x (Complier vs. Noncomplier)		
Depress0	−0.420	0.425
Age	0.078	0.015
Motivation	1.309	0.292
Education	0.304	0.071
Assertive	−0.338	0.149
Nonmarried	0.546	0.288
Econ-Hard	−0.225	0.155
Non-White	−0.424	0.330
Female	−0.396	0.259
Intercept	−4.208	1.623

because standard deviations may vary depending on CACE models specified to estimate treatment effects, and this makes the comparison between models very difficult.

Table 3.3 shows that the intervention had a positive impact on the level of depression for compliers (TX effect = −0.351, Effect size = 0.484). In this method, the treatment effect is significant, and its magnitude is much larger than that of the overall average effects in the ITT analysis (e.g., Effect size = 0.189). The level of depression is significantly lower for compliers in the intervention condition compared with that of control condition individuals who could have complied if they had been assigned to the intervention condition. In the CACE analysis, economic hardship was found to be a significant predictor of the level of depression. It was also found that subjects complied more if they were older, more motivated, more educated, and less assertive.

The difference in the results from the ITT approach (Table 3.2) and those from the CACE approach (Table 3.3) implies that quite different conclusions are possible depending on the estimation method used to evaluate the effect of intervention treatment. According to the ITT analysis, the intervention did not have a significant effect on depression, and the magnitude of the effect was trivial. In contrast, the CACE analysis showed that the intervention had a significant effect on depression level for compliers and had a practically meaningful effect size.

ESTIMATION OF CACE WITH A SINGLE CATEGORICAL OUTCOME

This section demonstrates the estimation of CACE with a single categorical outcome using the Study of Vitamin Supplement Effect on Survival Rates in young children in Indonesia (Aceh Study; Imbens & Rubin, 1997; Sommer & Zeger, 1991; Sommer et al., 1986). The Aceh Study is a large-scale randomized controlled community trial conducted through a joint collaboration of the Dana Center for Preventive Ophthalmology at Johns Hopkins University, Hellen Keller International, and the Indonesian government in a province (Aceh) in Indonesia. The major goal of the Aceh Study is to examine the effectiveness of the intervention in reducing the mortality rate among infants and young children due to vitamin A deficiency. The study was originally aimed for children from 12 to 85 months old, but some children under 12 months or over 85 months old were also included in the study. Therefore, the effect of the age of children needs to interpreted with caution in this study. In the intervention condition villages, there were village-based persons trained by the government to give out the capsules. They were supposed to give each child a capsule every 6 months. Parents were asked at the end of 1 year of intervention whether their children had received a vitamin A capsule in the past 6 months. A total sample size of 20,130 was analyzed in this

TABLE 3.4
Aceh Study: Sample Statistics ($N = 20,130$)

Variable	M	SD	Description
TX	0.52	0.50	Experimental condition (0 = control, 1 = treatment)
c	0.81	0.39	Compliance (0 = noncompliance, 1 = compliance) in TX group
Survival	0.993	0.08	Vital status at 1 year follow-up (0 = died, 1 = alive)
Age	37.55	20.97	Age in months
Male	0.51	0.50	Gender (0 = female, 1 = male)
SES	0.63	0.48	Land ownership (0 = does not own land, 1 = owns land)
Health	0.87	0.33	Health seeking in the past year by any household member (0 = no, 1 = yes)
Diepast	0.64	1.07	Number of children whom the mother has had died in the past
Nblind	0.008	0.09	Nightblindness in past six months (0 = no, 1 = yes)

study after listwise deletion of cases that had missingness in covariates and outcome variables. The variables used in the current study are described in Table 3.4.

In the Aceh Study, the vital status of children at 1-year follow-up is the major outcome measure and is used as a binary outcome in this section. Vital status was measured at the end of 1 year of intervention. Sixty children died in the first 6 months of the trial, 75 children died in the second 6 months of the trial, and 19,995 children were alive at the end of the trial. Children who died either in the first or second 6-month trials were categorized as *not survived*, and children who were alive at the end of the trial were categorized as *survived* in this study. The survival rate among 10,439 intervention condition children was 0.995, and the survival rate among 9,691 control condition children was 0.992.

Table 3.5 shows the results from the Aceh Study data analysis using the ITT approach. In this method, it is assumed that noncompliers receive the same effects from the intervention as compliers. Table 3.5 shows that the intervention had a significant effect on survival rates of young children (TX effect = 0.446, Odds ratio = 1.561). The logistic regression results show that the odds of survival are 1.561 times higher for children in the intervention condition than for children in the control condition. In the ITT analysis, child's age and mortality rate of child's siblings were found to be significant predictors of the survival rate. Children had a higher rate of survival if they were older and had fewer siblings who had died.

Figure 3.3 illustrates the model to estimate differential treatment effects in the Aceh Study using the CACE approach. The CACE estimation of the intervention effects in the Aceh Study has been previously analyzed without covariates using EM and data augmentation algorithms (Imbens & Rubin, 1997). The current study employs the EM algorithm and incorporates covariates in the model. For CACE estimation of the intervention, a dichotomous variable (c) was created based on the dosage of vitamin A each child had taken. Children who took one or two capsules were categorized as *compliers* (81% of intervention condition children) and the rest were categorized as *noncompliers*. In this model, covariates (x) are used as predictors of not only the outcome measure (Survival) but also the

TABLE 3.5
Intervention Effects on Survival: ITT Analysis

Parameter	Estimate	SE
Average treatment effects on survival	0.446	0.177
Age	0.046	0.006
Male	−0.194	0.174
SES	0.064	0.177
Health	0.036	0.254
Diepast	−0.264	0.052
Nblind	−1.400	0.727
Intercept	4.933	0.290

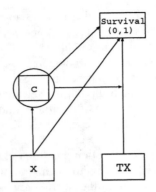

FIG. 3.3.   CACE estimation with a single categorical outcome.

TABLE 3.6
Intervention Effects on Survival: CACE Analysis

Parameter	Estimate	SE
CACE	0.813	0.274
Survival Regressed on x		
Age	0.043	0.005
Male	−0.189	0.174
SES	−0.014	0.182
Health	0.015	0.253
Diepast	−0.261	0.052
Nblind	−1.436	0.734
Intercept (Complier)	4.008	0.346
Intercept (Noncomplier)	3.351	0.342
c Regressed on x (Complier vs. Noncomplier)		
Age	0.005	0.001
Male	0.000	0.050
SES	0.394	0.051
Health	0.097	0.077
Diepast	0.004	0.025
Nblind	0.223	0.313
Intercept	0.938	0.094

compliance status (c) to improve precision in the prediction of compliance status and the quality of the treatment effect estimates.

Table 3.6 shows the results from the Aceh Study data analysis using the CACE approach. The logistic regression of vital status in the CACE approach shows that the intervention had a significant effect on survival rates of young children (TX effect = 0.813, Odds ratio = 2.254), and the odds ratio is considerably higher than in the ITT approach (i.e., 1.561). The odds of survival are 2.254 times higher for intervention condition children who actually took capsules than for control condition children who could have taken capsules if they had been assigned to the intervention condition. In the CACE analysis, child's age and mortality rate of child's siblings were found to be significant predictors of the survival rate. Children had a higher rate of survival if they were older and had fewer siblings who had died. It was also found that parents complied with the intervention more if they had higher socioeconomic status (SES) and if their children were older.

In the Aceh Study, both ITT and CACE approaches showed significant effects of the intervention on the vital status of young children. However, the magnitudes of the intervention effects are quite different in two approaches. These results imply that treatment effect estimates for categorical outcomes could be still sensitive to estimation method in the presence of noncompliance, although noncompliance rate is quite low (19%) and the sample size is very large.

ESTIMATION OF CACE WITH MULTIPLE OUTCOMES

This section demonstrates the estimation of CACE with multiple outcome measures using the JOBS II Study. The same subset of the JOBS II data with a sample size of 486 used earlier was analyzed in this section. The variables used in this section are described in Table 3.1. This section focuses on the estimation of the intervention effects on reemployment, which was one of the major goals of the JOBS II intervention. Reemployment status was determined 6 months after the intervention by classifying respondents working for 20 hours or more per week as reemployed (Employ6 $= 1$) and the rest as unemployed (Employ6 $= 0$).

Table 3.7 shows the results from the CACE analysis using a single categorical outcome (Employ6). The logistic regression of reemployment status in the CACE approach shows that the intervention did not have a significant effect on reemployment among intervention condition individuals, although they actually had complied with the intervention (TX effect $= 0.576$, Odds ratio $= 1.779$). In the CACE analysis using a single categorical outcome, it was found that age, education, and racial background were significant predictors of the reemployment. Individuals had a higher rate of reemployment if they were White, younger, and more educated. It was also found that individuals complied more if they were older, single, more motivated, more educated, and less assertive.

Figure 3.4 illustrates the model to estimate CACE using multiple outcomes in the JOBS II Intervention Study. In this method, compliance status (c) of control group individuals is estimated based on both outcomes, and intervention effects for compliers are also estimated for both outcomes. The binary and continuous outcomes are correlated through covariates, intervention assignment, and compliance status, but there is no direct relation between the binary outcome and the residual of the continuous outcome. The conditional independence between these

TABLE 3.7
Intervention Effects on Employment: CACE Analysis

Parameter	Estimate	SE
CACE	0.576	0.344
Employ6 Regressed on x		
Depress0	−0.058	0.323
Age	−0.023	0.011
Motivation	−0.267	0.215
Education	0.130	0.053
Assertive	0.075	0.118
Nonmarried	0.201	0.210
Econ-Hard	0.015	0.122
Non-White	−0.554	0.253
Female	−0.051	0.202
Intercept (Complier)	−0.761	1.290
Intercept (Noncomplier)	−0.499	1.191
c Regressed on x (Complier vs. Noncomplier)		
Depress0	−0.387	0.428
Age	0.078	0.016
Motivation	1.244	0.294
Education	0.301	0.070
Assertive	−0.347	0.152
Nonmarried	0.571	0.291
Econ-Hard	−0.239	0.157
Non-White	−0.386	0.331
Female	−0.386	0.260
Intercept	−4.193	1.648

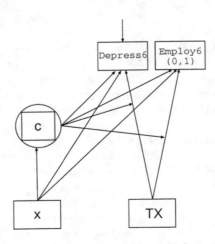

FIG. 3.4.   CACE estimation with multiple outcomes.

TABLE 3.8
Intervention Effects on Employment and Depression: CACE Analysis

Parameter	Estimate	SE	Estimate	SE
	Employ6		*Depress6*	
CACE	0.693	0.353	−0.369	0.142
	Employ6 Regressed on x		*Depress6 Regressed on x*	
Depress0	−0.062	0.324	0.066	0.107
Age	−0.022	0.011	−0.001	0.004
Motivation	−0.237	0.219	−0.005	0.077
Education	0.137	0.053	−0.031	0.017
Assertive	0.070	0.118	−0.038	0.038
Nonmarried	0.205	0.211	−0.119	0.075
Econ-Hard	0.007	0.123	0.152	0.041
Non-White	−0.565	0.253	0.064	0.092
Female	−0.053	0.203	0.100	0.069
Intercept (Complier)	−0.980	1.289	2.161	0.423
Intercept (Noncomplier)	−0.532	1.191	1.820	0.385
σ_y^2			0.488	0.036

	c Regressed on x (Complier vs. Noncomplier)	
	Estimate	SE
Depress0	−0.450	0.422
Age	0.078	0.015
Motivation	1.303	0.291
Education	0.306	0.070
Assertive	−0.351	0.151
Nonmarried	0.521	0.289
Econ-Hard	−0.223	0.156
Non-White	−0.384	0.333
Female	−0.403	0.257
Intercept	−4.119	1.616

two outcome measures is assumed for the simplicity in the model estimation, but this assumption may need to be relaxed. In this model, two major outcomes (Employ6 and Depress6) of the intervention are considered at the same time to improve the quality of parameter estimates in the categorical outcome (Employ6). The model is intended to increase the precision in the estimation of compliance status in the control condition by including a continuous outcome (Depress6), and consequently to increase the power to detect intervention effects on the categorical outcome (Employ6).

Table 3.8 shows the results from the CACE analysis of the JOBS II intervention using multiple outcomes illustrated in Fig. 3.4. The logistic regression of reemployment status shows that the intervention had a positive effect on reemployment for compliers (TX effect = 0.693, Odds ratio = 2.000). In this method, the intervention effect is significant, and its magnitude is larger than that in the CACE analysis using a single categorical outcome only. The odds of reemployment are two times higher for intervention condition individuals who actually participated in intervention seminars than for control condition individuals who could have participated if they had been assigned to the intervention condition. The logistic regression of reemployment status also shows that age, education, and racial background were significant predictors of the reemployment. Individuals had a higher rate of reemployment if they were White, younger, and more educated.

Table 3.8 also shows the estimation of intervention effects on the level of depression 6 months after the intervention. The results show that the intervention had a positive effect on depression for compliers (TX effect = −0.369, Effect size = 0.509). The intervention effects on depression are slightly stronger in this model than in the CACE model using a continuous outcome only (see Table 3.3). Among several covariates, economic hardship was found to be a significant predictor of the level of depression. It was also found that subjects complied more if they were older, more motivated, more educated, and less assertive.

The difference in the results from the CACE approach using a single outcome (Tables 3.3 and 3.7) and those from the CACE approach with multiple outcomes (Table 3.8) implies that the efficiency in CACE estimation can be improved by employing estimation models based on multiple outcomes. The difference between the two methods was not dramatic, but still affected the power to detect intervention effects.

GROWTH MIXTURE CACE ANALYSIS FOR MULTIPLE OUTCOMES WITH A TREND

This section demonstrates CACE estimation using repeated outcome measures with a trend using the Johns Hopkins Public School Preventive Intervention Study. In the previous section, multiple outcome measures are used in CACE estimation, but these outcomes were not repeated measures of the same outcome. When intervention studies are focused on the long-term effects of treatment, the outcome is often measured several times at specific intervals. In this case, one way to define the treatment effect is to use the difference between the treatment and the control group in the outcome measured at the last time point, conditioning on the outcome measured at the first time point (ANCOVA). Another way to define the treatment effect is to use a trend or growth trajectory of the subjects. This section demonstrates CACE estimation in these two alternative approaches.

The Johns Hopkins Public School Preventive Intervention Study was conducted by the Johns Hopkins University Preventive Intervention Research Center in 1993–1994 (Ialongo et al., 1999). The study was designed to improve academic achievement and reduce early behavioral problems of school children. Based on the life course/social field framework as described by Kellam and Rebok (1992), the study focused on successful adaptation to first grade as a means of improving social adaptational status over the life course. Teachers and first-grade children were randomly assigned to intervention conditions. The intervention impact was assessed in the spring of first and second grades. Two intervention programs were employed in the Johns Hopkins Public School Preventive Intervention Study: the Classroom-Centered Intervention and the Family-School Partnership Intervention. The present study focused on the comparison between the control group and the Family-School Partnership Intervention group. Intervention condition parents were asked to implement 66 take-home activities related to literacy and mathematics. Based on the level of completeness in home-learning activities, a dichotomous variable was created in this study. Parents who completed at least 35 activities were categorized as *compliers* (73% of parents) and the rest were categorized as *noncompliers*. The cutpoint was decided based on exploratory growth mixture analyses (Jo & Muthén, 2000), but the details are not discussed in this chapter. For illustration purpose, compliance in continuous measure was simply dichotomized in this example, but note that sensitivity of the CACE estimate to different thresholds needs to be carefully examined in practice (West & Sagarine, 2000). Figure 3.5 shows observed mean curves of attention deficit in the Johns Hopkins School Preventive Intervention Study.

A total sample size of 286 was analyzed in this study after listwise deletion of cases that had missingness in covariates and outcome variables. The two major outcome measures in the Johns Hopkins Public School Preventive Intervention Study were academic achievement (CTBS mathematics and reading test scores) and the score Teacher Observation of Classroom Adaptation–Revised (TOCA–R) score (Werthamer-Larsson, Kellam, & Wheeler, 1991). Among these two outcome meas-

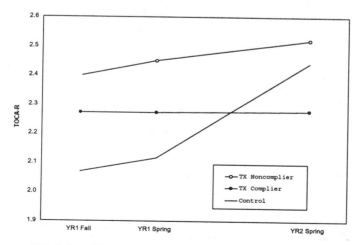

FIG. 3.5.   Observed mean curves of attention deficit.

TABLE 3.9

The Johns Hopkins Public School Prevention Data: Sample Statistics ($N = 286$)

Variable	M	SD	Description
TX	0.50	0.50	Experimental condition (0 = control, 1 = treatment)
Activity	40.78	15.96	Number of completed home-learning activities
c	0.73	0.45	Dichotomized home-learning activities (0 = 34 or fewer, 1 = 35 to 66)
AD0	2.19	0.92	TOCA teacher report mean attention deficit before TX (1st grade, fall)
AD6	2.22	0.95	TOCA teacher report mean attention deficit 6 month after TX
AD18	2.39	1.11	TOCA teacher report mean attention deficit 18 month after TX
Male	0.49	0.50	Student's gender (0 = female, 1 = male)
Lunch	0.62	0.49	Free lunch program (0 = no, 1 = yes)
Page	3.01	1.44	Parent's age in 5-year brackets
Pmale	0.07	0.26	Parent's gender (0 = female, 1 = male)
Non-White	0.87	1.03	Parent's ethnicity (1 = non-White, 0 = White)

TABLE 3.10

Intervention Effects on Attention Deficit: CACE Analysis

Parameter	Estimate	SE
CACE	−0.300	0.129
AD18 Regressed on x		
AD0	0.624	0.068
Male	0.330	0.107
Lunch	0.296	0.112
Page	0.037	0.037
Pmale	0.132	0.258
Non-White	−0.213	0.146
Intercept (Complier)	0.890	0.246
Intercept (Noncomplier)	0.765	0.276
σ_y^2	0.790	0.074
c Regressed on x (Complier vs. Noncomplier)		
AD0	−0.118	0.226
Male	0.203	0.390
Lunch	−0.147	0.382
Page	−0.197	0.126
Pmale	−0.781	0.637
Non-White	−0.306	0.639
Intercept	2.209	0.782

ures, the TOCA–R score was used as the final outcome measure in this study. The TOCA–R is designed to assess each child's adequacy of performance on the core tasks in the classroom as rated by the teacher. Among several areas that TOCA–R measures, attention deficit is the construct focused in this study. The attention deficit scale ranges from 1 to 6 and consists of TOCA–R items that measure hyperactivity, concentration problems, and impulsiveness. Table 3.9 shows the sample statistics for the variables used in the analyses of this study.

Table 3.10 shows the results from the CACE analysis using a single outcome measured approximately 18 months after the intervention (AD18). In this approach, the outcome measured before the treatment (AD0) is used as one of covariates, and the outcome measured in the spring of the first grade (AD6) is ignored (i.e., ANCOVA). The results show that the intervention had a positive impact on children's attention deficit when their parents were highly involved in the intervention activities (TX effect = -0.300, Effect size = 0.271). It was assumed that there was no effect of intervention assignment for children with parents who had a very low level of compliance with the intervention activities, but this assumption may need to be relaxed. The assumption of the exclusion restriction is critical for the identifiability of CACE models, but can be unrealistic in some situations (Hirano et al., 2000; Jo, 2000a, 2000b). In the CACE analysis based on a single outcome measure, baseline attention deficit, gender, and free lunch program were found to be significant predictors of the level of attention deficit. Children had a higher level of attention deficit in spring of the second grade if their baseline attention deficit was higher, if they were boys, and if their SES level was low.

Figure 3.6 illustrates the growth mixture CACE model using repeated outcome measures. In this approach, all three measures of attention deficit are considered

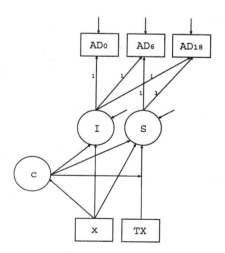

FIG. 3.6.   Growth mixture CACE estimation with repeated outcome measures.

in the analysis. This approach is in line with the CACE approach using a single outcome measure in the sense that compliance status of control group individuals is estimated, and average causal effects of the treatment are estimated only for compliers. One difference between CACE models using growth mixtures and CACE models using a single outcome is that the first time point measure (AD0) is one of the outcome measures instead of one of the covariates. Because initial status (I) and growth rate (S) are separated in this model, the influence of background variables can be estimated separately for initial level of attention deficit and change of attention deficit. Another difference is that the growth mixture CACE model utilizes not only covariates, but also trajectory information to identify compliance class and increase efficiency in the estimation of intervention effects. Including a growth process in the estimation of CACE utilizes the idea of

TABLE 3.11
Intervention Effects on Attention Deficit: Growth Mixture CACE Analysis

Parameter	Estimate	SE
CACE	−0.306	0.126
Growth rate Regressed on x		
Male	0.062	0.038
Lunch	0.063	0.039
Page	0.013	0.013
Pmale	0.061	0.084
Non-White	−0.107	0.050
Intercept (Complier)	0.103	0.074
Intercept (Noncomplier)	0.047	0.087
Initial Status Regressed on x		
Male	0.376	0.102
Lunch	0.277	0.104
Page	−0.002	0.036
Pmale	−0.131	0.128
Non-White	0.268	0.159
Intercept (Complier)	1.569	0.207
Intercept (Noncomplier)	1.673	0.234
ψ_S	0.042	0.011
ψ_I	0.536	0.061
σ_y^2	0.265	0.030
c Regressed on x (Complier vs. Noncomplier)		
Male	0.144	0.387
Lunch	−0.176	0.385
Page	−0.198	0.127
Pmale	−0.775	0.632
Non-White	−0.327	0.625
Intercept	2.025	0.713

a general latent variable modeling framework, where both categorical and continuous latent variables are incorporated (Muthén, 1998; Muthén et al., 1997; Muthén & Shedden, 1999). That is, latent variables that represent growth trajectories are continuous as in conventional structural equation models, whereas the latent variable that represents compliance status is categorical.

In Fig. 3.6, initial status I has equal loadings $(1, 1, 1)$ on three outcome measures representing initial status, which does not change over time. The time scores (h) are fixed at 0, 1, and 3 representing linear growth over time. The arrows from c to I and S mean that trajectory shapes are different between compliers and noncompliers in the control group. The arrow from TX to S corresponds to the mean shift in growth rate due to the treatment. The arrow from c to this path indicates that the treatment effect is different depending on the compliance status. The intervention effects for compliers (CACE) is defined as the difference in estimated attention deficit between the control and the treatment condition at the last time point (see Eq. [16]).

Table 3.11 shows the results from the estimation of treatment effects using growth mixture CACE modeling. The results show that the intervention had a positive impact on children's attention deficit change when their parents were highly involved in the intervention activities (TX effect = 0.306, Effect size = 0.276). It is also shown that growth mixture CACE analysis has a slightly larger effect size and tighter confidence interval than the CACE analysis using the ANCOVA approach shown in Table 3.10. In the growth mixture CACE analysis, child's gender and participation in the free lunch program were significant predictors of initial level of attention deficit, and parents' racial background was a

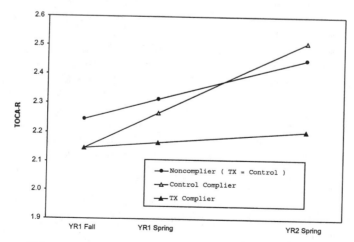

FIG. 3.7. Estimated mean curves of attention deficit.

significant predictor of growth rate of attention deficit. Initial level of attention deficit was higher for boys with low SES. The level of attention deficit increased significantly faster for children from White families.

Figure 3.7 shows estimated mean attention deficit curves over time based on results in Table 3.11. This figure shows how attention deficit changed over time depending on parents' compliance level and treatment assignment. It is shown that attention deficit among highly complying parents' children maintained a low level over time, but the deficit could increase to a level even higher than that of less involved parents' children at the second grade unless the intervention was given.

CONCLUSION

Noncompliance is a common problem in intervention studies, and one can arrive at different conclusions about the effect of the same intervention trial depending on how this problem is handled. Both ITT and CACE analyses are useful in their own contexts. However, the estimation of CACE was the focus of this study, because a major interest in intervention trials is often the estimation of treatment effects for individuals who actually receive the treatment.

The current study demonstrated that the problem of noncompliance can be dealt with in a broader framework of structural equation modeling by looking at compliance status as a categorical latent variable. To deal with compliance status as a latent variable, a broader framework of structural equation modeling was employed. This framework has two differences in the concept of latent variable from the conventional structural equation modeling. First, latent variable can be not only continuous but also categorical, whereas latent variable is only continuous in the conventional framework. Second, *latent* may mean missing for only a part of the total sample, whereas it usually means missing or unknown for everybody in the conventional framework.

This study demonstrated that the general latent variable approach is useful in improving the efficiency and interpretability of CACE estimation. Possibilities of flexible CACE modeling in a general latent variable modeling framework were demonstrated in various situations. The examples shown in this study imply that the difference in the estimation of treatment effects could be substantial depending not only on estimation approaches, but also modeling alternatives.

In the examples of intervention effect estimation using a single outcome measure, it was shown that the magnitude of treatment effects was considerably larger in the CACE approach than in the ITT approach. In the JOBS II study example using a continuous outcome measure, the intervention did not have a significant effect on depression, and the magnitude of the effect was trivial according to the ITT analysis. In contrast, the CACE analysis showed that the intervention had a significant effect on depression level for compliers and had a practically meaningful effect size. In the Aceh Study example using a categorical outcome measure, both ITT and CACE approaches showed significant effects of the intervention on vital status of young children. However, the magnitudes of the intervention effects were quite different in two approaches, implying that treatment effect estimates for categorical outcomes could still be sensitive to estimation method in the presence of noncompliance even with a high compliance rate and a large sample size. In both examples, covariates were incorporated in CACE models to increase the precision in the estimation of compliance class and improve the power to detect treatment effects.

This study also demonstrated the use of multiple outcomes and growth trajectories in the estimation of CACE. It was shown that the quality of intervention effect estimates could be improved further within the CACE approach by employing models that utilize the information from multiple outcomes and growth trajectories. In the CACE estimation of the JOBS II study, the intervention effect on reemployment status was not significant when reemployment status was the only outcome in the model. In contrast, the intervention effect was significant and its magnitude was larger when both outcomes (reemployment and depression) were included in the model. In the CACE estimation of the Johns Hopkins study, the difference between ANCOVA and growth mixture approaches was small in terms of the magnitude of the intervention effects. However, the growth mixture CACE approach provided more detailed information about the intervention effects. It was found that the intervention had a positive impact on attention deficit among highly complying parents' children. Initial level of attention deficit was higher for boys with low SES. The level of attention deficit increased significantly faster for children from White families.

APPENDIX

Mplus input for Table 3.3

title: CACE estimation with a single continuous outcome
data: file is jobs2.dat;
variable: names are depress6 TX depress0 age motivat educat;
           names are assert nonmarr econhard nonwhite female employ6 c1 c2;
           usev are depress6 TX depress0-female c1 c2;
           classes-c(2);
           training=c1-c2;
analysis: type=mixture;
model:
%OVERALL%
           C#1 ON depress0-female;
           depress6 ON TX depress0-female;
           depress6;
           [depress6];

```
%C#1%
        [depress6];
        depress6 ON TX;
%C#2%
        [depress6];
        depress6 ON TX@0;
```

Mplus input for Table 3.6

```
title: CACE estimation with a single categorical outcome
data: file is aceh.dat;
variable: names are survival TX age male ses health diepast nblind c1 c2;
        categorical are survival;
        classes = c(2);
        training = c1-c2;
analysis: type = mixture;
model:
%OVERALL%
        C#1 ON age-nblind;
        survival ON TX age-nblind;
%C#1%
        [survival$1*-4];
        survival ON TX;
%C#2%
        [survival$1*-3];
        survival ON TX@0;
```

Mplus input for Table 3.8

```
title: CACE estimation with multiple outcomes
data: file is jobs2.dat;
variable: names are depress6 employ6 TX depress0-female c1 c2;
        categorical are employ6;
        classes = c(2);
        training = c1-c2;
analysis: type = mixture;
model:
%OVERALL%
        C#1 ON depress0-female;
        depress6 ON TX depress0-female;
        employ6 ON TX depress0-female;
        [depress6];
        depress6;
```

%C#1%
     [depress6];
     [employ6$1*1.0];
     depress6 ON TX;
     employ6 ON TX;
%C#2%
     [depress6];
     [employ6$1*0.5];
     depress6 ON TX@0;
     employ6 ON TX@0;

Mplus input for Table 3.11

title: CACE estimation with repeated outcome measures
data: file is hopkins.dat;
variable: names are TX AD0 AD6 AD18;
     names are male lunch page pmale nonwhite c1 c2;
     usev are AD0 AD6 AD18 TX male-nonwhite c1 c2;
     classes = c(2);
     training = c1-c2;
analysis: type = mixture;
model:
%OVERALL%
     init by AD0-AD18@1;
     grow by AD0@0 AD6@1 AD18@3;
     [AD0-AD18@0];
     AD0-AD18 (1);
     grow ON TX male-nonwhite;
     init ON male-nonwhite;
     init;
     [init];
     grow;
     [grow];
     C#1 ON male-nonwhite;
%C#1%
     [init];
     [grow];
     grow ON TX;
%C#2%
     [init];
     [grow];
     grow ON TX@0;

ACKNOWLEDGEMENT

This study is supported by the NIMH grant P30MH38330, Michigan Prevention Research Center at the Institute for Social Research, Richard H. Price, P.I., University of Michigan. This study is also supported by grant 1 KO2 AA 00230-01 from NIAAA and by NIMH grant P50 MH38725, Epidemiologic Prevention Center for Early Risk Behaviors, Philip Leaf, P.I., Department of Mental Hygiene, Johns Hopkins School of Hygiene and Public Health. We would like to thank Amiram Vinkour, Nicholas Ialongo, and Joanne Katz for their data and helpful comments.

REFERENCES

Angrist, J. D., Imbens, G. W., & Rubin, D. B. (1996). Identification of causal effects using instrumental variables. *Journal of the American Statistical Association, 91*, 444–455.

Bloom, H. S. (1984). Accounting for non-compliers in experimental evaluation designs. *Evaluation Review, 8*, 225–246.

Dempster, A., Laird, N., & Rubin, D. B. (1977). Maximum likelihood from incomplete data via the EM algorithm. *Journal of the Royal Statistical Society* (Series B), *39*, 1–38.

Derogatis, L. R., Lipman, R. S., Rickles, K., Uhlenuth, E. H., & Covi, L. (1974). The Hopkins Symptom Checklist (HSCL). In P. Pichot (Ed.), *Psychological measurements in psychopharmacology: Modern problems in pharmacopsychiatry* 7 (pp. 79–110). New York: Karger, Basel.

Hirano, K., Imbens, G. W., Rubin, D. B., & Zhou, X. H. (1999). *Assessing the effect of an influenza vaccine in an encouragement design.* Unpublished manuscripts.

Holland, P. W. (1986). Statistics and causal inference. *Journal of the American Statistical Association, 81*, 945–970.

Holland, P. W. (1988). Causal inference, path analysis, and recursive structural equation models. *Sociological Methodology*, 449–484.

Ialongo, N. S., Werthamer, L., Kellam, S. G., Brown, C. H., Wang, S., & Lin, Y. (1999). Proximal impact of two first-grade preventive interventions on the early risk behaviors for later substance abuse, depression and antisocial behavior. *American Journal of Community Psychology, 27*, 599–642.

Imbens, G. W., & Angrist. J. (1994). Identification and estimation of local average treatment effects. *Econometrica, 62*, 467–476.

Imbens, G. W., & Rubin, D. B. (1997). Bayesian inference for causal effects in randomized experiments with non-compliance. *The Annals of Statistics, 25*, 305–327.

Jo, B. (2000a). *Estimating intervention effects with noncompliance: Alternative model specifications.* Submitted for publication.

Jo, B. (2000b). *Model misspecification sensitivity analysis in estimating causal effects of inverventions with noncompliance.* Submitted for publication.

Jo, B. (2000c). *Statistical power in randomized intervention studies wiht noncompliance.* Submitted for publication.

Jo, B., & Muthén, B. O. (2000). Intervention studies with noncompliance: Complier average causal effect estimation in growth mixture modeling. In N. Duan & S. Reise (Eds.), *Multilevel modeling: Methodological advances, issues, and applications, multivariate applications book series.* Mahwah, NJ: Lawrence Erlbaum Associates.

Kellam, S. G., & Rebok, G. W. (1992). Building developmental and etiological theory through epidemiologically based preventive intervention trials. In J. McCord & R. E. Trembley (Eds.),

Preventing anti-social behavior: interventions from birth through adolescence. New York; Guilford Press, pp. 162–195.

Little, R. J. A., & Rubin, D. B. (1987). *Statistical analysis with missing data.* New York: John Wiley.

Little, R. J. A., & Yau, L. (1998). Statistical techniques for analyzing data from prevention trials: Treatment of no-shows using Rubin's causal model. *Psychological Methods, 3,* 147–159.

McLachlan, G. J., & Krishnan, T. (1997). *The EM algorithm and extensions.* New York: Wiley.

Muthén, B. O. (1998). Second-generation structural equation modeling with a combination of categorical and continuous latent variables: new opportunities for latent class/latent growth modeling. In A. Sayer & L. Collins (Eds.), New methods for the analysis of change. Washington DC: American Psychological Association.

Muthén, B. O., Brown, C. H., Khoo, S. T., Yang, C. C., & Jo, B. (1997). *General growth mixture modeling of latent trajectory classes: Perspectives and prospects.* Unpublished manuscript.

Muthén, B. O., & Curran, P. J. (1997). General longitudinal modeling of individual differences in experimental designs: A latent variable framework for analysis and power estimation. *Psychological Methods, 3,* 371–402.

Muthén, L. K., & Muthén, B. O. (1998). *Mplus user's guide.* Los Angeles: Author.

Muthén, B. O., & Shedden, K. (1999). Finite mixture modeling with mixture outcomes using the EM algorithm. *Biometrics, 55,* 463–469.

Price, R.H., van Ryn, M., Vinokur, A.D. (1992). Impact of a preventive job search intervention on the likelihood of depression among the unemployed. *Journal of Health and Social Behavior, 33,* 158–167.

Rubin, D. B. (1974). Estimating causal effects of treatments in randomized and nonrandomized studies. *Journal of Educational Psychology, 66,* 688–701.

Rubin, D. B. (1978). Bayesian inference for causal effects: The role of randomization. *Annals of Statistics, 6,* 34–58.

Rubin, D. B. (1980). Discussion of "Randomization analysis of experimental data in the Fisher randomization test" by D. Basu. *Journal of the American Statistical Association, 75,* 591–593.

Rubin, D. B. (1990). Comment on "Neyman (1923) and causal inference in experiments and observational studies." *Statistical Science, 5,* 472–480.

Sommer, A., Tarwotjo, I., Djunaedi E., et al. (1986). Impact of vitamin A supplementation on childhood mortality: A randomised controlled community trial. *Lancet, i,* 1169–1173.

Sommer, A., & Zeger, S. (1991). On estimating efficacy from clinical trials. *Statistics in Medicine, 10,* 45–52.

Tanner, M. (1996). *Tools for statistical inference: Methods for the exploration of posterior distributions and likelihood functions.* New York: Springer.

Titterington, D. M., Smith, A. F. M., Makov, U. E. (1985). *Statistical analysis of finite mixture distributions.* Chichester, England: John Wiley.

Vinokur, A. D., Price, R. H., & Schul, Y. (1995). Impact of the JOBS intervention on unemployed workers varying in risk for depression. *American Journal of Community Psychology, 23,* 39–74.

Vinokur, A. D., & Schul, Y. (1997). Mastery and inoculation against setbacks as active ingredients in intervention for the unemployed. *Journal of Consulting and Clinical Psychology, 65,* 867–877.

Werthamer-Larsson, L., Kellam, S. G., & Wheeler, L. (1991). Effect of first-grade classroom environment on child shy behavior, aggressive behavior, and concentration problems. *American Journal of Community Psychology, 19,* 585–602.

West, S. G., & Sagarin, B. J. (2000) Participant selection and loss in randomized experiments. In L. Bickman (Ed.), Research design. Thousnad Oaks, CA: Sage. pp. 117–154.

4

Multilevel Modeling With SEM

Ronald H. Heck
University of Hawaii at Mānoa

Over the past two decades, concerns in various fields with conceptual and methodological issues in conducting research with hierarchical (or clustered) data have led to the development of multilevel modeling techniques. For example, research on organizations presents opportunities to study phenomena in hierarchical settings. Individuals work in departments nested within particular organizations within geographic regions and countries. These individuals interact with their social contexts in a variety of ways. Individuals within successive clusters may share some common characteristics (e.g., socialization patterns, traditions and values, and beliefs about work). Similarly, the individuals nested in these various contexts may also influence the properties of the groups.

Clustered data also result from the specific research design. In survey research, for example, individuals are often selected to participate in a study from some type of stratified random sampling design (e.g., individuals may be chosen from certain neighborhoods in particular cities and geographical areas). Longitudinal designs present another research situation where a series of measurements is nested within the individuals who participate in the study (Hox, 1998). In the past, researchers have had considerable difficulty analyzing data where individuals are nested within a series of hierarchical groupings. Ignoring such data structures can lead to false inferences about the relations among variables in a model, as well as missed insights about the social processes being studied.

A variety of names have been used to refer to methods for analyzing hierarchical data structures: multilevel regression models, hierarchical linear models, mixed- and random-effects models, random coefficients models, and multilevel covariance structure models. The statistical theory for multilevel models has developed out of several streams of methodological work in different fields of inquiry, including biometric applications of mixed-model analysis of variance (ANOVA), random coefficients regression models in econometrics, and developments in the statistical theory of covariance component models and Bayesian estimation of linear models (Bock, 1989; de Leeuw & Kreft, 1986; Efron & Morris, 1975; Fisher, 1918, 1925; Goldstein, 1987; Hartley & Rao, 1967; Laird & Ware, 1982; Lindley & Smith, 1972; Morris, 1995; Muthén, 1989; Muthén & Satorra, 1989; Raudenbush, 1988; Raudenbush & Bryk, 1986; Rubin, 1950; Shigemasu, 1976; Smith, 1973; Wald, 1947; Wong & Mason, 1985).

The intent of this chapter is to provide an introduction to multilevel modeling techniques using structural equation modeling (SEM). Several conceptual and methodological issues in multilevel modeling are discussed, followed by the mathematical models underlying multilevel SEM. Finally, examples of a multilevel confirmatory factor analysis, multilevel path analysis, and multilevel modeling with latent variables are presented. The examples are intended to show, in simple terms, how to set up and conduct analyses step by step. For this reason, substantive issues are kept at a minimum, and the focus is placed on the methodological and practical issues in multilevel modeling with SEM.

OVERVIEW OF MULTILEVEL MODELING

Multilevel modeling is one of several approaches that can be used in analyzing clustered data. In studying organizations, for example, multilevel modeling is an attractive approach because it allows the incorporation of substantive theory about individual and organizational processes into the clustered sampling designs of survey research. Despite the existence of hierarchical data structures in behavioral and social sciences, past empirical studies often did not address them adequately (Bryk & Raudenbush, 1992), although substantive concerns about multilevel modeling including proper model specification (e.g., unit of analysis, aggregation effects, contextual effects) and the precision of parameter estimates with single-level analyses were periodically raised (e.g., Burstein, 1980; Cronbach & Webb, 1975; Goldstein, 1987; Lindley & Smith, 1972; Strenio, 1981; Walsh, 1947). Applying the single-level linear model to hierarchical data produced several analytic difficulties, including a forced choice over the proper unit of analysis, trade-offs in measurement precision, and limitations in the methods used to estimate the model's parameters (Raudenbush, 1995). In a way, this represented a *blind spot* in how researchers approached the analysis of hierarchical data.

For many years, therefore, empirical work lagged behind the substantive theory of multilevel modeling because of the limitations of single-level analyses; that is, either individuals were the unit of analysis or groups were the unit of analysis. Researchers did not always consider the implications of the assumptions they made about measuring variables at their natural level and subsequently moving them from one level to another to maintain a single-level analysis. In hierarchical data sets, the lowest level of measurement is called the *microlevel*, with all higher level measurements called the *macrolevel*. Before multilevel techniques were available, researchers either had to disaggregate or aggregate variables in a hierarchical structure to construct a data set that could be analyzed on a single level. In the disaggregation approach to studying organizations, for example, the researcher would move variables conceptualized at the macrolevel (e.g., departmental and organizational levels) to the microlevel (e.g., the individual level) of the data structure. Organizational-level variables like productivity and organizational size might be combined with information about departmental leadership and individual employees' workplace attitudes and motivation. The unit of analysis would then be individuals, and the analysis would be conducted using the number of individuals in the study as opposed to the number of organizations or departments.

Treating individuals as if they were independent of their various macrolevel groupings ignores the complexity inherent in the data and can introduce potentially important biases into the analysis. Single-level analyses require the researcher to assume all observations are independent; that is, that individuals within similar subunits and organizations share no common characteristics or perceptions. As similarities among individuals within groups become more pronounced (i.e., where the individuals within groups are more homogeneous), however, the model's regression coefficients, standard errors, and associated tests of parameter significance become more biased (Muthén & Muthén, 1998; Muthén & Satorra, 1995). For example, the downward bias of standard errors in single-level analyses results in smaller estimates and, hence, more findings of significant parameters in the model.

Moreover, efficient estimation based on ordinary least squares (OLS) regression requires that the random errors in the equation are independent, normally distributed, and have constant variance (Bryk & Raudenbush, 1992). This assumption is often violated in hierarchical data sets. The random error components of multilevel data structures are more complex because the errors within each unit are dependent because they are common to every individual within the unit. Therefore, conducting an individual-level analysis implies that no systematic influence of macrolevel variables is expected. Hence, all *macrolevel influence* is incorporated into the error term of the model (Kreft & de Leeuw, 1998).

In the aggregation approach, the researcher would combine data from individuals and subunits within each organization to create an organizational-level set of measures and then investigate between-organizational variation in the aggregated measures. Because organizations are the unit of analysis in this case, the individual and department data would be used to develop mean scores on the variables for each organization. Unfortunately, the aggregation approach also presents problems for single-level analyses. One is that differences at the aggregate level typically appear stronger than they would be if within-organizational variation were also incorporated into the analysis because all the variability present within each organizational unit (or subunit) is reduced to a single mean (Draper, 1995; Kaplan & Elliott, 1997). Ignoring individual variability and then making statements about individuals through conducting a group-level analyses is known as the *ecological fallacy* (Robinson, 1950).

A second problem is developing efficient estimates at the group level, in cases where the individual-level data for particular variables (e.g., minority status, low socioeconomic status [SES]) may be more sparse in some groups. Similarly, there may be fewer individuals in some groups than in others. These situations can result in less efficient prediction equations for these groups (Bryk & Raudenbush, 1992).

The unit of analysis problem suggests that OLS regression estimates are not robust to misspecification of the number of levels in the data structure (Raudenbush, 1995). Prior to the development of multilevel analytic techniques and their increased accessibility to researchers through emergent computer software, few satisfactory solutions to the analysis of clustered data emerged, although several approaches were laid out (e.g., Aitken & Longford, 1986; Cronbach, 1976; Cronbach & Webb, 1975; Dempster, Laird, & Rubin, 1977; Goldstein, 1987; Lindley & Smith, 1972; Muthén, 1989, 1991; Schmidt, 1969; Wong & Mason, 1985). Although analysis of variance methods offered partial answers to some of the questions posed with nested data (Draper, 1995), the general formulation of the multilevel linear model was not presented until the early 1970s (e.g., see Lindley & Smith, 1972).

Most important, the multilevel linear model provided a mathematical modeling environment within which researchers could investigate theories about relationships among variables at each level of the organizational or sampling hierarchy. Multilevel modeling allows the researcher to avoid the aggregation or disaggregation problem by considering both levels simultaneously in the analysis. Multilevel analysis provides a means to partition an outcome's variance into different components (e.g., within and between units) and, within the analysis, a means to assign explanatory variables to different organizational levels.

Early use of multilevel modeling, however, was limited by the fact that only in cases of perfectly balanced sampling designs (i.e., equal group sizes) were closed-form mathematical formulas available to estimate the variance and covariance components (Bryk & Raudenbush, 1992). Because variance and covariance components must be estimated, when sampling designs are unbalanced, iterative estimation procedures must be used to obtain efficient estimates. Dempster, Laird, and Rubin (1977) and Harville's (1977) applications of maximum likelihood (ML) to the estimation of variance components provided an initial means to estimate multilevel covariance structures for both balanced and unbalanced sampling designs (Dempster, Rubin, & Tsutakawa, 1981; Little & Rubin, 1987). ML estimation is based on characteristics of multivariate normality within the sample covariance matrix that are used to produce optimal (i.e., consistent and asymptotically efficient) estimates of the population parameters. Because of this, it requires relatively large sample sizes. More recently, statistical concerns about multilevel modeling under different sampling conditions and emerging solutions have drawn the attention of researchers (e.g., Kaplan & Ferguson, 1999; Morris, 1995; Muthén & Satorra, 1995).

Determining the extent to which the clustering is present is often the first step in deciding whether multilevel modeling will offer an improvement in the precision of estimates over previously used, single-level techniques (Longford, 1993). Often single-level analyses will suffice quite well depending on the structure and characteristics of specific data sets. Where variability due to clustering is present across levels, however, multilevel analyses yield better calibrated estimates of population parameters (intercepts, slopes, standard errors) than analyses conducted at a single level without adjustments for clustering effects. Through the use of an iterative fitting function such as ML, the parameter coefficients can be more appropriately weighted by considering the more complex covariance structure among the errors in multilevel analyses (i.e., because the errors within each unit are dependent). This affects the precision of the structural coefficients between groups because the amount of data available in each organization will generally vary (Bryk & Raudenbush, 1992).

Multilevel Regression Models

As the previous discussion implies, the choice of analytic paradigm requires the investigator to consider the research questions, theoretical model, and the structure of the data before considering the strengths and limitations of various multilevel techniques and software programs. A first type of multilevel analytic framework is the multilevel regression (or random coefficients) model. Multilevel regression is a general type of linear model where the values of the coefficients are assumed to vary as a probability distribution. In a single-level regression analysis, the coefficients describing the model, such as the intercept and slope, are considered as fixed values estimated from the sample data. For example, the regression coefficient describing the impact of employee job satisfaction on outcomes would be fixed at some weight for the model.

Conceptually, the multilevel regression model can be viewed as a hierarchical system of regression equations (Bryk & Raudenbush, 1992; Hox, 1998). In the multilevel formulation, the coefficients within each group (referred to as Level 1 coefficients) can be treated as randomly varying. This general multilevel framework allows the formulation of several useful submodels that can be used to examine an outcome's variance components at different levels (e.g., individual and group), the variability in intercepts that may be explained by individual- and group-level variables, and the variability in slopes that may be explained by group-level variables. In this formulation, the level of organizational outcomes produced (i.e., the intercept) would be expected to be different in each organization in the study. Similarly, the effect of job satisfaction on outcomes (i.e., the slope) produced might be larger in some organizations than in others. The researcher might be interested in the average job satisfaction slope across the organizations, as well as how particular organizations deviate from the overall average slope. Organizational (Level 2) variables such as size and resource allocations might be included in the model to explain differences in outcome levels and differences in the effects of job satisfaction on outcomes.

The multilevel regression model can also be extended to examine multivariate models with latent variables by defining a measurement model at Level 1 that corrects observed indicators of the underlying constructs for measurement error. Individual- (Level 2) and group-level (Level 3) predictors and mediating variables can be added to the model to explain variation in the latent constructs. Until recently, the literature on multilevel regression modeling has not addressed the estimation of mediating effects (see Raudenbush & Sampson, 1999).

Multilevel Structural Equation Modeling

Hierarchical data structures may also be investigated with SEM. The SEM approach represents a synthesis of factor analytic techniques developed in psychology with simultaneous equation modeling (i.e., using a series of regression equations) modeling from econometrics and sociology (Kaplan, 1998). Structural equation models are particularly designed to accommodate latent variables (underlying constructs defined by observed indicators), measurement errors in both dependent and independent variables, direct and indirect effects, reciprocal causation, simultaneity, and interdependence (Jöreskog, 1977; Jöreskog & Sörböm, 1993). In recent years, researchers have worked to integrate multilevel regression modeling with SEM to provide a general methodological approach that would account for clustered sampling, population heterogeneity, measurement error, and simultaneous equations (e.g., Bryk & Raudenbush, 1992; Hox, 1995; Kaplan, 1998; Kaplan & Elliott, 1997; McArdle & Hamagami; 1996; Muthén, 1989; 1990, 1991, 1992, 1994; Muthén & Satorra, 1989, 1995; Raudenbush, Rowan, & Kang, 1991; Raudenbush & Sampson, 1999; Willett & Sayer, 1996).

Several types of multilevel models can be investigated with SEM techniques including two-level factor (measurement) models that focus on the definition of latent (underlying) constructs through their observed indicators, path models that investigate two-level relationships among observed variables, and two-level structural models that focus on the relationships among latent and observed variables. It should be emphasized that the general multilevel formulation with SEM allows the specification of separate structural models with direct and indirect effects within and between organizations. Moreover, SEM methods can also be used to model individual growth trajectories with latent variables (e.g., see Duncan & Duncan, 1996; Khoo & Muthén, 2000; Muthén & Muthén, 1998; Willett & Sayer, 1996, for a thorough discussion of SEM methods in growth modeling) while also incorporating features of organizations. These latter methods are relatively complex; as such, this discussion is outside the scope of this introductory chapter.

Much of the methodological work on multilevel SEM is continuing at present, so there is still considerable debate over specific statistical issues that have surfaced within initial multilevel modeling efforts (e.g., potential biases in parameters, standard errors, and fit indexes resulting from sampling issues, effects of missing data, violations of normality, statistical power). As multilevel modeling becomes more accepted into the mainstream of quantitative modeling, it is expected that many of these issues will be resolved. Of course, in applying any statistical model to the analysis of data, one must remember that models are representations of reality and not the reality itself. The statistical model utilized is never a substitute for having strong theory and a thorough understanding of one's data.

STRUCTURAL EQUATION MODELING WITH *MPLUS*

Although the SEM approach and corresponding computer software have been widely accepted in the analysis of single-level multivariate data, the techniques have not been widely applied to the analysis of multilevel data structures (Hox, 1995; Muthén, 1994). Presently, these structures are difficult to analyze properly with most existing SEM software packages. The SEM approach is attractive for multilevel modeling, however, because it provides a flexible framework that makes possible the specification and testing of a wide variety of theoretical models. McDonald and Goldstein (1989), Muthén (1989, 1991, 1994), and Muthén and Satorra (1989) have provided much of the work underlying multilevel covariance structure analysis. More recently, there is an expanding literature on the use of SEM techniques in defining and testing multilevel models (e.g., Goldstein & McDonald, 1988; Hox, 1995, 1998; Kaplan, 1998; Kaplan & Elliott, 1997; McArdle & Hamagami, 1996; Muthén, 1997; Muthén & Muthén, 1998; Muthén & Satorra, 1995).

One new software program that is designed to analyze multilevel data structures is *Mplus* (Muthén & Muthén, 1998). It represents a redesign, considerable extension, and replacement of the second author's LISCOMP program (Muthén, 1988) and is designed for easy use by applied researchers. A defining feature of the program is its flexibility in handling numerous types of models with categorical observed and latent variables. *Mplus* can be used for analyzing single-level univariate and multivariate designs, multiple group designs with mean and threshold structures, designs with missing values, longitudinal (growth) designs, mixture model designs (i.e., where different individuals are hypothesized to belong to different subpopulations whose membership must be inferred from the data), complex sample modeling using sampling weights and a cluster variable, and multilevel designs with hierarchical data obtained through cluster sampling.

The flexibility of the program in analyzing multilevel data should considerably enhance the analytic possibilities with SEM for research designs where individuals are nested in groups. Some of the general models include multilevel confirmatory factor analysis (used to examine the measurement properties of latent constructs within and across groups), multilevel path analysis, and multilevel SEM (which can include multilevel factor models and separate sets of predictors within and between groups). The program is also capable of examining multilevel models of individual growth.

The SEM used in *Mplus* consists of two interrelated submodels. Readers familiar with the general form of the SEM will notice slight differences in notation (see the *Mplus User's Guide* for further discussion). The first is the measurement model that relates unobserved (latent) variables to their observed indicators. The general equation for the measurement model described in *Mplus* is

$$y_i = \nu + \Lambda \eta_i + K x_i + \varepsilon_i, \tag{1}$$

where y_i is described as a vector of observed dependent variables observed for individual i, ν is a vector of measurement intercepts, Λ is a matrix of measurement slopes, η_i is a set of latent variables, x_i is a vector of independent (background) variables, K is a matrix of regression slopes, and ϵ_i is a vector of measurement errors that is uncorrelated with other variables (Muthén & Muthén, 1998). The covariance matrix of ϵ is denoted θ. As the reader can see from Eq. 1, the observed variables are linked to the underlying factors through the factor loading matrix (Λ).

The second model, the structural model, specifies the causal relationships among a set of latent variables to be explained (called *endogenous variables*). They are explained by specifying that they are causally dependent on other endogenous variables or a vector of exogenous (x) variables. Exogenous or independent variables are determined by causes outside of the model, and therefore are not explained by the model. The structural relationships in a model may be written as

$$\eta_i = \alpha + B \eta_i + \Gamma x_i + \zeta_i, \tag{2}$$

where η_i is a vector of endogenous factors for individual i, α is a parameter vector, B is a matrix of regression coefficients relating the endogenous factors to other endogenous factors, Γ is a matrix of regression coefficients relating the exogenous variables (x_i) to the endogenous variables, and ζ_i is a vector of residuals (or errors in the equations), indicating that the endogenous variables are not perfectly predicted by the structural equations. The covariance matrix of ζ is denoted ψ.

In cases where all variables are observed, the model of structural relationships reduces to a standard path analytic model:

$$y_i = \alpha + By_i + \Gamma x_i + \zeta_i. \tag{3}$$

The approach was presented by Jöreskog in 1977. Since then, a great number of technical strides have been made in using SEM with real-world data, including problems of statistical power, violations of normality, strategies for handling missing data, indexes to assess the fit of models, and model modification strategies (Kaplan, 1998). For the interested reader, extended introductions to SEM can be found in Bollen (1989), Marcoulides and Hershberger (1997), Pedhazur and Schmelkin (1991), and Schumacker and Lomax (1996).

Options for Analyzing Multilevel Data

Researchers should be mindful of the multilevel structure of data present in many types of research (e.g., school or organizational studies). However, even if the multilevel nature of the data is taken into account, there are a variety of modeling options that can be considered (de Leeuw & Kreft, 1995). *Mplus* offers a couple of ways to deal with clustering effects that result from the study's sampling design. For example, modeling with sample weights and a clustering variable allows for the standard errors and tests of model fit to take into account the weights (which yields a more accurate or unbiased estimation of the population parameters) as well as the nonindependence of the observations due to clustering (Kaplan & Ferguson, 1999; Muthén & Muthén, 1998). In applying sampling weights, observations may be weighted inversely proportional to their probability of selection from the population.

In a design-based approach, a single-level SEM analysis can be maintained using the conventional covariance matrix (i.e., based on the number of individuals in the study), after adjustments are made for design effects including the unequal subject selection probabilities and nonindependence of observations (Muthén & Satorra, 1995). Equal weighting of the estimates (as would occur in simple random sampling) would bias the estimates of the model's parameters because of the oversampling of certain subpopulations. Essentially, the multilevel features in the data are treated as noise that is filtered out of the analysis to provide more precise estimates of the population parameters. This approach corresponds to single-level regression with weighting (see Muthén & Satorra, 1995, for further discussion).[1]

---

[1] Normalized sample weights may be applied to individual-level data in *Mplus*. In one example not included in the chapter, the *Mplus* weighted coefficients were identical to SPSS-weighted, single-level regression coefficients. The standard error estimates were found to be somewhat larger using *Mplus*, however, because of adjustments made to also consider the effects of clustering (Muthén & Muthén, 1998).

Mplus provides correct (robust) standard errors and chi-square test of model fit for clustered data and sampling weights. Readers interested in this approach can consult Chapter 10 in the *Mplus User's Guide* (Muthén & Muthén, 1998).

An example of the design-based approach to clustered data might be where participants are selected at random from a set of organizations of differing sizes with the intent of producing an analysis focusing on the motivations of individuals. In this hypothetical analysis, the researcher would not be interested in examining how group-level variables that might account for variation in motivation levels between the groups, but she or he still wants to adjust the estimates for possible clustering effects (i.e., similarities among individuals within groups). Moreover, without applying sample weights, the subjects in oversampled groups, perhaps from smaller organizations, would exert undue influence on the population estimates of individuals' work-related motivations.

Two-Level Disaggregated Analysis

In contrast to modeling with sampling weights, model-based approaches tend to focus more on the effects due to clustering than the effects due to design (Muthén & Satorra, 1995), although design effects can also be incorporated into multilevel modeling. The general statistical model for multilevel covariance structure analysis is complicated and difficult to implement as a practical matter because of the inherent complexities of computing separate covariance matrices for each unit (Hox, 1995; McArdle & Hamagami, 1996). This is because SEM techniques generally depend on large sample sizes for efficient estimation. One way to simplify the analysis of multilevel data structures using SEM techniques is to assume that there is one population of individuals that are clustered in groups. Instead of developing a separate covariance matrix for each unit, the individual data are decomposed into two separate models for the within- and between-groups structures (e.g., Cronbach & Webb, 1975; Muthén, 1991, 1994; Muthén & Satorra, 1989, 1995).

The goal of the analysis is to decompose the variation in a set of dependent variables into variance components associated with each level of a hierarchical data structure and explain the variation present at each level simultaneously using sets of predictors (Muthén & Muthén, 1998). For each individual, the total score is decomposed into an individual component (i.e., the individual deviation from the group mean) and a group component (i.e., the disaggregated group mean). This individual decomposition is used to compute separate within- and between-groups covariance matrixes (Hox, 1995).

As suggested previously, ignoring the presence of substantial similarities among individuals within groups can result in substantially biased estimates of the model's parameters, standard errors, and fit indexes. The intraclass correlation describes the degree of correspondence within clusters or groups and may be expressed as

$$\rho = \sigma_b^2/(\sigma_b^2 + \sigma_w^2), \tag{4}$$

where σ_b^2 is the variability between groups and σ_w^2 is the within-group variability.

Therefore, ρ indicates the proportion of the total variability that can be attributed to variability between the groups. The intraclass correlation should be zero when the data are independent—thus, its magnitude depends on characteristics of the variable measured and the attributes of the groups. The larger the intraclass correlation, the larger the distortion in parameter estimation that results from ignoring this similarity. For example, in studies of school outcomes, intraclass correlations are often in the range of .10 to .25 (Hill & Rowe, 1996; Reynolds & Packer, 1992), suggesting considerable similarities due to clustering. In the absence of between-group variability (i.e., where the intraclass correlation is less than .05), however, there is little need to perform a multilevel analysis. In such cases where the observations are nearly independent, a single-level analysis would provide correct estimates of the parameters and standard errors.

To represent the hierarchical nature of the data in a multilevel SEM analysis, the subscript c is added to represent the cluster (group) component and i again represents the individual component. As an example, consider a number of items that are proposed to measure an underlying organizational leadership factor. Following Muthén's (1991, 1994) discussion of multilevel covariance structure analysis, the multilevel measurement model can be expressed as

$$y_{ci} = v + \lambda\ \eta_{ci} + \varepsilon_{ci}, \tag{5}$$

where y_{ci} is a vector of observed leadership variables, v is a vector of intercepts (means), λ is a vector of factor loadings, η_{ci} is the latent leadership factor, and ϵ_{ci} is a vector of residuals. Unlike conventional single-level analyses, where independence of observation is assumed over all N observations, in multilevel SEM, independence is only assumed over the C clusters (Muthén, 1991, 1994).

Because the groups are viewed as being randomly sampled, however, we need to specify the factor mean as randomly varying across organizations (Muthén, 1991, 1994). We can express these relationships as:

$$\eta_{ci} = \alpha + \eta_{Bc} + \eta_{Wci}, \tag{6}$$

where α is the overall expectation (grand mean) for η_{ci}, η_{Bc} is a random factor component capturing organizational effects, and η_{Wci} is a random factor component varying over individuals within their organizations. The between-group component contains the group contribution to the individual's score. The advantage of this technique is that group-centered deviation scores (for the pooled within-group covariance matrix) are uncorrelated with the disaggregated group means used for the between-groups matrix (Hox, 1995). The between-factor component (η_{Bc}) and the within-factor component (η_{Wci}) are therefore independent, as in conventional random effects analysis of variance (ANOVA). Conditional on individual i being in organization c, the mean of factor η_{ci} is $\alpha + \eta_{Bc}$, where η_{Bc} varies randomly across organizations (Muthén, 1994). It is therefore possible to specify organizational differences in two parameters; that is, α and the variance of η_{Bc} (which we denote as ψ_B).

If we wish to examine the variance components of the latent factor, which we described in ψ, we can break the total factor variance down into a between-organization variance component and a within-organization variance component:

$$V(\eta_{ci}) = \Psi_T = \Psi_B + \Psi_W. \tag{7}$$

As Muthén (1994) noted, from a substantive point of view, because the observed scores are not independent for individuals in the same organization, we can estimate the proportion of the factor variance that is between-organizations (ψ_B) relative to the total factor variance (ψ_T). This corresponds to an adjustment made for the individual measurement properties of the observed variables comprising each factor (e.g., differing intraclass correlations). The latent variable counterpart of an intraclass correlation for observed variables (Eq. 4) can therefore be expressed as

$$\Psi_B/(\Psi_B + \Psi_W). \tag{8}$$

Similarly, we can also look at the residual variation ϵ_{ci} as the sum of a between-group and a within-group component

$$V(\varepsilon_{ci}) = \Theta_B + \Theta_W. \tag{9}$$

We may also add observed and latent predictors at both the within- and between-group levels. This allows the specification of separate structural models at each level (Kaplan & Elliott, 1997). Following Muthén and Muthén's (1998) discussion (see also Muthén & Satorra, 1995), the general two-level model considers a vector of observed variables that can contain cluster-specific, group-level variables z_c (c = 1, 2, ..., C) and within-group variables (y_{ci} and x'_{ci}) for individual i in cluster c, where

$$\nu_{ci} = \begin{pmatrix} z_c \\ y_{ci} \\ x_{ci} \end{pmatrix} = \nu_c^* + \nu_{ci}^* = \begin{pmatrix} \nu_{zc}^* \\ \nu_{yc}^* \\ \nu_{xc}^* \end{pmatrix} + \begin{pmatrix} 0 \\ \nu_{yci}^* \\ \nu_{xci}^* \end{pmatrix}. \tag{10}$$

The asterisked components are independent between and within components of the respective variable vector (Muthén & Satorra, 1995). The between-group matrix contains the between-group predictors (z_c), group-level variation in intercepts (y_c), and group-level variation in the individual-level predictors (x_c). Note that the within-group matrix contains the intercepts and individual-level predictors and zeros (0) for the group-level variables.

In the *Mplus* modeling framework, for example, variation in dependent variables such as organizational outcomes can be explained by several sources. These sources could include between-group predictors (z_c) like organizational size, which are conceived of as affecting only the between-group variability in organizational outcomes; individual-level predictors (e.g., individual demographics) that may be considered in some models as varying only within groups (x_{ci})— that is, having no between-group variation; or individual-level predictors that may be decomposed into their own within- and between-group components (x_c and x_{ci}). An example of this latter formulation might be a predictor such as employee motivation, which could vary across individuals in an organization and across the set of organizations. In some cases, the researcher might want to consider certain individual background variables (e.g., socioeconomic status [SES], minority status) as having between-group components as well.

This multilevel model can be translated into a between-cluster model with latent variables, which is written as

$$v_c^* = \nu_B + \Lambda_B \eta_{Bc} + \varepsilon_{Bc}, \tag{11}$$

$$\eta_{Bc} = \alpha_B + B_B \eta_{Bc} + \zeta_{Bc}, \tag{12}$$

and a within-cluster model with latent variables, which can be written as

$$v_{ci}^* = \Lambda_w \eta_{Wci} + \varepsilon_{Wci}, \tag{13}$$

$$\eta_{Wci} = B_w \eta_{Wci} + \zeta_{Wci}. \tag{14}$$

Equations (11) and (13) represent the measurement models liking observed variables to underlying factors for each level, and Eqs. (12) and (14) represent the latent variable structural models at each level. The general mean and covariance structure model (i.e., consisting of within- and between-group components) for two-level data (Muthén & Muthén, 1998) can be expressed as:

$$\mu = \nu_B + \Lambda_B (I - B_B)^{-1} \alpha_B, \tag{15}$$

$$\Sigma_B = \Lambda_B (I - B_B)^{-1} \Psi_B (I - B_B)'^{-1} \Lambda_B' + \Theta_B, \tag{16}$$

$$\Sigma_w = \Lambda_w (I - B_w)^{-1} \Psi_w (I - B_w)'^{-1} \Lambda_w' + \Theta_w. \tag{17}$$

For the interested reader, SEMs that are more general are also formulated in Schmidt and Wisenbaker (1986), McDonald and Goldstein (1989), and Muthén and Satorra (1995), and Muthén (1989, 1990).

Developing the Within- and Between-Group Covariance Matrixes

As suggested previously, the decomposition of variables from the sample data into their component parts can be used to compute a between-groups covariance matrix S_B (the covariance matrix of the disaggregated group means Y_B) and a within-groups covariance matrix S_W (the covariance matrix of the individual deviations from the group means Y_w). The covariance matrixes are also orthogonal and additive:

$$S_T = S_B + S_W. \tag{18}$$

Muthén (1989, 1994) demonstrated that the pooled within-group sample covariance matrix S_{PW} (instead of S_W) is the unbiased estimate of the population within-groups covariance matrix (Σ_W). This is calculated in a sample as

$$S_{PW} = (N - C)^{-1} \sum_{c=1}^{C} \sum_{i=1}^{nc} (y_{ci} - \overline{y}_c)(y_{ci} - \overline{y}_c)'. \tag{19}$$

This equation corresponds to the conventional equation for the covariance matrix of individual deviation scores, with $N-C$ in the denominator instead of the usual $N-1$ (Muthén, 1994). It is important to note that analyzing the pooled within-group matrix instead of the total covariance matrix is one useful strategy for dealing with the bias resulting from cluster sampling (Muthén, 1989).[2] Because the pooled-within group covariance matrix is an unbiased estimate of the population within-groups covariance matrix (Σ_W), we can now estimate the population within-group structure by constructing this matrix.

The between-groups covariance matrix S_B for the disaggregated group means for the sample is written as

$$S_B = (C - 1)^{-1} \sum_{c=1}^{C} n_c (\overline{y}_c - \overline{y})(\overline{y}_c - \overline{y})', \tag{20}$$

with $\overline{y}$ denoting the overall sample mean vector (Muthén & Satorra, 1995). It is important to note that S_B is not a simple estimator of the population between-groups covariance matrix (Σ_B). It turns out that S_B is a consistent and unbiased estimator of

$$\Sigma_W + c\Sigma_B, \tag{21}$$

where the scalar c reflects the group size (Muthén, 1994; Muthén & Muthén, 1998),

$$c = [n^2 - \sum_{c=1}^{C} n_c^2][n(C - 1)]^{-1}. \tag{22}$$

---

[2] Two-level disaggregated modeling with SEM results in estimates of the within-group parameters that are the same as those obtained through multilevel regression modeling (e.g., using Bryk, Raudenbush, & Congdon's [1996] HLM program with group mean centering).

For balanced data, c is the common group size. For unbalanced data and a large number of groups, one can proceed as if the group sizes were equal and calculate the scaling factor c as a combination of the observed cluster sizes similar to the mean (Muthén, 1994).

The ML estimate of Σ_W is S_{PW}. Because the population counterpart of S_B is a function of both $\Sigma_W + \Sigma_B$, as Muthén (1990) indicated, the ML estimate for Σ_B is

$$c^{-1} = (S_B - S_{PW}). \qquad (23)$$

The S_B and S_{PW} sample matrixes are produced in *Mplus* as part of the two-level analysis (see Muthén & Muthén, 1998).

Estimation With Balanced and Unbalanced Groups

With balanced group sizes, ML can be used to estimate the model's parameters. It should be remembered that ML estimation techniques depend on large sample sizes, preferably at both levels, for the estimates to have desirable asymptotic properties (e.g., Bassiri, 1988; Fotiu, 1989; Muthén, 1989). With unbalanced group sizes, it is often not practical to use conventional SEM estimation techniques such as ML because the fitting function involves terms for each distinct group size, including information on the mean vectors (Muthén, 1990, 1994). When ML estimation is used with unbalanced groups, it produces incorrect chi-square values, fit indexes and standard errors (Kaplan, 1998; Muthén, 1994).

With unbalanced group sizes, Muthén's quasi-likelihood estimator (called MLM in *Mplus*) can be used to estimate the model's parameters.[3] This estimator is similar to a conventional two-population covariance structure analysis using ML estimation under normality (Muthén, 1994). Muthén (1991) demonstrated that the MLM fitting function is a consistent estimator of the population between-group covariance matrix, where sample sizes are sufficiently large. Where the group sizes are not extremely different, MLM has produced satisfactory solutions, although it makes use of less information than ML (Hox, 1993, 1995; McDonald, 1994; Muthén, 1990, 1994; Muthén & Muthén, 1998). MLM estimation in *Mplus* contains the Muthén-Satorra (1995) rescaling of chi-square statistic and standard errors, which produce corrected estimates for unbalanced group sizes (Muthén & Muthén, 1998). *Mplus* also offers another quasi-likelihood estimator (MLMV) that includes robust standard errors and a mean- and variance-adjusted chi-square test statistic (Muthén & Muthén, 1998).

---

[3] Bayesian estimates can also be used to estimate the parameters in multilevel models (e.g., see Bryk & Raudenbush, 1992) especially when the number of groups in the study is small. These methods have not yet been widely applied to SEM.

Statistical Power

In investigating multilevel data structures, researchers should also consider issues surrounding statistical power and the sensitivity of their models to hypothesis testing. Because *power* is defined as the probability of finding a significant effect if it indeed exists, power is closely tied to hypothesis testing. Tests of significance were designed to provide evidence with respect to an event having arisen because of sampling error. A *t* test is one statistical test that is often used to determine the significance of a model parameter, defined as the ratio of the estimate to its standard error (i.e., for a large sample, the required *t* ratio is 1.96 at $p = .05$). The test of significance will therefore depend heavily on the accuracy of the standard error estimate. Unfortunately, in multilevel studies, when models are estimated with small numbers of groups (or imbalanced groups), the error variance is likely to be underestimated, resulting in standard error estimates of parameters that are too small and a greater likelihood of committing *Type I* errors (i.e., falsely rejecting the null hypothesis).

Estimating power also requires the researcher to consider the magnitudes (called *effect sizes*) and direction of any anticipated effects, the sample size (i.e., number of clusters or groups needed and their within-group sizes), and the likely within- and between-group variance (intraclass correlation) associated with the observations (see Cohen, 1988; Hoyle & Panter, 1995; Kaplan, 1995; Kish, 1957, 1965; MacCallum, Roznowski, & Necowitz 1992; Muthén & Satorra, 1995; Saris & Satorra, 1993; Satorra & Saris, 1985, for further discussion). For example, larger anticipated effects are related to greater statistical power. Detecting smaller effects would of course require larger numbers of groups to be included in the study. Of course, the best time to think about statistical power is in the design phase of studies. These issues and statistical power are so related that a small change in one can have a profound influence on power.

We also must consider the size of the interclass correlation. Barcikowski (1981) demonstrated that ignoring intraclass correlations in ANOVA studies can greatly inflate the chances of making *Type I* errors. For example, in a study with 10 individuals in each group and a relatively small intraclass correlation of .2 (20% of the variance is between groups), the significance level of .05 is raised to .28. Of course, using this inflated alpha level would result in many more findings of significance.

It is therefore important to note that, in the presence of small intraclass correlations (e.g., studies on school effects), it would be desirable to increase the number of groups included in the study to achieve more accurate estimates of parameters, standard errors, and error variances. This is especially important for obtaining accurate estimates of the model's between-group parameters, because the number of individuals contributing information to the calculation of the model's within-group parameters with maximum likelihood will generally be accurate if there are at least 200 or so subjects in the study (Boomsma, 1987; Chou & Bentler, 1995; Mok, 1995). Determining the required number of groups needed in a study, however, is more problematic and depends on the anticipated effects and the complexity of the model being estimated. In samples that include a large number of groups, a change in the number of individuals within each group will have only a minimal impact on statistical power. However, when the sample is composed of a small number of groups, a relatively small change in the within-group size can have a substantial impact on statistical power (Duncan, T. E. personal communication, 1998).

Most discussions of sample size and related issues are based on the use of probability samples. Although individuals may be chosen at random within units, they are seldom assigned at random to their existing units. When convenience samples are used for groups, it is unclear what the effects might be. As emphasized by others (e.g., Busing, 1993; Hox, 1998; Kreft & de Leeuw, 1998; Mok, 1995), caution should certainly be exercised in putting strong credibility in results where the number of groups is small (i.e., $N < 100$). Under these types of conditions, it is quite likely that the groups are not normally distributed. Accurately modeling the distribution of effects across a sample of groups that either may be nonrandom or depart from normality, therefore, is generally more of a problem in multilevel modeling than problems presented by the number of individuals sampled within each unit (e.g., Morris, 1995).

Similarly, missing data may potentially bias the analysis (Byrne, 1995). Of course, the best data-collection procedure is to have large numbers of observations per unit, relatively large numbers of units (Mason, 1995), and little or no missing data. Changes in any one of those conditions affect the completeness of our knowledge. In the real world, however, it is not always possible to utilize optimal sampling methods. Therefore, each individual study must be judged on its strengths and weaknesses, as well as how it contributes (whether flawed or not) to the development of research knowledge.

MULTILEVEL CONFIRMATORY FACTOR ANALYSIS

A first type of multilevel model is where researchers may wish to investigate underlying constructs through factor analysis. Many social processes are conceived as structural processes operating among unobserved constructs. Factor analysis is a useful general approach for investigating the relationships between constructs and their observed indicators because it provides a mathematical model that links the observations or manifestations of the underlying processes to the theories and constructs through which we interpret and understand them (Ecob & Cuttance, 1987). Through confirmatory factor analysis (CFA), the researcher can assess the reliability and validity of the measurements through the careful specification of constructs and their indicators prior to their actual testing with data. This is often a step that is given little attention in the preliminary stages of investigating theoretical models. The lack of measurement quality in defining constructs can be an important limitation to the credibility of results stemming from the test of a particular theory.

With multilevel factor analysis, we can examine the stability of factor models within and across groups. For example, we can examine the amount of measurement error in the observed variables that define latent factors both within and between groups. The unreliability of these measures affects the decomposition of variance, which can affect the intraclass correlations (Muthén, 1991). The individual-level error variance tends to inflate the contribution of within-level variation to the calculation of the intraclass correlation. Multilevel factor analysis, therefore, gives results that correspond to those that would be obtained from perfectly reliable measures (Muthén, 1994). When we look at an error-free variance ratio for the intraclass correlation, we are gaining a more precise estimate of the within- and between-level contributions. Through this process, we can test the construct validity of our proposed model and, hence, improve the credibility of our results by paying more attention to the reliability and validity of constructs comprising the theoretical model.

Although it is relatively easy to conceptualize multilevel factor models, actually fitting the models has presented sizable problems in the past because of the necessity of estimating the fixed and random coefficients across levels. As Muthén (1994) argued, factor analyses have typically ignored the multilevel character of the data. In part, this is because creating the proper within- and between-group covariance matrices, especially for unbalanced sampling designs, has been somewhat problematic in the past given the limitations of SEM software programs. As suggested previously, for multilevel analysis, *Mplus* (Muthén & Muthén, 1998) has the capability to create the necessary within- and between-group matrixes, although in the case of balanced group sizes, these matrixes can also be created (with some alterations) from other SEM software programs.

Specifying a Multilevel Factor Model

In this example, 384 employees in 56 organizations rated their managers' leadership in 36 areas. We concentrate on a subset of the data—six items that we propose define two leadership factors. It is important to note that ML estimation is best applied to interval data because of assumptions about the normality of the data. Its use with ordinal data has been open to considerable debate (e.g., effects on fit indexes, parameter estimates). As the number of scale points increases, however, ordinal data behave more closely to interval data (Boomsma, 1987; Rigdon, 1998). However, one should look at the measurement properties of ordinal data (and scales developed) closely before deciding which estimation method to use. Currently, however, only ML and Muthén's quasi-maximum likelihood estimator (MLM) are available for analyzing multilevel data with SEM techniques in *Mplus*.

The proposed multilevel factor model is presented in Fig. 4.1. The two latent factors of leadership (i.e., governance and evaluation) are enclosed in circles. Each factor is defined by arrows leading to the three observed indicators

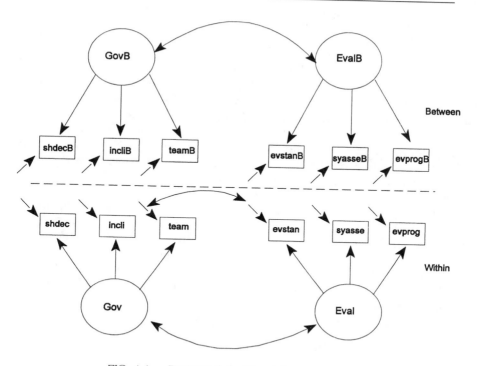

FIG. 4.1.   Proposed multilevel factor model.

(enclosed in rectangles) and their corresponding unique factors (i.e., with short arrows representing measurement error). The governance factor consists of the extent to which the manager involves employees in shared decision making (shdec), uses a team approach internally (team), and encourages the involvement of clients in policymaking (inclin). The evaluation factor consists of the extent to which the manager develops evaluation standards for assessing employee performance (evstan), uses systematic assessment procedures (syasse), and evaluates programs that are implemented (evprog).

As summarized in the figure, the multilevel factor model suggests that there are four orthogonal sources of variation for each observed variable. The within-group sources of variation are the (a) individual variability common to the variables that load on each common factor, and (b) individual variability that is specific to each variable (its residual). The between-group sources are the (c) group variability common to the variables (i.e., shown at the group level with B as a suffix) that load on each factor, and (d) group variability specific to each observed variable (the group-level residual).

The goal of the multilevel analysis is to summarize the within- and between-group variation in this leadership model and establish whether the same individual-level model holds at the organizational level. It is likely that there may be differences in the quality of measurement of items defining the factors that result from the multilevel nature of the data. For example, we may reasonably expect that employees within each organization differ to some extent in their assessments of a manager's performance with respect to these two leadership dimensions. The within-groups model addresses the portion of variance in the factors that results from variation among individuals.

Similarly, we can expect that there are also differences in managers' leadership performance across the organizations (i.e., between-organization variance). The between-groups model addresses across-group variation rather than across-individual variation (Muthén, 1991). Hence, we hypothesize that the same two-model factor holds across organizations, but that there may be likely differences in the measurement quality of the items used to define the two leadership factors. Some of this difference is also likely due to the differing amounts of variance contributed by each variable across levels (i.e., the intraclass correlation). Alternately, we could also hypothesize that one general leadership factor may be sufficient to account for the variation in leadership between organizations. Of course, there are many additional possibilities to consider when multilevel factor models are conceptualized and tested.

Testing the Model

Muthén (1994) outlined four steps to examine multilevel data structures with SEM. At the first step, the researcher can propose and test a conventional, single-level model (using the total sample covariance matrix S_T). Of course, the conventional analysis using the total sample ($N = 384$) will be biased to some extent (e.g., depending on the size of the intraclass correlations) because of its failure to consider the nested effects of the data, but this will likely give some indication of the variables that can be used to serve as indicators of the latent constructs. The tests of model fit are likely to give rough estimates of the model's adequacy. Moreover, we may be able to spot obvious misspecification, such as weak items or the presence of correlated error.

In this first, single-level test, the proposed two-factor model fit the data marginally (not tabled). After looking at the modification indexes, one covariance between errors was freed (i.e., the path between team and evstan in Fig. 4.1). The resulting model fit the data reasonably well [χ^2 (7f) = 20.06, $p = .01$, and RMSEA = .07, $p = .16$]. Each set of three items loaded well on its corresponding latent variable (with loadings ranging from .52–.81), and the errors were generally low (.35–.73).

Because the single-level model fit the data adequately, as a second step, we can examine the intraclass correlations for the observed indicators. The intraclass correlation summarizes the proportion of the total variation that lies between groups.

They are examined to check whether $\Sigma_B = 0$. In this case, there was considerable variation between groups for the six measures of leadership, with intraclass correlations ranging from about 4% to 23%. Because there was sufficient between-organizational variation in the observed variables, we can proceed to the third step (i.e., testing the within- and between-group models separately if desired) and the fourth step (i.e., testing the between and within components simultaneously) in the analysis.

At Step 3, we may wish to estimate only the pooled within-group covariance matrix ($N = 328$). This step can also be useful in determining where possible sources of misspecification may reside because there are no modification indexes available in *Mplus* for multilevel models. This pooled within-group analysis can be viewed as a model with no between-group structure imposed (Muthén, 1994). Once again, the resulting model estimated with maximum likelihood (not tabled) fit the data reasonably well [χ^2 (7f) = 23.7, $p = .001$, RMSEA = .085, $p = .054$].

At Step 4, the complete within- and between-group models are tested simultaneously. Figure 4.2 provides the *Mplus* input statements for this model. The initial lines in Fig. 4.2 identify the data file and variables used in the analysis. The variable statement also requires the user to identify the variable used to form the clusters (group). To test the complete (i.e., two-group) multilevel model with unbalanced group sizes, Muthén's robust quasi-likelihood estimator (MLM) should be used because it provides the correct chi-square coefficient and standard errors. With unbalanced group sizes, the RMSEA is incorrect, so only the chi-square can

TITLE:	Two-level Confirmatory Factor Analysis
DATA:	FILE IS C: \Mplus\nlead.raw; Format is 1f2 . 0, 6f1 . 0, 2x;
VARIABLE:	Names are group shdec incli syasse evprog team evstan; CLUSTER IS group;
ANALYSIS:	TYPE = General Twolevel; ESTIMATOR IS MLM;
Model:	
	%BETWEEN% bgov by shdec incli team; beval by syasse evprog evstan;
	%WITHIN% gov by shdec incli team; eval by syasse evprog evstan; team WITH evstan;
OUTPUT:	SAMPSTAT STANDARDIZED;
Fit Index: χ^2 (15) = 30 . 148, $p = . 01$.	

FIG. 4.2. *Mplus* input instructions for multilevel leadership CFA.

be used to estimate the overall model fit. Parameter estimates, however, are the same with either the MLM or ML estimation.

The model statements for a two-level analysis require a separate model to be specified between and within groups. For example, each between-group leadership factor is measured by three observed variables. This is specified using the BY statement, which is short for *measured by*. As part of the default specifications, *Mplus* fixes the first observed indicator specified for each factor at 1.0 to provide a metric for measuring the factor. The covariance between factors is automatically estimated by the program. In the within-groups measurement model, each leadership factor is similarly defined by three observed indicators. There is also one covariance between errors (identified in the initial analysis) that needs to be estimated. This parameter is included by using the WITH statement.

The actual output from *Mplus* is presented in Table 4.1. The information includes the cluster sizes, the intraclass correlations for the observed variables, the between- and within-group covariance matrixes, fit indexes, the unstandardized and standardized parameter estimates, and squared multiple correlations of the observed variables on the factors.

First, we can examine the fit of the proposed model to the data. The χ^2 (15f) for the within- and between-groups models was 30.148 ($p = .01$). Therefore, the addition of the between- structure added only about 6.5 chi-square points (from the χ^2 in Step 3) with an additional 8 degrees of freedom.[4] This increase in chi-square does not seem to be large. We can accept the model as a plausible representation of the data.

Once the fit of the model is determined to be adequate, it is important to assess the size of the parameter estimates. The *Mplus* standardized parameter estimates are summarized in Fig. 4.3. There are a number of different ways to standardize estimates in multilevel modeling with SEM. *Mplus* standardizes the between-level parameters by the between-level variances for latent and observed variables and the within-group parameters by the within-group variances for latent and observed variables. This is helpful in determining how much variance is explained at each level separately (L. Muthén, personal communication, 1998).

On the individual level, the loadings on the governance factor ranged from .50 to .57 and were all substantial and statistically significant (i.e., tested as the ratio of the unstandardized estimate to its standard error). This provides evidence that the observed variables serve as reliable indicators of the latent governance

---

[4] The reader may recall that for the single-level model, there were 7 degrees of freedom. In conventional covariance structure analysis with p variables and r parameters, the degrees of freedom are equal to $p(p+1)/2 - r$. In this case, we have six variables and 14 parameters (i.e., the degrees of freedom is calculated as $42/2 - 14 = 7$). To calculate the degrees of freedom in the multilevel case, we have $p(p+1) - r$ parameters because there are both within- and between-groups covariance matrixes ($42 - 27 = 15$). The extra degree of freedom in the between-groups model is the result of not estimating the error covariance between team and evstan.

TABLE 4.1
Mplus Output for Two-Factor Model

Input Reading Terminated Normally
two-level confirmatory

SUMMARY OF ANALYSIS

Number of groups	1
Number of observations	384
Number of y-variables	6
Number of x-variables	0
Number of continuous latent variables	4

Observed variables in the analysis
   SHDEC   INCLI   SYASSE   EVPROG   TEAM   EVSTAN

   Cluster variable   GROUP
Continuous latent variables in the analysis
   BGOV   BEVAL   GOV   EVAL

Estimator	MLM
Maximum number of iterations	1000
Convergence criterion	.100D-05

Input data file(s)
   C: \Mplus\nlead.raw
Input data format
   (1F2.0, 6F1. 0, 2X)
SUMMARY OF DATA

Number of clusters   56
   Size (s)   Cluster ID with Size s

Size (s)	Cluster ID with Size s							
3	3	38						
4	1	16	21	27	28	29	2	
5	11	6	10	25	44			
6	13	26	4	19	8	31	22	39
42	23	48	52					
7	5	20	30	12	36	9	14	24
15	7	18	54					
8	45	34	37	35	56			
9	51	47	53	46	49			
10	33	41	17	43	55	32		
12	40	50						

   Average cluster size   6.845

Mplus VERSION 1.0
two-level confirmatory

Estimated Intraclass Correlations for the Y Variables

Variable	Intraclass Correlation	Variable	Intraclass Correlation	Variable	Intraclass Correlation
SHDEC	.227	INCLI	.128	SYASSE	.112
EVPROG	.037	TEAM	.120	EVSTAN	.120

continued

TABLE 4.1

Mplus Output for Two-Factor Model (*continued*)

SAMPLE STATISTICS
    NUMBER OF CLUSTERS: 56
        SAMPLE STATISTICS FOR BETWEEN
            Means/Intercepts/Thresholds

1	2	3	4	5	6
3.956	4.258	4.029	3.964	3.768	3.904

Covariances/Correlations/Residual Correlations

	SHDEC	INCLI	SYASSE	EVPROG	TEAM	EVSTAN
SHDEC	2.812					
INCLI	.654	1.293				
SYASSE	.855	1.012	2.491			
EVPROG	.862	.766	.909	2.548		
TEAM	1.822	.915	1.246	1.893	4.370	
EVSTAN	1.145	1.041	1.844	1.872	2.622	3.504

        SAMPLE STATISTICS FOR WITHIN
            Means/Intercepts/Thresholds

	1	2	3	4	5	6
1	.000	.000	.000	.000	.000	.000

Covariances/Correlations/Residual Correlations

	SHDEC	INCLI	SYASSE	EVPROG	TEAM	EVSTAN
SHDEC	.938					
INCLI	.270	.647				
SYASSE	.367	.273	1.340			
EVPROG	.302	.264	.766	2.022		
TEAM	.286	.359	.598	.773	2.262	
EVSTAN	.358	.239	.840	1.103	.930	1.813

THE MODEL ESTIMATION TERMINATED NORMALLY
TESTS OF MODEL FIT
Chi-Square Test of Model Fit
        Value   30.148[*]
        Degrees of Freedom   15
        P-value   .0114

[*]The chi-square value for MLM, MLMV, WLSM and WLSMV cannot be used for chi-square difference tests.

MODEL RESULTS

	Estimates	S.E.	Est./S.E.	Std	StdYX
Between Level					
BGOV By					
SHDEC	1.000	.000	.000	.332	.634
INCLI	.546	.212	2.569	.181	.613
TEAM	1.658	.641	2.586	.550	.996

BEVAL BY					
EVSTAN	1.000	.000	.000	.490	.999
SYASSE	.578	.187	3.092	.283	.671
EVPROG	.570	.166	3.440	.279	.825
BEVAL WITH					
BGOV	.147	.061	2.419	.904	.904
Residual Variances					
SHDEC	.163	.055	2.981	.163	.598
INCLI	.054	.024	2.242	.054	.624
SYASSE	.098	.032	3.033	.098	.550
EVPROG	.037	.038	.957	.037	.320
TEAM	.003	.082	.031	.003	.008
EVSTAN	.001	.052	.010	.001	.002
Variances					
BGOV	.110	.064	1.713	1.000	1.000
BEVAL	.240	.114	2.106	1.000	1.000
Intercepts					
SHDEC	3.956	.081	48.984	3.956	7.563
INCLI	4.258	.060	70.879	4.258	14.421
SYASSE	4.029	.079	50.912	4.029	9.554
EVPROG	3.964	.083	47.704	3.964	11.707
TEAM	3.768	.100	37.501	3.768	6.820
EVSTAN	3.904	.091	42.911	3.904	7.966
Within Level					
GOV BY					
SHDEC	1.000	.000	.000	.479	.495
INCLI	.896	.245	3.658	.429	.532
TEAM	1.790	.411	4.356	.857	.568
EVAL BY					
SYASSE	1.000	.000	.000	.805	.697
EVPROG	1.213	.212	5.734	.977	.692
EVSTAN	1.298	.222	5.845	1.045	.777
EVAL WITH					
GOV	.294	.057	5.123	.762	.762
TEAM WITH					
EVSTAN	.232	.082	2.839	.232	.114
Residual Variances					
SHDEC	.708	.115	6.152	.708	.755
INCLI	.467	.084	5.563	.467	.717
SYASSE	.686	.150	4.559	.686	.514
EVPROG	1.036	.211	4.911	1.036	.521
TEAM	1.540	.329	4.683	1.540	.677
EVSTAN	.715	.132	5.434	.715	.396

continued

TABLE 4.1
Mplus Output for Two-Factor Model (*continued*)

Variances					
GOV	.229	.068	3.364	1.000	1.000
EVAL	.648	.162	3.993	1.000	1.000

R-SQUARE
Between Level

Variable	R-Square
SHDEC	.402
INCLI	.376
SYASSE	.450
EVPROG	.680
TEAM	.992
EVSTAN	.998

Within Level

Variable	R-Square
SHDEC	.245
INCLI	.283
SYASSE	.486
EVPROG	.479
TEAM	.323
EVSTAN	.604

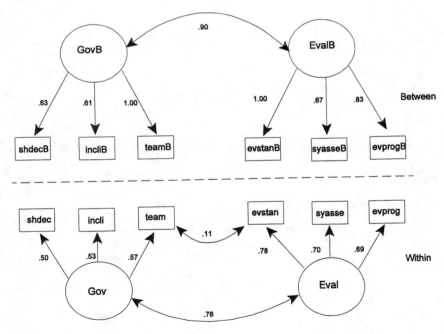

FIG. 4.3.   Standardized *Mplus* parameter estimates.

variable. The evaluation factor seems to be a bit better measured (with loading ranging from .69 to .78). The correlation between the factors within groups was .76.

Similarly, on the group level, the factor loadings were also relatively high (ranging from .61 to 1.00). We would, of course, be a bit more cautious with this part of the model because of the relatively small number of groups in the study ($N = 56$). There was a substantial correlation between the factors (.90), which suggests that perhaps one leadership factor would be enough to capture the between-group variation. Subsequent testing of one general between-group leadership factor, however, did not result in an improved model fit.

Finally, we may also wish to determine what proportion of the factor variance lies between groups. After adjusting for the measurement errors associated with each observed indicator, the factor variance components in Table 4.1 for governance were .110 (between groups) and .229 (within groups). The intraclass correlation for this factor was .32 [.110/(.110 + .229)]. The factor variance components for evaluation were .240 (between groups) and .648 (within groups). The intraclass correlation for this factor was .27 [.240/(.240 + .648)]. This suggests that measurement errors due to the observed indicators definitely affect the individual-level variance contributing to the intraclass correlations for each observed variable (Muthén, 1991).

MULTILEVEL PATH MODELS

A second type of multilevel SEM model is the multilevel path model. This is a simplified model that uses only observed variables instead of latent constructs. Unlike the general multilevel regression model, however, the path model allows researchers to investigate more complex relationships that include multiple dependent variables, intervening variables, and, therefore, indirect effects (i.e., combined effects through several paths). This can facilitate specifying separate sets of structural relationships within and between groups. Another advantage of formulating this type of multilevel model is that it allows the researcher to investigate simultaneously both direct effects and indirect effects (through other paths in the model). Indirect effects would be overlooked within the typical multilevel regression study. Although we could define a series of separate models, an advantage of using a multilevel structural model is that we can specify all of the hypothesized relations within one model (see Raudenbush & Sampson, 1999, for a discussion of how to formulate similar models within a multilevel regression framework).

The multilevel path model, however, does not include separate error terms for the variables in the model (because all variables are observed), which potentially introduces sources of bias into the analysis of the model's parameters. This is an important limitation for several reasons. First, as we noted in the previous multilevel factor model, the unreliability of the observed measures affects, to some extent, the variance decomposition of the variables across organizational levels into their within- and between-organizational components (Muthén, 1991). Second, in the multilevel path model, measurement error in an outcome variable will affect precision, whereas measurement error in the input variables will affect the accuracy of the estimates (Kaplan, 1998). Where observed variables (e.g., scales) are being used, it would be important to examine the reliability of the items preliminarily. Where the specific focus is not on measurement error, however, path models can be a useful approach to the multilevel modeling of organizational processes.

Currently, *Mplus* is able to formulate and test multilevel structural models that contain random variation in intercepts, but not random variation in within-group regression slopes (Muthén & Muthén, 1998).[5] One recent formulation by Chou, Bentler, and Pentz (1998) opens this latter possibility, however, by using a two-stage estimation method that draws on the slopes-as-outcomes approach (Burstein, 1980). The slope estimates are first computed within each unit based on the independent observations within that unit. These estimates are then placed in a new data matrix that can be analyzed through SEM. A major limitation of the approach, however, is that the error within each unit is not incorporated into the analysis (Chou et al., 1998).

Specifying a Multilevel Path Model

Consider an example where eighth-grade students ($N = 9,410$) in 51 schools are measured on a standardized test of math skills at Grades 6 and 8. We can define separate structural models consisting of individual (within-school) student composition variables including female (coded 1), participation in the federally funded free or reduced school lunch program (coded 1), minority (coded 1), and previous student learning (as measured on the sixth-grade standardized math test). It is hypothesized that the student composition factors affect Grades 6 and 8 learning. Moreover, it is hypothesized that Grade 6 math scores will affect Grade 8 math scores.

In the between-schools model, we can define a set of school-level variables that may impact Grades 6 and 8 school scores. These variables include community socioeconomic status (CSES), whether the student attends a middle school from Grade 6 to Grade 8 or stays in a K–8 school (coded 0 = K–8 and 1 = middle), and a composite indicator of school quality (ESS) collected from a survey of staff, parents, and students. The composite consists of six observed subscales including the quality of principal leadership, school emphasis on academics, high expectations for achievement, frequent monitoring of school progress, positive school climate, and positive home-school relations. Additionally, variables in the within-groups model can also be included in the

---

[5] It is of interest to note that in *Mplus* each slope can be decomposed into a within-groups and a between-groups component.

between-groups model (see Eq. [10]). In this case, it is hypothesized that Grade 6 math scores (i.e., defined as the school mean math score) will affect Grade 8 school outcomes in math.

The *Mplus* input file is shown in Fig. 4.4. Structural relations between variables can be easily defined through model statements. They are specified by ON statements, which are short for *regressed on*. As shown in the *Mplus* model statements, there are no latent variables included in this model (i.e., there are no BY statements). Notice in Fig. 4.4 that the within-group predictors (lunch, minority, female) must be referred to in the between-group model (even if they are fixed at zero). This requires researchers to think about the theoretical reasons for how these variables are conceptualized in the between-groups model. In this example, all three within-group predictors were first fixed at zero; however, minority status was subsequently freed and estimated in the model statements in Fig. 4.4. Although participation in the lunch program would likely vary across schools, in

TITLE:	Two-level Path Model For Math;
DATA:	FILE IS C:\DOE97\math.txt;
VARIABLE:	Names are schcode read8 math8 lang8 read6 math6 lang6 gender lunch minor slep sped middle cses ess; usevariables are schcode math8 math6 gender lunch minor middle cses ess;
	CLUSTER IS schcode; BETWEEN is middle cses ess;
DEFINE:	math8 = math8/100; math6 = math6/100;
ANALYSIS:	TYPE = General Twolevel; Estimator is MLM; Iterations = 5000;
Model:	
	%BETWEEN% math8 on math6*.9 cses*.1 ess*.1 middle*.1; math6 on cses middle; math8 on minor lunch@0 gender@0; math6 on minor lunch@0 gender@0;
	%WITHIN% math8 on math6*.8 lunch*-.1 minor*-.1 gender*-.1; math6 on lunch*-.1 minor*-.1 gender;
OUTPUT:	SAMPSTAT STANDARDIZED;

Fit index: χ^2 (5) = 21.8, p=.001.

FIG. 4.4. *Mplus* input statements for multilevel path model.

this example, this variable was fixed because of multicollinearity problems (i.e., between lunch participation and CSES). Percent of females in the school was not conceptualized as varying across schools.

MLM estimation was used to estimate the model's parameters because the group sizes were unbalanced. Although in typical modeling it is not necessary to set starting values because default values are automatically used, in multilevel modeling sometimes the model will not converge with default starting values. The model estimated in Fig. 4.4 required some individual starting values. These may be set by using asterisks in *Mplus*. At times, the starting values for the model's parameters may need to be adjusted carefully to achieve a solution (i.e., sometimes shifting a starting value by .1 may make the difference in a model converging).

In this example, we begin by examining the intraclass correlations of the observed variables from the *Mplus* file (Step 2). The intraclass correlations for math6 and math8 were .11 and .12, respectively. This suggests that a bit over 10% of the variance in math scores lies between schools. This is sufficient between-group variation to proceed with the multilevel analysis.

The first attempt to test the complete within- and between-groups model (Step 4) produced a chi-square coefficient (7) of 117 ($p = .000$). This did not represent a satisfactory fit of the model to the data. Although modification indexes are not available for multilevel models in *Mplus*, the user can often get a sense of the misspecification present by running the within- and between-group models separately (using ML estimation). On closer inspection, in this case the misfit was in the between-school model, because the individual model as specified (i.e., all variable paths estimated) fit the data perfectly [$\chi^2(0) = 0$].

The between-level model was then examined separately [$\chi^2(7) = 33$]. The modification indexes suggested freeing the parameters between minority status (minor) and math6 and between minority status and math8 to improve the model's fit (see Fig. 4.4). When a within-group variable such as minority status is defined in the between-groups model, the between-groups component can be thought of as the percentage of students in the school who are minority. Once these two parameters were freed, the resulting fit of the full multilevel model was considered acceptable [$\chi^2(5) = 21.8$, $p = .001$]. Although better fitting models could be obtained by freeing more between-group parameters, these modifications might make little sense substantively.

Given that the multilevel model fit the data reasonably well, the parameter estimates can be examined. The standardized estimates are summarized in Fig. 4.5. Correlations among the predictors are not included in the figure for ease of presentation. The within- and between-groups models summarize a variety of direct and indirect effects. At the within-school level, sixth-grade math scores had the largest direct effect on eighth-grade math scores (.85). In contrast, the direct effects of the student composition variables on eighth-grade math outcomes were small. Additionally, the student composition variables produced small direct

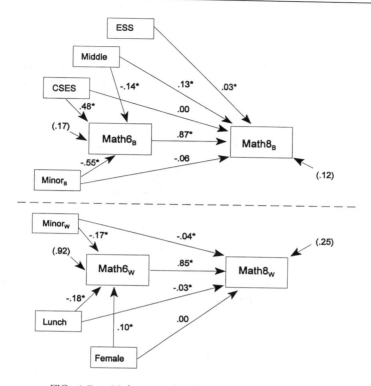

FIG. 4.5.   *Mplus* standardized estimates (*p <.05).

effects on six-grade math scores. In turn, these variables exerted small indirect effects on Grade 8 math outcomes through grade 6 learning outcomes.

For the between-school model, the strongest predictor of eighth-grade school scores in math was sixth-grade school scores (.87). There was a weak direct effect associated school type (middle) on Grade 8 math scores (.13). This advantage, however, was negated by the negative indirect effect of school type on Grade 8 outcomes through Grade 6 outcomes (−.14 × .87). Percent of minority students in the school (Minor B) also exerted a moderate indirect effect on Grade 8 school outcomes (−.55 × .87). The effect of CSES on Grade 8 outcomes was entirely indirect. Finally, the composite measure of school quality (ESS) was also significantly related to outcomes, but the effect was small.

We can also determine the variance accounted for at each level. Between schools, the variables in the model accounted for 88% of the between-school variance in eighth-grade math scores (with the 12% representing the errors in the equations) and 83% of the between-school variance in sixth-grade math scores. The within-school variables accounted for 75% of the within-school variance in eighth-grade math scores and 8% of the within-school variance in sixth-grade math scores.

Multilevel Structural Models With Latent Variables

We can also incorporate latent variables into the multilevel analysis, which can bring several benefits to the measurement of variables in a model and, hence, the accuracy of its structural relations. To illustrate this type of model, we also use the data set on organizational leadership ($N = 384$ individuals within 56 organizations), where the sampling design is unbalanced. To simplify the presentation, let us assume that we have three leadership scales (i.e., each scale composed of several survey items). As summarized in Fig. 4.6, the three scales are proposed to define a single leadership latent variable. The three observed indicators are governance practices (e.g., shared decision making, client involvement, team-oriented work environment), organizational culture and climate (e.g., two-way communication, morale, high work standards, support for risk-taking), and task organization (e.g., effective assessment and evaluation procedures, staff development, utilization of employee skills, effective allocation of resources).

We hypothesize that the leadership factor varies across organizations and wish to examine how a set of variables within and between groups accounts for variance in perceptions of leadership. The proposed structural model may be con-

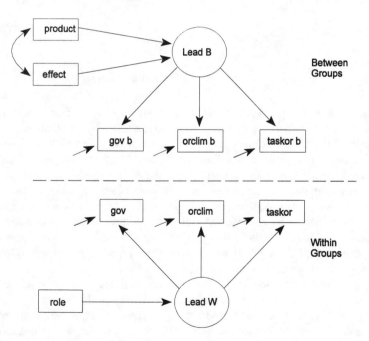

FIG. 4.6.   Proposed model of variables affecting leadership.

ceptualized in a manner that is very similar to the multilevel factor model presented previously. For the within-group model, we propose that the individual's organizational role affects leadership. For example, we can ask managers (coded 1) to complete a self-report of their leadership, and we can ask employees (coded 0) to complete a performance assessment of their immediate supervisor. We suspect that managers will systematically rate their leadership skills and activities more favorably than their employees will rate their managers' leadership.

As in the multilevel factor model, the intercepts of the observed variables comprising leadership are hypothesized to vary across organizations. The group-level variation is modeled in terms of a latent leadership factor (Lead B), which accounts for variance in the three indicators (gov B, orgclim B, taskor B). Similar to the MCFA example presented earlier, for each group-level variable, there is also a residual (represented by an arrow) that represents the group-level variability remaining after the observed variable has been taken into account (Gustafsson & Stahl, 1996).

One or more group-level predictors (z variables) can also be introduced to explain variation in factor mean across groups. In this example, the group-level variables are organizational effectiveness and organizational type. In the between-group model, organizations are referred to as ineffective (coded 0) and effective (coded 1) according to the levels of outputs they produce. In this example, organizational type refers to service- (coded 0) and product-oriented (coded 1) organizations.

The proposed model presented in Fig. 4.6 provides a simple illustration of how separate structural models at both levels may be used to account for variance in leadership performance ratings while incorporating measurement error into the analysis at both levels. This allows a more refined estimation of the model's structural parameters. Although beyond the scope of this simple example, we could also model separate sets of intervening variables if we wished.

For the variables comprising leadership, the intraclass correlations were .17 for governance, .22 for climate, and .24 for task organization. It appears, therefore, that there is sufficient variance in our measures of leadership at the organizational level to proceed with a multilevel analysis. Role is conceptualized as having no organizational-level variance and therefore is constrained to 0 in the between-groups model input statements in Fig. 4.7.

The *Mplus* model input statements in Fig. 4.7 identify the variable that is used to form the clusters and any variables that exist only at the group level (i.e., effectiveness and product). In the between-group model, group variation in leadership (Lead B) is measured by the three observed variables. Structural relations are defined by on statements. Once again, any within-group predictors must be defined in the between-groups model (i.e., blead on role@0). In the within-group measurement model, leadership (Lead) is similarly defined by the observed indicators. The single structural relationship examines the impact of organizational role on within-group ratings of leadership.

TITLE:	Two-level SEM Example;
DATA:	File is C:\Mplus\leadmod.txt;
VARIABLE:	Names are group product effect gov orgclim taskorg role;
	CLUSTER IS group; Between = effect product;
ANALYSIS:	TYPE=Twolevel; Estimator is MLM;
MODEL:	
	%BETWEEN% blead by orgclim gov taskorg; blead on effect product; blead on role@0;
	%WITHIN% lead by gov orgclim taskorg; lead on role;
OUTPUT:	SAMPSTAT STANDARDIZED;

Fit index: χ^2 (9) = 18.79, p=.03.

FIG. 4.7.   *Mplus* input statements for multilevel SEM.

Output From the Analysis

The overall fit of the model was good [$\chi^2(9) = 18.79$, $p = .03$]. In Fig. 4.8, standardized estimates are presented. The three indicators of leadership loaded substantially on the within- and between-group leadership factor. This suggests the factor accounts for substantial within- and between-group variability in the observed variables. Organizational role exerted a small, but statistically significant, effect on leadership ratings (.21), suggesting that managers rate their leadership higher than their employees rate it. At the organizational level, effectiveness had a substantial effect on between-group leadership ratings (.41). Moreover, managers in product organizations were rated lower (-.44) in terms of their leadership. The organizational-level variables accounted for 44% of the between-group variance in leadership, whereas the one individual-level predictor accounted for only 4% of the within-group variance. Given the variety of information and the sensibility of the estimates, therefore, we can accept the model as a plausible representation of the data.

We can also determine how much of the factor variance is between groups. The within-group variance for leadership (lead) was .20. The between-level variance for leadership (Blead) was .08. The factor intraclass correlation was [.08/(.08 + .20)], or about 29%. As the reader notes, although there is a relatively small amount of measurement error, especially within organizations,

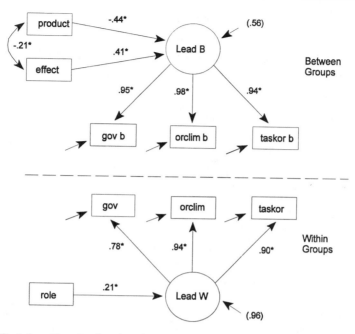

FIG. 4.8.   Standardized *Mplus* parameter estimates (*p <.05).

the factor intraclass correlation of .29 is a bit higher than the separate intraclass correlations of the observed variables (i.e., ranging from .17 to .24). This gives a more accurate view of the amount of variation in leadership that exists across organizations.

CHAPTER SUMMARY

The goal of this chapter was to provide an overview of two-level, or disaggregated, modeling with SEM techniques. This is one approach that can be used to examine data obtained from cluster sampling. The examples were provided to give readers a sense of a few of the many substantive problems that can be addressed using these techniques. It is important to keep in mind the role of theory in defining and testing multilevel models. Multilevel SEM using *Mplus* allows the investigation of a wide range of theoretical models (e.g., multilevel models with latent variables, multilevel models with direct and indirect effects, separate models within and between groups). Despite some problems that may be encountered in setting up and running multilevel models with SEM, the approach can yield answers to a variety of research questions in the social and behavioral sciences concerning individual processes, group processes, and outcomes.

ACKNOWLEDGEMENT

The author is grateful to Bengt Muthén, Linda Muthén, Vicki Rosser, and George Marcoulides for helpful comments on earlier versions of the manuscript.

REFERENCES

Aitken, M., & Longford, N. (1986). Statistical modeling issues in school effectiveness studies. *Journal of Royal Statistical Society (Series A), 149*, 1–43.

Barcikowski R. (1981). Statistical power with group mean as the unit of analysis. *Journal of Educational Statistics, 6*(3), 267–285.

Bassiri, D. (1988). *Large and small sample properties of maximum likelihood estimates for the hierarchical model.* Unpublished doctoral dissertation, Michigan State University.

Bock, R. D. (1989). *Multilevel analysis of educational data.* San Diego: Academic.

Bollen, K. (1989). *Structural equations with latent variables.* New York: Wiley.

Boomsma, A. (1987). The robustness of maximum likelihood estimation in structural equation models. In P. Cuttance & R. Ecob (Eds.), *Structural modeling by example* (pp. 160–188). Cambridge: Cambridge University Press.

Bryk, A. S., & Raudenbush, S. W. (1992). *Hierarchical linear models: Applications and data analysis methods.* Newbury Park, CA: Sage.

Bryk, A. S. Raudenbush, S. W., & Condon, R. (1996). *HLM: Hierarchical linear and nonlinear modeling with the HLM/2L and HLM/3L programs.* Chicago: Scientific Software.

Burstein, L. (1980). The analysis of multilevel data in the educational research in evaluation. *Review of Research in Education, 8*, 158–233.

Busing, F. M. (1993). *Distribution characteristics of variance estimates in two-level models.* Preprint PRM 93-04. Department of Psychometrics and Research Methodology, Leiden University, Netherlands.

Byrne, B. (1995). One application of structural equation modeling from two perspectives: Exploring with EQS and LISREL. In R. Hoyle (Ed.), *Structural equation modeling: Concepts, issues and applications* (pp. 138–157). Newbury Park, CA: Sage.

Chou, C. P., & Bentler, P. (1995). Estimates and tests in structural equation modeling. In R. Hoyle (Ed.), *Structural equation modeling: Concepts, issues, and applications* (pp. 37–55). Newbury Park, CA: Sage.

Chou, C.P., Bentler, P., & Pentz, M. (1998). *A two-stage approach to multilevel structural equation models: Application to longitudinal data.* Unpublished paper, Department of Preventive Medicine, University of Southern California, Los Angeles.

Cohen, J. (1988). *Statistical power analysis for the behavioral sciences* (2nd ed.). Hillsdale, NJ: Lawrence Erlbaum Associates.

Cronbach, L. J. (1976). *Research in classrooms and schools: Formulation of questions, designs and analysis.* Occasional Paper, Stanford Evaluation Consortium, Palo Alto, CA.

Cronbach, L. J., & Webb, N. (1975). Between and within class effects in a reported aptitude-by-treatment interaction: Reanalysis of a study by G.L. Anderson. *Journal of Educational Psychology, 6*, 717–724.

de Leeuw, J., & Kreft, I. (1986). Random coefficient models for multilevel analysis. *Journal of Educational Statistics, 11*(1), 57–85.

de Leeuw, J., & Kreft, I. G. (1995). Questioning multilevel models. *Journal of Educational Statistics, 20*(2), 171–189.

Dempster, A., Laird N., & Rubin, D. (1977). Maximum likelihood from incomplete data via the EM algorithm. *Journal of the Royal Statistical Society (Series B)*, *30*, 1–38.

Dempster, A., Rubin, D., & Tsutakawa, R. (1981). Estimation in covariance components models. *Journal of the American Statistical Association*, *76*, 341–353.

Draper, D. (1995). Inference and hierarchical modeling in the social sciences. *Journal of Educational Statistics*, *20*(2), 115–148.

Duncan, S. C., & Duncan, T. E. (1996). A multivariate growth curve analysis of adolescent substance abuse. *Structural Equation Modeling*, *3*, 323–347.

Ecob, R., & Cuttance, P. (1987). An overview of structural equation modeling. In P. Cuttance & R. Ecob (Eds.), *Structural modeling by example* (pp. 9–23). Cambridge: Cambridge University Press.

Efron, B., & Morris, C. (1975). Data analysis using Stein's estimator and its generalizations. *Journal of the American Statistical Association*, *74*, 311–319.

Fisher, R. A. (1918). The correlation between relatives on the supposition of Mendelian inheritance. *Transactions of the Royal Society of Edinburgh*, *52*, 399–433.

Fisher, R. A. (1925). *Statistical methods for research workers*. London: Oliver & Boyd.

Fotiu, R. (1989). *A comparison of the EM and data augmentation algorithms on simulates small sample hierarchical data from research on education*. Unpublished doctoral dissertation, Michigan State University, East Lansing.

Goldstein, H. (1987). *Multilevel models in educational and social research*. London: Oxford University Press.

Goldstein, H., & McDonald, R. (1988). A general model for the analysis of multilevel data. *Psychometrika*, *53*, 455–467.

Gustafsson, J. E., & Stahl, P. A. (1996). *STREAMS User's Guide. Version 1.6 for Windows*. Mölndal, Sweden: Multivariate Ware.

Hartley, H. O., & Rao, J. N. (1967). Maximum likelihood estimation from the mixed analysis of variance model. *Biometrika*, *54*, 93–108.

Harville, D. A. (1977). Maximum likelihood approaches to variance component estimation and to related problems. *Journal of the American Statistical Association*, *72*, 320–340.

Hill, P., & Rowe, K. (1996). Multilevel modelling in school effectiveness research. *School Effectiveness and School Improvement*, *7*(1), 1–34.

Hox, J. (1993). Factor analysis of multilevel data: Guaging the Muthén model. In J. Oud & R. van Blokland-Vogelesang (Eds.), *Advances in longitudinal and multivariate analysis in the behavioural sciences*. (pp. 141–156). Nijmegen, NL: ITS.

Hox, J. J. (1995). *Applied multilevel analysis*. Amsterdam: T.T. Publikaties.

Hox, J. J. (1998). Multilevel modeling: When and why? In I. Balderjahn, R. Mathar, & M. Schader (Eds.), *Classification, data analysis, and data highways* (pp. 147–154). New York: Springer Verlag.

Hoyle, R., & Panter, A. (1995). Writing about structural equation models. In R. Hoyle (Ed.), *Structural equation modeling: Concepts, issues, and applications* (pp. 158–176). Newbury Park, CA: Sage.

Jöreskog, K. G. (1977). Structural equation modeling in the social sciences: Specification, estimation, and testing. In P. R. Krishnaih (Ed.), *Applications of statistics* (pp. 265–287). Amsterdam: North-Holland.

Jöreskog, K. G., & Sörbom, D. (1993). *LISREL 8: User's reference guide*. Chicago: Scientific Software.

Kaplan, D. (1995). Statistical power in SEM. In R. Hoyle (Ed.), *Structural equation modeling: Concepts, issues, and applications* (pp. 100–117). Newbury Park, CA: Sage.

Kaplan, D. (1998). Methods for multilevel data analysis. In G. A. Marcoulides (Ed.), *Modern methods for business research* (pp. 337–358). Mahwah, NJ: Lawrence Erlbaum Associates.

Kaplan, D., & Elliott, P.R. (1997). A didactic example of multilevel structural equation modeling applicable to the study of organizations. *Structural Equation Modeling*, *4*(1), 1–23.

Kaplan, D., & Ferguson, A. (1999). On the utilization of sample weights in latent variable models. *Structural Equation Modeling, 6*(4), 305–321.

Khoo, S.T., & Muthén, B. O. (2000). Longitudinal data on families: Growth modeling alternatives. In J. Rose, L. Chassin, C. Presson, & J. Sherman (Eds.), *Multivariate applications in substance use research.* (pp 43–78). Mahwah, NJ: Lawrence, Erlbaum Associates.

Kish, L. (1957). Confidence limits for cluster samples. *American Sociological Review, 22,* 154–165.

Kish, L. (1965). *Survey sampling.* New York: Wiley.

Kreft, I., & De Leeuw, J. (1998). *Introducing multilevel modeling.* Newbury Park, CA: Sage.

Laird, N. M., & Ware, J. H. (1982). Random-effects models for longitudinal data. *Biometrics, 38,* 963–974.

Lindley, D., & Smith, A. (1972). Bayes estimates for the linear model. *Journal of the Royal Statistical Society, B34,* 1–41.

Little, R., & Rubin, D. (1987). *Statistical analysis with missing data.* New York: Wiley.

Longford, N. (1993). *Random coefficient models.* Oxford: Clarendon.

MacCallum, R.C., Roznowski, M., & Necowitz, L. B. (1992). Model modifications in covariance structure analysis. The problem of capitalization on chance. *Psychological Bulletin, 111,* 490–504.

Marcoulides, G. A., & Hershberger, S. (1997). *Multivariate statistical methods: A first course.* Mahwah, NJ: Lawrence Erlbaum Associates.

Mason, W. (1995). Comment. *Journal of Educational and Behavioral Statistics, 20*(2), 221–227.

McArdle, J., & Hamagami, F. (1996). Multilevel models from a multiple group structural equation perspective. In G. Marcoulides & R. Schumacker (Eds.), *Advanced structural equation modeling: Issues and techniques* (pp. 89–124). Mahwah, NJ: Lawrence Erlbaum Associates.

McDonald, R. P. (1994). The bilevel reticular action model for path analysis with latent variables. *Sociological Methods and Research, 22,* 399–413.

McDonald, R. P., & Goldstein, H. (1989). Balanced versus unbalanced designs for linear structural relations in two-level data. *British Journal of Mathematical and Statistical Psychology, 42,* 215–232.

Mok, M. (1995). *Sample size requirements for 2-level designs in educational research.* Unpublished manuscript, Macquarie University, Sydney, Australia.

Morris, C. (1995). Hierarchical models for educational data: An overview. *Journal of Educational Statistics, 20*(2), 190–200.

Muthén, B. O. (1988). *LISCOMP: Analysis of linear structural equations with a comprehensive measurement model.* Mooresville, IN: Scientific Software.

Muthén, B. O. (1989). Latent variable modeling in heterogenous populations. *Psychometrika, 54,* 557–585.

Muthén, B. O. (1990). *Mean and covariance structure analysis of hierarchical data.* Los Angeles: UCLA Statistics Series #62.

Muthén, B. O. (1991). Multilevel factor analysis of class and student achievement components. *Journal of Educational Measurement, 28,* 338–354.

Muthén, B. O. (1992, September). *Latent variable modeling of growth with missing data and multilevel.* Paper presented at the seventh international conference on Multivariate Analysis. Barcelona, Spain.

Muthén, B. O. (1994). Multilevel covariance structure analysis. *Sociological Methods & Research, 22*(3), 376–398.

Muthén, B. O. (1997). Latent variable modeling with longitudinal and multilevel data. In Raftery (Ed.), *Sociological methodology* (pp. 453–480). Boston: Blackwell.

Muthén, B. O., & Muthén, L. (1998) *Mplus user's guide.* Los Angeles, CA: Author.

Muthén, B. O., & Satorra, A. (1989). Multilevel aspects of varying parameters in structural models. In R. D. Bock (Ed.), *Multilevel analysis of educational data* (pp. 87–99). San Diego: Academic Press.

Muthén, B. O., & Satorra, A. (1995). Complex sample data in structural equation modeling. In P. Marsden (Ed.), *Sociological methodology 1995* (pp. 267–316). Washington, DC: American Sociological Association.

Pedhazur, E., & Schmelkin, L. (1991). *Measurement, design, and analysis: An integrated approach.* Hillsdale, NJ: Lawrence Erlbaum Associates.

Raudenbush, S. W. (1988). Educational applications of hierarchical linear model: A review. *Journal of Educational Statistics, 13*(2), 85–116.

Raudenbush, S. W. (1995). Reexamining, Reaffirming, and improving application of hierarchical models. *Journal of Educational Statistics, 20*(2), 210–220.

Raudenbush, S. W., & Bryk, A. S. (1986). A hierarchical model for studying school effects. *Sociology of Education, 59*, 1–17.

Raudenbush, S. W. Rowan, B., & Kang, S. J. (1991). A multilevel multivariate model of school climate and estimation via the EM algorithm and application to U.S. high school data. *Journal of Education Statistics, 1*, 295–330.

Raudenbush, S., & Sampson, R. (1999). Assessing direct and indirect effects in multilevel designs with latent variables. *Sociological Methods & Research, 28*(2), 123–153.

Reynolds, D., & Packer, A. (1992). School effectiveness and school improvement in the 1990s. In D. Reynolds & P. Cuttance (Eds.), *School effectiveness: Research, policy, and practice.* (pp. 171–188). London: Cassell.

Rigdon, E. (1998). Structural equation models. In G. Marcoulides (Ed.), *Modern methods for business research* (pp. 251–294). Mahwah, NJ: Lawrence Erlbaum Associates.

Robinson, W. S. (1950). Ecological correlations and the behavior of individuals. *Sociological Review, 15*, 351–357.

Rubin, H. (1950). Note on random coefficients. In T. C. Koopmans (Ed.), *Statistical inference in dynamic economic models.* (pp 419–421). New York: Wiley.

Saris, W. E., & Satorra, A. (1993). Power evaluations in structural equation models. In K. Bollen & J. S. Long (Eds.), *Testing structural equation models* (pp. 181–204). Newbury Park, CA: Sage.

Satorra, A., & Saris, W. E. (1985). Power of the likelihood ratio test in covariance structure analysis. *Psychometrika, 50*, 83–90.

Schmidt, W. H. (1969). *Covariance structure analysis of the multivariate random effects model.* Unpublished doctoral dissertation, University of Chicago.

Schmidt, W., & Wisenbaker, J. (1986). *Hierarchical data analysis: An approach based on structural equations* (Technical Report No. 4). East Lansing, MI: Department of Counseling Psychology and Special Education.

Schumacker, R., & Lomax, R. (1996). *Structural equation modeling for beginners.* Mahwah, NJ: Lawrence Erlbaum Associates.

Shigemasu, K. (1976). Development and validation of a simplified m-group regression model. *Journal of Educational Statistics, 1*(2), 157–180.

Smith, A. F. (1973). A general Bayesian linear model. *Journal of the Royal Statistical Society (Series B), 35*, 61–75.

Strenio, J. L. (1981). *Empirical Bayes estimation for a hierarchical linear model.* Unpublished doctoral dissertation, Department of Statistics, Harvard University.

Wald, A. (1947). A note on regression analysis. *Annals of Mathematical Statistics, 18*, 586–589.

Walsh, J. E. (1947). Concerning the effect of the intraclass correlation on certain significance tests. *Annals of Mathematical Statistics, 18*, 88–96.

Willett, J., & Sayer, A. (1996). Cross-domain analysis of change over time: Combining growth modeling and covariance structure analysis. In G. Marcoulides & R. Schumacker (Eds.), *Advanced structural equation modeling: Issues and techniques* (pp. 125–158). Mahwah, NJ: Lawrence Erlbaum Associates.

Wong, G. T., & Mason, W. M. (1985). The hierarchical logistic regression model for multilevel analysis. *Journal of the American Statistical Association, 80*(391), 513–524.

5

Bayesian Structural Equation Models for Multilevel Data

Kamel Jedidi
Asim Ansari
Columbia University

Multilevel structural equation models (SEM) have become increasingly popular in the psychometric literature (Goldstein & McDonald, 1988; Longford & Muthén, 1992; McDonald & Goldstein, 1989; Muthén & Sattora, 1989; Muthén, 1989, 1994). The rapid growth of multilevel modeling stems from the importance of accounting for population heterogeneity to make valid inferences from data that have a *nested* or *hierarchical* structure. Such nested data structures are common in the social sciences. Here are some examples:

- In the educational literature, student performance data are often collected from a cluster sample obtained by first drawing a random sample of schools and then drawing a random sample of students from within each selected school. For example, in the Second International Mathematics Study (SIMS; Crosswhite, Dossey, Swafford, McKnight, & Cooney 1985), a national probability sample of school districts was selected, a sample of schools was drawn from within district, and a sample of two classes were selected from within each school. Here students are nested within classrooms, classrooms are nested within schools, and schools are nested within districts, thus forming a four-level nesting structure. Background variables are observed at all the four levels of the hierarchy, and interest could be in understanding how district-level, school-level, class-level, and student-specific variables influence test performance.

- In marketing, firms interested in understanding the determinants of customer satisfaction often collect satisfaction and product/service quality data from an ongoing panel of customers. The resulting data have a two-level structure. Here the multiple replications per customer constitute the Level 1 observation units, whereas the customer can be considered Level 2 units or clusters. Explanatory variables are observed at the two levels of the hierarchy. Associated with the Level 1 units (i.e., the replications) are Level 1 variables such as service quality, which can affect customer satisfaction. Similarly, the Level 2 units (customers) can be described by demographic variables (e.g., income and age).

Additional examples of multilevel structures include data from longitudinal studies (e.g., Ansari, Morrin, & Gupta 1996; MacArdle & Hamagami, 1995) and data from surveys of various populations segments (e.g., different age group, different cultures). When examining such data structures, the researcher is often interested in drawing substantive conclusions regarding the nature of dependence of the response variable on the explanatory variables at different levels of the hierarchy. A qualitative understanding of this dependence can be achieved by constructing multilevel models of such data.

In this chapter, we focus on the substantive and methodological issues that arise in the Bayesian modeling of SEM of multilevel data. We describe the details of the hierarchical Bayesian approach and illustrate how to use Markov Chain Monte Carlo procedures (Gibbs sampling) to obtain sampling-based inferences for multilevel SEM. These procedures circumvent the need for evaluating multidimensional integrals and are therefore especially suitable for multilevel data. We also discuss model comparison and model adequacy of multilevel SEM and how they can be handled using the simulation output from MCMC procedures. Previous multilevel SEM capture only mean heterogeneity by typically allowing individuals or groups (e.g., classrooms) to have different measurement intercepts. We generalize these approaches to capture both mean and covariance heterogeneity by allowing individuals to have different intercepts as well as different structural parameters. We also discuss how mean heterogeniety can be captured through factor means instead of measurement intercepts. We illustrate the Bayesian multilevel SEM using data from a longitudinal customer satisfaction study.

Because multilevel SEM models have been available for more than one decade, one might ask about the advantages of a hierarchical Bayesian approach relative to the traditional maximum likelihood (ML) approach. The hierarchical Bayesian approach provides several theoretical and practical advantages. From a practical viewpoint, Bayesian methods allow one to flexibly incorporate prior information, whenever possible, about model parameters. In addition, Bayesian methods allow the estimation of individual-specific parameters while accounting for the uncertainty in such estimates. Specifically, the Bayesian multilevel SEM permits the direct estimation of factor scores along with the other model parameters, and therefore allows a proper accounting of uncertainty in making inferences regarding all unknown quantities in the model. From a theoretical viewpoint, Bayesian procedures do not rely on asymptotic inference and can be especially useful in nonlinear models (Arminger & Muthén, 1998) and binary data situations (Ansari & Jedidi, 2000) because these may require very large sample sizes for asymptotic properties to hold. Moreover, as we discuss later, by using MCMC procedures, we obtain simulation-based estimates of the parameters, hence circumventing the need for evaluating complex multidimensional integrals that are often required to implement ML methods on multilevel data.

The rest of the chapter is organized as follows. First, it describes the structure of a two-level factor analysis model in terms of the hierarchical Bayesian framework. Second, it discusses the Bayesian multilevel SEM. Third, it outlines the MCMC simulation procedure for estimating the multilevel SEM. Fourth, it illustrates the hierarchical Bayesian SEM using a customer satisfaction study. Fifth, it provides a summary and discusses directions for future research.

THE MULTILEVEL FACTOR ANALYSIS MODEL

Multilevel models mimic the hierarchical structure of the data and are natural tools for analyzing the structural relationships among the variables across the different levels of the hierarchy (Draper, 1995). In a multilevel model, the statistical formulation proceeds in stages. Submodels are specified at each level of the hierarchy; these different submodels are then linked together to arrive at a hierarchical model of the phenomenon of interest. For example, in modeling student achievement data, researchers typically begin by specifying a confirmatory factor analysis model for each student (Level 1 model) to capture *within*-classroom (or school) variations in test scores. Then they specify a second-level confirmatory factor model that describes the across-classroom variability of measurement intercepts (*between*-classroom variation). Thus, the second-level model captures the heterogeneity of students across classrooms. It is very well known in the psychometric literature that failure to control for such heterogeneity would lead to improper inferences about model parameters (e.g., inflated measurement reliabilities).

In this section, we describe a two-level factor analysis model. We focus on two-level models for ease of exposition. Generalizing to more than two levels is straightforward in a Bayesian hierarchical representation. Mean heterogeneity in factor analysis models can be captured at either the measurement intercepts level or the factor means level. We discuss both of these specifications in turn.

Heterogeneous Intercepts

Suppose data come from I distinct individuals[1] or groups (e.g., classrooms) indexed $i=1$ to I. Each individual i provides $j=1$ to n_i observations (e.g, student responses) on a p dimensional vector x_{ij} of indicator (manifest) variables. The total number of observations in the two-level data is then given by $N=\Sigma_i n_i$.

We assume that the manifest variables for the Level 1 observations for individual (e.g., classroom) i have a common factor structure:

$$x_{ij} = \alpha_i + \Lambda\xi_{ij} + \delta_{ij}, \tag{1}$$

$$\xi_{ij} \sim N(0, \Phi), \quad j=1 \text{ to } n_i, \tag{2}$$

$$\delta_{ij} \sim N(0, \Theta), \tag{3}$$

where α_i $(p \times 1)$ is individual i's mean vector, Λ is a $p \times r$ matrix of factor loadings $(r \leqslant p)$, Φ is a $r \times r$ positive definite covariance matrix of the factors, and $\Theta(p \times p)$ is a diagonal matrix of measurement error variances. The vectors ξ_{ij}, which represent the first-level factor scores, are assumed to be independent of the measurement error terms δ_{ij}.

At the second level, the individual vector means α_i vary in the population as follows:

$$\alpha_i = \alpha + \Lambda_b\xi_{b,i} + \delta_{b,i}, \tag{4}$$

$$\xi_{b,i} \sim N(0, \Phi_b), \quad i = 1 \text{ to } I, \tag{5}$$

$$\delta_{b,i} \sim N(0, \Theta_b). \tag{6}$$

Here Λ_b is a loading matrix of dimension $p \times r_b$ $(r_b < p)$, Φ_b is a factor covariance matrix of dimensions $r_b \times r_b$, and Θ_b, is a diagonal covariance matrix. The second-level factor scores $\xi_{b,i}$ are assumed to be independent of $\delta_{b,i}$.

To examine the consequences of ignoring individual heterogeneity for multilevel data, we derive the implied unconditional mean μ and unconditional

---

[1] In this chapter, we use the word *individual* to denote either a set of observations from a group of individuals who belong to the same Level 1 unit of analysis (e.g., classroom) or a set of replications from one individual (e.g., longitudinal observations).

covariance matrix Σ for an arbitrary observation x_{ij}. These quantities are given next:

$$E[E[x_{ij}|i]] = E[\alpha_i]$$
$$= E[\alpha + \Lambda_b \xi_{b,i} + \delta_{b,i}] \qquad (7)$$
$$= \alpha,$$

$$V[x_{ij}] = E[V(x_{ij}|i)] + V[E(x_{ij}|i)]$$
$$= E[\Lambda \Phi \Lambda' + \Theta] + V[\alpha_i] \qquad (8)$$
$$= \Lambda \Phi \Lambda' + \Theta + \Lambda_b \Phi_b \Lambda_b' + \Theta_b.$$

Thus, the total covariance matrix $\Sigma = V[x_{ij}]$ is the sum of a common *within*-individual covariance matrix ($\Sigma_W = \Lambda \Phi \Lambda' + \Theta$) and a common *between*-individual covariance matrix ($\Sigma_B = \Lambda_b \Phi_b \Lambda_b' + \Theta_b$). Consequently, an aggregate analysis that ignores heterogeneity in measurement intercepts leads to misleading inferences about all model parameters. For example, suppose $\Lambda = \Lambda_b$; then the unconditional covariance matrix reduces to $\Lambda(\Phi + \Phi_b)\Lambda' + \Theta + \Theta_b$. Thus, an aggregate analysis that estimates $\Lambda_{Agg} \Phi_{Agg} \Lambda_{Agg}' + \Theta_{Agg}$ will recover Λ, but will fail to separate Φ from Φ_b and Θ from Θ_b.

The identification of the factor model in Eqs. (1) to (6) requires certain restrictions that depend on whether we have a confirmatory or an exploratory factor model. In confirmatory models, the loadings matrixes Λ and Λ_b should have certain elements restricted to zero. Furthermore, to fix the scale of the latent factors, one can either impose restrictions via the loadings matrixes (e.g., set the scale of the factor to the scale of an *a priori* chosen variable) or assume that Φ and Φ_b are correlation matrixes. It is also possible to impose cross-level constraints such as $\Lambda = \Lambda_b$ if the factor structure is *invariant* across levels. In exploratory factor analysis, Φ and Φ_b are typically assumed to be identity matrixes. Inaddition, we need to impose $r(r-1)/2$ restrictions on Λ and $r_b(r_b-1)/b$ restrictions on Λ_b to account for rotational indeterminacies. Bock and Gibbons (1996) suggest one form in which these restrictions can be applied.

Equation (4) only captures the *unobserved* heterogeneity in measurement intercepts. However, as in consumer psychology, researchers may have *a priori* hypotheses on how the manifest variable means (or equivalently the measurement intercepts α_i) vary as a function of individual-specific covariates (e.g., gender, age). In such situations, we can easily extend Eq. (4) to include both observed and unobserved sources of heterogeneity as follows:

$$\alpha_i = \alpha + Z_i \beta + \Lambda_b \xi_{b,i} + \delta_{b,i},$$

where Z_i is a matrix that contains individual specific covariates. The parameters in the vector β explain the individual differences in the measurement intercepts in terms of the individual-level covariates. In the remainder of the chapter, we mainly focus on the unobserved heterogeneity case for ease of exposition.

The prior setup for continuous variables can be extended to handle binary and mixed variable situations. Ansari and Jedidi (2000) developed a hierachichal Bayesian procedure for estimating multilevel factor models when the manifest variables are binary. The factor model in Eqs. (1) to (6) can be considered as a special case of the binary data situation. Because the manifest variables are binary, the x_{ij} in Eq. (1) can be treated as a latent (unobserved) variable, and the link between the observed binary variable $\tilde{x}_{ij}$ and the underlying latent variables for observation j of individual i can be written in terms of a threshold specification as follows:

$$\tilde{x}_{ijk} = \begin{cases} 1 & \text{if } x_{ijk} > 0 \\ 0 & \text{otherwise.} \end{cases} \quad \text{for } k = 1 \text{ to } p.$$

The latent variables have meaning that depends on the context of the application. In psychometric studies dealing with achievement data, the latent variables refer to underlying ability variables. In biometric applications, these describe tolerances, whereas in consumer psychology studies, they refer to unobserved utility for products. Ansari and Jedidi discussed the identification restrictions for the binary multilevel factor analysis model and provided the details of the Markov Chain Monte Carlo procedures (Gibbs sampling and Metropolis–Hastings) that they developed for parameter estimation. They also discussed and illustrated how to use the simulation output from the MCMC procedure to perform model checking and model comparison. In this chapter, we focus on the simpler situation involving continuous variables.

Heterogeneous Factor Means

It is clear that the multilevel factor model in Eqs. (1) to (6) captures group differences in measurement intercepts.[2] However, in many situations, researchers are interested in modeling individual or group differences in latent constructs. For example, in achievement studies, researchers may be interested in comparing classrooms in terms of their mean levels on different types of abilities (e.g., spa-

---

[2]Because we set the factors means to zero in Eq. (2), differences in measurement intercepts are equivalent to differences in indicator variable means.

tial reasoning). Such individual differences can be modeled using different factor means ξ_i for the individuals. As heterogeneity is introduced using different factor means, the measurement intercepts α_i can be assumed to be invariant (i.e., $\alpha_i = \alpha$ for $i=1$ to I). Using the same notation as in Eqs. (1) to (3), the (heterogeneous factor means) Level 1 model can be written as:

$$x_{ij} = \alpha + \Lambda\xi_{ij} + \delta_{ij}, \tag{9}$$

$$\xi_{ij} \sim N(\nu_i, \Phi), \quad j = 1 \text{ to } n_i, \tag{10}$$

$$\delta_{ij} \sim N(0, \Theta), \tag{11}$$

where ν_i is $(r \times 1)$ vector of individual-specific factor means.

The population distribution specifying the heterogeneity in individual-level parameters (Level 2) can be written as

$$\nu_i \sim N(0, \Delta), \tag{12}$$

for $i=1$ to I. In Eq. (12), the factor means ν_i for each individual come from a population normal distribution with mean zero and a covariance matrix Δ. We assume a zero mean for this distribution to fix the location of the grand mean and ensure identification of parameters. This is analogous to setting the factor means of the first group to zero in a multigroup (i.e., fixed effects) factor analysis model. The covariance matrix Δ describes the covariation in the factor means across individuals (between-individual variation). Note that our specification for the multilevel factor analysis model allows for heterogeneity in factor means, but assumes invariant Λ, Φ, and Θ. Ansari, Jedidi, and Dube (2001) discussed a general multilevel factor model where these parameters are heterogeneous in the population.

To further examine the impact of ignoring heterogeneity and compare the implications of capturing heterogeneity at the factor means level, we compute the unconditional mean and covariance matrix for an arbitrary observation. Taking into account the differences in factor means across groups, the unconditional mean for an arbitrary observation y_i can be written as

$$E[E[x_{ij} \mid i]] = E[\alpha + \Lambda\nu_i] = \alpha, \tag{13}$$

and the unconditional covariance can be written as

$$V[x_{ij}] = E[V(x_{ij} \mid i)] + V[E(x_{ij} \mid i)]$$

$$= E[\Lambda\Phi\Lambda' + \Theta] + V[\alpha + \Lambda\nu_i] \tag{14}$$

$$= \Lambda(\Phi + \Delta)\Lambda' + \Theta$$

$$= \Lambda(\Phi^{Agg})\Lambda' + \Theta. \tag{15}$$

Comparing Eq. (8) and Eq. (15), it is clear that the heterogeneous factor means model is a special case of the heterogeneous intercepts model where the first- and second-level loading matrixes are invariant (i.e., $\Lambda = \Lambda_b$) and where the second-level error covariance matrix is null (i.e., $\Theta_b = 0$). Therefore, the identification of the heterogeneous factor means model does not pose any additional restrictions beyond the ones that we discussed for the heterogeneous intercepts model.

Moreover, a close examination of Eq. (14) reveals that an analysis that ignores heterogeneity in factor means should recover Λ and Θ, but will fail to separate Φ and Δ. Consequently, two types of misleading inferences will result from using such an analysis. First, because the diagonal elements in Φ^{Agg} are necessarily larger than the corresponding elements in Φ, factor reliability estimates will be inflated (Lord & Novick, 1968; Muthen, 1989). Second, the magnitude and signs of factor covariances in Φ^{Agg} can be distorted. For example, if the elements Φ and Δ are of the same sign, then the magnitude of the elements of Φ^{Agg} would be amplified. Alternatively, if the off-diagonal elements of Φ and Δ are of opposite sign, then the off-diagonal elements Φ^{Agg} may get attenuated or may indeed have the wrong sign.

To capture observed heterogeneity, the individual factor means ν_i can be specified to vary according to some *a priori* specified covariates (e.g., gender). As in MIMIC modeling (see Muthen, 1989), we treat this case by making each latent factor ξ_{ij} a function of the individual covariates. This specification puts us within the framework of the full structural equation model that we discuss next. We treat the estimation of the multilevel factor model in Eqs. (9) to (12) as a special case of the full SEM.

THE MULTILEVEL STRUCTURAL EQUATION MODEL

As in the factor model, a multilevel SEM is specified in two stages. In the first stage, structural and measurement models are specified for each individual. In the second stage, a population distribution is specified to model the variation of the parameters across all individuals. In this section, we consider an SEM where mean heterogeneity is modeled through the factor means. Extension to the case where mean heterogeneity is represented through the measurement intercepts follows the same approach, and therefore we do not discuss it.

Let $i=1$ to I represent individuals or groups and let $j=1$ to n_i index the observations belonging to the ith individual. Suppose each individual provides multivariate observations on q endogenous and p exogenous indicator (manifest) variables y_{ij} and x_{ij}, respectively. The associations among these manifest variables can be described in terms of latent constructs using an SEM. Let the $(r \times 1)$ vector ξ_{ij} and the $(m \times 1)$ vector η_{ij}, respectively, contain the exogenous and endogenous latent variables. As is well known, the complete model for individual i consists of a measurement model that describes the relationship among the observed and latent variables and a structural model that relates the exogenous and endogenous latent variables. Specifically, the measurement model for individual i can be written as

$$x_{ij} = \alpha_x + \Lambda_x \xi_{ij} + \delta_{ij}$$

$$y_{ij} = \alpha_y + \Lambda_y \eta_{ij} + \varepsilon_{ij} \tag{16}$$

for $j=1$ to n_i, where α_x and α_y are $p \times 1$ and $q \times 1$ measurement intercept vectors, respectively, for the exogenous and endogenous indicator variables. The $(p \times r)$ matrix Λ_x and the $(q \times m)$ matrix Λ_y contain the factor loadings. The terms $\delta_{ij} \sim N(0, \Theta_x)$ and $\epsilon_{ij} \sim N(0, \Theta_y)$ represent the vectors of measurement errors. The $p \times p$ matrix Θ_x and the $q \times q$ matrix Θ_y are diagonal and contain the measurement error variances. The r latent factors in ξ_{ij} are assumed to be normally distributed $N(v_i, \Phi)$, where v_i is a r vector of individual-specific factor means and Φ is a $r \times r$ covariance matrix of the exogenous factor scores.

The structural model that relates the latent constructs ξ_{ij} and η_{ij} for each individual i is

$$B_i \eta_{ij} = \gamma_{0i} + \Gamma_i \xi_{ij} + \zeta_{ij}, \tag{17}$$

where B_i is a triangular $(m \times m)$ matrix of structural parameters specifying the links among the endogenous latent variables, γ_{0i} is a vector of structural intercept terms, Γ_i is a $(m \times r)$ coefficient matrix denoting the effects of ξ_{ij} on η_{ij}, and ζ_{ij} is a $m \times 1$ vector of disturbances. The disturbances ζ_{ij} are assumed to be uncorrelated with ξ_{ij} and are distributed $N(0, \Psi)$, where Ψ is a $(m \times m)$ covariance matrix that captures the residual variation in the structural model. Note that, in this chapter, we only consider a recursive SEM (i.e., triangular B_i) with unrestricted (nondiagonal) error covariance matrix, Ψ.

The structural model is crucially important to researchers because it includes structural parameters that measure the impact of key antecedent variables on outcomes. In many research studies, this relationship is of primary interest, and researchers often focus on studying the individual differences in structural parameters. For example, market researchers are usually interested in determining how consumers react differentially to market stimuli (see Jedidi et al., 1997, for an example). Previous research on multilevel models has not allowed for such forms of heterogeneity. In contrast, we allow the structural coefficients $(B_i, \gamma_{0i}, \Gamma_i)$ to vary across individuals. As we show later, this specification captures both mean and covariance heterogeneity.

To complete the specification of the multilevel SEM, we now describe how the individual-level measurement parameters $\{v_i\}$ and the structural parameters

$\pi_i = \{B_i, \gamma_{0i}, \Gamma_i\}$ are distributed in the population. As in the multilevel factor model, we assume that ν_i is distributed multivariate normal $N(0, \Delta)$ in the population. Recall that we assume a zero mean for this population distribution to fix the location of the grand factor mean and ensure identification. For the structural model, π_i is assumed to be distributed multivariate normal $N(Z_i\vartheta, Y)$, where Z_i is a matrix that contains individual specific covariates (e.g., gender, ethnic group). Such a specification allows for both observed and unobserved sources of heterogeneity. Specifically, the inclusion of covariates through Z_i allows a researcher to test for specific moderating effects. If individual-level covariates are not available, then Z_i reduces to an identity matrix. The parameters in ϑ explain the individual differences in the structural parameters in terms of the individual-level covariates (e.g., demographics). The Y matrix captures the covariation in the structural parameters resulting from unobserved individual-level variables. Because of the scale indeterminacy of the endogenous factors, we impose $E(\gamma_{0i})=0$ for identification. Although the population mean of the structural intercepts is fixed to zero, the individual-level intercepts are estimable subject to this constraint. This is analogous to fixing the intercept of one group to zero in a multigroup analysis (see Joreskog, 1971; Sorbom, 1981).

Taking into account the individual-level models and the heterogeneity specifications, the complete two-stage model can be written as:

Stage 1:

$$x_{ij} = \alpha_x + \Lambda_x \xi_{ij} + \delta_{ij}$$

$$y_{ij} = \alpha_y + \Lambda_y \eta_{ij} + \epsilon_{ij}$$

$$B_i \eta_{ij} = \gamma_{0i} + \Gamma_i \xi_{ij} + \zeta_{ij}$$

$$\delta_{ij} \sim N(0, \Theta_x) \tag{18}$$

$$\epsilon_{ij} \sim N(0, \Theta_y)$$

$$\xi_{ij} \sim N(\nu_i, \Phi)$$

$$\zeta_{ij} \sim N(0, \Psi)$$

Stage 2:

$$\nu_i \sim N(0, \Delta)$$

$$\pi_i \sim N(Z_i\vartheta, Y). \tag{19}$$

We now develop a Bayesian methodology for estimating the parameters of the full hierarchical SEM described in Eqs. (18) and (19). Our Bayesian procedure allows the estimation of the multilevel factor model in Eqs. (9) to (12) as a special case.

INFERENCE

Let $w_{ij} = \{y_{ij}, x_{ij}\}$ be the joint vector of manifest variables for an arbitrary observation j for individual i. According to the model represented in Eqs. (18) and (19), this observation comes from a multivariate normal distribution $f_i(w_{ij}; \mu_i, \Sigma_i)$ with conditional mean vector

$$\mu_i = \begin{pmatrix} \alpha_y + \Lambda_y B_i^{-1}(\gamma_{0i} + \Gamma_i \nu_i) \\ \alpha_x + \Lambda_x \nu_i \end{pmatrix} \qquad (20)$$

and conditional covariance matrix

$$\Sigma_i = \begin{pmatrix} \Lambda_y B_i^{-1}(\Gamma_i \Phi \Gamma_i' + \Psi) B_i^{-1'} \Lambda_y' + \Theta_y & \Lambda_y B_i^{-1} \Gamma_i \Phi \Lambda_x' \\ \Lambda_x \Phi \Gamma_i' B_i^{-1'} \Lambda_y' & \Lambda_x \Phi \Lambda_x' + \Theta_x \end{pmatrix}. \qquad (21)$$

Both the conditional mean and covariance matrix in Eqs. (20) and (21), respectively, vary across individuals. Therefore, the SEM specified in Eqs. (18) and (19) captures both *mean* and *covariance* heterogeneity. However, the traditional multilevel structural model, where the structural coefficients are set to be invariant across individuals (i.e., $\Gamma_i = \Gamma$ and $B_i = B$), captures only mean heterogeneity.

The likelihood for individual i is

$$L_i = \prod_{j=1}^{n_i} (2\pi)^{\frac{-(p+q)}{2}} |\Sigma_i|^{-1/2} \exp\left(-\frac{1}{2}(w_{ij} - \mu_i)' \Sigma_i^{-1}(w_{ij} - \mu_i) \right), \qquad (22)$$

and the unconditional likelihood for a random sample of I individuals is given by the continuous mixture

$$L = \prod_{i=1}^{I} \iint \cdots \int L_i(\mu_i(\varphi), \Sigma_i(\varphi)) h(\varphi) d\varphi, \qquad (23)$$

where $h(\varphi)$ is the continuous population distribution that captures the heterogeneity in the parameters for the individuals. The unconditional likelihood L given in Eq. (23) is a function of the parameters $\varphi = \{\alpha_x, \alpha_y, \Lambda_x, \Lambda_y, \Phi, \Delta, \Theta_x, \Theta_y, \vartheta, \Upsilon, \Psi\}$ and cannot be written in closed form, making maximum likelihood estimation extremely difficult. We therefore use a simulation-based Bayesian approach that uses MCMC methods to estimate the parameters.

Bayesian inference requires the specification of priors for the model parameters. Let $\Lambda = \begin{pmatrix} \Lambda_x & 0 \\ 0 & \Lambda_y \end{pmatrix}$, $\alpha = \begin{pmatrix} \alpha_x \\ \alpha_y \end{pmatrix}$, and $\Theta = \begin{pmatrix} \Theta_x & 0 \\ 0 & \Theta_y \end{pmatrix}$. The unknown parameters for the model are then given by $\varphi = \{\alpha, \Lambda, \Phi, \Delta, \Theta, \vartheta, \Upsilon, \Psi\}$. Lee (1981) and

Arminger and Muthen (1998) discussed different forms of prior distributions for factor analysis and covariance structure models. Appendix 1 describes the prior distributions over the parameters in our model.

Inference in the Bayesian framework also requires one to summarize the joint posterior of all unknowns. Because this posterior density is very complex, we use simulation-based methods to obtain random draws from the posterior density (see Appendixes 1 and 2 for details). Inference can then be based on the empirical distribution of the draws. The complexity of the posterior density precludes the use of direct methods for obtaining these draws. Therefore, we use Markov Chain Monte Carlo (MCMC) methods to obtain these draws (see Gamerman, 1997; Gelman et al., 1996; Robert & Casella, 1999, for details regarding Bayesian inference and Markov Chain Monte Carlo methods). Specifically, our MCMC procedure involves Gibbs sampling (Gelfand & Smith, 1990; Geman & Geman 1984) steps in tandem with data augmentation (Tanner & Wong, 1987) to obtain the requisite draws. The MCMC methods require sampling parameter estimates from the full conditional distribution of each block of parameters. In the context of our multilevel SEM we need to generate random draws for the blocks $(\alpha, \Lambda, \{\xi_{ij}\}, \{\eta_{ij}\}, \{\nu_i\}, \Phi, \Delta, \Theta, \pi_i, \vartheta, \Upsilon, \Psi)$. Each iteration of the MCMC procedure involves sequentially sampling from the full conditional distributions associated with each block of parameters. The MCMC procedure also provides samples of the factor scores $f_{ij} = \{\xi_{ij}, \eta_{ij}\}$ and ν_i, thus enabling posterior inference about these quantities.

The MCMC sampler is run for a large number of iterations. This iterative scheme of sequential draws generates a Markov chain that converges in distribution to the joint posterior under general conditions (Tierney, 1994). After passing through an initial transient phase, the chain converges to the posterior distribution of parameters. Geyer (1992) recommended a single long run to obtain a sample from the posterior, whereas Gelman and Rubin (1992) proposed multiple chains from different starting values to help diagnose convergence. Although convergence cannot be proved, a number of convergence diagnostics that use the statistical properties of the chain have been proposed in the literature. Cowles and Carlin (1996) and Brooks and Roberts (1998) provided detailed reviews of many of the methods proposed in the literature. After the chains have converged, a large sample of draws can be obtained to approximate the posterior distribution to any desired degree of accuracy. Appendix 2 describes the full conditional distributions and the simulation steps involved in each iteration of the MCMC procedure.

A CUSTOMER SATISFACTION APPLICATION

Many researchers have analyzed the antecedents of customer satisfaction (see Oliver, 1997, for a review). Typically, researchers have postulated that overall customer satisfaction with a product or service is affected by its perceived performance and by the extent to which a customer's expectations are met or disconfirmed (e.g., Johnson, Anderson, & Fornell, 1995; Oliver, 1993).

We used the hierarchical Bayesian approach to estimate an SEM of satisfaction using panel data from a study on campus-dining services conducted at a large northeastern university. The data were collected using the following procedure. The population of interest consisted of students who had purchased all-inclusive meal plans for the fall semester. At the beginning of the semester during registration week, subjects from the population were recruited using sign-up sheets circulated by experimenters in booths set up in dining outlets and dormitories at the university. Sixty individuals signed up to attend an information session; of these, 55 agreed to participate in the panel. Each subject who participated in the study was paid $50 and was required to complete a daily diary for 39 consecutive days using the following procedure. As soon as possible after dinner every day, subjects were required to record their degree of Satisfaction with the dining service and their perception of the service provider's performance along key dimensions including Food, Service, and the Dining Environment. Subjects also recorded their expectancy Disconfirmation (i.e., the degree to which their expectations of performance were met or disconfirmed). All the observable variables (items) were measured using seven-point scales. We excluded two subjects from the analysis because of limited data for those individuals. Because of missing data for some subjects, our final data set contains 1,542 observations from the remaining 53 subjects. Therefore, we have an average of 29 observations per subject.

We specified a model in which customers' Satisfaction (η) with the dining service depends on perception of the dining service's performance on Food (ξ_1), Service (ξ_2), and the Dining Environment (ξ_3). In addition, Satisfaction depends on Disconfirmation (ξ_4). Satisfaction for each service episode was measured using the following three items: *very dissatisfied* to *very satisfied* (y_1), *felt terrible* to *delighted* (y_2), and *liked very little* to *liked very much* (y_3). Food performance was measured using the following three observable indicators: *unpalatable* to *palatable* (x_1), *bad taste* to *good taste* (x_2), and *not nutritious* to *nutritious* (x_3). Service performance was measured on four items: *indifferent* to *responsive* (x_4), *unfriendly* to *friendly* (x_5), *inefficient* to *efficient* (x_6), and *uncaring* to *caring* (x_7). Dining Environment was measured using three items: *unpleasant* to *pleasant* (x_8), *dirty* to *clean* (x_9), and *stressful* to *relaxing* (x_{10}). Finally, Disconfirmation was measured using two *much better than expected* to *much worse than expected* items (x_{11} and x_{12}). Figure 5.1 presents a graphical summary of the structure of the Satisfaction model. Note that, to avoid clutter, Figure 5.1 does not show the covariances among the factors.

To understand the nature of heterogeneity in the customer satisfaction process, we specified and estimated three models. The base model, Model 1, is the conventional SEM that assumes that the data come from a homogeneous population (i.e., no heterogeneity across respondent). Model 2, consistent with the extant literature on multilevel modeling, assumes that individuals differ only in their factor means. Model 3 allows for both heterogeneity in factor means and heterogeneity in structural coefficients, and therefore subsumes the multilevel formulation (Model 2).

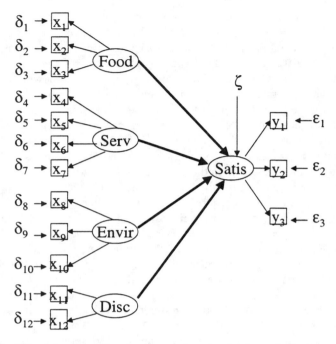

FIG. 5.1.   The structural equation model for satisfaction.

Because of the indeterminacy in the scales and origins of the factors, we imposed the following constraints to achieve identification. In all three models, for each factor we set the loading of one indicator variable to unity. In addition, following the usual practice in SEM, we set the mean of each factor to zero for Model 1. In contrast, for Models 2 and 3, we assume that the factor means ν_i vary across individuals with a grand mean $E(\nu_i)=0$. As discussed earlier, we also set the population mean of the structural intercept to zero [i.e., $E(\gamma_{0i})=0$]. Note that the measurement parameters in Models 1, 2, and 3 are identified because each factor has at least two indicators and the factors are allowed to covary (see Bollen, 1989). The structural parameters in Models 1, 2 and 3 are also identified because the structural model is a multiple regression equation.

We used the MCMC procedure described in Section 4 and Appendix 2 to estimate Models 1 through 3 inclusive. The MCMC algorithm was coded using the C programming language. Furthermore, we estimated Model 1 using Proc Calis in SAS to compare our Bayesian estimates with those obtained from the maximum likelihood estimator (MLE). Appendix 1 reports the prior distributions we used. The parameter estimates for all models are based on 20,000 draws obtained after discarding the first 10,000 iterations.

Model Evaluation

Bayes factors (Kass & Raftery, 1995) have traditionally been used in Bayesian analysis to compare two models. The calculation of Bayes factors from the MCMC output is difficult for complex models. Therefore, we use the pseudo-Bayes factor (PsBF; Geisser & Eddy, 1979; Gelfand, 1996) as a surrogate for the Bayes factor. The PsBF is based on the cross-validation predictive density of the data instead of the prior predictive density used in the calculation of Bayes factors. It can therefore be used even with improper priors. Moreover, it can be conveniently computed for SEM using the MCMC draws.

Let w be the observed data and let $w_{(ijk)}$ represent the data with the kth variable of observation j from individual i deleted. The cross-validation predictive density can then be written as

$$\pi(w_{ijk}| w_{(ijk)}) = \int \pi(w_{ijk}|\varphi, w_{(ijk)})\pi(\varphi| w_{(ijk)})d\varphi, \qquad (24)$$

where φ is the vector of all parameters in the model. The PsBF for comparing two models (M1 and M2) is expressed in terms of the product of cross-validation predictive densities and can be written as

$$\text{PsBF} = \prod_{i=1}^{I}\prod_{j=1}^{n_i}\prod_{k=1}^{p+q} \frac{\pi(w_{ijk} | w_{(ijk)}, \text{M1})}{\pi(w_{ijk} | w_{(ijk)}, \text{M2})}. \qquad (25)$$

The PsBF summarizes the evidence provided by the data for M1 against M2, and its value can be interpreted as the number of times model M1 is more (or less) probable than model M2.

The PsBF for the multilevel SEM can be calculated easily from a sample of d MCMC draws ($\varphi_1, \ldots, \varphi_d$). Because φ is the vector of all parameters, including the factor scores, the responses w_{ijk}, $i = 1$ to I, $j = 1$ to n_i, and $k = 1$ to $p+q$ are conditionally independent given φ. In such a situation, a Monte Carlo estimate of $\pi(w_{ijk}|w_{(ijk)})$ can be obtained as

$$\pi(w_{ijk}| w_{(ijk)}) = [\frac{1}{d}\sum_{t=1}^{d} \frac{1}{f(w_{ijk};\varphi^{(t)})}]^{-1}, \qquad (26)$$

where the univariate normal density $f(w_{ijk};\varphi^{(t)})$ is evaluated at tth draw, $\varphi^{(t)}$ of the MCMC sampler. Gelfand (1996) provided the derivation for the prior equation. In practice, we can calculate the logarithms of the numerator and denominator of the PsBF, and these can be used for comparing different models. These can be considered as a surrogate for the log-marginal data likelihoods $\log(\Pr(D))$ from the models.

To determine which model best represents the heterogeneity in the satisfaction data, we compared the three models using the PsBF. A model with a higher log(P(D)) is the preferred model. The log-marginal likelihood for the three models are $\log(Pr(D|M1)) = -28462.63$; $\log(Pr(D|M2)) = -28358.49$ and $\log(Pr(D|M3)) = -28316.03$, respectively, where M1, M2, and M3 denote, respectively, Models 1, 2, and 3. Hence, the data strongly support Model 2 over Model 1 and Model 3 over Model 2 and Model 1.

To further assess the fit of each model and investigate the diagnostic potential of goodness-of-fit measures when applied to heterogeneous data, we computed the aggregate Goodness-of-Fit Index (GFI) for each model. The aggregate GFI compares the estimated implied covariance matrix $\Sigma(\bar{\varphi})$, for an arbitrary observation, with the sample covariance matrix S. For all models, we computed the implied covariance matrix using the mean parameter estimates $\bar{\varphi}$ from the simulation output. The GFI statistics for Models 1, 2, and 3, respectively, are 0.99, 0.97, and 0.98. The close correspondence between the aggregate GFI measures for the three models demonstrates that a goodness-of-fit measure that is based on the aggregate covariance matrix S (which is computed from the aggregate data) fails to discriminate among models when the data are heterogeneous. The reason is that S is not a sufficient statistic for model parameters in the presence of heterogeneity. See Jedidi, Jagpal, and DeSarbo (1997) for an example that illustrates this point.

Because the main focus of Models 2 and 3 is on capturing heterogeneity at the individual level, we computed individual-specific GFI statistics using the data and the implied covariance matrices for each individual (see Eq. [21] for the implied covariance matrix from Model 3). Table 5.1 reports these GFI statistics for the 53 individuals in the sample. A comparison of the columns for Models 1 and 2 shows that the individual-level GFIs for both these models are low for most individuals. In fact, the GFI statistics from Models 1 and 2 are negative[3] for a number of individuals, showing that the two models do not fit the data for these individuals. Although Model 2 subsumes Model 1, the GFI statistics show that solely accounting for heterogeneity in factor means does not improve model fit at the individual level. It is apparent from comparing the GFI statistics from Model 3 with those obtained from the other two models that Model 3 provides a marked improvement in fit for each individual. This shows that the traditional psychometric methods (e.g., multilevel models) do not fully capture the heterogeneity in our data.

In summary, regardless of which statistic we use (marginal likelihoods or the individual-level GFI statistics), Model 3, which includes heterogeneous structural parameters, is the preferred model. In addition, it is clear that the aggregate GFI statistic is not suitable for assessing model adequacy in the presence of heterogeneous data.

---

[3] The GFI statistic could be negative if the model does not fit the data well (see Bollen, 1989).

TABLE 5.1
Model Fit: GFI Statistics for Each Subject

ID	Model 1	Model 2	Model 3	ID	Model 1	Model 2	Model 3
1	0.65	0.54	0.87	28	0.87	0.80	0.92
2	−0.38	0.43	0.82	29	−0.80	0.18	0.86
3	0.13	0.62	0.93	30	0.87	0.86	0.96
4	−9.81	−4.38	0.84	31	0.89	0.80	0.93
5	−1.19	−0.01	0.87	32	0.09	0.43	0.72
6	0.92	0.82	0.92	33	0.72	0.59	0.86
7	−2.15	−0.41	0.80	34	−1.43	−0.19	0.51
8	0.83	0.78	0.87	35	−0.41	0.39	0.89
9	0.83	0.75	0.94	36	0.31	0.76	0.94
10	0.59	0.81	0.91	37	0.11	0.68	0.91
11	0.82	0.82	0.88	38	0.07	0.68	0.95
12	0.70	0.79	0.82	39	0.81	0.89	0.92
13	−1.03	0.02	0.79	40	−11.57	−5.38	0.83
14	0.84	0.72	0.94	41	0.76	0.64	0.92
15	−1.10	0.10	0.84	42	0.65	0.55	0.83
16	−0.42	0.37	0.89	43	0.68	0.86	0.92
17	−0.06	0.63	0.95	44	0.87	0.75	0.92
18	−7.20	−2.86	0.87	45	0.53	0.65	0.90
19	−4.09	−1.35	0.76	46	−1.04	0.13	0.85
20	0.80	0.77	0.85	47	0.84	0.72	0.88
21	−0.30	0.42	0.88	48	0.88	0.88	0.93
22	−4.54	−1.59	0.87	49	−0.21	0.40	0.82
23	0.80	0.84	0.91	50	0.33	0.62	0.85
24	−4.23	−1.66	0.55	51	−1.30	−0.24	0.64
25	−0.46	−0.40	0.86	52	0.84	0.72	0.83
26	0.81	0.69	0.93	53	0.69	0.56	0.78
27	−0.37	0.48	0.85				

PARAMETER ESTIMATES

We now examine the parameter estimates from Models 1, 2, and 3. We first discuss the results from the measurement model and then analyze the structural model estimates. Table 5.2 shows the factor loadings from the measurement model. The MLE factor loadings reported in Column 3 are virtually identical to those obtained from the nonheterogeneous Bayesian model, Model 1 (see Column 4). This close similarity in estimates is expected because we used diffuse priors and our sample size is large (1,542 observations). It is also clear from Table 5.2 that the loading estimates differ only slightly across all three models. This finding is not surprising because we assumed common factor loadings for all individuals. Overall, all factor loadings are significant, suggesting that the indicators are reliable measures for the underlying factors.

TABLE 5.2
Measurement Model Results: Factor Loadings

Factor	Indicator	MLE	Model 1	Model 2	Model 3
Food	x_1	1	1	1	1
	x_2	1.106 (0.023)	1.109 (0.023)	1.067 (0.023)	1.072 (0.022)
	x_3	0.717 (0.026)	0.719 (0.026)	0.723 (0.026)	0.732 (0.025)
Service	x_4	1	1	1	1
	x_5	1.028 (0.025)	1.028 (0.024)	1.031 (0.025)	1.035 (0.025)
	x_6	0.994 (0.028)	0.996 (0.029)	1.009 (0.030)	1.012 (0.031)
	x_7	1.015 (0.027)	1.016 (0.028)	1.027 (0.028)	1.031 (0.030)
Envir.	x_8	1	1	1	1
	x_9	1.220 (0.029)	1.216 (0.030)	1.234 (0.029)	1.24 (0.031)
	x_{10}	1.016 (0.029)	1.018 (0.029)	1.027 (0.029)	1.035 (0.031)
Disc.	x_{11}	1	1	1	1
	x_{12}	0.984 (0.024)	0.984 (0.024)	0.984 (0.024)	0.985 (0.023)
Satis.	y_1	1	1	1	1
	y_2	1.038 (0.019)	1.040 (0.019)	1.042 (0.019)	1.032 (0.019)
	y_3	1.080 (0.019)	1.082 (0.019)	1.083 (0.019)	1.072 (0.019)

Note. Posterior standard deviations are shown in parentheses.

Table 5.3 reports the measurement error variances. First, as in Table 5.2, the maximum likelihood estimates (MLE) are almost identical to those obtained from the nonheterogeneous Bayesian model, Model 1. Second, a comparison of the estimates from Models 1 and 2 and Models 1 and 3 suggests that ignoring factor mean heterogeneity and /or structural heterogeneity induces a slight estimation bias.

Table 5.4 reports the estimated covariance matrix Φ of the exogenous factors, ξ_{ij} for Models 1, 2, and 3. For Models 2 and 3, the table also reports the covariance matrix Δ of the mean factor scores ν_i across individuals. As in the previous tables, the MLE estimates are very similar to those from Model 1. Recall that Model 2 only captures heterogeneity in the factor means, ν_i. It is well known that ignoring heterogeneity in factor means results in a confounding of the within- and between-covariance matrixes of the factors (i.e., $\Phi_{Model1} = \Phi_{Model2} = \Delta_{Model2}$, see Eq. [14]).

TABLE 5.3
Measurement Model Results: Measurement Error Variances

Factor	Indicator	MLE	Model 1	Model 2	Model 3
Food	x_1	0.458 (0.021)	0.460 (0.025)	0.403 (0.026)	0.415 (0.024)
	x_2	0.345 (0.027)	0.348 (0.026)	0.420 (0.029)	0.419 (0.026)
	x_3	1.217 (0.046)	1.213 (0.045)	1.173 (0.047)	1.160 (0.044)
Service	x_4	0.469 (0.023)	0.471 (0.025)	0.478 (0.025)	0.480 (0.026)
	x_5	0.428 (0.023)	0.429 (0.024)	0.437 (0.023)	0.440 (0.025)
	x_6	0.697 (0.030)	0.697 (0.032)	0.681 (0.032)	0.681 (0.032)
	x_7	0.609 (0.028)	0.609 (0.030)	0.597 (0.027)	0.597 (0.029)
Envir.	x_8	0.703 (0.032)	0.696 (0.032)	0.720 (0.032)	0.720 (0.033)
	x_9	0.217 (0.028)	0.235 (0.029)	0.203 (0.027)	0.210 (0.027)
	x_{10}	0.838 (0.036)	0.836 (0.034)	0.828 (0.37)	0.825 (0.036)
Disc.	x_{11}	0.568 (0.034)	0.570 (0.036)	0.594 (0.034)	0.585 (0.036)
	x_{12}	0.561 (0.033)	0.562 (0.034)	0.584 (0.032)	0.583 (0.033)
Satis.	y_1	0.487 (0.021)	0.486 (0.021)	0.487 (0.021)	0.492 (0.021)
	y_2	0.294 (0.016)	0.294 (0.016)	0.293 (0.015)	0.292 (0.015)
	y_3	0.258 (0.015)	0.256 (0.015)	0.258 (0.015)	0.256 (0.014)

Note. Posterior standard deviations are shown in parentheses.

The results for the three models confirm this theoretical relationship. For example, the first row of Table 5.4 reveals that $\Phi_{Food-Food}$ for Model 1 is 1.569. This value is approximately equal to the sum of the estimates $\Phi_{Food-Food} = 1.165$ and $\Delta_{Food-Food} = 0.426$ obtained from Model 2. Thus, if the factor means are heterogeneous (Model 2), the results from a conventional model that ignores heterogeneity will always underestimate the factor variances and inflate the measurement reliability. A similar relationship exists between the estimates for Models 1 and 3.

Focusing on the estimates for Φ for Model 3, we see that all the exogenous factors are positively correlated. The estimates of Δ show that the mean factor

TABLE 5.4
Estimated Covariance Structure of Antecedent Factors

Parameter	Φ				Δ	
	MLE	Model 1	Model 2	Model 3	Model 2	Model 3
Food-Food	1.569	1.562	1.165	1.150	0.426	0.423
	(0.074)	(0.074)	(0.055)	(0.055)	(0.093)	(0.089)
Food-Service	0.617	0.618	0.399	0.396	0.216	0.215
	(0.043)	(0.043)	(0.032)	(0.032)	(0.063)	(0.061)
Food-Envir.	0.764	0.765	0.414	0.410	0.331	0.324
	(0.048)	(0.047)	(0.032)	(0.031)	(0.080)	(0.078)
Food-Disc.	1.232	1.230	0.997	0.982	0.229	0.233
	(0.061)	(0.061)	(0.050)	(0.049)	(0.062)	(0.058)
Service-Service	1.170	1.170	0.881	0.873	0.285	0.283
	(0.059)	(0.060)	(0.046)	(0.046)	(0.064)	(0.063)
Service-Envir.	0.691	0.694	0.409	0.405	0.266	0.262
	(0.042)	(0.044)	(0.029)	(0.028)	(0.066)	(0.066)
Service-Disc.	0.602	0.603	0.428	0.425	0.161	0.163
	(0.046)	(0.046)	(0.037)	(0.037)	(0.049)	(0.046)
Envir.-Envir.	1.297	1.297	0.852	0.840	0.426	0.414
	(0.070)	(0.070)	(0.046)	(0.048)	(0.093)	(0.100)
Envir.-Disc.	0.704	0.707	0.462	0.456	0.218	0.217
	(0.050)	(0.050)	(0.038)	(0.036)	(0.059)	(0.056)
Disc.-Disc.	1.801	1.799	1.534	1.552	0.231	0.218
	(0.087)	(0.087)	(0.079)	(0.077)	(0.056)	(0.051)

Note. Posterior standard deviations are in parentheses.
Φ = Unduplicated elements in covariance matrix of exogenous factors.
Δ = Unduplicated elements in covariance matrix of mean factor scores for exogenous factors.

scores are also positively correlated across individuals. In addition, the large magnitudes of the diagonal elements of Δ show that there is considerable heterogeneity in factor means across individuals.

Table 5.5 reports the regression coefficients from the structural model. In interpreting the table, recall that Model 3 captures heterogeneity in the impact of the antecedent constructs on Satisfaction by assuming that the individual-specific coefficients come from a multivariate normal population distribution $N(\vartheta, \mathbf{Y})$. The population mean, ϑ, for the structural coefficients and the standard deviation of the individual specific coefficients $\sqrt{Y_{kk}}$ are reported in Column 5 of the table. The mean estimates for Model 3 show that Satisfaction is significantly affected by perceived performance on Food, Service, and Environment. In addition, the positive coefficient for Disconfirmation confirms the previous findings in the literature that better-than-expected performance increases Satisfaction. The magnitudes of the across-individuals standard deviations (see the last

TABLE 5.5
Structural Model: Regression Coefficients

Exogenous Factor	MLE	Model 1	Model 2	Model 3	
				ϑ	$\sqrt{\mathbf{Y}}_{kk}$
Food	0.311	0.311	0.258	0.418	0.265
	(0.027)	(0.028)	(0.028)	(0.049)	(0.038)
Service	0.108	0.108	0.110	0.085	0.199
	(0.022)	(0.023)	(0.022)	(0.038)	(0.025)
Envir.	0.058	0.057	0.053	0.094	0.22
	(0.022)	(0.023)	(0.021)	(0.040)	(0.030)
Disc.	0.536	0.536	0.588	0.440	0.256
	(0.027)	(0.027)	(0.028)	(0.046)	(0.036)
Ψ	0.285	0.285	0.266	0.151	
	(0.019)	(0.019)	(0.019)	(0.015)	

Note. Posterior standard deviations are shown in parentheses.

ϑ denotes the population mean of the structural coefficients.

$\sqrt{\mathbf{Y}}_{kk}$ denotes the population standard deviation of the structural coefficients.

Column) are large and confirm that the importance weights of the antecedant dimensions on Satisfaction vary significantly across subjects.

The differences in the magnitudes of the coefficients across the models show that ignoring heterogeneity leads to biased estimates of the structural parameters. Furthermore, both Models 1 and 2 seriously overstate statistical significance because they understate the posterior standard deviations of all structural parameter estimates. For example, the posterior standard deviation for Food is 0.049 for M3, but only 0.028 for M1 and M2. In addition, the last row of Table 5.5 shows that, by failing to allow for structural heterogeneity, Models 1 and 2 understate the goodness-of-fit of the structural regression model (i.e., larger estimated structural error variance ψ). This result is not surprising because the unaccounted heterogeneity is absorbed by the structural error term.

Figure 5.2 presents a plot of the estimated exogenous mean factor scores for each individual. These scores represent the average perception for the individuals along the three dimensions of the service. The figure also shows how individuals differ on their mean disconfirmation scores. It is clear from the figure that there is considerable heterogeneity in the mean factor scores for the individuals.

SUMMARY AND CONCLUSIONS

We illustrate procedures for performing simulation based Bayesian inference and model assessment for multilevel SEM. These procedures are appropriate if the heterogeneity in the population can be measured on a continuum and multiple obser-

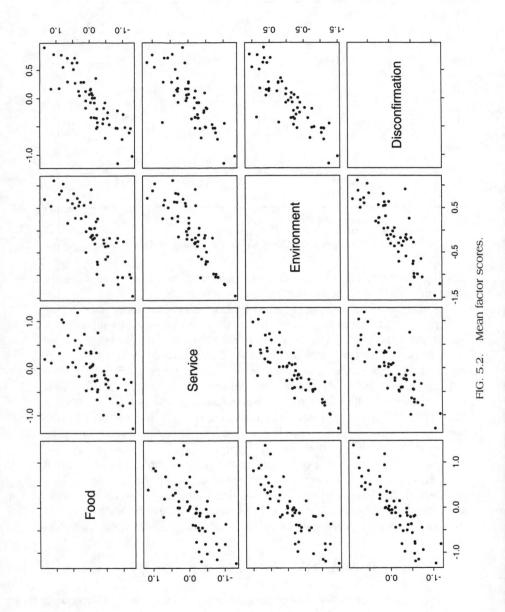

FIG. 5.2. Mean factor scores.

vations are available for each individual. The MCMC approach discussed in this chapter uses data augmentation and therefore circumvents the need for complex multidimensional integration, which is necessary for MLE. An important feature of this approach is that it automatically provides individual-specific estimates of model parameters and factor scores. Thus, it is possible to adequately account for the uncertainty in these quantities because as these are not computed based on the plug-in estimates of the other parameters. The procedures we report in this chapter can be naturally extended to data structures with multiple levels of nesting and can also be modified easily to handle binary, ordered, and censored multilevel data. Our multilevel SEM specification assumes that all the individuals have common factor loadings, factor covariance matrix, measurement error variances, and structural error covariance matrix. Our procedures can be extended to allow for more general form of covariance structure heterogeneity. Ansari et al. (2001) illustrate covariance heterogeneity in the context of factor analysis models. Ansari, Jedidi, and Jagpal (2000) made this extension for the SEM model.

We illustrate the Bayesian methodology using data from a satisfaction study. The results show that the structural parameters vary significantly in the population (i.e., it is incorrect to analyze the pooled data set using a conventional SEM). The estimates obtained by applying the standard (MLE) and the Bayesian procedures to a conventional SEM model (i.e., a model that does not allow for unobservable heterogeneity) were misleading, although the aggregate goodness-of-fit statistic was high (GFI = 0.99). In particular, the simple model understated the goodness of fit for the structural equation and provided biased estimates of the structural parameters. Perhaps most importantly, the simple model seriously understated the standard errors of the structural parameters. Finally, we show that the traditional multilevel methods do not fully capture the heterogeneity in our data. Thus, accounting for heterogeneity in both mean and covariance structures is important for obtaining proper inferences.

APPENDIX 1: PRIOR DISTRIBUTIONS

We specify the prior distribution over φ as a product of independent priors

$$p(\varphi) = p(\alpha)p(\Lambda)p(\Phi)p(\Delta)p(\Theta)p(\vartheta)p(\Upsilon)p(\Psi). \qquad (i)$$

We use proper but diffuse priors over all model parameters. The priors for the measurement intercepts α are assumed to be multivariate normal $N(\kappa, A)$. The covariance matrix A can be specified to be diagonal with the elements (variances) set to large values to represent vague knowledge. The exact location of this distribution is no longer critical once a large variance is assumed; therefore, without loss of generality, κ can be set to zero. For the application we used $N(0, 100I)$, where I is an identity matrix with appropriate dimensionality.

The combined factor loading matrix Λ has a patterned structure owing to the identification restrictions that require setting some of the elements of Λ to zero or one. We therefore specified independent multivariate normal priors over the free elements within each row of the matrix. We have for row k a prior $N(g_k, H_k)$. The covariance matrix H_k is specified to be diagonal with large variances to ensure a diffuse prior. Thus, the prior over the loading matrix is the product of the independent priors associated with the rows of Λ. In the application, we specified the prior distribution for each row to be $N(0, 100I)$.

The precision matrix Δ^{-1} associated with the population distribution $\nu_i \sim N(0, \Delta)$ is a $r \times r$ positive definite matrix. In keeping with standard Bayesian analysis of linear models, we assumed a Wishart prior $W(\delta, (\delta\Omega)^{-1})$, where Ω^{-1} can be considered the expected prior precision of the ν_is. Smaller δ values correspond to vaguer prior distributions. For the application, we set $\delta = 5$ and $\Omega = I$ to ensure a proper prior.

The $r \times r$ precision matrix Φ^{-1} associated with the population distribution $\xi_{ij} \sim N(\nu_i, \Phi)$ is assumed to come from a Wishart prior $W(\rho, (\rho R)^{-1})$. Here R^{-1} can be considered the expected prior precision of the ξ_{ij}s. Smaller values of ρ correspond to vaguer prior distributions. For the satisfaction application, we used a prior of $W(5, 5I)$.

We assume independent inverse gamma prior for each of the $v = (p+q)$ measurement error precisions contained in Θ^{-1}. That is, $\theta_k \sim IG(a_k, b_k)$, $k = 1$ to v. In the application, we assumed $a_k = 3$ and $b_k = 1,000$ for all k.

The prior for the vector ϑ is specified to be multivariate normal $N(c, C)$. The covariance matrix C can be assumed to be diagonal and its entries chosen to represent vague knowledge. The exact location vector c is no longer critical once a large variance is assumed; hence, without loss of generality, we set c to zero. In the application we therefore set $c = 0$ and $C = 100I$.

We assumed a Wishart prior $W(\rho_v, (\rho_v R_v)^{-1})$ over the precision matrix Y^{-1} associated with the structural parameters π_i. Smaller ρ_v values correspond to vaguer distributions. We therefore set $\rho_v = 5$ and $R_v = 0.1I$. Finally, we assumed a Wishart prior $W(\rho_\psi, (\rho_\psi R_\psi)^{-1})$ over the precision matrix Ψ^{-1} of the structural model. If the structural model consists of a single equation, then an Inverse gamma prior over the single structural error variance parameter can be assumed instead. In the application we chose $IG(3, 1000)$ for the prior over the univariate ψ.

APPENDIX 2: FULL CONDITIONAL DISTRIBUTIONS

The MCMC methods require sampling parameter estimates from the full conditional distribution of each block of parameters. In the context of our multilevel structural equation model, we need to generate random draws for the following blocks of parameters: $\{\alpha, \Lambda, \{\xi_{ij}\}, \{\eta_{ij}\}, \{\nu_i\}, \Phi, \Delta, \Theta, \{\pi_i\}, \vartheta, Y, \Psi\}$.

Each iteration of the MCMC procedure involves sequentially sampling from the full conditional distributions associated with each block of parameters.

The $(l+1)$th iteration of the MCMC algorithm requires us to generate random draws from the following full conditional distributions:

(a) The full conditional for the measurement intercepts α is a multivariate normal distribution. Using standard Bayesian theory regarding conjugacy, we see that the normal sampling density of w_{ij} and the normal prior $N(\kappa, A)$ for α combine to give the conditional

$$p(\alpha \mid \Lambda, \{f_{ij}\}, \Theta, \{w_{ij}\}) = N(\hat{\alpha}, V_\alpha),$$ (i)

where $V_\alpha^{-1} = A^{-1} + N\Theta^{-1}$, $\hat{\alpha} = V_\alpha \left[A^{-1}\kappa + \sum_{i=1}^{I} \sum_{j=1}^{n_i} \Theta^{-1}(w_{ij} - \Lambda f_{ij}) \right]$ and $f_{ij} = \{\xi_{ij}, \eta_{ij}\}$.

(b) The loading matrix Λ is a patterned matrix containing both fixed and free elements. Of the fixed elements, some are fixed to zero, while others are fixed at one to impose identifiability constraints. Given the choice of the prior distributions, the full conditionals pertaining to the different rows are independent. Therefore, the rows can be handled sequentially. The normal priors combined with the normal likelihood for the manifest variables yield multivariate normal full conditional distributions for the free elements in each row of the loadings matrix Λ. Let λ_k be the vector of free elements in row k. The prior for λ_k is given by $p(\lambda_k) = N(g_k, H_k)$.

Let $\tilde{f}_{ijk}$ be the vector of factor scores corresponding to the elements in row k of Λ that are set to one and let f_{-ijk} contain the remaining factor scores from f_{ij}. Form the adjusted variable $\tilde{w}_{ijk} = w_{ijk} - \iota' \tilde{f}_{ijk} - \alpha_k$, where ι is a vector of ones. Given the prior, the vector λ_k can be sampled from the full conditional distribution given by

$$p(\lambda_k \mid \{\tilde{w}_{ijk}\}, \{f_{-ijk}\}, \theta_k) = N\left(D_k \left[\sum_{i=1}^{I} \sum_{j=1}^{n_i} \theta_k^{-1} f_{-ijk} \tilde{w}_{ijk} + H_k^{-1} g_k \right], D_k \right),$$ (ii)

where $D_k^{-1} = \sum_{i=1}^{I} \sum_{j=1}^{n_i} \theta_k^{-1} f_{-ijk} f_{-ijk}' + H_k^{-1}$.

(c) The full conditional distribution for the factor scores ξ_{ij} is a multivariate normal distribution. The mean and variance of this distribution can be obtained by considering the prior $\xi_{ij} \sim N(\nu_i, \Phi)$ and the two data sources for ξ_{ij}. The first data we consider are η_{ij}. Consider the SEM $B_i \eta_{ij} = \gamma_{0i} + \Gamma_i \xi_{ij} + \zeta_{ij}$. Define $\tilde{\eta}_{ij} = B_i \eta_{ij} - \gamma_{0i}$. An intermediate posterior distribution for ξ_{ij} can be written as $N(\tilde{\xi}_{1,ij}, V_{1,\eta_i})$, where $V_{1,\eta,i}^{-1} = \Phi^{-1} + \Gamma_i' \Psi^{-1} \Gamma_i$ and $\tilde{\xi}_{1,ij} = V_{1,\eta,i}[\Phi^{-1}\nu_i + \Gamma_i' \Psi^{-1}\tilde{\eta}_{ij}]$. This intermediate posterior acts as a prior for the other data source x_{ij}. Taking into account the measurement equation, $x_{ij} = \alpha_x + \Lambda_x \xi_{ij} + \delta_{ij}$, the full conditional for ξ_{ij} can be written as $N(\tilde{\xi}_{ij}, V_{\eta,i})$, where $V_{\eta,i}^{-1} = V_{1,\eta,i}^{-1} + \Lambda_x' \Theta_x^{-1} \Lambda_x$ and $\tilde{\xi}_{ij} = V_{\eta,i}[V_{1,\eta,i}^{-1} \tilde{\xi}_{ij} + \Lambda_x' \Theta_x^{-1}(x_{ij} - \alpha_x)]$.

(d) The full conditional distribution for the individual-level factor means ν_i is a multivariate normal distribution. This can be derived by combining the normal sampling density $\xi_{ij} \sim N(\nu_i, \Phi)$ with the automatic prior $\nu_i \sim N(0, \Delta)$. We have

$$p(\nu_i \mid \{\xi_{ij}\}, \Phi, \Delta) = N(\hat{\nu}_i, V_{\nu i}), \qquad \text{(iii)}$$

where $V_{\nu_i}^{-1} = \Delta^{-1} + n_i \Phi^{-1}$ and $\hat{\nu}_i = V_{\nu_i} \Phi^{-1} \sum_{j=1}^{n_i} \xi_{ij}$.

(e) From standard Bayesian theory, we see that the full conditional distribution for the precision matrix Φ^{-1} of the individual-level factor scores is a Wishart distribution. This can be written as

$$p(\Phi^{-1} \mid \{\xi_{ij}\}, \{\nu_i\}) = W(\rho_{pos}, R_{pos}), \qquad \text{(iv)}$$

where $\rho_{pos} = \rho + N$ and $R_{pos} = \left[\sum_{i=1}^{I} \sum_{j=1}^{n_i} (\xi_{ij} - \nu_i)(\xi_{ij} - \nu_i)' + \rho R \right]^{-1}$.

(f) The full conditional for the precision matrix Δ^{-1} of the factor means is a Wishart distribution. Given the prior $W(\delta, (\delta\Omega)^{-1})$, the full conditional can be written as

$$p(\Delta^{-1} \mid \{\nu_i\}) = W\left(\delta + I, \left[\sum_{i=1}^{I} \nu_i \nu_i' + \delta\Omega \right]^{-1} \right). \qquad \text{(v)}$$

(g) The full conditional distributions for the diagonal elements of the measurement error variances Θ (i.e., θ_k, $k = 1$ to r) are independent inverse gamma distributions. These distributions follow from standard Bayesian theory and can be written as

$$p(\theta_k \mid \lambda_k, \alpha_k, \{f_{ij}\}) = IG\left(\frac{N}{2} + a_k, \left[\frac{\sum_{i=1}^{I} \sum_{j=1}^{n_i}(w_{ijk} - \alpha_k - \lambda_k' f_{ij})^2}{2} + b_k^{-1} \right]^{-1} \right), \qquad \text{(vi)}$$

where λ_k is a vector containing the elements of row k of Λ.

(h) The full conditional for the factor scores η_{ij} is a multivariate normal distribution. Consider the reduced form for the structural model $\eta_{ij} = B_i^{-1}(\gamma_{0i} + \Gamma_i \xi_{ij} + \zeta_{ij})$. Let $\Omega = B_i^{-1} \Psi B_i^{-1'}$. Then the full conditional is given by $N(\tilde{\eta}_{ij}, V_\eta)$, where $V_\eta^{-1} = \Omega^{-1} + \Lambda_y' \Theta_y^{-1} \Lambda_y$ and

$$\tilde{\eta}_{ij} = V_\eta \left[\Omega^{-1}(B_i^{-1} \gamma_{0i} + B_i^{-1} \Gamma_i \xi_{ij}) + \Lambda_y^{-1} \Theta_y^{-1}(y_i - \alpha_y) \right].$$

(i) The full conditional for the structural parameters $\boldsymbol{\pi}_i = \{\boldsymbol{B}_i, \boldsymbol{\gamma}_0, \boldsymbol{\Gamma}_i\}$ associated with individual i is a multivariate normal distribution. For a recursive system of simultaneous equations, the structural model $\boldsymbol{B}_i \boldsymbol{\eta}_{ij} = \boldsymbol{\gamma}_{i,0} + \boldsymbol{\Gamma}_i \boldsymbol{\xi}_{ij} + \boldsymbol{\zeta}_{ij}$ is a general triangular system (See Zellner, 1971). This system can be recast as $\boldsymbol{\eta}_{ij} = \boldsymbol{\Xi}_{ij} \boldsymbol{\pi}_i + \boldsymbol{\zeta}_{ij}$, where $\boldsymbol{\Xi}_{ij}$ is an appropriately dimensioned matrix containing both the exogenous and endogenous factor scores. The key feature of a triangular system is that the determinant of the matrix of the coefficients of the endogenous variables $\boldsymbol{\eta}$ vanishes. Thus, we can treat the system $\boldsymbol{\eta}_{ij} = \boldsymbol{\Xi}_{ij} \boldsymbol{\pi}_i + \boldsymbol{\zeta}_{ij}$ as a seemingly unrelated regression (SUR) system. Given the prior $p(\boldsymbol{\pi}_i) = N(\boldsymbol{Z}_i \boldsymbol{\vartheta}, \boldsymbol{\Upsilon})$, the full conditional is given by $N(\widetilde{\boldsymbol{\pi}}_i, \boldsymbol{V}_\pi)$, where $\boldsymbol{V}_\pi^{-1} = \boldsymbol{\Upsilon}^{-1} + \sum_{j=1}^{n_i} \boldsymbol{\Xi}_{ij}' \boldsymbol{\Psi}^{-1} \boldsymbol{\Xi}_{ij}$ and $\widetilde{\boldsymbol{\pi}}_i = \boldsymbol{V}_\pi [\boldsymbol{\Upsilon}^{-1} \boldsymbol{Z}_i \boldsymbol{\vartheta} + \sum_{j=1}^{n_i} \boldsymbol{\Xi}_{ij}' \boldsymbol{\Psi}^{-1} \boldsymbol{\eta}_{ij}]$.

(j) From standard Bayesian theory pertaining to linear models, the full conditional distribution for the precision matrix $\boldsymbol{\Psi}^{-1}$ of the structural model is Wishart and is given by

$$p(\boldsymbol{\Psi}^{-1} \mid \{\boldsymbol{\xi}_{ij}\}, \{\boldsymbol{\eta}_{ij}\}, \{\boldsymbol{\gamma}_{i,0}, \boldsymbol{\Gamma}_i, \boldsymbol{B}_i\}) = W(\rho_{pos}, R_{pos}), \qquad \text{(vii)}$$

where $\rho_{pos} = \rho_\psi + N$ and $R_{pos} = \left[\sum_{i=1}^I \sum_{j=1}^{n_i} \widetilde{\boldsymbol{\eta}}_{ij} \widetilde{\boldsymbol{\eta}}_{ij}' + \rho_\psi R_\psi \right]^{-1}$ and $\widetilde{\boldsymbol{\eta}}_{ij} = \boldsymbol{B}_i \boldsymbol{\eta}_{ij} - \boldsymbol{\gamma}_{i,0} - \boldsymbol{\Gamma}_i \boldsymbol{\xi}_{ij}$.

(k) The full conditional for the population structural parameters $\boldsymbol{\vartheta}$ is a multivariate normal distribution and can be written as

$$p(\boldsymbol{\vartheta} \mid \{\boldsymbol{\pi}_i\}, \boldsymbol{\Upsilon}) = N(\hat{\boldsymbol{\vartheta}}, V_\vartheta), \qquad \text{(viii)}$$

where $V_\vartheta^{-1} = C^{-1} + \sum_{i=1}^I Z_i' \boldsymbol{\Upsilon}^{-1} Z_i$ and $\hat{\boldsymbol{\vartheta}} = V_\vartheta (C^{-1} c + \sum_{i=1}^I Z_i' \boldsymbol{\Upsilon}^{-1} \boldsymbol{\pi}_i)$.

(l) The full conditional for the precision matrix $\boldsymbol{\Upsilon}^{-1}$ of the individual-level structural parameters $\boldsymbol{\pi}_i$ is a Wishart distribution. Given the prior $W(\rho_\nu, (\rho_\nu R_\nu)^{-1})$, the full conditional can be written as

$$p(\boldsymbol{\Upsilon}^{-1} \mid \{\boldsymbol{\pi}_i\}) = W\left(\rho_\nu + I, \left[\sum_{i=1}^I (\boldsymbol{\pi}_i - Z_i \boldsymbol{\vartheta})(\boldsymbol{\pi}_i - Z_i \boldsymbol{\vartheta})' + \rho_\nu R_\nu \right]^{-1} \right). \qquad \text{(ix)}$$

REFERENCES

Ansari, A., & Morrin, M., and Gupta, A. (1996). *Bayesian approaches for modeling multilevel data in marketing.* Working paper, Columbia University.

Ansari, A., & Jedidi, K. (2000). Bayesian factor analysis for multilevel binary observations. *Psychometrika.* In press for Volume 65, issue #4.

Ansari, A., Jedidi, K., & Dube, L. (2001). *Random coefficient cactor analysis: A Bayesian approach.* Psychometrika. Conditionally accepted.

Ansari, A., Jedidi, K., & Jagpal, S. (2000). *A hierarchical Bayesian approach for modeling heterogeneity in structural equation models.* Marketing Science, 19, 328–347.

Arminger, G., & Muthén, B. (1998). A Bayesian approach to nonlinear latent variable models using the Gibbs sampler and the Metropolis-Hastings algorithm. *Psychometrika, 63*, 271–300.

Best, N. G., Cowles, M. K., & Vines, S. K. (1995). *CODA: Convergence diagnostics and output analysis software for Gibbs sampler output: Version 0.3.* Technical report, Biostatistics Unit-MRC, Cambridge, England.

Bock, R. D. (Ed.). (1989). *Multilevel analysis of educational data,* New York: Academic Press.

Bollen, K. A. (1989). *Structural equations with latent variables,* New York: Wiley.

Brooks, S. P., & Gelman, A. (1998). General methods for monitoring convergence of iterative simulations. *Journal of Computational and Graphical Statistics, 7*, 434–455.

Brooks, S. P., & Roberts, G. O. (1998). Convergence assessment techniques for Markov chain Monte Carlo, *Journal of Computational and Graphical Statistics, 8*, 319–335.

Chib, S., & Greenberg, E. (1995). Understanding the Metropolis-Hastings algorithm. *American Statistician, 49*, 327–335.

Cowles, M. K., & Carlin, B. P. (1996). Markov chain Monte Carlo convergence diagnostics: A comparative review. *Journal of the American Statistical Association, 91*, 883–904.

Crosswhite, F. J., Dossey, J. A., Swafford, J. O., McKnight, C. C., & Cooney, T. J. (1985), *Second International Mathematics Study: Summary report for the United States.* Champaign, IL: Stipes.

Draper, D. (1995). Inference and hierarchical modeling in the social sciences. *Journal of Educational and Behavioral Statistics, 20*, 115–147.

Gamerman, D. (1997). *Markov Chain Monte Carlo.* London: Chapman & Hall.

Geisser, S., & Eddy, E. (1979). A predictive approach to model selection. *Journal of the American Statistical Association, 74*, 53–160.

Gelfand, A. E. (1996). Model determination using sampling-based methods. In W. R. Gilks, S. Richardson, & D. J. Spiegelhalter (Eds.), *Markov Chain Monte Carlo in Practice* London: Chapman & Hall. (pp. 145–161).

Gelfand, A. E., & Smith, A. F. M. (1990). *Sampling-based approaches to calculating marginal densities.* Journal of the American Statistical Association, 85, 972–985.

Gelman, A., Carlin, J. B., Stern, H. S., & Rubin D. B. (1995). *Bayesian data analysis.* London: Chapman & Hall.

Gelman, A., & Rubin, D. R. (1992). Inference from iterative simulation using multiple sequences. *Statistical Science, 7*, 457–511.

Geman, S., & Geman, D. (1984). Stochastic relaxation, Gibbs distributions and the Bayesian restoration of images. *IEEE Transactions of Pattern Analysis and Machine Intelligence, 6*, 721–741.

Geyer, C. J. (1992). Practical Markov chain Monte Carlo (with discussion). *Statistical Science, 7*, 473–511.

Goldstein, H., & McDonald, R. P. (1988). A general model for the analysis of multilevel data. *Psychometrika, 553*, 455–467.

Jedidi, K., Jagpal, H. S. & DeSarbo, W. S. (1997). Finite-mixture structural equation models for response-based segmentation and unobserved heterogeneity. *Marketing Science, 16*(1), 39–59.

Johnson, M. D., Anderson, E. W., & Fornell, C. (1995). Rational and adaptive performance expectations in a customer satisfaction framework. *Journal of Consumer Research, 21*, 695–707.

Joreskog, K. G. (1971). Simultaneous factor analysis in several populations. *Psychometrika, 36*, 409–426.

Kass, R. E., & Raftery, A. E. (1995). Bayes factors. *Journal of American Statistical Association, 90*, 773–795.

Lee, S.-Y. (1981). A Bayesian approach to confirmatory factor analysis. *Psychometrika, 46*, 153–160.

Longford, N. T., & Muthén, B. (1992). Factor analysis for clustered observations. *Psychometrika, 57*, 581–597.

Marcoulides, G. A. & Schumacker, R. E. (1996). *Advanced structural equation Modeling.* Mahwah, NJ: Lawrence Erlbaum Associates.

McArdle, J. J., & Hamagami, F. (1996). Multilevel models from a multiple group structural equation perspective. In G. A. Marcoulides & R. R. Schumacker (Eds.), *Advanced structural equation modeling*, (pp. 89–124). Hillsdale Lawrence Erlbaum Associates.

McDonald, R. P., & Goldstein , H. (1989). Balanced versus unbalanced designs for linear structural relations in two-level data. *British Journal of Mathematical and Statistical Psychology, 42,* 214–232.

Muthén, B. & Satorra, A. (1989). Multilevel aspects of varying parameters in structural models. In R. D. Bock (Ed.), *Multilevel analysis of educational data*, (pp. 87–99). San Diego: Academic Press.

Muthén, B. (1989). Latent variable modeling in heterogeneous populations. *Psychometrika, 54,* 557–585.

Muthén, B. (1994). Multilevel covariance structure analysis. *Sociological Methods & Research, 22,* 376–398.

Newton, M. A., & Raftery, A. E. (1994). Approximate Bayesian inference by the weighted likelihood bootsrap (with discussion). *Journal of the Royal Statistical Society* (Series B), *56,* 3–18.

Oliver, R. L. (1993). Cognitive, affective, and attribute bases of the satisfaction response. *Journal of Consumer Research, 20,* 418–430.

Oliver, R. L. (1997). *Satisfaction: A behavioral perspective on the consumer.* New York: McGraw-Hill.

Robert, C. P., & Casella, G. (1999). *Monte Carlo statistical methods,* New York: Springer-Verlag.

Scheines, R., Hoijtink, H., & Boomsma, A. (1999). Bayesian estimation and testing of structural equation models. *Psychometrika, 64,* 37–52.

Shi, J., & Lee, S. (1997). A Bayesian estimation of factor score in confirmatory factor model with polytomous, censored or truncated data. *Psychometrika, 62*(1), 29–50.

Sorbom, D. (1981). Structural equation models with structured means. In K. G. Joreskog & H. Wold (Eds.), *Systems under indirect observation: Causality, structure, and prediction* (pp. 193–195). Amsterdam; North Holland.

Tanner, M. A., & Wong, W. H. (1987). The calculation of posterior distributions by data augmentation (with discussion). *Journal of the American Statistical Association, 82,* 528–550.

Tierney, L. (1994). Markov chains for exploring posterior distributions (with discussion). *Annals of Statistics, 22,* 1701–1762.

Yung, Y.-F. (1997). Finite mixtures in confirmatory factor-analysis models. *Psychometrika, 62*(3), 297–330.

6

Robust Standard Errors and Chi-Squares for Interaction Models

Fan Yang-Wallentin
Karl G. Jöreskog
Uppsala University

Kenny and Judd (1984) formulated a model with interaction effects of two latent variables and suggested using product variables to estimate the model. Using one and four product variables and simulation techniques, Yang-Jonsson (1997) studied the estimation of this model with three methods: maximum likelihood (ML), weighted least squares (WLS), and weighted least squares based on the augmented moment matrix (WLSA). Because the model implies non-normality, one would expect WLS and WLSA to be better than ML at least in large samples, but Yang-Jonsson (1997) found that ML often works well over a range of sample sizes from 400 to 3,200, except that asymptotic standard errors and chi-squares of ML estimates are, in principle, incorrectly computed. In this chapter, we show that both asymptotic standard errors and chi-squares for ML can be corrected for non-normality using Satorra–Bentler type scaling corrections.

The Kenny–Judd model is used as an example of a general model with non-linear relationships between latent variables. Most of the arguments presented apply more generally than just to the Kenny–Judd model.

The Kenny–Judd model was defined earlier. Jöreskog and Yang (1996) and Yang-Jonsson (1997) showed that this model is identified using products of observed variables. Kenny and Judd suggested using four product variables, but in fact only one product variable is necessary for identification.

The implications of using product variables are non-normality and constraints on the mean vector as well as on the covariance matrix. Hence, both the mean vector and the covariance matrix must be used in the analysis.

THE KENNY–JUDD MODEL

Kenny and Judd (1984) formulated a nonlinear regression equation:

$$y = \alpha + \gamma_1\xi_1 + \gamma_2\xi_2 + \gamma_3\xi_1\xi_2 + \zeta, \tag{1}$$

with the idea that there is an interactive effect of ξ_1 and ξ_2 on y in addition to the direct effects of each of ξ_1 and ξ_2 alone, and this interactive effect is manifesting itself in terms of an effect of the product of ξ_1 and ξ_2.

The variables ξ_1 and ξ_2 are latent variables that are not directly observable. Kenny and Judd (1984) considered the case when there are two observable indicators x_1 and x_2 of ξ_1 and two observable indicators x_3 and x_4 of ξ_2, such that

$$\begin{bmatrix} x_1 \\ x_2 \\ x_3 \\ x_4 \end{bmatrix} = \begin{bmatrix} \tau_1 \\ \tau_2 \\ \tau_3 \\ \tau_4 \end{bmatrix} + \begin{bmatrix} \lambda_1 & 0 \\ \lambda_2 & 0 \\ 0 & \lambda_3 \\ 0 & \lambda_4 \end{bmatrix} \begin{bmatrix} \xi_1 \\ \xi_2 \end{bmatrix} + \begin{bmatrix} \delta_1 \\ \delta_2 \\ \delta_3 \\ \delta_4 \end{bmatrix}. \tag{2}$$

Kenny and Judd (1984) did not include the constant intercept terms α and τ_i in Eqs. (1) and (2). The usual argument for leaving these out—that one can work with the observed variables in deviation scores from their means—is not valid here. The point is that even if y, ξ_1, ξ_2, and ζ in Eqs. (1) all have zero means, α will still be nonzero. As is seen later, the means of the observed variables are functions of other parameters in the model, and therefore the intercept terms have to be estimated jointly with all the other parameters.

We make the following assumptions:

1. ξ_1 and ξ_2 are bivariate normal with zero means
2. $\zeta \sim N(0, \psi)$
3. $\delta_i \sim N(0, \theta_i)$, $i = 1, \ldots, 4$
4. δ_i is independent of δ_j for $i \neq j$
5. δ_i is independent of ξ_j for $i = 1, \ldots, 4$ and $j = 1, 2$
6. ζ is independent of δ_i and ξ_j for $i = 1, \ldots, 4$ and $j = 1, 2$

Of these, Assumptions 4 to 6 are crucial and untestable, whereas Assumptions 1 to 3 are not essential and testable.

The model includes the product variable $\xi_1\xi_2$. To estimate the model, one needs some indicators of this. Kenny and Judd (1984) suggested using product variables x_1x_3, x_1x_4, x_2x_3, x_2x_4 together with (y, x_1, x_2, x_3, x_4) to estimate the model, but any number of these product variables can be used. It is of interest to know if it is better to use one product variable or more than one. In this chapter, we refer to the model with one product variable as Model 1 and the model with four product variables as Model 2.

The consequences of product variables in the model are:

- y is not normal, although ξ_1 and ξ_2 are. The joint distribution of (y, x_1, x_2, x_3, x_4) is not multivariate normal, although that of (x_1, x_2, x_3, x_4) is.
- The mean of y is $\mu_y = \alpha + \gamma_3\phi_{21}$. So the mean vector of (y, x_1, x_2, x_3, x_4) is a function not only of $(\alpha, \tau_1, \tau_2, \tau_3, \tau_4)$ but also of γ_3 and ϕ_{21}. So both the mean vector and the covariance matrix of the observed variables should be used to estimate the model.
- Using one or more product variables x_1x_3, x_1x_4, x_2x_3, x_2x_4 together with y, x_1, x_2, x_3, x_4 to estimate the model implies still more non-normality and even more complicated constraints on both the mean vector and the covariance matrix of the observed variables.

For the model with one product variable,

$$x_5 = x_1x_3 = (\tau_1 + \xi_1 + \delta_1)(\tau_3 + \xi_2 + \delta_3)$$

$$= \tau_1\tau_2 + \tau_3\xi_1 + \tau_1\xi_2 + \xi_1\xi_2 + \delta_5, \tag{3}$$

where

$$\delta_5 = \tau_1\delta_3 + \tau_3\delta_1 + \xi_1\delta_3 + \xi_2\delta_1 + \delta_1\delta_3, \tag{4}$$

the mean vector and covariance matrix of $(y, x_1, x_2, x_3, x_4, x_5)$ are

$$\mu' = (\alpha + \gamma_3\phi_{21}, \tau_1, \tau_2, \tau_3, \tau_4, \tau_1\tau_3 + \phi_{21}), \tag{5}$$

$$\Sigma = \begin{bmatrix} \sigma_{yy} \\ \gamma_1\phi_{11} + \gamma_2\phi_{21} & \phi_{11} + \theta_1 \\ \gamma_1\lambda_2\phi_{11} + \gamma_2\lambda_2\phi_{21} & \lambda_2\phi_{11} & \lambda_2^2\phi_{11} + \theta_2 \\ \gamma_1\phi_{21} + \gamma_2\phi_{22} & \phi_{21} & \lambda_2\phi_{21} & \phi_{22} + \theta_3 \\ \gamma_1\lambda_4\phi_{21} + \gamma_2\lambda_4\phi_{22} & \lambda_4\phi_{21} & \lambda_4\lambda_2\phi_{21} & \lambda_4\phi_{22} & \lambda_4^2\phi_{22} + \theta_4 \\ \sigma_{61} & \sigma_{62} & \sigma_{63} & \sigma_{64} & \sigma_{65} & \sigma_{66} \end{bmatrix} \tag{6}$$

where

$$\sigma_{yy} = \gamma_1^2\phi_{11} + \gamma_2^2\phi_{22} + 2\gamma_1\gamma_2\phi_{21} + \gamma_3^2(\phi_{11}\phi_{22} + \phi_{21}^2) + \psi, \tag{7}$$

$$\sigma_{61} = \tau_3\gamma_1\phi_{11} + \tau_3\gamma_2\phi_{21} + \tau_1\gamma_1\phi_{21} + \tau_1\gamma_2\phi_{22} + \gamma_3(\phi_{21}^2 + \phi_{11}\phi_{22}), \tag{8}$$

$$\sigma_{62} = \tau_3\phi_{11} + \tau_1\phi_{21} + \tau_3\theta_1, \tag{9}$$

$$\sigma_{63} = \tau_3\lambda_2\phi_{11} + \tau_1\lambda_2\phi_{21}, \tag{10}$$

$$\sigma_{64} = \tau_3\phi_{21} + \tau_1\phi_{22} + \tau_1\theta_3, \tag{11}$$

$$\sigma_{65} = \tau_3\lambda_4\phi_{21} + \tau_1\lambda_4\phi_{22}, \tag{12}$$

$$\sigma_{66} = \tau_3^2\phi_{11} + \tau_1^2\phi_{22} + \phi_{12}^2 + \phi_{11}\phi_{22} + \tau_1^2\theta_3 + \tau_3^2\theta_1 + \phi_{11}\theta_3 + \phi_{22}\theta_1 + \theta_1\theta_3. \tag{13}$$

The parameter vector representing the independent parameters is

$$\theta = (\alpha,\, \gamma_1,\, \gamma_2,\, \gamma_3,\, \psi,\, \tau_1,\, \tau_2,\, \tau_3,\, \tau_4,\, \lambda_2,\, \lambda_4,\, \phi_{11},\, \phi_{21},\, \phi_{22},\, \theta_1,\, \theta_2,\, \theta_3,\, \theta_4).$$

Model 1 has 9 degrees of freedom. This is obtained as the number of elements in μ (Eq. [6]) plus the number of distinct elements in Σ (Eq. [21]) minus the number of parameters in θ (Eq. [18]). With four product variables, the number of parameters is the same, but μ and Σ are extended with three more rows. Model 2 has 36 degrees of freedom.

MAXIMUM LIKELIHOOD METHOD

Let $\mathbf{z}_1, \mathbf{z}_2, \ldots, \mathbf{z}_N$ be N independent observations of the random vector

$$\mathbf{z} = (y, x_1, x_2, x_3, x_4, x_5),$$

and let $\bar{\mathbf{z}}$ and $\mathbf{S}$ be the sample mean vector and covariance matrix. Let μ and Σ be the corresponding population mean vector and covariance matrix. These are functions of the parameter vector

$$\theta = (\alpha,\, \gamma_1,\, \gamma_2,\, \gamma_3,\, \psi,\, \tau_1,\, \tau_2,\, \tau_3,\, \tau_4,\, \lambda_2,\, \lambda_4,\, \phi_{11},\, \phi_{21},\, \phi_{22},\, \theta_1,\, \theta_2,\, \theta_3,\, \theta_4).$$

The maximum likelihood (ML) method will estimate θ by minimizing the fit function

$$F(\theta) = \log\|\Sigma\| + \mathrm{tr}(S\Sigma^{-1}) - \log\|S\| - k + (\bar{\mathbf{z}} - \mu)'\Sigma^{-1}(\bar{\mathbf{z}} - \mu), \tag{14}$$

where k is the number of variables in $\mathbf{z}$ (here $k = 6$). This fit function is derived from the ML principle based on the assumption that the observed variables $\mathbf{z}$ have a multinormal distribution (see e.g., Anderson, 1984, for a derivation of the multinormal likelihood). Because of the product variables, this assumption does not hold for the Kenny–Judd model. As stated previously, the random vector $\mathbf{z}$ is not multivariate normal. The approach studied here is that of using ML estimates of parameters, but with standard errors and chi-squares corrected for non-normality.

In this chapter, we consider ML estimation via the augmented moment matrix. The reason for this is that it implies skewness so that the sample mean vector and covariance matrix are not independent. Therefore, one should analyze a matrix that contains both the mean vector and the covariance matrix. Such a matrix is the augmented moment matrix. The correction of standard errors and chi-squares involves the use of the asymptotic covariance matrix of the elements of the augmented moment matrix.

The sample augmented moment matrix is defined as

$$\mathbf{A} = (1/N) \sum_{c=1}^{N} \binom{\mathbf{z}_c}{1} (\mathbf{z}_c'\ 1) = \begin{pmatrix} S + \bar{\mathbf{z}}\bar{\mathbf{z}}' & \bar{\mathbf{z}} \\ \bar{\mathbf{z}}' & 1 \end{pmatrix}. \tag{15}$$

This is the matrix of sample moments about zero for the vector $\mathbf{z}$ augmented with a variable, which is constant equal to 1 for every case. The corresponding population matrix is

$$Y = (\alpha_{ij}) = E\binom{\mathbf{z}}{1}(\mathbf{z}'\ 1) = \begin{pmatrix} \Sigma + \mu\mu' & \mu \\ \mu' & 1 \end{pmatrix}. \tag{16}$$

Let

$$\mathbf{a}' = (a_{11}, a_{21}, a_{22}, a_{31}, \ldots, a_{k+1,k}, 1)$$

be a vector of the nonduplicated elements of $\mathbf{A}$, and let

$$\alpha' = (\alpha_{11}, \alpha_{21}, \alpha_{22}, \alpha_{31}, \ldots, \alpha_{k+1,k}, 1)$$

be a vector of the corresponding population moments. Note that the last element in these matrices is a fixed constant equal to 1.

We first show that the ML fit function (Eq. [14]) is identically the same function $\boldsymbol{\theta}$ as

$$F(\theta) = \log\|Y\| + \text{tr}(AY^{-1}) - \log\|A\| - k. \tag{17}$$

Using well-known formulas for the determinant and inverse of a partitioned matrix, it is readily verified that

$$\|Y\| = \|\Sigma + \mu\mu' - \mu\mu'\| = \|\Sigma\|, \tag{18}$$

$$\|A\| = \|S + \bar{\mathbf{z}}\bar{\mathbf{z}}' - \bar{\mathbf{z}}\bar{\mathbf{z}}'\| = \|S\|, \tag{19}$$

$$Y^{-1} = \begin{pmatrix} \Sigma^{-1} & -\Sigma^{-1}\mu \\ -\mu'\Sigma^{-1} & 1 + \mu'\Sigma^{-1}\mu \end{pmatrix}. \tag{20}$$

Because

$$A = \begin{pmatrix} S + \bar{z}\,\bar{z} & \bar{z} \\ \bar{z}' & 1 \end{pmatrix}, \tag{21}$$

the trace of $Y^{-1}A$ becomes

$$tr\,(Y^{-1}A) = tr[\Sigma^{-1}(S + \bar{z}\bar{z}') - \Sigma^{-1}\mu\bar{z}' - \mu'\Sigma^{-1}\bar{z} + 1 + \mu'\Sigma^{-1}\mu] \tag{22}$$

$$= tr[\Sigma^{-1}(S + \bar{z}\bar{z}' - \mu\bar{z}' - \bar{z}\mu' + \mu\mu')] + 1 \tag{23}$$

$$= tr\{\Sigma^{-1}[S + (\bar{z} - \mu)(\bar{z} - \mu)']\} + 1 \tag{24}$$

$$= tr\,(\Sigma^{-1}S) + (\bar{z} - \mu)'\Sigma^{-1}(\bar{z} - \mu). \tag{25}$$

Substitution of Eqs. (18), (19), and (25) into Eq. (17) shows that the right-hand side of Eq. (17) is identically the same as the right-hand side of Eq. (14), except for the additive constant 1.

ASYMPTOTIC STANDARD ERRORS AND CHI-SQUARES

The asymptotic standard errors given by LISREL for ML estimates assumes that the observed variables have a multivariate normal distribution, which is not the case here. These standard errors are obtained from the inverse of the Fisher information matrix. This means that the standard errors are not asymptotically correct. However, Browne (1984) pointed out that it is possible to obtain correct asymptotic standard errors under non-normality if one has a consistent estimate of the asymptotic covariance matrix **W** of the vector **s** of the nonduplicated elements of the sample covariance matrix **S**. Browne (1984), gave a general formula for the asymptotic covariance matrix of $\hat{\theta}$ for ML estimates. This formula does not apply directly to our problem for two reasons. First, it applies only to covariance structures and not to a simultaneous mean and covariance structure. Second, it involves the inverse of **W**, which does not exist for Model 2. Satorra and Bentler (1988) and Satorra (1989) gave another asymptotically equivalent formula that does not require the inverse of **W**. However, this formula still applies only to covariance structures, although it can easily be extended to more general moment structures. In this section, it is shown how Satorra and Bentler's formula can be applied. This will facilitate a direct comparison of the two asymptotic standard errors and χ^2 of ML estimates.

Consider the fit function

$$F(\theta) = F[A, Y(\theta)], \tag{26}$$

where F is Eq. (17).

Let $\Delta(s \times t) = \partial \alpha / \partial \theta'$, where $s = (k+1)(k+2)/2$ and $t =$ the number of independent parameters in θ. Let $n = N-1$. Assume that $\mathbf{A}$ converges in probability to Y_0 as the sample size increases and let θ_0 be the value of θ that minimizes $F[Y_0, Y(\theta)]$. We say that the model holds if $Y_0 = Y(\theta_0)$. Furthermore, let

$$V_0 = \frac{1}{2} \partial^2 F / \partial a \partial a',\tag{27}$$

evaluated at $A = Y_0$, $Y = Y_0$ and let

$$E_0 = \Delta_0' V_0 \Delta_0,\tag{28}$$

where Δ_0 is Δ evaluated at $\theta = \theta_0$. The matrix V_0 is

$$V_0 = \mathbf{D}'(Y_0^{-1} \otimes Y_0^{-1})\mathbf{D},$$

where $\mathbf{D}(k^2 \times s)$ is the duplication matrix of Magnus and Neudecker (1988). Then the asymptotic covariance matrix of $\hat{\theta}$ is given by (Satorra, 1989)

$$nACov(\hat{\theta}) = E_0^{-1}(\Delta_0' V_0 \Omega V_0 \Delta_0)E_0^{-1},\tag{29}$$

where Ω is the asymptotic covariance matrix $\mathbf{a}$. Because of the last element of $\mathbf{a}$, both V_0 and Ω are singular, but none of them need's to be inverted.

Furthermore, let $\hat{\Delta}$ and $\hat{E}$ be Δ and $\mathbf{E}$ evaluated at $\theta = \hat{\theta}$ and let $\mathbf{W}_{NNT}$ be a consistent estimate of $n\Omega$ under non-normality. Then a consistent estimate of $nACov(\hat{\theta})$ may be obtained by substituting $\hat{\Delta}$ $\mathbf{W}_{NNT}$, and $\hat{E}$ for Δ_0, Ω, and E_0 in Eq. (29). Note that $\mathbf{W}_{NNT}$ need not be inverted.

To test the model, one can use

$$c = \frac{d}{h_1} c_2\tag{30}$$

as a test statistic (Satorra & Bentler 1988), where[1]

$$c_2 = n(s - \hat{\sigma})' \hat{\Delta}_c (\hat{\Delta}_c' W_{NT} \hat{\Delta}_c)^{-1} \hat{\Delta}_c' (s - \hat{\sigma})\tag{31}$$

$$h_1 = tr[(\hat{\Delta}_c' W_{NT} \hat{\Delta}_c)^{-1}(\hat{\Delta}_c' W_{NNT} \hat{\Delta}_c)].\tag{32}$$

---

[1] Jöreskog et al. (1999) incorrectly gave the formula for h_1 without the exponent-1.

$\mathbf{W}_{NT}=2n\mathbf{K}'(\hat{\mathbf{Y}}\otimes\hat{\mathbf{Y}})\mathbf{K}$ is the weight matrix under normality, where $\mathbf{K}=\mathbf{D}(\mathbf{D}'\mathbf{D})^{-1}$. $\hat{\Delta}_c(s\times s-t)$ is an orthogonal complement to $\hat{\Delta}$ satisfying $\hat{\Delta}'\hat{\Delta}_c=0$, and $\mathbf{W}_{NNT}$ is computed by PRELIS under non-normality. The elements of $\mathbf{W}_{NNT}$ are given by

$$w_{gh,ij} = n\,\mathrm{Est}[\mathrm{ACov}(a_{gh},a_{ij})] = n_{ghij} - a_{gh}a_{ij}, \tag{33}$$

where

$$n_{ghij} = (1/N)\sum_{a=1}^{N} z_{ag}z_{ah}z_{ai}z_{aj} \tag{34}$$

is a fourth-order sample moment about zero.

If the model holds and is identified, c in Eq. (30) is approximately distributed as χ^2 with d degrees of freedom, where $d=s-t$ for ML.

SIMULATION DESIGN

Following the assumptions in the first section, we can generate data for the Kenny–Judd model. Although we are generating normal variables, the product variables used in the analysis are not normal. As stated previously, there are 18 parameters in the Kenny–Judd model—namely, γ_1, γ_2, γ_3, λ_2, λ_4, ϕ_{11}, ϕ_{21}, ϕ_{22}, ψ, θ_1, θ_2, θ_3, θ_4, α, and τ_i, $i=1,2,3,4$. These must all be specified to generate data on the observed variables. We have chosen the following population parameter values:

$$\gamma_1 = 0.2,\ \gamma_2 = 0.4,\ \gamma_3 = 0.7,\ \lambda_2 = 0.6,\ \lambda_4 = 0.7,$$

$$\phi_{11} = 0.49,\ \phi_{21} = 0.2352,\ \phi_{22} = 0.64,\ \psi = 0.20,$$

$$\theta_1 = 0.51,\ \theta_2 = 0.64,\ \theta_3 = 0.36,\ \theta_4 = 0.51,$$

$$\alpha = 1.00,\ \tau_i = 0.00,\ i = 1, 2, 3, 4.$$

The sample sizes used in the simulation are shown in Table 6.1

These sample sizes are considered to be from sufficiently small to sufficiently large. We chose 600 replications in this study (i.e., 600 parameter estimates of each sample size was estimated). Because of nonconvergence in ML, the actual number of replicates is less than 600. Table 6.2 shows the number of converged samples for each sample size. It is seen that nonconvergence is a serious problem for ML, particularly for $N=100$, but even for $N=3,200$ we did not get all samples to converge.

TABLE 6.1
Sample Sizes

N=100	N=200	N=400	N=800	N=1,600	N=3,200

TABLE 6.2
Converged Samples

N=100	N=200	N=400	N=800	N=1,600	N=3,200
268	500	548	544	552	564

RESULTS

Asymptotic Standard Errors

LISREL computes estimated asymptotic standard errors for each parameter and each sample. It is well known (see e.g., Browne, 1984; Satorra, 1989) that these asymptotic standard errors for ML are incorrect when the observed variables are not multivariate normal, as they are in our study due to the use of product variables. The bias in standard errors is measured by a standard error ratio that is the ratio of the average estimated standard error and the empirical standard error of the parameter estimates. In this context, the latter is the standard deviation in the distribution of the parameter estimates and is taken to be the true standard error. A value of 1 for the standard error ratio indicates no bias, values below 1 indicate underestimation, and values above 1 indicate overestimation.

The estimated standard error ratios are given in Table 6.3 for Model 1 and in Table 6.4 for Model 2. It is seen that before the correction the standard errors are almost always underestimated. The degree of underestimation does not decrease with increasing sample size; it is quite the contrary. The standard errors are more underestimated for Model 2 than for Model 1. This is in line with the interpretation that Model 2 introduces more non-normality in the observed variables due to the use of four product variables instead of only one product variable in Model 1. For $N = 3,200$, the largest bias is -27% for Model 1 and -39% for Model 2. For γ_3 and $N = 3,200$, the bias is -9% for Model 1 and -29% for Model 2.

Using the formulas developed by Satorra and Bentler (1988) and Satorra (1989) the corrected asymptotic standard errors are computed and shown in the bottom half of Tables 6.3 and 6.4. It is seen that the corrected standard errors for Model 1 are slightly better for sample sizes 400 and larger. For sample sizes 100 and 200, there are ups and downs. The correction works for some parameters and not for others for these two samples sizes.

For Model 2, the correction works much better for all parameters and all sample sizes. For $N = 100$, the bias is -28% on average before the correction and -14% after correction. For $N = 3,200$, the largest bias is -39% before correction and -27% after correction. For γ_3 at the same sample size, the bias comes down from -29% to -7%.

TABLE 6.3
Standard Error Ratios for Model 1
Model 1: One Product Variable

Before correction

Parameter	$N = 100$	$N=200$	$N=400$	$N=800$	$N=1,600$	$N=3,200$
α	1.00	0.96	0.99	1.08	0.95	0.96
γ_1	0.95	0.95	0.89	0.95	0.89	0.94
γ_2	0.89	0.91	0.93	0.93	0.94	0.88
γ_3	1.01	0.88	0.90	0.93	0.91	0.91
ψ	0.98	0.92	0.91	1.01	0.95	0.94
λ_2	0.82	0.92	1.00	0.96	0.98	0.93
λ_4	0.98	0.97	0.98	0.95	0.97	0.96
ϕ_{11}	1.14	0.87	0.93	0.94	0.93	0.93
ϕ_{21}	0.69	0.64	0.64	0.62	0.65	0.63
ϕ_{22}	0.86	0.87	0.90	0.85	0.88	0.86
θ_1	1.12	0.90	0.98	0.99	0.96	0.96
θ_2	0.90	0.98	1.03	1.02	1.02	1.00
θ_3	0.80	0.98	1.02	0.98	0.98	0.99
θ_4	0.99	0.98	0.96	0.99	0.98	1.05

After correction

Parameter	$N = 100$	$N=200$	$N=400$	$N=800$	$N=1,600$	$N=3,200$
α	1.02	1.01	1.04	1.14	1.02	1.03
γ_1	0.99	0.98	0.93	0.99	0.94	0.99
γ_2	0.92	0.97	1.00	1.00	1.01	0.95
γ_3	0.96	0.87	0.90	0.94	0.93	0.94
ψ	0.94	0.92	0.92	1.02	0.96	0.96
λ_2	0.81	0.91	1.00	0.97	0.99	0.94
λ_4	0.97	0.96	0.98	0.96	0.98	0.97
ϕ_{11}	1.13	0.89	0.95	0.97	0.97	0.97
ϕ_{21}	0.76	0.73	0.73	0.72	0.77	0.73
ϕ_{22}	0.93	0.95	0.99	0.85	0.98	0.97
θ_1	1.11	0.91	0.99	1.00	0.97	0.97
θ_2	0.88	0.97	1.03	1.02	1.02	1.00
θ_3	0.83	0.99	1.02	0.99	1.00	1.00
θ_4	0.96	0.98	0.96	1.00	0.99	1.05

Chi-Squared Goodness-of-Fit Statistic

To test a model, an asymptotic χ^2 goodness-of-fit test is used. If the model holds, which is the case here, this χ^2 should be distributed, in large sample, as χ^2 with specified degrees of freedom. We investigate the extent to which this is the case by computing the mean and standard deviation of the chi-square values obtained from each sample. We also compute the percentage of chi-square values exceeding the 95th and 99th percentile (P95 and P99) of the chi-square distribution. Table 6.5 shows the results for before and after the corrections.

It is seen that, before corrections, there is a tendency to reject the models too often when the models hold. After the correction the χ^2 are all underestimated for all the sample sizes and for both models. For Model 1, P95 and P99 perform worse for sample sizes 100 and better for other sample sizes. For sample size 3,200, the P95 is exactly 5% as expected. For Model 2, P95 is worse after correction than

TABLE 6.4
Standard Error Ratios for Model 2
Model 2: Four Product Variables

Before correction

Parameter	N=100	N=200	N=400	N=800	N=1,600	N=3,200
α	0.85	0.85	0.80	0.85	0.78	0.82
γ_1	0.79	0.84	0.77	0.86	0.84	0.87
γ_2	0.77	0.82	0.81	0.83	0.86	0.81
γ_3	0.78	0.69	0.69	0.68	0.68	0.71
ψ	0.76	0.80	0.78	0.78	0.76	0.79
λ_2	0.62	0.64	0.66	0.66	0.67	0.63
λ_4	0.72	0.64	0.69	0.66	0.65	0.66
ϕ_{11}	0.63	0.63	0.63	0.65	0.65	0.64
ϕ_{21}	0.65	0.62	0.62	0.62	0.62	0.61
ϕ_{22}	0.72	0.65	0.69	0.62	0.66	0.65
θ''_1	0.62	0.69	0.70	0.68	0.69	0.71
θ''_2	0.69	0.61	0.62	0.65	0.67	0.64
θ''_3	0.73	0.76	0.80	0.74	0.77	0.79
θ''_4	0.67	0.67	0.67	0.68	0.65	0.73

After correction

Parameter	N=100	N=200	N=400	N=800	N=1,600	N=3,200
α	0.98	0.99	0.95	1.02	0.94	0.98
γ_1	0.95	0.96	0.88	0.97	0.95	0.99
γ_2	0.91	0.95	0.95	0.97	1.02	0.95
γ_3	0.91	0.86	0.88	0.88	0.89	0.93
ψ	0.88	0.95	0.94	0.95	0.93	0.97
λ_2	0.72	0.79	0.83	0.87	0.88	0.83
λ_4	0.86	0.80	0.88	0.87	0.86	0.87
ϕ_{11}	0.74	0.84	0.88	0.94	0.95	0.94
ϕ_{21}	0.77	0.74	0.73	0.74	0.75	0.73
ϕ_{22}	0.93	0.90	0.98	0.89	0.97	0.96
θ_1	0.70	0.87	0.90	0.91	0.93	0.95
θ_2	0.92	0.89	0.93	1.00	1.03	0.98
θ_3	0.84	0.90	0.96	0.90	0.95	0.98
θ_4	0.88	0.93	0.94	0.96	0.92	1.04

TABLE 6.5
Distribution of χ^2
TV=Target Value
Model 1: One Product Variable

Before the corrections

	TV	100	200	400	800	1,600	3,200
$M(\chi^2)$	9	7.24	7.70	7.92	8.09	7.75	7.95
$S(\chi^2)$	4.24	4.05	3.85	3.97	3.89	3.69	3.86
$P95$	5	8.2	9.8	8.9	7.9	8.3	8.2
$P99$	1	2.1	2.4	2.2	1.8	1.8	2.1

After the corrections

	TV	100	200	400	800	1,600	3,200
$M(\chi^2)$	9	6.86	7.54	8.02	8.25	8.16	8.07
$S(\chi^2)$	4.24	4.65	4.39	4.56	4.15	4.03	3.99
$P95$	5	11.6	8.6	5.3	5.3	5.3	5.0
$P99$	1	4.1	1.8	1.3	0.7	0.5	0.5

Model 2: Four Product Variables

Before correction

	TV	100	200	400	800	1,600	3,200
$M(\chi^2)$	36	35.49	36.81	38.85	38.33	37.90	38.75
$S(\chi^2)$	8.49	10.75	11.55	11.72	10.83	10.95	11.68
$P95$	5	9.7	11.0	6.2	5.0	6.9	6.6
$P99$	1	3.4	2.6	1.6	0.9	2.7	1.4

After correction

	TV	100	200	400	800	1,600	3,200
$M(\chi^2)$	36	22.30	24.06	26.58	26.69	26.60	27.17
$S(\chi^2)$	8.49	13.03	10.77	10.79	8.63	8.71	8.48
$P95$	5	18.6	21.0	13.1	7.5	8.2	7.1
$P99$	1	4.6	8.8	3.5	1.5	2.4	1.2

before correction for all sample sizes. *P99* is slightly better for sample sizes 1,600 and 3,200.

CONCLUSION

Using the formulas of Satorra (1989) and Satorra and Bentler (1988), one can compute the correct asymptotic standard errors and chi-squares of ML estimates under non-normality. The corrections work better for the model with four product variables (the model has more non-normality). Chi-squares after the corrections are not as good as we expected especially for the model with four product variables. For the model with one product variable they were better for larger sample sizes. A plausible explanation for the poor performance of the chi-square corrections is that the asymptotic covariance matrix involves eight- order moments which are difficult to estimate accurately unless one has a very large sample.

ACKNOWLEDGEMENT

The research reported in this chapter has been supported by the Swedish Council for Research in the Humanities and Social Sciences (HSFR) under the program *Non-Linear Structural Equation Modeling*.

REFERENCES

Anderson, T. W. (1984). *An introduction to multivariate statistical analysis*. (2nd ed.). New York: Wiley.

Browne, M. W. (1984). Asymptotically distribution-free methods for the analysis of covariance structures. *British Journal of Mathematical and Statistical Psychology, 37*, 62–83.

Jöreskog, K. G., Sörbom, D., du Toit, S., & du Toit, M. (1999). *New statistical features in LISREL 8.30*. Chicago: Scientific Software international.

Jöreskog, K. G., & Yang, F. (1996). Nonlinear structural equation models: The Kenny–Judd model with interaction effects. In G. A. Marcoulides & R. E. Schumacker (Eds.), *Advanced structural equation modeling: Issues and techniques* (pp 57–82). Hillsdale, NJ: Lawrence Erlbaum Associates.

Kenny, D. A., & Judd, C. M. (1984). Estimating the nonlinear and interactive effects of latent variables. *Psychological Bulletin, 96*, 201–210.

Magnus, J., & Neudecker, H. (1988). *Matrix differential calculus*. New York: Wiley.

Satorra, A. (1989). Alternative test criteria in covariance structure analysis: A unified approach. *Psychometrika, 54*, 131–151.

Satorra, A., & Bentler, P. M. (1988). Scaling corrections for chi-square statistics in covariance structure analysis Proceeding of the Business and Economic Statistics Section of the American Statistical Association, 1988, 308–313.

Yang-Jonsson, F. (1997). *Non-linear structural equation models: Simulation studies of the Kenny–Judd model*. dpublished doctoral Dissertation, Uppsala University, Sweden.

Yang-Jonsson, F. (1998). Modeling interaction and nonlinear effects: A step-by step LISREL Example. In G. A. Marcoulides & R. E. Schumacker (Eds); *Interaction and nonlinear effects in structural equation models*. (pp. 17–42). Mahwah, NJ: Lawrence Erlbaum Associates.

7

Interaction Models in Latent Growth Curves

Fuzhong Li
Terry E. Duncan
Susan C. Duncan
Oregon Research Institute

Fan Yang-Wallentin
Uppsala University

Alan C. Acock
Oregon State University

Hyman Hops
Oregon Research Institute

Researchers in the behavioral and social sciences often deal with complex models involving interaction and nonlinear effects in addition to main effects of variables. For hypotheses about interaction and nonlinear effects between continuous variables, analyses are frequently conducted using multiple regression techniques (e.g., Aiken & West, 1991; Jaccard, Turrisi, & Wan, 1990). However, concerns with these techniques have been raised regarding measurement error that often introduces bias in regression coefficients and lowers the power of statistical tests for these nonlinear effects (Busemeyer & Jones, 1983; Jaccard & Wan, 1995). Therefore, methods such as structural equation modeling (SEM) with latent variables, which can account for errors in measurement, have generally been recommended for modeling interaction and quadratic effects (Jaccard & Wan, 1996).

In the 1980s, Kenny and Judd (1984) provided one of the first examples of estimating structural equation models with interactions and quadratics in latent variables. Unfortunately, the procedure was difficult to use due to limitations in standard SEM softwares for handling of nonlinear constraints. Subsequent extensions of Kenny and Judd's procedure have made their method more accessible to a broad audience of substantive researchers. Recent developments in software (LISREL 8; Jöreskog & Sörbom, 1993) and contributions by Jaccard and Wan (1995), Jöreskog and Yang (1996), and Ping (1995, 1996) have made Kenny and Judd's technique easier to apply and have provided a fresh look at the statistical issues involved. Other methods such as a multisample/multigroup method (Neale, 1998; Rigdon, Schumacker, & Wothke, 1998) and a two-stage least squares approach (Bollen, 1995) have also been proposed and recommended as viable alternatives. These developments have provided new opportunities for modeling interactions and quadratics within the SEM framework, which allow the incorporation of measurement error into model tests and parameter estimation (Jaccard & Wan, 1995).

EXTENDING THE ANALYSIS OF INTERACTION EFFECTS TO LATENT GROWTH MODELS

The existing SEM-based methods for interaction analysis are readily applicable for cross-sectional models involving interaction terms between continuous variables. Their utility in longitudinal studies, however, remains largely unexplored. Given an increasing interest in the analysis of change using longitudinal data (Collins & Horn, 1991; Collins & Sayer, in press), a method that allows consideration of interaction between dynamic, longitudinal change variables would be beneficial to gain a better understanding of issues related to the pattern of change over time. In this chapter, we consider interaction analysis in the context of latent growth modeling (LGM; McArdle, 1988; Meredith & Tisak, 1990; Muthén, 1991). LGM allows for the analysis of intra- and interindividual trajectories in developmental models and has been shown to be quite flexible in addressing various questions related to growth or change (e.g., Duncan, Duncan, Strycker, Li, & Alpert, 1999; McArdle, 1998; Muthén, 1997; Muthén & Curran, 1997; Raykov, 1996; Stoolmiller, 1995; Willett & Sayer, 1994, 1996). For example, questions and hypotheses about determinants and outcomes of growth can be parameterized by focusing on predictors of slope scores and/or slope scores as predictors (e.g., Stoolmiller, Duncan, Bank, & Patterson, 1993; Walker, Acock, Bowman, & Li, 1996).

Although it is clear that latent curve analysis can be a useful tool for analyzing patterns and predictors of change, it is also important to consider extensions of the method to the analysis of more complex forms of dynamic system models (McArdle & Hamagami, in press), such as models involving interactive relationships between growth parameters. Modeling the interaction among change scores (slope factors) may be of substantive interest in hypotheses testing to determine how change in two latent attributes interact with one another to produce a joint effect on growth of an outcome (criterion) variable. This chapter provides an extension of latent variable interaction analysis to longitudinal models involving growth parameters. In the following section, a discussion of the extension of Jöreskog and Yang's (1996) interaction method to latent growth curve models is provided. Specifically, we focus on interactions between two latent growth slope factors and their joint effect on the slope factor of a criterion variable.

LATENT GROWTH MODELS WITH INTERACTION BETWEEN LATENT GROWTH (SLOPE) FACTORS

Suppose we are interested in a hypothesis about the dynamic influence of two exogenous latent growth variables, X and Z, on the rate of change in Y, in which X and Z are operationalized as time-changing latent slope predictors. For simplicity, we use a two-factor growth model of change (i.e., intercept, slope) for X, Z, and Y. In this hypothetical situation, we want to investigate the extent to which the impact of joint changes in X and Z influences changes in Y. More specifically, we examine whether the effect of longitudinal change in X on Y is influenced or moderated by the level of simultaneous change in Z, the moderator variable, by testing the interactive relationship between the two growth parameters (i.e., slope factors) on the slope of Y. As such, we question whether there is an interaction between two dynamic predictors, the growth trajectories of X and Z, that jointly influence the change in the criterion variable in addition to the direct effects of change in X and Z. In the following example, we present a model that illustrates the situation where two exogenous latent variables, consisting of growth curve factors, are hypothesized to interact with each other longitudinally to influence an endogenous latent growth slope factor. This hypothetical model is depicted in Fig. 7.1.

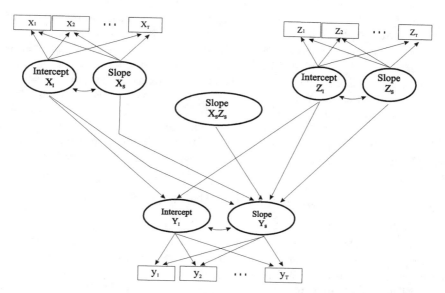

FIG. 7.1.   A hypothetical latent growth model with interaction between two slope factors.

In Fig. 7.1, two growth variables (X and Z) are each measured by the time series of the repeated variables ($x_1, x_2, ..., x_T$ for X and $z_1, z_2, ..., z_T$ for Z). The latent product term of the exogenous variables, denoted by XZ, represents a multiplicative interaction between the latent slope factors X and Z, with its cross-product indicators (not shown) formed by multiplying each of the corresponding observed indicators of X and Z. Details on the formulation of these two-way cross-product terms are presented in the section on model specification. Similar to the exogenous latent variables, there is a two-factor latent growth outcome variable (symbolized by Y) with Intercept and Slope, measured again by the time series of repeated variables $Y[t]$, for $t = 1$ to T.

Although the model shown in Fig. 7.1 is acknowledged to be complex compared with the conventional latent variable interaction models, in that it involves a time dimension, this specification is central to basic questions that are asked by many social science researchers in the study of change: Does longitudinal change in predictor variables influence the rate of change in an outcome variable? If so, does the simultaneous change in predictor variables interact to jointly influence the rate of change in the outcome variable?

There are various techniques for estimating latent interaction effects (see Schumacker & Marcoulides, 1998, for a review of currently available procedures). Among the full information-based methods (i.e., fitting a model to all parameters simultaneously), the Jöreskog and Yang (1996) procedure is the most relevant for applications within the latent growth curve modeling framework. This is because the Jöreskog and Yang approach involves specification of both first and second moments (i.e., the mean vector and covariance matrix) in model estimation. Other procedures (e.g., Jaccard & Wan, 1995; Ping, 1995, 1996) require centering of the raw scores (Jaccard & Wan, 1996) and therefore are not directly applicable to latent curve analysis, which utilizes both covariance and mean structures. In what follows, we outline the model specification for the interaction analysis of growth models within the LISREL framework (see Willett & Sayer's 1994, well-regarded article on modeling growth/change using the LISREL approach). For the sake of continuity, we begin the presentation using a univariate two-factor growth model. We then build on to this example by specifying a multivariate growth model involving an interaction term between two exogenous latent slope factors.

Model Specifications Using the LISREL Approach

A Growth Model. We consider a univariate, two-factor (intercept, slope) growth model within a two-level latent variable growth modeling framework (Willett & Sayer, 1994). Assuming four equal-interval time points, Level 1 is a LISREL measurement model for endogenous variables Y:

$$Y = \tau_y + \Lambda_y \eta + \epsilon, \tag{1}$$

where Y is a 4×1 vector of observed outcomes for the T=4 time points, τ a 4×1 intercept vector, Λ a 4×2 matrix of factor loadings, η a 2×1 vector of latent variables representing the growth (i.e., intercept, slope) parameters involving means and variances, and ϵ a 4×1 vector of time-specific errors in the measurement of Y that are uncorrelated with η. As in classic factor analysis, it is assumed that the errors are normal and uncorrelated—that is, $\epsilon \sim N(0, \Theta)$ with $\Theta = \text{diag}[\Theta_{\epsilon 11}, \ldots, \Theta_{\epsilon 44}]$.

Equation (1) can be written as follows to represent the observed status Y_i of an individual i at time t:

$$\begin{bmatrix} y_1 \\ y_2 \\ y_3 \\ y_4 \end{bmatrix} = \begin{bmatrix} \tau_1 \\ \tau_2 \\ \tau_3 \\ \tau_4 \end{bmatrix} + \begin{bmatrix} 1t_1 \\ 1t_2 \\ 1t_3 \\ 1t_4 \end{bmatrix} \begin{bmatrix} \eta_{1i} \\ \eta_{2i} \end{bmatrix} + \begin{bmatrix} \epsilon_1 \\ \epsilon_2 \\ \epsilon_3 \\ \epsilon_4 \end{bmatrix}$$

$$\mathbf{Y}_i = \tau_y + \Lambda_y \eta + \epsilon_i,$$

Note that the elements of τ_y and Λ_y parameter matrixes are entirely constrained to contain prespecified values and constants (Willett & Sayer, 1994). The columns of Λ represent specific aspects of changes and are termed *basis functions* (Meredith & Tisak, 1990). There are various approaches to specifying the elements in Λ to reflect true change. Commonly used approaches include use of fixed numerical values or estimated values from the data. For example, a linear growth function can be specified using the loadings of constant 1s in the first column (defining intercept) and $t_1=0$, $t_2=1$, $t_3=2$, and $t_4=3$ in the second column (defining slope) in Λ, so that η_1 represents the initial status of individual i on his or her growth trajectory and η_2 represents his or her linear growth rate across t_1 to t_4 on this trajectory. Alternatively, the growth can be specified as of $t_1=0$, $t_2=1$, $t_3=*$, and $t_4=*$ in the second column of Λ, where $*$ means that the loading is freely estimated from the data. With this formulation, the model becomes an unspecified growth function, where η_1 represents the initial level of the growth trajectory and η_2 corresponds to an optimal shape function on the growth trajectory.

Level 2 is a structural model that shows the influence of latent variables on each other:

$$\eta = \alpha + \mathbf{B}\eta + \zeta, \tag{2}$$

where α (2×1) is a vector of intercepts (for endogenous ηs) or means (for exogenous ηs), $\mathbf{B}$ is a null matrix, and ζ (2×1) is a vector of deviations of the parameters from their respective means and distributed as $\zeta \sim N(0, \Psi)$ with $Cov(\zeta)$ Ψ. In estimating the model in Eqns. (1) and (2), one obtains estimates of the basis function loadings in Λ, the variances and covariance of latent growth factors in

Ψ, the error variances (or uniqueness variances) in Θ_ϵ, and latent growth mean estimates in α.

Growth Curve Model With a Product Term.
Having briefly described the basic feature of an LGM, we now turn to the model shown in Fig. 7.1 and outline the model specification for the interaction analysis using Jöreskog-Yang's (1996) method. To facilitate the presentation, a latent growth curve interaction model is presented in Fig. 7.2 using LISREL notation. Note that X in Fig. 7.1 is replaced by the Greek letter ξ_j (where $j=1,2$), Z by ξ_k (where $k=3,4$), and Y by η_l (where $l=1,2$). The first two-factor (ξ_1 and ξ_2) univariate growth model on the upper-left-hand side of Fig. 7.2 includes four repeated measures $(x_1, \ldots, x_4)$ with error variables $\delta_1, \ldots, \delta_4$. The second two-factor (ξ_3 and ξ_4) univariate growth model on the upper right-hand-side of Fig. 7.2 includes four repeated measures $(x_5, \ldots, x_8)$ with error variables $\delta_5, \ldots, \delta_8$. Finally, the two-factor (η_1 and η_2) univariate growth model on the bottom of Fig. 7.2 includes four repeated measures $(y_1, \ldots, y_4)$, with error variables $\varepsilon, \ldots, \varepsilon_4$. To recap, the top two growth components contain exogenous latent growth predictors and the bottom growth component contains an endogenous latent outcome variable. Note that we have used the unspecified growth specification with the third (λ_3) and fourth (λ_4) loadings free for the exogenous latent predictor variables (the rationale for doing so in this context is provided in the section on model specification).

Because our primary interest is in the interaction between the two slope factors (i.e., the rates of change in the exogenous latent growth variables), we focus on the slope factors of ξ_2 (for the exogenous latent variable X) and ξ_4 (for the exogenous latent variable Z) and their latent product term $\xi_2\xi_4$. The model in Fig. 7.2 contains two structural equations:

$$\eta_1 = \alpha_1 + \gamma_{11}\xi_1 + \gamma_{13}\xi_3 + \zeta_1, \text{ and} \tag{3}$$

$$\eta_2 = \alpha_2 + \gamma_{21}\xi_1 + \gamma_{22}\xi_2 + \gamma_{23}\xi_3 + \gamma_{24}\xi_4 + \gamma_{25}\xi_2\xi_4 + \zeta_2, \tag{4}$$

where α in both equations denotes an intercept term and the variable of ζ is a disturbance term (assumed to be $\zeta \sim N[0, \Psi]$), and γ_{11} through γ_{25} are regression parameters that relate the exogenous latent variables ξs and the latent product variable $\xi_2\xi_4$ to the intercept and slope components of growth in η. Equation (3) only contains the main effects of ξ_1 and ξ_3 on η_1, and it defines the cross-sectional relationship between exogenous latent variables and the endogenous latent variable. This is because these latent variables (ξ_1, ξ_3, and η_1) are defined by the Time 1 measures and as such represent relationships among the latent attributes at the initial time point. Because of our focus on the slope factors, we do not consider an interaction term in Eq. (3). Equation (4) contains an interaction effect of ξ_2 (slope or shape) and ξ_4 (slope or shape) on η_2 (slope or shape) in addition to the direct effects emanating from the initial level and shape factors in the equation, and this interaction effect is manifesting itself in terms of an effect of the latent product of ξ_2 and ξ_4.

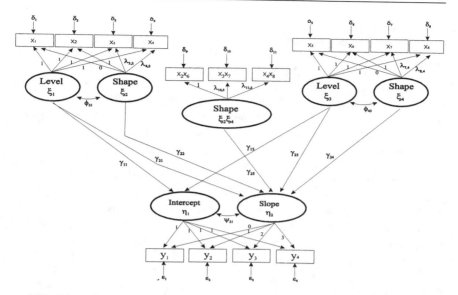

FIG. 7.2. A LISREL model with interaction between two slope factors.

In the conventional analysis of latent interaction models, the interaction effect γ_{25} (in Eq. [4]) is of special interest because this parameter indicates how much the slope of η_2 on ξ_2 is predicted to change given a one unit change in the moderator variable ξ_4 (Jaccard & Wan, 1996). In the context of longitudinal models, the prediction of either $\xi_2 \rightarrow \eta_2$ or $\xi_4 \rightarrow \eta_2$ represents the effect of a ξ's slope on the slope of η. It is best viewed as a slope-to-slope relationship in a growth curve analysis. The $\xi_2 \xi_4$ interaction signifies that the regression of η_2 on the slope factor ξ_2 depends on the specific slope value of ξ_4 (a moderator) at which the effect of ξ_2 slope on the η_2 slope is measured. For example, to examine the regression of η_2 on ξ_2 at the particular slope value of ξ_4, Eq. (4) can be rearranged as:

$$\eta_2 = (\gamma_{22} + \gamma_{25}\xi_4)\xi_2 + (\alpha_2 + \gamma_{24}\xi_4) + \zeta_2. \tag{5}$$

The term $[(\gamma_{22} + \gamma_{25}\xi_4)\xi_2]$ is often referred to as the *simple slope* of the regression of η_2 on ξ_2 for a given ξ_4 (Aiken & West, 1991; Jöreskog, 1998). Because of the slope-to-slope relationship in the growth model depicted in Fig. 7.2, this effect reflects the dynamic longitudinal influence of the exogenous latent variable ξ (operationalizing the slope of X) on the endogenous latent variable η (operationalizing the slope of Y).

Before presenting the LISREL X-measurement model for ξs and Y-measurement model for η, we briefly mention the cross-product formulation in the context of latent growth models. When the two latent growth factors are measured by different indicators taken at the same time intervals (e.g., Time 1 measure of factor ξ_2 corresponds to Time 1 measure of factor ξ_4), it is reasonable to form cross-product indicators based on measures corresponding to the same time point. To allow for formulation of cross-product terms at the observed variable level, a two-factor (level-shape) unspecified growth model (Meredith & Tisak, 1990) has to be considered in parameterizing the latent product term $\xi_2\xi_4$. In an unspecified model, only loadings representing the first two time points have to be constrained (i.e., $t_1=0$, $t_2=1$) for identification purposes. The remaining two loadings are freely estimated providing a shape model. Because the shape factor loading for the first time measurement point is fixed to zero (necessary for providing a reference point for the slope factor), only the measurement of t_2, t_3, and t_4 for ξ_2 and ξ_4 can be used to form product variables as indicators of the latent product variable ($\xi_2\xi_4$). Although the selection of a reference point is largely arbitrary, future research needs to determine the consequences of this selection on product term exclusion.

Within the framework mentioned earlier, measures of the latent variables are selected from t_2 and subsequent time points to form cross-product terms of x_2x_6, x_3x_7, and x_4x_8 as shown in Fig. 7.2. The x_1x_5 product variable is not used in the model because the loadings of the two original nonproduct observed variables (x_1 and x_5) on ξ_2 and ξ_4, respectively, are constrained to zero for identification purposes (see Fig. 7.2; $x_1=x_5=0$). Therefore, instead of using the x_1x_5 product indicator as a reference variable for scaling the latent product variable $\xi_2\xi_4$, the product indicator x_2x_6 is used (see Fig. 7.2; $x_2=x_6=1$ on ξ_2 and ξ_4, respectively).

Detailed formulation of the model presented in Fig. 7.2 using Jöreskog and Yang's (1996) model specification and maximum likelihood estimation is presented next. The reader is referred to Jöreskog and Yang for more details (see also Yang-Jonsson, 1997). The reader is also encouraged to refer to the work by Jaccard and Wan (1996), which provides a simplified overview at the Jöreskog and Yang technique.

The LISREL specification for the Y-measurement model expressed in Eq. (1) can be used for the dependent growth variable, η_l ($l=1,2$ for the intercept and slope, respectively), with factor loadings for t_1 through t_4 either constrained to values of 0, 1, 2, or 3 or freely estimated loadings with the first two prespecified value constraints for identification. In Fig. 7.2, we have chosen values that represent linear changes in the latent variable η. The Y-measurement model shown in Fig. 7.2 is expressed as

$$\begin{bmatrix} y_1 \\ y_2 \\ y_3 \\ y_4 \end{bmatrix} = \begin{bmatrix} \tau_1 \\ \tau_2 \\ \tau_3 \\ \tau_4 \end{bmatrix} + \begin{bmatrix} 1 & t_1 \\ 1 & t_2 \\ 1 & t_3 \\ 1 & t_4 \end{bmatrix} \begin{bmatrix} \eta_1 \\ \eta_2 \end{bmatrix} + \begin{bmatrix} \epsilon_1 \\ \epsilon_2 \\ \epsilon_3 \\ \epsilon_4 \end{bmatrix}$$

$$\mathbf{Y} = \tau_y + \Lambda_y\eta + \epsilon, \tag{6}$$

where t_1 through $t_4=0, 1, 2, 3$.

The LISREL specification for the X-measurement model of exogenous latent variables, ξs, including the exogenous latent product variable, $\xi_2\xi_4$, is outlined in the following matrix form:

$$
\begin{bmatrix} x_1 \\ x_2 \\ x_3 \\ x_4 \\ x_5 \\ x_6 \\ x_7 \\ x_8 \\ x_2x_6 \\ x_3x_7 \\ x_4x_8 \end{bmatrix} =
\begin{bmatrix} \tau_1 \\ \tau_2 \\ \tau_3 \\ \tau_4 \\ \tau_5 \\ \tau_6 \\ \tau_7 \\ \tau_8 \\ \tau_2\tau_6 \\ \tau_3\tau_7 \\ \tau_4\tau_8 \end{bmatrix} +
\begin{bmatrix}
1 & 0 & 0 & 0 & 0 \\
1 & 1 & 0 & 0 & 0 \\
1 & \lambda_{32} & 0 & 0 & 0 \\
1 & \lambda_{42} & 0 & 0 & 0 \\
0 & 0 & 1 & 0 & 0 \\
0 & 0 & 1 & 1 & 0 \\
0 & 0 & 1 & \lambda_{74} & 0 \\
0 & 0 & 1 & \lambda_{84} & 0 \\
0 & \tau_6 & 0 & \tau_2 & 1 \\
0 & \tau_7\lambda_{32} & 0 & \tau_3\lambda_{74} & \lambda_{32}\lambda_{74} \\
0 & \tau_8\lambda_{42} & 0 & \tau_4\lambda_{84} & \lambda_{42}\lambda_{84}
\end{bmatrix}
\begin{bmatrix} \xi_1 \\ \xi_2 \\ \xi_3 \\ \xi_4 \\ \xi_2\xi_4 \end{bmatrix} +
\begin{bmatrix} \delta_1 \\ \delta_2 \\ \delta_3 \\ \delta_4 \\ \delta_5 \\ \delta_6 \\ \delta_7 \\ \delta_8 \\ \delta_9 \\ \delta_{10} \\ \delta_{11} \end{bmatrix}
$$

$$\mathbf{X} = \tau_x + \Lambda_x\xi + \delta. \tag{7}$$

As can be seen from Eq. (7), the latent product variable $\xi_2\xi_4$ has a set of indicators consisting of observed cross-product variables (i.e., x_2x_6, x_3x_7, and x_4x_8). The multiplication of indicator variables for the latent product variable (a set of nonlinear constraints necessary for model estimation) in Eq. (7) can be derived using the method outlined by Jöreskog and Yang (1996). These are formulated as

$$x_2x_6 = x_9 = \tau_2\tau_6 + \tau_6\xi_2 + \tau_2\xi_4 + \xi_2\xi_4 + \delta_9, \tag{8}$$

$$x_3x_7 = x_{10} = \tau_3\tau_7 + \tau_7\lambda_{32}\xi_2 + \tau_3\lambda_{74}\xi_4 + \lambda_{32}\lambda_{74}\xi_2\xi_4 + \delta_{10}, \tag{9}$$

$$x_4x_8 = x_{11} = \tau_4\tau_8 + \tau_8\lambda_{42}\xi_2 + \tau_4\lambda_{84}\xi_4 + \lambda_{42}\lambda_{84}\xi_2\xi_4 + \delta_{11} \tag{10}$$

Error parameters δ_9, δ_{10}, and δ_{11} in Eqs. (8) through (10) are outlined in a later part of this section. As can be seen, the multiplication of indicator variables leads to a series of nonlinear terms, including the factor loadings and factor and error variances. These terms, shown next, can be implemented in the latent variable interaction model using the LISREL 8 SEM program (Jöreskog & Sörbom, 1993).

The structural program of the model shown in Fig. 7.2 is:

$$
\begin{bmatrix} \eta_1 \\ \eta_2 \end{bmatrix} =
\begin{bmatrix} \alpha_1 \\ \alpha_2 \end{bmatrix} +
\begin{bmatrix}
\gamma_{11} & 0 & \gamma_{13} & 0 & 0 \\
\gamma_{21} & \gamma_{22} & \gamma_{23} & \gamma_{24} & \gamma_{25}
\end{bmatrix}
\begin{bmatrix} \xi_1 \\ \xi_2 \\ \xi_3 \\ \xi_4 \\ \xi_2\xi_4 \end{bmatrix} +
\begin{bmatrix} \zeta_1 \\ \zeta_2 \end{bmatrix}
$$

$$\eta = \alpha + \mathbf{B}\eta + \Gamma\xi + \zeta, \tag{11}$$

where $\mathbf{B}$ is a null matrix. In this structural model, the interaction effect $\xi_2\xi_4$ is of special interest in our presentation, because this parameter indicates how much the slope of η_2 on ξ_2 is predicted to change given a one unit change in the moderator variable ξ_4.

As in the conventional modeling of interactions, exogenous latent variables are centered (i.e., variables given in mean deviation form). We maintain this convention in the growth model because it will not be necessary to answer the question about the influence of ξs on η. Even if ξs have zero means [i.e., $E(\xi_1)=E(\xi_2)=E(\xi_3)=E(\xi_4)=0$], the product term $\xi_2\xi_4$ does not have a zero mean in general. The latent exogenous latent mean vector (κ) is specified as:

$$\kappa = \begin{pmatrix} 0 \\ 0 \\ 0 \\ 0 \\ \phi_{42} \end{pmatrix}.$$

Note that because the observed intercepts (the X-intercept vector τ in Eq. [7]) are freely estimated, the nonproduct exogenous latent variable means are constrained to zero ($\kappa_1=\kappa_2=\kappa_3=\kappa_4=0$) to impose model identification restrictions. This specification implies that the means of κ have been recast into the vector of τs. Alternatively, τ can be set at zero while estimating the means of κs. The mean of the product variable $\xi_2\xi_4$ equals $Cov(\xi_2, \xi_4)=\phi_{42}$. The variance/covariance matrix (Φ) of (ξ_1, ξ_2, ξ_3, ξ_4, $\xi_2\xi_4$) is written as:

$$\phi = \begin{pmatrix} \phi_{11} & & & & \\ \phi_{21} & \phi_{22} & & & \\ \phi_{31} & \phi_{32} & \phi_{33} & & \\ \phi_{41} & \phi_{42} & \phi_{43} & \phi_{44} & \\ 0 & 0 & 0 & 0 & \phi_{22}\phi_{44}+\phi_{42}^2 \end{pmatrix}.$$

The only nonlinear constraint in the Φ matrix is the variance of the latent product variable, which must equal $Var(\xi_2)Var(\xi_4) + Cov(\xi_2\xi_4)^2$. The ζ vector in Eq. (11) contains latent residuals distributed with zero mean vector and covariance matrix Ψ:

$$\Psi = \begin{bmatrix} \psi_{11} & \\ \psi_{21} & \psi_{22} \end{bmatrix}.$$

Finally, the variance/covariance matrix of Θ_δ is:

$$
\Theta_\delta = \begin{pmatrix}
\theta_1 \\
0 & \theta_2 \\
0 & 0 & \theta_3 \\
0 & 0 & 0 & \theta_4 \\
0 & 0 & 0 & 0 & \theta_5 \\
0 & 0 & 0 & 0 & 0 & \theta_6 \\
0 & 0 & 0 & 0 & 0 & 0 & \theta_7 \\
0 & 0 & 0 & 0 & 0 & 0 & 0 & \theta_8 \\
0 & \theta_{92} & 0 & 0 & 0 & \theta_{96} & 0 & 0 & \theta_9 \\
0 & 0 & \theta_{10,3} & 0 & 0 & 0 & 0 & \theta_{10,7} & 0 & \theta_{10} \\
0 & 0 & 0 & \theta_{11,4} & 0 & 0 & 0 & 0 & \theta_{11,8} & 0 & \theta_{11}
\end{pmatrix} .
$$

The error variance for the product variables of $x_2 x_6$, $x_3 x_7$, and $x_4 x_8$ are indicated as θ_9, θ_{10}, and θ_{11} in Θ_δ, which are formulated as:

$$\theta_9 = \tau_2^2 \theta_6 + \tau_6^2 \theta_2 + \phi_{22}\theta_6 + \phi_{44}\theta_2 + \theta_2 \theta_6,$$

$$\theta_{10} = \tau_3^2 \theta_7 + \tau_7^2 \theta_3 + \lambda_{32}^2 \phi_{22}\theta_7 + \lambda_{74}^2 \phi_{44}\theta_3 + \theta_3 \theta_7,$$

$$\theta_{11} = \tau_4^2 \tau_8^2 \theta_4 + \lambda_{42}^2 \phi_{22}\theta_8 + \lambda_{84}\phi_{44}\theta_4 + \theta_4 \theta_8.$$

Finally, the covariances of θ_{92}, θ_{96}, $\theta_{10,3}$, $\theta_{10,7}$, $\theta_{11,4}$, and $\theta_{11,8}$ Θ_δ are $\theta_{92} = \tau_6 \delta_2$, $\theta_{96} = \tau_2 \delta_6$, $\theta_{10,3} = \tau_7 \delta_3$, $\theta_{10,7} = \tau_3 \delta_7$, $\theta_{11,4} = \tau_8 \delta_4$, and $\theta_{11,8} = \tau_4 \delta_8$. More details on the derivation of nonlinear constraints of this model can be found in Li, Duncan, and Acock (2000).

Implementation of linear and nonlinear constraints for this model in LIS-REL 8 (Jöreskog & Sörbom, 1993) is demonstrated next using an empirical example.

AN ILLUSTRATION

In this section, we provide an empirical example of the methodology described earlier. The example arises from an ongoing longitudinal study of the social influences of peers and family on the onset and maintenance of various substances in adolescence (for details of this study, see Duncan, Duncan, & Hops, 1994; Hops, Tildesley, Lichtenstein, Ary, & Sherman, 1990).

Research Question

Peer substance use is consistently one of the best predictors of adolescent substance use (e.g., Brook, Brook, Gordon, Whiteman, & Cohen, 1990; Curran, Stice, & Chassin, 1997; Dishion & Loeber, 1985). Contact with drug-using peers and/or association with deviant peers is clearly the strongest proximal correlate of adolescent substance use. However, it has also been suggested that parental discipline exerts important influences on the development of early adolescent substance use and other problem behaviors (Patterson, 1982; Patterson, Reid, & Dishion, 1992). It is not surprising that parental supervision and involvement with their children would impact an adolescent's level of contact with deviant peers and could limit access to unsupervised settings in which mutual influence processes unfold unabated by adult intervention (Ary, Duncan, Duncan, & Hops, 1999; Dishion, Capaldi, Spracklen, & Li, 1995). It is therefore plausible that the impact of deviant peer association and/or peer substance use on adolescent substance use is moderated by parental discipline such as rule/limit setting. When levels of parental discipline are low, peer substance use will have greater impact on adolescent substance use; however, when the levels of parental discipline are high, the effect of peer substance use is diminished.

In line with this reasoning, it is postulated that change in peer substance use and parental discipline leads to change in adolescent substance use, and there is an interaction of the changes in peer substance use and parental discipline. Specifically, we hypothesize that the interaction between peer substance use and parental discipline is such that the relationship between the rate of change in peer substance use and the rate of change in adolescent substance use wanes as the rate of change in parental discipline practices increases over time.

Data

For illustration purposes, a subset of the study data from Year 4 through Year 7 was obtained. Of the 530 participants at Year 4, those whose ages were 14 through 16 ($N=441$) were selected. Preliminary analyses indicate that there were no differences in the variables of interest across the four age groups in the sample data. After removing the participants with missing values, the final sample size was 328, which was used for the interaction analysis. Measures of adolescent substance use, substance use by peers, and parental discipline were used in the current interaction analysis. Details of these measures are described next.

Measures

Adolescent Substance Use.   The measure of adolescent substance use was constructed from items assessing frequency of use as well as from self-reports of current use on alcohol, cigarettes, and marijuana. Use of each specific substance was measured on a 5-point scale via an algorithm incorporating self-reports of use and frequency. The five levels on the scales represent: (0) *never used*, (1) *use prior to the past 6 months*, (2) *current use less than four times a month*, (3) *current use between 4 and 29 times a month*, and (4) *current use 30 or more times a month*. Although these scales were created from status and frequency information, the assumption is made that the underlying properties are continuous in nature. A sum of these three substance use items was created to form a general measure of adolescent substance use. This indicator of adolescent substance use ranges from 0 to 15, with higher scores indicating increased substance use.

Peer Substance Use.   Target adolescents were asked to identify how many of their five closest friends had used alcohol, cigarette, or marijuana in the past year. Adolescents responded to the item ranging from 0 to 5, with 0 indicating *no friends used a substance* and 5 indicating *five or more friends used a substance*. An average of the three substance use items was created to represent a general measure of adolescents' association with substance using peers. This indicator of peer substance use ranges from 0 to 5, with higher scores indicating greater levels of substance using peers.

Parental Discipline.   Target adolescents were asked to respond to items that asked whether their parents had said or done anything to stop/criticize/punish the use of alcohol, cigarette, and marijuana during the last year. For example, on the use of cigarettes, adolescents were asked, "During the last year, my Mother/Father has punished me for smoking cigarettes." There were four items per substance, each measured on a 4-point scale with 1 indicating *never* and 4 *repeatedly*. Items were averaged to form a measure of parental discipline with higher scores indicating greater parental discipline.

Model Testing

Tests of fit for the interaction model presented previously were conducted using the LISREL (Jöreskog & Sörbom, 1993) maximum likelihood estimation procedure. The analyses involved both covariance and mean structures. We conducted the interaction analyses in two steps: (a) preliminary analyses of change on each variable over time, and (b) the interaction analysis. Step 1 analyses are considered prerequisite for the longitudinal interaction analysis because they allow us to establish evidence about change in the variables of interest. In the presence of observed change in the variables of interest, Step 2 allows us to examine whether changes in the independent variables (i.e., substance-using peers, parental discipline) jointly influence longitudinal change in the dependent variable (i.e., adolecent substance use). The LISREL script for the interaction analysis is presented in Appendix A.

Model fit evaluation will rely on the Root Mean Square Error of Approximation (RMSEA; Steiger & Lind, 1980), Comparative Fit Index (CFI; Bentler, 1990), and Non-Normed Fit Index (NNFI; also known as Tucker–Lewis index; Tucker & Lewis, 1973). Values of the RMSEA less than 0.05 are considered an indication of good fit, with values between 0.05 and 0.08 indicating a reasonable fit. Values of CFI and NNFI greater than 0.90 are usually taken as evidence of a good fit (Hu & Bentler, 1995). In our interaction analysis, evaluation of fit also includes other aspects of the model such as the admissibility of various parameter estimates.

RESULTS OF THE EXAMPLE DATA

Table 7.1 displays univariate descriptive statistics for all measured variables used in our analyses. First, note that skewness and kurtosis are minimal, indicating that it is reasonable to assume the constructs are approximately normally distributed. Approximate normality justifies the use of normal theory maximum likelihood estimation techniques. Second, note that all observed variables show increases in mean level over time. However, variance increases were observed only in adolescent substance use.

Preliminary Analyses of Change: Step 1 Analyses

As a preliminary analysis to examine change in both the independent variables (peer substance use, parental discipline) and dependent variable (adolescent substance use), a univariate growth model was first tested for each variable of interest. A two-factor linear growth model was chosen that consisted of intercept and slope factors for each variable. Thus, the factor loadings for the four observed measures were fixed to 1.0 on the intercept factor and 0, 1, 2, and 3 on the slope factor. Main growth parameters in the model included the means and variances of the two latent growth factors and their covariance. Results of these univariate growth model analyses are summarized in Table 7.2.

The overall fit of each model was generally acceptable, suggesting a reasonable fit of the model to the observed data. Model parameter estimates revealed significant mean intercept and slope estimates ($p < .05$) for each latent variable. Of particular interest is the estimated growth rate in the latent growth factors where a significant increase in adolescent substance use, substance use by peers, and parental discipline existed over time. The variance of the intercept and slope is also statistically significant ($p < .05$), indicating individual variation around the mean at the initial level of the assessment (Year 4) and mean rate of change over time (Year 4 through Year 7). Finally, there was a significant ($p < .05$) estimate for the correlation between the intercept and slope factors, indicating adolescents who reported higher initial levels in all three measures tended to report smaller rates of increase in these measures over time.

TABLE 7.1
Univariate Descriptive Statistics for All Measured Variables

	Adolescent Substance Use				Peer Substance Use				Parental Discipline			
	T1	T2	T3	T4	T1	T2	T3	T4	T1	T2	T3	T4
Mean	7.232	7.607	8.000	8.527	2.540	2.636	2.830	3.090	3.483	3.502	3.670	3.868
Variance	8.149	8.386	9.034	9.394	2.746	2.998	2.540	2.250	1.725	1.797	1.785	1.644
Skewness	.556	.429	.466	.195	-.071	-.041	-.146	-.279	-.376	-.436	-.597	-.858
Kurtosis	.375	-.528	-.461	-.515	-1.245	-1.366	-1.217	-1.040	-1.066	-1.066	-.926	-.467
N	328	328	328	328	328	328	328	328	328	328	328	328

TABLE 7.2
Mode Fit Statistics and Parameter Estimates

	Adolescent Substance Use	Peer Substance Use	Parental Discipline
Overall model fit	χ^2 (5) = 1.264	χ^2 (5) = 9.657	χ^2 (5) = 18.767
	p = .939	p = .086	p = .002
	RMSEA = .00	RMSEA = .057	RMSEA = .094
	NNFI = 1.006	NNFI = .990	NNFI = .958
	CFI = 1.00	CFI = .992	CFI =.965
Mean (intercept)	7.214	2.501	3.428
Variance (intercept)	7.078	2.039	1.011
Mean (slope)	.424	.186	.134
Variance (slope)	.561	.124	.056
Correlation between intercept and slope	−.490	−.496	−.346

Note. All parameter estimates are significantly significant at .05 level.

Interaction Analyses: Step 2 Analyses

Given significant mean level changes and variability in intra-individual differences in the developmental growth trajectories of all three latent variables, we now turn our attention to determining whether longitudinal change in peer substance use interacts with the longitudinal change in parental discipline to jointly influence adolescent developmental trajectories in substance use over the 4-year measurement period. To model this interaction, we regressed the two latent growth factors (intercept, slope) of adolescent substance use on the latent growth variable predictors of peer substance use and parental discipline as well as the latent product of the two slope factors.

The model shown in Fig. 7.2 resulted in a chi-square of χ^2(89, N=328)=457.926, $p < .001$, RMSEA=.093, NNFI=.905, and CFI=.911, indicating a marginal fit of the model to the observed data. Although the overall fit is somewhat problematic, it is good enough to use this model to illustrate how the procedure is applied for two reasons: (a) this model was specified *a priori*, and (b) examination of the solution indicated the absence of out-of-bounds parameter estimates. Appendix B presents an abbreviated LISREL output, including LISREL maximum likelihood estimates of interest (shown in the GAMMA matrix).

Although not particularly interesting, for completeness, we first focus briefly on the estimates of the regression parameters linking the exogenous latent intercept factors to the intercept of the endogenous latent variable. These estimates capture the predictability of individual differences in the initial level of adolescent substance use as a function of the initial level of exogenous latent variables in the prediction equation (see Eq. [3]). Therefore, they provide the cross-sectional information with regard to the relationship between the independent variables and the dependent variable. The maximum likelihood estimates for the effects of ξ_1 (initial level of peer substance use) and ξ_3 (initial level of parental discipline) on η_1 (initial level of adolescent substance use) and their corresponding test statistics are as follows:

$$\eta_1 = 6.745 + .992(\xi_1) + (-1.098)(\xi_3)$$

$$(.249) \qquad\qquad (.260)$$

$$3.982 \qquad\qquad -4.217$$

Results indicate that both peer substance use and parental discipline were significantly associated with initial level of adolescent substance use ($p<.05$). The estimates indicate that peer substance use at Year 4 (initial assessment) was related to adolescent initial substance use. The analysis also indicates that greater parental discipline tended to decrease the likelihood of adolescents' substance use in the earlier years.

More interesting, however, are the estimates of the regression parameters linking the slope predictors involving the latent product interaction term to the outcome slope factor – adolescent substance use (see Eq. [4]). The maximum likelihood estimates for the ξs, including the covariate influence of initial levels and the effect of the interaction term ($\xi_2\xi_4$) on the growth factor (η_2) of adolescent substance use and their corresponding test statistics are as follows:

$$\eta_2 = .355 + .627(\xi_1) + .518(\xi_2) + .632(\xi_3) + (-.233)(\xi_4) + (-.147)(\xi_2\xi_4)$$

$$(.203) \quad\; (.083) \quad\; (.186) \qquad (.099) \qquad\quad (.063)$$

$$3.091 \quad\; 6.266 \quad\; 3.402 \qquad -2.377 \qquad -2.333$$

The interaction effect ($\gamma_{25} = -.147$) in the prior regression equation was statistically significant, as shown by the z value of -2.333 ($p< .05$). This significance term indicates an interaction between the two dynamic latent growth predictor variables (the slopes of ξ_2 and ξ_4), suggesting a joint influence of longitudinal changes in peer substance use and parental discipline on longitudinal changes in adolescent substance use. The estimated latent growth variable squared multiple correlation was .726 for the intercept factor and .663 for the slope factor, respectively, indicating that the latent growth predictor variables in the equation accounted for 73% of the variance in the initial level of adolescent substance use (η_1) and, more important, 66% in the rate of change over time (η_2).

Post Hoc Interaction Analyses

To better understand the interaction, it is helpful to further probe the effect following the conventional post hoc analyses similar to that of ANOVA interactions (see Aiken & West, 1991; Jaccard & Wan, 1996; Jaccard, Turrisi, & Wan, 1990).

Specifically, we examined whether the relationship between the longitudinal change in peer substance use and the longitudinal change in adolescent substance use varied as a function of different rates of change in parental discipline, the moderator variable, over time. First, we examined the slope of adolescent substance use on peer substance use at high and low slope (growth trajectory) values of parental discipline. Specifically, we used high (defined as one standard deviation above the mean) and low (defined as one standard deviation below the mean) slope values of parental discipline. The slope, b, at a given high or low value of parental discipline is given by

$$b \text{ at } \quad S_{\xi 4} = b_1 + b_3 S_{\xi 4}, \tag{12}$$

where S_{ξ_4} is a specific slope value of ξ_4. From the PHI matrix in the LISREL output, the variance of the latent slope factor of the parental discipline variable is 1.714, and the square root of this is the estimated latent variable standard deviation (1.309), resulting in a low value of -1.309 (i.e., one estimated standard deviation below its mean) and a high value of 1.309 (i.e., one estimated standard deviation above its mean). Substituting these low and high values into the prior b slope equation, we obtained estimated values of 2.323 for low and 1.939 for high of parental discipline. The analyses indicate a stronger longitudinal effect of peers on adolescent substance use development when the longitudinal change in parental discipline trajectories is less pronounced (i.e., smaller rates of positive change).

The significant interaction between parental discipline and substance using peers also indicates that the impact of either one on adolescent substance use is conditional on the level of the other. Therefore, we extended the previous post hoc analyses and selected high and low values of both predictors. This analysis is summarized in Table 7.3. Estimated values are plotted in Fig. 7.3. The analysis showed an ordinal interaction (Lubin, 1961), with the largest difference between high and low parental discipline found at high peer substance use. The result suggests a stronger relationship between the rates of change in peer substance use and adolescent substance use when the positive rate of change in parental discipline is less pronounced.

Taken together, the interaction analyses indicate that the relationship between longitudinal change in peer substance use and longitudinal change in adolescent substance use, becomes weakened over time as parents' rate of change in discipline

TABLE 7.3
Interpreting the Interaction Term

Condition in ξ_2 and ξ_4	Values in ξ_2 and ξ_4	Expected Change
High in peers and high in parents	1.059, 1.309	1.653
High in peers and low in parents	1.059, -1.309	2.670
Low in peers and high in parents	-1.059, 1.309	.964
Low in peers and low in parents	-1.059, -1.309	1.116

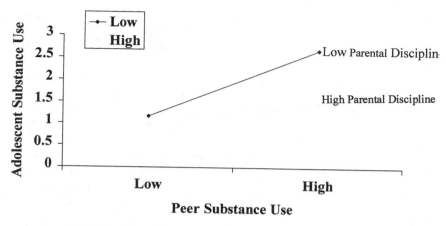

FIG. 7.3.   Graphic representation of interaction analysis.

regarding their child's substance use increases. Thus, the analysis appears to suggest that, to offset the strong impact of peers in the development of adolescent substance use, parents must increase their discipline efforts during adolescence.

DISCUSSION

In the fields of developmental research, a variety of interactive (moderator) models can be described. Interaction effects are common in the study of adolescent problem behavior development. For example, stressors such as maternal depression, daily hassles, separating and unemployment or health problems may serve to disrupt parental attention to the child's behavior. This could, in turn, lead to difficulties in the parents' ability to monitor their child effectively (Wahler & Dumas, 1989). In the same vein, parents' use of substances could disrupt their monitoring practices (Dishion, Reid, & Patterson, 1988; Loeber, Farrington, Stouthamer-Loeber, & Van Kammen, 1998). Therefore, it is essential that we have suitable methods for incorporating these factors into our structural models that allow testing of functional complexities in relationships.

Using standard SEM-based procedures (i.e., Jöreskog & Yang, 1996), this chapter presented an extension of latent growth curve models that includes interactions between latent growth (slope) parameters. Model specifications for these interaction effects were discussed within the LISREL framework (Jöreskog & Sörbom, 1993). An illustrative example in the field of adolescent substance use followed. The results of the analyses show that it is possible to statistically capture interaction effects in the context of latent growth modeling.

Many methodologists have noted the complexities of latent variable interaction analysis (see Jaccard & Wan, 1996; Schumacker & Marcoulides, 1998). We refer the reader to the work by Jöreskog (1998) for reviews of various SEM-based procedures and Jaccard and Wan (1996) for their excellent discussion on practical issues in designing studies for SEM-based analyses of interaction effects. Various contributing chapters in the SEM interaction book edited by Schumacker and Marcoulides (1998) are also excellent sources for recent updates and issues in analyzing interaction and nonlinear effects in SEM. Here we highlight a few issues relevant to the application of the method presented in this chapter.

First, it is important to focus on interpretation of the interaction effect in the model because it involves simultaneous, dynamic change scores of the latent continuous predictors. In multiple regression involving interactions, values of change in η_2 are predicted by a regression coefficient (slope), which gives the increase in Y resulting from a one unit increase in XZ. In the context of latent growth modeling, this would indicate change in η_2 that is predicted by simultaneous and joint change in ξ_2 and ξ_4. So the interaction in this context represents a joint and concurrent change between two latent growth shape factors, ξ_2 and ξ_4. In the example used in this chapter, this would mean that when there are concurrent changes in parental discipline practices (positively increasing) and substance use peers (less steep but still positively increasing), their joint effect is enhanced. That is, steeper and positively increasing parental discipline over time is likely to slow down the impact of change in peer influence on the developmental trajectories of adolescent substance use. It is important to note that the negative interaction effect between the two slope factors in no way indicates decreases in the peer influence over time. Instead, this implies that higher rates of change in parental discipline along with smaller rates of positive change in peers is associated with low growth rates in adolescent substance use.

Second, we have not incorporated an interaction term in modeling the impact of initial levels of exogenous latent variables on either the initial levels or the rates of change of the endogenous variable because this would make the model more complex and more difficult to estimate. Therefore, considering model parsimony is a desirable characteristic of any interaction analysis. It is generally recommended that analyses be limited to tests of specific hypotheses under investigation (Rigdon, Schumacker, & Wothke, 1998). However, researchers may choose to use a two-step approach by modeling the static influence of the exogenous predictors on the growth factor of the endogenous variable and then conducting a longitudinal model such as the one presented in this chapter. This two-step approach is shown in the work by Li et al. (2000).

Third, we presented a common model of interest in latent growth modeling: The intercept-slope model (or level-shape model). This model is admittedly complex with regard to its specification because it involves latent intercepts of the growth parameters that may complicate model estimation as well as interpretation. A much simpler version of this model is a shape-only model in which the rate of growth is defined by a single shape factor (see Meredith & Tisak, 1990).

However, the highly restrictive set of model expectations (i.e., zero mean and zero variance in the intercept) often makes justification of these assumptions unlikely in practice. Thus, the choice between the level-shape and shape-only models must be made based on substantive theory and empirical data. If it is reasonable to assume that the intercept factor can be eliminated or if it is strictly proportional to the slope, the predictive model with the fewer parameters (in this case, the shape model) represents the preferred model. An example of this model is given by Duncan et al. (1999).

Fourth, a well-known problem in latent interaction analysis is that of the joint distribution of the observed variables. We need to point out that this problem also applies to growth curve models involving interaction effects where products of indicator variables are not normally distributed. For this reason, use of maximum likelihood estimation in the analysis of interaction in latent variables has been cautioned (see Jöreskog, 1998). Although Jöreskog and Yang (1996) proposed alternative estimation procedures, they are not without cost and may not be suitable for longitudinal studies, which often have small or medium sample sizes. Other techniques such as Bollen's (1995) two-stage least squares procedure and Arminger and Muthén's (1998) Bayesian approach, may provide future hope for longitudinal models.

Finally, although it is a useful tool for studying nonlinear dynamic relations, the extension of Jöreskog and Yang's (1996) procedure to LGMs requires careful model parameterization. Because of the procedure's complexity, specification of the nonlinear constraints is a tedious and error-prone task. This is a common concern that has been echoed by a number of researchers (Jaccard & Wan, 1996; Jöreskog & Yang, 1996; Laplante, Sabourin, Cournoyer, & Wright, 1998; Li et al., 1998; Neale, 1998; Ping, 1998). As such, "utmost care must be taken to specify the constraints in the model correctly" (Jöreskog & Yang, 1996, p. 85). One solution to this is to simplify the estimating procedure. For example, Jöreskog, Sörbom, du Toit, and du Toit (1999) have shown a simple way of estimating nonlinear models by means of latent variable scores. This method involves estimating a measurement model using observed variables and generating the latent variable scores. In a follow-up step, the structural model of interest is estimated using these latent variable scores as observed variables. As illustrated by Jöreskog et al. (1999) and Yang-Jonsson (1998), the method may represent a simpler way to model interaction compared with the one proposed by Jöreskog and Yang (1996).

In summary, the modeling method illustrated in this chapter shows that interaction analyses with latent variables can be extended to analyses of more complex, dynamic models involving interactive relationships between growth (slope) parameters. Although the method described has potential, much remains to be done on its applicability. Applications of modeling interactions among change scores (growth factors) are likely to expand theoretical models, in which structural relationships among a set of variables have conventionally been lim-

ited to either direct or indirect effects. These analytic tools will also allow
researchers to more vigorously test hypotheses concerning the effects of interactions between dynamic latent attributes on the development of behavioral
outcomes of interest.

APPENDIX A

The following LISREL script is used for estimating the interaction presented
in this chapter. The raw data file specified (lgmint.dat) can be obtained on our
website.

```
Interaction: an intercept-slope model using LISREL 8
DATA NI=16 NO=328
RAW FILE=lgmint.dat
LABEL
y1 y2 y3 y4 x1 x2 x3 x4 z1 z2 z3 z4 int1 int2 int3 int4
SELECT
1 2 3 4 9 10 11 12 5 6 7 8 14 15 16/
MODEL NY=4 NX=11 NE=2 NK=5 TD=sy TE=di PS=sy GA=fu KA=fr
   TX=fu TY=fu
LK
Int_Peer Slp_Peer Int_Par Slp_Par Pe_by_pa
LE
Intcept Slope
FIX ly(1,1) ly(2,1) ly(3,1) ly(4,1)
VALUE 1 ly(1,1) ly(2,1) ly(3,1) ly(4,1)
FIX ly(1,2) ly(2,2) ly(3,2) ly(4,2)
VALUE 0 ly(1,2)
VALUE 1 ly(2,2)
VALUE 2 ly(3,2)
VALUE 3 ly(4,2)
FIX lx(1,1) lx(2,1) lx(3,1) lx(4,1)
VALUE 1 lx(1,1) lx(2,1) lx(3,1) lx(4,1)
FIX lx(1,2) lx(2,2) lx(3,2) lx(4,2)
VALUE 0 lx(1,2)
VALUE 1 lx(2,2)
FREE lx(3,2)
FREE lx(4,2)
START .60 lx(3,2) lx(4,2)
FIX lx(5,3) lx(6,3) lx(7,3) lx(8,3)
VALUE 1 lx(5,3) lx(6,3) lx(7,3) lx(8,3)
```

```
FIX lx(5,4) lx(6,4) lx(7,4) lx(8,4)
VALUE 0 lx(5,4)
VALUE 1 lx(6,4)
FREE lx(7,4)
FREE lx(8,4)
START .3 lx(7,4) lx(8,4)
PA PH
1
1 1
1 1 1
1 1 1 1
0 0 0 0 1
PA GA
1 0 1 0 0
1 1 1 1 1
FIX lx(9,5)
VALUE 1 lx(9,5)
CO lx(10,5)=lx(3,2)*lx(7,4)
CO lx(11,5)=lx(4,2)*lx(8,4)
CO lx(9,2)=tx(6)
CO lx(9,4)=tx(2)
CO lx(10,2)=tx(7)*lx(3,2)
CO lx(10,4)=tx(3)*lx(7,4)
CO lx(11,2)=tx(8)*lx(4,2)
CO lx(11,4)=tx(4)*lx(8,4)
PA AL
1 1
START 3.5 al 1
START 1.3 al 2
PA TX
1 1 1 1 1 1 1 1 1 1 1
CO tx(9)=tx(2)*tx(6)
CO tx(10)=tx(3)*tx(7)
CO tx(11)=tx(4)*tx(7)
CO ph(5,5)=ph(2,2)*ph(4,4)+ph(4,2)**2
CO td(9,9)=tx(2)**2*td(6,6)+tx(6)**2*td(2,2)+ph(2,2)*td(6,6)+c
ph(4,4)*td(2,2)+td(2,2)*td(6,6)
CO td(10,10)=tx(3)**2*td(7,7)+tx(7)**2*td(3,3)+lx(3,2)**2*ph(2,2)*td(7,7)+c
lx(7,4)**2*ph(4,4)*td(3,3)+td(3,3)*td(7,7)
CO td(11,11)=tx(4)**2*td(8,8)+tx(8)**2*td(4,4)+lx(4,2)**2*ph(2,2)*td(8,8) + c
lx(8,4)**2*ph(4,4)*td(4,4)+td(4,4)*td(8,8)
CO td(9,2)=tx(6)*td(2,2)
CO td(9,6)=tx(2)*td(6,6)
```

CO td(10,3)=tx(7)*td(3,3)
CO td(10,7)=tx(3)*td(7,7)
CO td(11,4)=tx(8)*td(4,4)
CO td(11,8)=tx(4)*td(8,8)
PA KA
0 0 0 0 1
CO ph(5,5)=ph(2,2)*ph(4,4)+ ph(4,2)**2
CO ka(5)=ph(4,2)
START .5 td(1,1)–td(4,4)
START 1 td(5,5)–td(8,8)
START 1.8 te(1,1)
START .9 te(2,2)–te(3,3)
START 1 ty 1–ty 4
START 2.0 tx 1–tx 4
START 2.0 tx 5–tx 8
START 6.0 tx 9–tx 11
START .1 ga 1 1
START .9 ga 2 5
START .02 phi(4,4) phi(1,1) phi(2,2) phi(5,5)
START .01 phi(3,3)
START 1.6 ps(1,1)
START 1.5 ps(2,2)
FREE ps(2,1)
START .01 ps(2,1)
OUT SC AD=OFF NS ND=4 EP=.00001

APPENDIX B

The following presents abbreviated LISREL output for the interaction analysis.

LISREL ESTIMATES (MAXIMUM LIKELIHOOD)
GAMMA

	Int_Peer	Slp_Peer	Int_Par	Slp_Par	Pe_by_pa
Intercept	0.9921	—	−1.0983	—	—
	(0.2491)		(0.2604)		
	3.9823		−4.2169		
Slope	0.6273	0.5176	0.6317	−0.2328	−0.1468
	(0.2030)	(0.0826)	(0.1857)	(0.0996)	(0.0629)
	3.0910	6.2663	3.4019	−2.3368	−2.3331

PHI

	Int_Peer	Slp_Peer	Int_Par	Slp_Par	Pe_by_pa
Int_Peer	1.5357				
	(0.1497)				
	10.2557				
Slp_Peer	−0.6141	1.1216			
	(0.0904)	(0.1301)			
	−6.7914	8.6214			
Int_Par	−1.3719	0.5868	1.1270		
	(0.1392)	(0.0908)	(0.1398)		
	−9.8531	6.4601	8.0601		
Slp_Par	1.3953	−1.1384	−0.7528	1.7144	
	(0.1281)	(0.0775)	(0.1209)	(0.1603)	
	10.8947	−14.6865	−6.2292	10.6938	
Pe_by_pa	—	—	—	—	3.2188
					(0.3521)
					9.1429

PSI

	Intercept	Slope
Intercept	2.2119	
	(0.4862)	
	4.5497	
Slope	−0.3208	0.2551
	(0.1793)	(0.0960)
	−1.7890	2.6586

SQUARED MULTIPLE CORRELATIONS FOR STRUCTURAL EQUATIONS

Intercept	Slope
0.7260	0.6633

SQUARED MULTIPLE CORRELATIONS FOR Y-VARIABLES

y1	y2	y3	y4
0.8798	0.7351	0.6757	0.7837

SQUARED MULTIPLE CORRELATIONS FOR X-VARIABLES

z1	z2	z3	z4	x1	x2
0.5436	0.5544	0.6535	0.6375	0.4196	0.6477

SQUARED MULTIPLE CORRELATIONS FOR X-VARIABLES

x3	x4	int2	int3	int4
0.6703	0.5942	0.2702	0.3470	0.3053

ALPHA

Intercept	Slope
6.7448	0.3545
(0.1512)	(0.0904)
44.6211	3.9228

ACKNOWLEDGEMENT

Preparation of this article was supported in part by Grants No. DA 09548 and DA 09306 from the National Institute on Drug Abuse, and by Grant No. AA12385 from the National Institute on Alcohol Abuse and Alcoholism.

REFERENCES

Aiken, L. S., & West, S. G. (1991). *Multiple regression: Testing and interpreting interactions.* Newbury Park, CA: Sage.

Arminger, G., & Muthén, B. O. (1998). A Bayesian approach to nonlinear latent variable models using the Gibbs sampler and the Metropolis-Hastings Algorithm. *Psychometrika, 63,* 271–300.

Ary, D., Duncan, T. E., Duncan, S. C., & Hops, H. (1999). Adolescent problem behavior: The influence of parents and peers. *Behavior Research and Therapy, 37,* 217–230.

Bentler, P. (1990). Comparative fit indexes in structural models. *Psychological Bulletin, 107,* 238–246.

Bollen, K. A. (1995). Structural equation models that are nonlinear in latent variable: A least squares estimator. In P. M. Marsden (Ed.), *Sociological methodology* (pp. 223–251). Cambridge, MA: Blackwell.

Brooks, J. S., Brook, D. W., Gordon, A. S., Whiteman, M., & Cohen, P. (1990). The psychosocial ecology of adolescent drug use: A family interactional approach. *Genetic, Social and General Psychology Monographs,* 116.

Busemeyer, J. R., & Jones, L. E. (1983). Analysis of Multiplicative combination rules when the causal variables are measured with error. *Psychological Bulletine, 93,* 549–562.

Collins, L., & Horn, J. L. (1991). *Best methods for the analysis of change.* Washington, DC: American Psychological Association.

Collius, L., & Sayer, A. (in press). *New methods for the analysis of change,* Washington DC: American Psychological Association.

Curran, P. J., Stice, E., & Chassin, L. (1997). The relation between adolescent alcohol use and peer alcohol use: A longitudinal random coefficient model. *Journal of Consulting and Clinical psychology, 65,* 130–140.

Dishion, T. J., Capaldi, D., Spracklen, K. M., & Li, F. (1995). Peer ecology of male adolescent drug use. *Development and Psychopathology, 7,* 803–824.

Dishion, T. J., & Loeber, R. (1985). Male adolescent marijuana and alcohol use: The role of parents and peers revisited. *American Journal of Drug and Alcohol Abuse, 11*, 11–25.

Dishion, T. J., Reid, J. B., & Patterson, G. R. (1988). Empirical guidelines for a family intervention for adolescent drug use. *Journal of Chemical Dependency Treatment, 1*, 189–222.

Duncan, T. E., Duncan, S. C., & Hops, H. (1994). The effects of family cohesiveness and peer encouragement on the development of adolescent alcohol use: A cohort-sequential approach to the analysis of longitudinal data. *Journal of Studies on Alcohol, 55*, 588–599.

Duncan, T. E., Duncan, S. C., Strycker, A. L., Li, F., & Alpert, A. (1999). *An introduction to latent variable growth curve modeling: Concepts, Issues, and Applications.* Mahwah, NJ: Lawrence Erlbaum Associates.

Hops, H., Tildesley, E., Lichtenstein, E., Ary, D., & Sherman, L. (1990). Parent–adolescent problem-solving interactions and drug use. *American Journal of Drug and Alcohol Abuse, 16*, 239–258.

Hu, L., & Bentler, P. M. (1995). Evaluating model fit. In R. H. Hoyle (Ed.), *Structural equation modeling: Issues and applications* (pp. 76–99). Thousand Oaks, CA: Sage.

Jaccard, J., Turrisi, R., & Wan, C. K. (1990). *Interaction effects in multiple regression.* Newbury Park, CA: Sage.

Jaccard, J., & Wan, C. K. (1995). Measurement error in the analysis of interaction effects between continuous predictors using multiple regression: Multiple indicator and structural equation modeling. *Psychological Bulletin, 117*, 348–357.

Jaccard, J., & Wan, C. K. (1996). *LISREL approaches to interaction effects in multiple regression.* Thousand Oaks, CA: Sage.

Jöreskog, K. G. (1998). Interaction and nonlinear modeling: Issues and approaches. In R. E. Schumacker & G. A. Marcoulides (Eds.), *Interaction and nonlinear effects in structural equation modeling* (pp. 239–250). Mahwah, NJ: Lawrence Erlbaum Associates.

Jöreskog, K. G., & Sörbom, D. (1993). *LISREL8: Structural equation modeling with the SIMPLIS command language.* Chicago, IL: Scientific Software International.

Jöreskog, K. G., Sörbom, D., du Toit, S., & du Toit, M. (1999). *LISREL 8: New statistical features.* Chicago, IL: Scientific Software International.

Jöreskog, K. G., & Yang, F. (1996). Non-linear structural equation models: The Kenny–Judd model with interaction effects. In G. A. Marcoulides & R. E. Schumacker (Eds.), *Advanced structural equation modeling: Issues and techniques* (pp. 57–88). Mahwah, NJ: Lawrence Erlbaum Associates.

Kenny, D., & Judd, C. M. (1984). Estimating the nonlinear and interaction effects of latent variables. *Psychological Bulletin, 96*, 201–210.

LaPlante, B., Sabourin, S., Cournoyer, L.-G., & Wright, J. (1998). Estimating nonlinear effects using a structured means intercept approach. In R. E. Schumacker & G. A. Marcoulides (Eds.), *Interaction and nonlinear effects in structural equation modeling* (pp. 183–202). Mahwah, NJ: Lawrence Erlbaum Associates.

Li, F., Duncan, T. E., & Acock, A. (2000). Modeling interaction effects in latent growth curve models. *Structural Equation Modeling, 7*, 497–533.

Li, F., Harmer, P., Duncan, T. E., Duncan, S. C., Acock, A., & Boles, S. (1998). Approaches to testing interaction effects using structural equation modeling methodology. *Multivariate Behavioral Research, 33*, 1–39.

Loeber, R., Farrington, D. P., Stouthamer-Loeber, M., & Van Kammen, W. B. (1998). *Antisocial behavior and mental health problems: Explanatory factors in childhood and adolescence.* Mahwah, NJ: Lawrence Erlbaum Associates.

Lubin, A. (1961). The interpretation of significant interaction. *Educational and Psychological Measurement, 21*, 807–817.

McArdle, J. J. (1988). Dynamic but structural equation modeling of repeated measures data. In R. B. Cattel & J. Nesselroade (Eds.), *Handbook of multivariate experimental psychology* (second ed., pp. 561–614). New York: Plenum.

McArdle, J. J., & Hamagami, F. (in press). Linear dynamic analyses with incomplete longitudinal data using raw data structural equation modeling techniques. In L. Collins, & A. Sayer (Eds.), *New methods for the analysis for change*. Washington DC: American Psychological Association.

Meredith, W., & Tisak, J. (1990). Latent curve analysis. *Psychometrika, 55*, 107–122.

Muthén, B. O. (1991). Analysis of longitudinal data using latent variable models with varying parameters. In L. M. Collins & J. L. Horn (Eds.), *Best methods for the analysis of change: Recent advances, unanswered questions, future directions* (pp. 1–17). Washington, DC: American Psychological Association.

Muthén, B. O. (1997). Latent variable modeling of longitudinal and multilevel data. In A. Raftery (Ed.), *Sociological methodology* (pp. 453–480). Boston: Blackwell.

Muthén, B., & Curran, P. J. (1997). General growth modeling of individual differences in experimental designs: A latent variable framework for analysis and power estimation. *Psychological Methods, 2*, 371–402.

Neale, M. C. (1998). Modeling interaction and nonlinear effects with Mx: A general approach. In R. E. Schumacker & G. A. Marcoulides (Eds.), *Interaction and nonlinear effects in structural equation modeling* (pp. 43–62). Mahwah, NJ: Lawrence Erlbaum Associates.

Patterson, G. R. (1982). *Coercive family process*. Eugene, OR: Castalia.

Patterson, G. R., Reid, J. B., & Dishion, T. J. (1992). *Antisocial boys: A social interactional approach* (Vol. 4). Eugene, OR: Castalia.

Ping, R. A., Jr. (1995). A parsimonious estimating technique for interaction and quadratic latent variables. *The Journal of Marketing Research, 32*, 336–347.

Ping, R. A., Jr. (1996). Latent variable interaction and quadratic effect estimation: A two-step technique using structural equation analysis. *Psychological Bulletin, 119*, 166–175.

Ping, R. A., Jr. (1998). EQS and LISREL examples using survey data. In R. E. Schumacker & G. A. Marcoulides (Eds.), *Interaction and nonlinear effects in structural equation modeling* (pp. 63–100). Mahwah, NJ: Lawrence Erlbaum Associates.

Raykov, T. (1996). Plasticity in fluid intelligence of older adults: An individual latent growth curve modeling application. *Structural Equation Modeling, 3*, 248–265.

Rigdon, E. E., Schumacker, R. E., & Wothke, W. (1998). A comparative review of interaction and nonlinear modeling. In R. E. Schumacker & G. A. Marcoulides (Eds.), *Interaction and nonlinear effects in structural equation modeling* (pp. 1–16). Mahwah, NJ: Lawrence Erlbaum Associates.

Schumacker, R. E., & Marcoulides, G. (1998). *Interaction and nonlinear effects in structural equation modeling*. Mahwah, NJ: Lawrence Erlbaum Associates.

Steiger, J. H., & Lind, J. C. (1980, May). *Statistically based tests for the number of common factors*. Paper presented at the annual spring meeting of the Psychometric Society, Iowa City, IA.

Stoolmiller, M. (1995). Using latent growth curve models to study developmental processes. In J. M. Gottman (Ed.), *The analysis of change* (pp. 103–138). Hillsdale, NJ: Lawrence Erlbaum Associates.

Stoolmiller, M., Duncan, T. E., Bank, L., & Patterson, G. R. (1993). Some problems and solutions in the study of change: Significant patterns in client resistance. *Journal of Consulting and Clinical Psychology, 61*, 920–928.

Tucker, L. R., & Lewis, C. (1973). A reliability coefficient for maximum likelihood factor analysis. *Psychometrika, 38*, 1–10.

Wahler, R. G., & Dumas, J. E. (1989). Attentional problems in dysfunctional mother–child interactions: An interbehavioral model. *Psychological Bulletin, 105*, 116–130.

Walker, A. J., Acock, A. C., Bowman, S. R., & Li, F. (1996). Amount of care given and caregiving satisfaction: A latent growth curve analysis. *Journal of Gerontology: Psychological Sciences, 51B*, 130–142.

Willett, J. B., & Sayer, A. G. (1994). Using covariance structure analysis to detect correlates and predictors of individual change over time. *Psychological Bulletin, 116*, 363–381.

Willett, J. B., & Sayer, A. G. (1996). Cross-domain analyses of change over time: Combining growth modeling and covariance structure analysis. In G. A. Marcoulides & R. E. Schumacker (Eds.), *Advanced structural equation modeling: Issues and techniques* (pp. 125–157). Mahwah, NJ: Lawrence Erlbaum Associates.

Yang-Jonsson, F. (1997). *Non-linear structural equation models: Simulation studies of the Kenny-Judd model.* Published doctoral dissertation, Uppsala University.

Yang-Jonsson, F. (1998). Interaction modeling: A step-by-step example. In R. E. Schumacker & G. A. Marcoulides (Eds.), *Interaction and nonlinear effects in structural equation modeling* (pp. 17–42). Mahwah, NJ: Lawrence Erlbaum Associates.

8

Advanced Studies
of Individual Differences
Linear Dynamic Models for
Longitudinal Data Analysis

Fumiaki Hamagami
John J. McArdle
University of Virginia

In developmental studies, we often sample data from numerous subjects on numerous occasions. We hypothesize for a model of certain attributes and attempt to test its validity empirically (Diggle, Liang, & Zeger, 1994; Kessler & Greenberg, 1981; Lindsey, 1993). In fitting and evaluating these models, we pay attention to several issues such as serial dependency (Jones, 1991; Jones & Ackerson, 1990; Jones & Boadi-Boateng, 1991; Nunez-Anton & Woodworth, 1994; Rosner & Nunoz, 1988), deterministic models (Tuma & Hannan, 1984), and individual variations in developmental processes (Baltes & Nesselroade, 1973; Nesselroade & Baltes, 1979; Nesselroade, 1991; Nesselroade & Boker, 1994; Wohlwill, 1973). Dynamical system models deal with serial autodependency and cross-variable dependency among variables across time (Brown, 1988; Coleman, 1964; Huckfeldt, Kohfeld, & Likens, 1982; Newell & Molenaar, 1998; Sheinerman, 1996; Tuma & Hannan, 1984; Vallicher & Nowak, 1994). However, most dynamic system models do not deal effectively with individual variations in a developmental process (Allison, 1990; Arminger, 1986; Brown, 1988, 1995; Coleman, 1964, 1968; cf. Nesselroade & Boker, 1994; Tuma & Hannan, 1984).

There are many common problems in longitudinal data collection that need to be dealt with in subsequent analyses. In a typical longitudinal study, for example, we invariably encounter missing observations due to subject refusal in follow-up, death, inability to locate subjects, schedule conflicts, unavoidable illness, and so forth. It is advisable to investigate how missing observations might influence the results of data analyses. This investigation helps impinge on our ability to draw inferences (see Little & Rubin, 1987; Schafer, 1997). Monte Carlo simulations enable us to draw some reasonable conclusions concerning how missing patterns can affect dynamic structures of some system. These Monte Carlo simulations need to be likened to our real situation as close as possible (McArdle & Hamagami, 1991, 1992).

There are also many statistical issues in longitudinal data analyses. For example, the simple and practical use of a "change score as a dependent variable" has been popular in much prior research (e.g., Burr & Nesselroade, 1990; Collins & Horn, 1991; Rogosa, Brandt, & Zimowski, 1982). Previous critiques of simple change score models have focused on: (a) initial value dependencies, (b) unreliability of difference score measurements, and (c) regression to the mean (Cronbach & Furby, 1970; Foerster, 1995; Kessler, 1977; Raykov, 1999). However, practical use of change scores as a dependent variable is also defended (Allison, 1990) as long as level and slope dependencies are taken into account in modeling (Kessler, 1977). The model distinguishes between a true change score and raw change score to remove measurement errors (Cronbach & Furby, 1970; Raykov, 1993).

Here we focus on some recently developed linear discrete dynamic system models (McArdle & Hamagami, 1999). The analyses presented here are designed to overcome some of these problems. These dynamic models combine three important aspects: (a) linear dynamic processes, (b) the methodology of structural equation models to account for data collected by sparse repeated measures due to data attrition or data-collection design (McArdle, 1994; McArdle & Hamagami, 1992; McArdle & Woodcock, 1997), and (c) individual variations about dynamic processes. The dynamic models presented here are also compared with a new multilevel regression model with change scores as a dependent variable. We also demonstrate why the traditional change score model is unable to capture dynamic characteristics when missing data problems are introduced.

To provide a practical overview of these models, we use Monte Carlo simulation methods (Bratley, Fox, & Schrage, 1987; Gamerman, 1998; Gilbert & Troitzsch, 1999; Keen & Spain, 1994; Law & Kelton, 1999; Mooney, 1997; Ross, 1996; Rubinstein, 1981; Zeigler, Kim, & Praehofer, 2000). Prior simulation models related to dynamic system are discussed elsewhere (Cacciabue, 1998; Pooch & Wall, 1998; van den Bosch & van der Klauw, 1994). In the first part of these analyses, we simulate a longitudinal data set that is balanced (i.e., all subjects are possibly measured on all occasions), and we compare the recovery of a structural dynamic model and the traditional regression model. In the second set of analyses, we degrade this balanced data in one way or another so that the observations are formed as unbalanced and evaluate the same dynamic system parameter estimates. Finally, we summarize results of the balanced data and the unbalanced data and conclude with some cautionary notes about dynamic modeling.

METHODS

Dynamic System Approaches

Dynamic processes generally are represented by one or more differential equations or difference equations simultaneously (Brown & Rothery, 1993; Goldberg, 1986; Sheinerman, 1996). A differential equation describes a process of change phenomenon. A dependent variable in a differential equation is a *rate of change*, whereas a predictor can be a constant or exogenous variables that have some functional relationship with how the outcome variable changes.

A model of univariate growth curve analysis (e.g., Anderson, 1993; McArdle & Epstein, 1987; Meredith & Tisak, 1990; Raykov, 1993; Rogosa, Brandt, & Zimowski, 1982) is far easier than multivariate dynamic models due to the fact that, with simultaneous parallel time series, we need to introduce a concept of *coupling* among target variables over time. Coupling in dynamic systems refers to a condition that a rate of change of one variable is perturbed by a state of another variable. This concept needs to be discerned from the cross-lagged effect in time series models where the previous state variable predicts the present state (not rate of change).

In contrast, when we have a system of repeated measures, coupling at each successive time is cumulatively compounded, propagated, or contaminated by coupling effects of all the previous time points (for details, see McArdle & Hamagami, 1999). It is well known that cross-sectional data collections are inadequate in analyzing dynamic characteristics of repeated measures (Bell, 1953; Collins & Horn, 1991; Wohlwill, 1973). To these classical statements we add the fact that most cross-sectional analyses ignore the dynamic propagations of preceding coupling effects from one variable to another (see Coleman, 1968; Tuma & Hannan, 1984).

In scientific terms, any dynamic system is based on a set of rates of change or difference scores as dependent variables (Alligood, Sauer, & Yorke, 1996; Cambel, 1993). However, in general, the complexity of the underlying system creates a limit on the number of data points needed for an accurate dynamic analysis. For instance, if we were interested in an interrelationship between two variables X and Y and we assume that the dynamic system is linear in a mathematical form, we express the dynamic system in terms of a system of differential equations as

$$dy/dt = \beta_y y + \gamma_x x$$
$$dx/dt = \beta_x x + \gamma_y y, \tag{1}$$

where dy/dt and dx/dt are instantaneous rates of change and parameters β and γ are parameters of the system that determine longitudinal profiles of X and Y. Analytical solutions for a dynamic system are solutions of differential equations (or difference equations). Unfortunately, complicated dynamic systems do not yield analytical solutions. They are often put in a form of multivariate nonlinear regression models, where X and Y are treated as dependent variables rather than rates of change for X and Y. In computational science, dynamical systems are usually solved by numerical approximations such as Runge–Kutta methods (see technical expositions of numerical analysis of differential equation modeling in Lindfield and Penny (1995), DeWolf and Wiberg (1993), Kamenski and Dimitrov (1993), Fox (1963), Hertzberg and Asbjornsen (1977). Data analyses of the dynamic system model have been often based on nonlinear least squares approaches (e.g., Brown, 1988, 1995; Tuma & Hannan, 1984). Arminger (1986) applied a two-step method to decompose dynamic effects by means of the maximum likelihood estimation for the linear dynamic system. However, this approach requires analytical solutions of the dynamic system to be known.

Dynamic Data Simulation

The equations according to which simulation data are generated are presented in Table 8.1. (The appendix gives simplified or pseudocodes for generating simulation data.) We generated a data set of 100 subjects, each of which is measured on 20 different occasions.

The process of simulation begins by establishing a set of population parameters. The initial conditions and additive constants of both X and Y variables are generated. Then a difference score between the previous score and current score is computed as a function of a dual change score model. Then a latent score is generated by adding a latent difference score and the previous latent score. Finally, the current manifest score is computed by adding the current latent score and the current error term. Using this computational approach, scores are recursively generated from occasion 1 to occasion $T = 20$ based on self-feedback, coupling, and constant change parameters. Scores for each subject on both the X and Y variables are generated for each occasion. This 100 by 40 matrix constitutes the balanced data matrix. This data-generation procedure is repeated 100 times for Monte Carlo simulation analyses. Simulated latent growth trajectories are shown in Fig. 8.1, and manifest growth trajectories are shown in Fig. 8.2. Latent growth curves portray developmental trajectories without adding random disturbances or uniqueness, whereas manifest growth curves simulate real data that include measurement errors and uniqueness.

In the next step, we generated incomplete data by degrading the 100 by 40 balanced data using various incomplete data paradigms. For each incomplete data

TABLE 8.1
Specification of Equations and Population Values Used in Monte Carlo Simulation

	X Variable	Y Variable
Fixed Equation		
Deterministic latent Initial condition	$\mu_{x0} = 5$	$\mu_{y0} = 5$
Stochastic latent Initial condition	$x[0]_n = \mu_{x0} + \phi_{x0}*Z_n$ $= 5 + 5 *Z_n$	$y[0]_n = \mu_{x0} + \phi_{x0} *Zn$ $= 5 + 5 *Z_n$
Manifest Initial condition	$X[0]_n = \mu_{x0} + \phi_{x0} *Z_n + \Psi_x *Z_n$ $= 5 + 5 *Z_n + 5 *Z_n$	$Y[0]_n = \mu_{x0} + \phi_{x0}*Z_n + \Psi_x *Z_n$ $= 5 + 5 *Z_n + 5 *Z_n$
Deterministic additive slope	$\mu_{xs} = 32.5$	$\mu_{ys} = 47.5$
Stochastic latent additive constant	$sx_n = \mu_{xs} + \phi_{xs} *Z_n$ $= 32.5 + 2.5 *Z_n$	$sy_n = \mu_{ys} + \phi_{ys} *Z_n$ $= 47.5 + 2.5 *Z_n$
General Recursive Equation (used from time 1 to t)		
Dynamic Parameters	$\alpha_x = 1$ $\beta_x = -.5$ $\gamma_x = .25$	$\alpha_y = 1$ $\beta_y = -.5$ $\gamma_y = -.25$
Latent Difference Score	$\Delta x[t]_n = x[t]_n - x[t-1]_n$ $= \alpha_x sx_n + \beta_x x[t-1]_n + \gamma_x y[t-1]_n$ $= sx - .5*x[t-1]_n + .25*y[t-1]_n$	$\Delta y[t]_n = y[t]_n - y[t-1]_n$ $= \alpha_y sy + \beta_y y[t-1]_n + \gamma_y x[t-1]_n$ $= sy - .5*y[t-1]_n - .25*x[t-1]_n$
Latent Integral Score	$x[t]_n = x[t-1]_n + \Delta x[t]_n$ $= \alpha_x sx_n + (1 + \beta_x)x[t-1]_n + \gamma_x y[t-1]_n$ $= sx_n + .5*x[t-1]_n + .25*y[t-1]_n$	$Y[t]_n = y[t-1]_n + \Delta y[t]_n$ $= \alpha_y sy + (1 + \beta_y)y[t-1]_n + \gamma_y x[t-1]_n$ $= sy_n + .5*y[t-1]_n - .25*x[t-1]_n$
Manifest Integral Scores	$X[t]_n = x[t-1]_n + \Delta x[t]_n + \Psi_x *Z_n$ $= \alpha_x sx_n + (1 + \beta_x)x[t-1]_n + \gamma_x y[t-1]_n + \Psi_y *Z_n$ $= sx_n + .5*x[t-1]_n + .25*y[t-1]_n + 5*Z_n$	$Y[t]_n = y[t-1]_n + \Delta y[t]_n + \Psi_y *Z_n$ $= \alpha_y sy_n + (1 + \beta_y)y[t-1]_n + \gamma_y x[t-1]_n + \Psi_y *Z_n$ $= sy_n + .5*y[t-1]_n - .25*x[t-1]_n + 5*Z_n$

Note: $X[t]$ is a manifest score at time t, $x[t]$ is a latent score at time t, $\Delta x[t]$ is a difference score at time t, Z is a standardized score, α_x is a basis coefficient of slope, β_x is a self-feedback parameter, γ_x is a coupling from y to x, $Y[t]$ is a manifest score at time t, $y[t]$ is a latent score at time t, $\Delta y[t]$ is a difference score at time t, Z is a standardized score, α_y is a basis coefficient of slope, β_y is a self-feedback parameter, γ_y is a coupling from x to y.

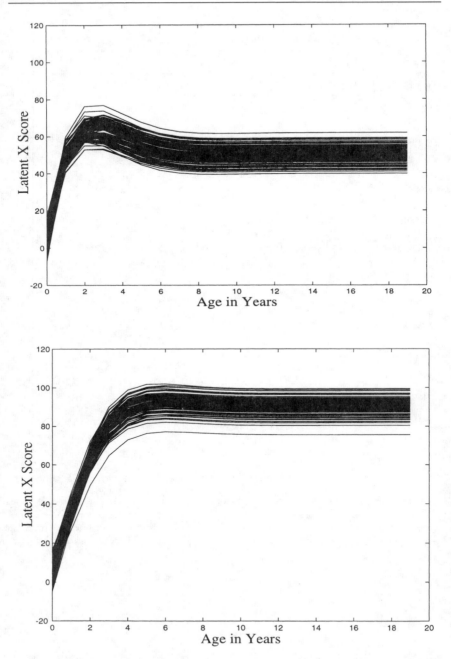

FIG. 8.1. $N = 100$ individual growth trajectories of X and Y latent scores simulated based on a bivariate dual-change score model.

type, we repeated the data-generation procedure 100 times, and we analyzed these data separately. The listing of types of incomplete data is provided in Table 8.2. Also Fig. 8.3 depicts an example of how missing patterns are constructed. In this figure, numerals in circles or rectangles indicate temporal events. (A circle indicates a missing observation, whereas a square indicates that Variables X and Y are measured.) Figures 8.4 and 8.5 depict manifest growth curves for these alternative incomplete data structures.

MODELS

Latent Difference Score Dynamical Models

A structural equation modeling (SEM) approach was used to solve the linear dynamic system. This SEM does not require analytical solutions of dynamic systems. We address five critical issues about our dynamic modeling approach:

1. The change models apply directly to the latent variables (true scores) but only indirectly to the observed variable. We separate true scores and error scores at each time point. Then we apply a dynamic model directly to true scores.

2. The change models are defined as deterministic over time. That is, rate of change does not show intra-individual variation across time. A rate of change is mathematically defined as error-free across time. However, a rate of change should show interindividual differences.

3. The change models are based on differences for observed scores measured discretely over periods of time. We stress this because, to model change phenomena with differentials, we need finely tuned measurement schemes that allow continuous observation of variables. One example of this is a chart of EKG or EEG, where measurements are obtained without interruptions.

4. The change model accounts for the means, variances, and covariances of the observed data.

5. The change model is defined as a linear difference equation rather than a nonlinear difference equation. Nonlinear dynamic systems are extremely complex and volatile because they are sensitive to the initial conditions of multiple time series and nonlinear models would provide an unpredictable result (see Alligood et al., 1996). In addition, fitting nonlinear models demands a lot of information to estimate parameters with precision.

Further, we recognize that there are individual differences among subjects in terms of how people start and grow (McArdle & Esptein, 1987; Nesselroade, 1991). These individual differences for the level and rate of change should be

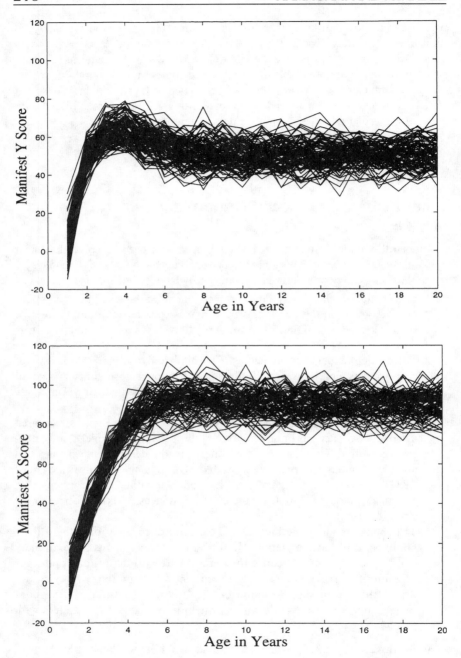

FIG. 8.2. $N = 100$ individual growth trajectories of X and Y manifest
variable scores simulated based on bivariate dual-change score model.

TABLE 8.2
Listing of the Incomplete Data Structure

Types of Incompleteness	Description of Generating Incomplete Data
(1) Odd-number occasion	We extracted data points of odd-number occasions (i.e., 1, 3, 5, … , 17,19).
(2) Random five consecutive occasions	We extracted five consecutive data points out of 20 occasions. The initial occasion of five consecutive events is randomly determined for each subject.
(3) Random three consecutive occasions	We extracted three consecutive data points out of 20 occasions. The initial occasion of three consecutive events is randomly determined for each subject.
(4) Random two consecutive occasions	We extracted three consecutive data points out of 20 occasions. The initial occasion of two consecutive events is randomly determined for each subject.
(5) Evenly spaced occasion data	We extracted data points of approximately 5 years apart between two observations. We extracted occasions 1, 5, 10, 15, and 20. So each subject provides five data points from Occasions 1, 5, 10, 15, and 20.
(6) First five occasions	We extracted only first five data points for each subject. Data from occasions 1, 2, 3, 4, and 5 are extracted.
(7) Middle five occasions	We extracted information of middle Occasions 6, 7, 8, 9, and 10 for each subject.
(8) Last five occasions	We extracted data points of the last five occasions (16, 17, 18, 19, and 20).
(9) Nonrandom level selection	In the selection by the level score, (a) subjects are sorted by the level scores from the lowest to highest, (b) original five occasions (1, 5, 10, 15, and 20) are measured, (c) the first 50% of lowest level scores provide all five occasion information, (d) the next 15% provide information of four occasions (1, 5, 10, and 15), (e) the next 15% provide information of four occasions (1, 5, 10, and 20), and (f) the last 20% provide information of three occasions (1, 5, and 10).
(10) Nonrandom slope selection	In the selection by the slope score, (a) subjects are sorted by the slope scores from the lowest to highest, (b) original five occasions (1, 5, 10, 15, and 20) are measured, (c) the first 50% of lowest level scores provide all five occasion information, (d) the next 15% provide information of four occasions (1, 5, 10, and 15), (e) the next 15% provide information of four occasions (1, 5, 10, and 20), and (f) the last 20% provide information of three occasions (1, 5, and 10).
(11) First three occasions	We extracted only first three data points for each subject.
(12) Only first and last occasions	We used only the first and last occasions.
(13) Random single occasion	We randomly selected a single occasion out of 20 for each subject.

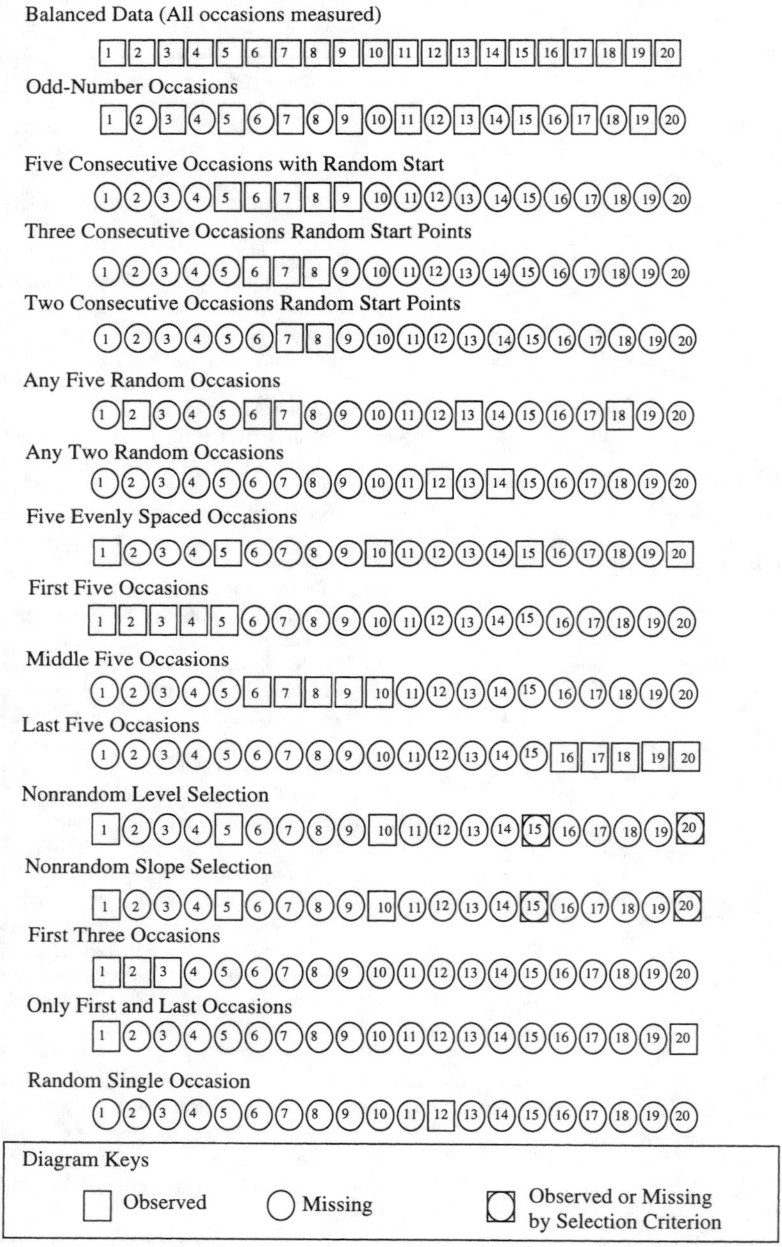

Balanced Data (All occasions measured)

Odd-Number Occasions

Five Consecutive Occasions with Random Start

Three Consecutive Occasions Random Start Points

Two Consecutive Occasions Random Start Points

Any Five Random Occasions

Any Two Random Occasions

Five Evenly Spaced Occasions

First Five Occasions

Middle Five Occasions

Last Five Occasions

Nonrandom Level Selection

Nonrandom Slope Selection

First Three Occasions

Only First and Last Occasions

Random Single Occasion

Diagram Keys

☐ Observed   ○ Missing   ⬡ Observed or Missing by Selection Criterion

FIG. 8.3. Designs of missing data structures (square denotes observed; circle denotes unobserved; numerals show occasion numbers).

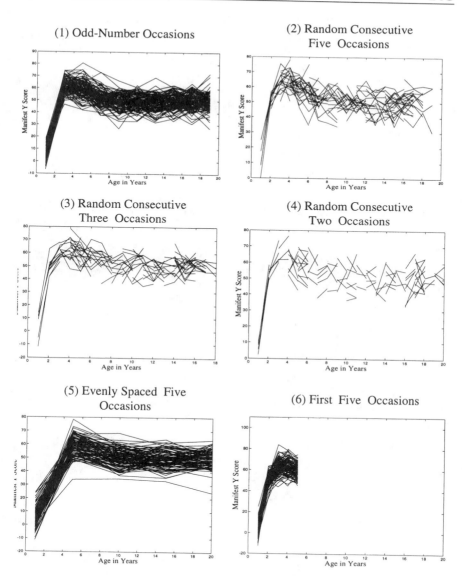

(1) Odd-Number Occasions

(2) Random Consecutive Five Occasions

(3) Random Consecutive Three Occasions

(4) Random Consecutive Two Occasions

(5) Evenly Spaced Five Occasions

(6) First Five Occasions

FIG. 8.4. $N = 100$ Y manifest variable growth curves generated by alternative strategies of degrading data.

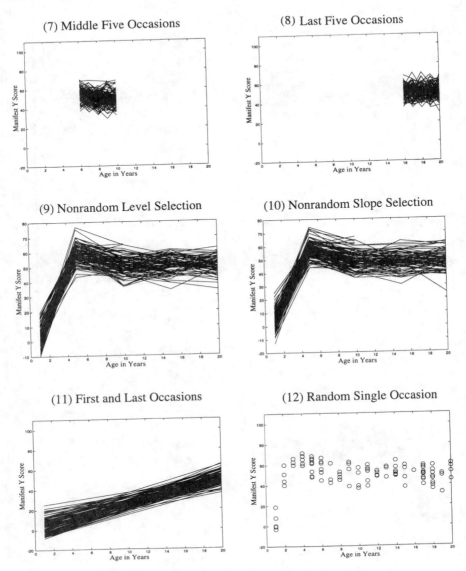

FIG. 8.5. $N = 100$ Y manifest variable growth curves generated by
alternative strategies of degrading data.

incorporated into the dynamic system models. In other words, we dismiss the idea of a single-subject approach (a time series model) to analyze multivariate multiple-subject repeated measures data.

The bivariate dynamic models we use here are an extended version of univariate dynamic models (McArdle, 1994). A significant difference between univariate and bivariate models is that, in the latter, a dynamic effect of one variable on the other variable comes into existence. Dynamic effects between variables is called *coupling* effects. Therefore, in the bivariate model, there are two dynamic parameters (i.e., *self-feedback* [we call it β] and coupling [we call it γ]).

Latent Difference Score Algebra

Technical details of the bivariate change score model, along with a univariate change score model, are provided in McArdle and Hamagami (1999). The bivariate dual-change score model is characterized by three components of dynamics. They are the proportionate change parameter (self-feedback, β), the constant change parameter (additive change, μ_s), and the proportionate external impact (coupling, γ).

Also, it is very important to note that a self-feedback effect at each successive time represents cumulatively compounding or propagation of a variable from all the previous time points, as well as an interaction effect at each successive time consisting of cumulative coupling effects of all the previous time points. These compound effects are nonlinear and multiplicative over time. Thus, cross-sectional approaches are clearly inappropriate in analyzing dynamic characteristics of repeated measures because they ignore propagations of preceding coupling effects and self-feedback effects.

We assume that a manifest score ($Y[t]$ or $X[t]$) is sum of a true score ($y[t]$ or $x[t]$) and a disturbance score ($ey[t]$ or $ex[t]$):

$$Y[t]_n = y[t]_n + ey[t]_n$$
$$X[t]_n = x[t]_n + ex[t]_n. \tag{2}$$

We define $\Delta y[t]$ (or $\Delta x[t]$) as a latent difference score between two adjacent occasions. So algebraically difference scores for x and y are expressed as

$$\Delta y[t]_n = y[t]_n - y[t-1]_n \tag{3}$$
$$\Delta x[t]_n = x[t]_n - x[t-1]_n.$$

In a dynamic system, a temporal index or time plays a critical role. The nature of the dynamic system is determined by mathematical forms of these difference scores. In the dual-change score model, we express a dynamic system algebraically at time **t** in a temporal scale as

$$\Delta y[t]_n = \alpha_y \, sy_n + \beta_y \, y[t-1]_n + \gamma_x \, x[t-1]_n \tag{4}$$

$$\Delta x[t]_n = \alpha_x \, sx_n + \beta_x \, x[t-1]_n + \gamma_y \, y[t-1]_n.$$

This representation simply says that a difference score between time t and time t-1 ($\Delta y[t]_n$) is the sum of three terms: a self-feedback effect ($\beta_y \, y[t-1]_n$), a linear constant effect ($\alpha_y \, sy_n$), and a coupling effect by the counterpart ($\gamma_x \, x[t-1]_n$). Mathematical terms are defined in Table 8.3. With a difference score mathematically defined, we algebraically manipulate a difference equation, a current score, and a preceding score. In the end, we express a system that has current scores as dependent variables and immediate past scores as predictors, symbolically expressed as,

$$y[t]_n = y[t-1]_n + \Delta y[t]_n \tag{5}$$

$$= (1+\beta_y)y[t-1]_n + \alpha_y sy_n + \gamma_x x[t-1]_n$$

$$x[t]_n = x[t-1]_n + \Delta x[t]_n$$

$$= (1+\beta_x)x[t-1]_n + \alpha_x sx_n + \gamma_y y[t-1]_n.$$

This dynamic model true score is then disturbed by an error term of the observed variable (i.e., uniqueness). This uniqueness term is a part of interindividual or between-persons differences. Other parts of the interindividual difference comes from variability in the initial score (or level score) and variability in the slope score.

$$Y[t]_n = y[t]_n + + \, ey[t]_n \tag{6}$$

$$= y[t-1]_n + \Delta y[t]_n + ey[t]_n$$

$$= (1+\beta_y)y[t-1]_n + \alpha_y sy_n + \gamma_x x[t-1]_n + ey[t]_n$$

$$X[t]_n = x[t]_n + + \, ex[t]_n$$

$$= x[t-1]_n + \Delta x[t]_n + ex[t]_n$$

$$= (1+\beta_x)x[t-1]_n + \alpha_x sx_n + \gamma_y y[t-1]_n + ex[t]_n.$$

Refer back to Table 8.3 for definition of all variables and dynamic parameters in the model. Figure 8.6 represents a path diagram (Wright, 1934) of the bivariate difference score dynamic model. In a path diagram, a circle represents an unobserved variable, whereas a square represents a measured variable. A single-headed arrow represents a deterministic structural coefficient, whereas a double-

TABLE 8.3

Definition of Mathematical Symbols and Variables of a Difference Score Dynamic Model

Variable and Parameters	Description of Variables and Parameters in the Dynamic System Model
$y[t]_n$	A true score at time t for an observed variable $Y[t]$
$y[t-1]_n$	An immediately preceding true score at time t for an observed variable $Y[t]$
$x[t]_n$	A true score at time t for an observed variable $X[t]$
$x[t-1]_n$	An immediately preceding true score at time t} for an observed variable $X[t]$
$\Delta y[t]_n$	A rate of change of true scores Y for a subject n at time t
$\Delta x[t]_n$	A rate of change of true scores X for a subject n at time t
β_y	A proportional change parameter for $y[t]$ or a self-feedback of y
β_x	A proportional change parameter for $x[t]$ or a self-feedback of x
γ_y	A coupling parameter for $y[t]$ (an effect of $x[t]$ on $y[t]$)
γ_x	A coupling parameter for $x[t]$ (an effect of $y[t]$ on $x[t]$)
$ey[t]_n$	A unique score for $Y[t]$ at time t for an observed variable $Y[t]$
$ex[t]_n$	A unique score for $X[t]$ at time t for an observed variable $X[t]$
α_y	A basis coefficient for the constant term (i.e., slope) for y
α_x	A basis coefficient for the constant term (i.e., slope) for x
sy_n	An individual subject's constant term (i.e., slope) for y
ex_n	An individual subject's constant term (i.e., slope) for x
μ_{x0}	A mean of initial conditions for X
μ_{y0}	A mean of initial conditions for Y
ϕ_{x0}	Standard deviation of initial condition for X
ϕ_{y0}	Standard deviation of initial condition for X
μ_{xs}	Mean of an additive component of X (sx)
μ_{ys}	Mean of an additive component of Y (sy)
ϕxs	Standard Deviation of an additive component of X (sx)
ϕ_{ys}	Standard Deviation of an additive component of Y (sy)
$\rho_{y0,ys}$	Correlation between a Y's initial condition and Y's additive component
$\rho_{y0,x0}$	Correlation between a Y's initial condition and X's initial condition
$\rho_{y0,xs}$	Correlation between a Y's initial condition and X's additive component
$\rho_{ys,x0}$	Correlation between a Y's additive component and X's initial condition
$\rho_{ys,xs}$	Correlation between a Y's additive component and X's additive component
$\rho_{x0,xs}$	Correlation between an X's initial condition and X's additive component

headed arrow represents a stochastic coefficient. Labels in Fig. 8.6 correspond to mathematical symbols in the prior equations. In Fig. 8.6, three dots mean that there are more repeated measures, latent true scores, and a latent rate of change between the initial and terminal sequences.

Multilevel Change Score Regression Model

A practical approach to examining a change phenomenon is the use of multiple regression models with the raw change score as the dependent variable

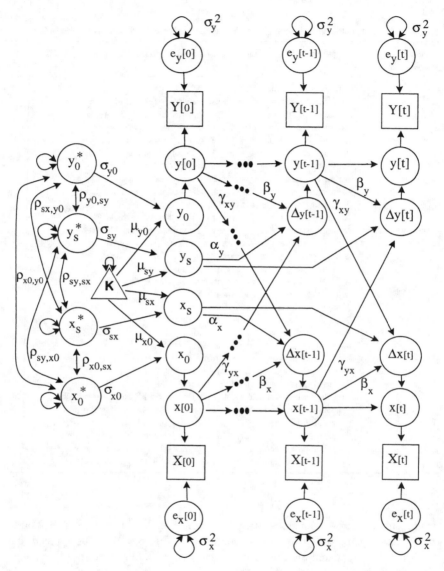

FIG. 8.6.   A path diagram representing a bivariate dual-change score model.

(Allison, 1987). This methodology is easy to implement. However, ease of implementation does not necessarily yield unbiased estimates of the true nature of change.

This traditional approach regresses a raw change score of Y (ΔY) on scores at a previous occasion ($Y[t-1]$ and $X[t-1]$) and separately regresses a change score of X (ΔX) on scores at a previous occasion ($Y[t-1]$ and $X[t-1]$). Note that the simultaneous nature of the system approach is ignored in the traditional regression model. Yet the regression model can be used to represent a dynamic structure of the bivariate dual-change score model, and the regression estimates may be close to the estimates obtained from more complex models (i.e., the regression model estimates self-feedback, coupling, and a constant linear change parameters).

We want to recognize that this simple method has been supported by some (Allison, 1990; Cronbach & Furby, 1970; Kessler, 1977; Raykov, 1999), but criticized by others (Cronbach & Furby, 1970; Foerster, 1995; Kessler, 1977; Raykov, 1999). From these critiques we know that the traditional regression method does not permit an accurate estimation of initial conditions, individual differences of initial conditions and true linear change scores, and covariation between initial conditions and true linear change scores.

Estimation With Incomplete Data

Incompleteness of longitudinal data is inevitable. Many researchers have dealt with missingness in the repeated measures (Allison, 1987; Bell, 1953; Helms, 1992; Kiiveri, 1987; Lange, Westlake, & Spence, 1976; Little & Rubin, 1987; Schafer, 1997). Structural equation models have been applied to incomplete data structures (Allison, 1987; McArdle & Aber, 1990; McArdle & Anderson, 1990; McArdel, 1994; McArdle & Hamagami, 1991, 1992; McArdle & Nesselroade, 1994). Neal (1995) developed the computer program called Mx (see Hamagami, 1997) capable of the missing data analysis. The Mx program is designed to perform the full information structural equation modeling as well as raw data incomplete structural equation modeling. Parameterization of dynamic models with incomplete data is executed by the Mx individualized structural equation modeling approach (Neal, 1995).

During Mx's estimation, each individual vector of repeated measures is fitted to a certain structural equation model and deviation between the expectation based on estimated parameters and an individual observed vector is summed over all subjects and used as a model fit criterion. These computational steps are repeated until convergence criteria are satisfied.

The traditional change score regression models presented next were performed with SAS PROC MIXED to deal with nested repeated measures effects. The Mx was used to analyze structural dynamic system models.

Evaluation of Goodness-of-Fit

Three sets of model fit indexes were used to evaluate the overall fit of each incomplete data paradigm against the population dynamic system. We provide some definitions here because some aspects are novel.

The first misfit index was computed as the sum of squared deviations between parameter estimates and population parameter values. Mathematically, the squared deviation index is computed as

$$f_\theta = \sum (q - \theta)^2,$$

where q is a bootstrap parameter estimate and θ is a population parameter value.

The second misfit index expresses the deviation of the sample eigen-system of a model from that of the population eigen-system. Eigenvalues of the dynamic system are calculated by eigen-system decompostion of the community matrix of the dynamic model. Specifically, if a dynamic system is expressed in a matrix form as

$$\begin{bmatrix} \Delta x \\ \Delta y \\ \Delta 1 \end{bmatrix} = \begin{bmatrix} \beta_x & \gamma_x & \mu_{sx} \\ \gamma_y & \beta_y & \mu_{sy} \\ 0 & 0 & 0 \end{bmatrix} \begin{bmatrix} x \\ y \\ 1 \end{bmatrix},$$

then, the community matrix of the dynamic system is the second matrix that includes all dynamic parameters in the above equation. The eigenvalues of the community matrix characterize the nature of the dynamic system (see Tuma et al., 1984). Thus, deviation from the population eigenvalues is a discrepancy between the sample dynamic system and the population dynamic system. An eigen deviation index (f_λ) is defined as the sum of squared difference between the sample eigenvalue and expected eigenvalue divided by the squared population eigenvalue. Namely,

$$f_\lambda = \sum_i \frac{(l_i - \lambda_i)^2}{\lambda_i^2}$$

where l_i is a sample eigenvalue, λ_i is a population eigenvalue of the community matrix and f_λ is a defined as follows. When the sample model replicates the population model exactly, f_λ is 0. However, when the eigen system is the complex value, f_λ becomes the complex number as well. Thus, there needs to be some generalized eigen fit index that enables comparison between a real number fit index and a complex number fit index. A solution is the use of a distance measure of the complex number in the complex plane. In the complex plane, the real part of the complex number is evaluated at the abscissa and the imaginary part is evaluated at the ordinate in the complex Cartesian coordinate. Thus, if $f_\lambda = a + bi$, where a is the real part and bi is the imaginary part of the complex number, the distance measure of the complex plane (f_c) is defined as the distance between a real-imaginary coordinate and the origin of the complex plane—that is,

$$f_c = (a^2 + b^2)^{1/2}.$$

Furthermore, this distance measure, f_c, can be rescaled as a normed centrality index, f_e (McDonald & Marsh, 1990), of the dynamic parameters using the equation

$$f_e = \exp(-.5f_c).$$

This normed index of centrality ranges from 0 to 1. The perfect reproduction of the dynamic eigen structure is 1, whereas 0 indicates that the estimated dynamic characteristics and population dynamics do not match.

The three misfit indexes, f_θ, f_c, and f_e, are used to evaluate how well the population dynamic system is reconstructed across different estimation methods.

RESULTS

Results of Complete Data Analyses

We use the acronym DSEM to designate the dual-change score structural equation model and MDIF to represent multilevel difference score regression model. Balanced data sets are generated using several different population parameter sets. We were able to recover population parameter values at all attempts using a balanced data structure. Therefore, to avoid redundancy, we limit reporting to data analyses based on one population parameter set.

Table 8.4 summarizes the results of bivariate difference equation SEM analyses based on the complete data. The first column of Table 8.4 designates all the parameters involved in the model, the second column enumerates their respective parametric values (θ), the third column enumerates parameter estimates (q), the fourth column enumerates differences between the population parameters and the parameter estimates (i.e., q-θ), the fifth column enumerates standard errors of parameters (i.e., $\sigma_q / \sqrt{n-1}$), and the sixth column enumerates a ratio between a difference between parameter and its estimate and its standard errors (i.e., $(q-\theta)/\sigma_q / \sqrt{n-1}$). Both self-feedback ($\beta_x$ and β_y) and coupling parameters (γ_{xy} and γ_{yx}) are accurately recovered. Means and standard deviations of initial conditions and constant slopes are accurately recovered as well. Uniqueness parameters for both X and Y variables were accurately recovered. All in all, the linear latent difference equation model has correctly and accurately recovered the dynamic characteristics of the complete data.

Table 8.5 summarizes results of the multilevel regression analyses of change scores. In these simulations, two kinds of balanced data were compared: one set contained measurement errors in time series, whereas the second set excluded

TABLE 8.4

Results of Bivariate Dual-Change Score Model for Latent Difference Dynamics Fitted to the Complete Data ($N = 100$, $T = 20$)

Parameters	Symbol	Population Parameter θ	Estimate q	Diff. $q - \theta$	Std. Error $\dfrac{\sigma_q}{\sqrt{n-1}}$	t value $\dfrac{q - \theta}{\sigma_q / \sqrt{n-1}}$
Self-feedback for X	β_x	**−.50**	−.50	0	.00	.00
Self-feedback for Y	β_y	**−.50**	−.50	0	.00	.00
Coupling from X	γ_x	**.25**	.25	0	.00	.00
Coupling from Y	γ_y	**−.25**	−.25	0	.00	.00
Standard deviation of X initial condition	ϕ_{x0}	**5.00**	4.96	−.04	.06	−.71
Standard deviation of X additive component	ϕ_{xs}	**2.50**	2.52	.02	.02	.99
Standard deviation of Y initial condition	ϕ_{y0}	**5.00**	4.50	−.50	.06	−7.77
Standard deviation of Y additive component	ϕ_{ys}	**2.50**	2.47	−.03	.02	−1.66
Mean of X initial condition	μ_{x0}	**5.00**	4.98	−.02	.07	−.30
Mean of X additive component	μ_{xs}	**47.50**	47.54	.04	.06	.70
Mean of Y initial condition	μ_{y0}	**5.00**	5.05	.05	.07	.75
Mean of Y additive component	μ_{ys}	**32.50**	32.56	.06	.05	1.11
Correlation between X level and X slope	$\rho_{x0,xs}$	**.00**	−.001	−.00	.01	−.07
Correlation between X level and Y level	$\rho_{x0,y0}$	**.00**	.02	.02	.02	1.33
Correlation between X level and Y slope	$\rho_{x0,ys}$	**.00**	.01	.01	.01	.77
Correlation between X slope and Y level	$\rho_{xs,y0}$	**.00**	.001	.00	.02	.06
Correlation between X slope and Y slope	$\rho_{xs,ys}$	**.00**	.01	.01	.01	.90
Correlation between Y level and Y slope	$\rho_{y0,xs}$	**.00**	.01	.01	.01	.71
Standard deviation of error term for X	ψ_x	**5.00**	4.99	−.01	.01	−1.24
Standard deviation of error term for Y	ψ_y	**5.00**	4.97	−.03	.01	−3.32

Note: Population values are boldfaced; Estimate is a parameter estimate based on maximum likelihood estimation; Diff. denotes a difference between a population parameter (θ) and its estimate (q); Std. Error is a bootstrap standard error, (i.e., $\sigma_q / \sqrt{n-1}$, where σ_q is a standard deviation of parameter estimates based on 100 Monte Carlo simulations); and t value denotes a ratio of a difference value and a bootstrap standard error (i.e, $(q - \theta)/(\sigma_q/\sqrt{n-1})$).

TABLE 8.5
Results of Multilevel Difference Score Regression (MDIF) Models Applied to Simulation Data Generated
Based on Bivariate Dual-Change Score Dynamic Models

Parameters	Symbol	Population Parameter θ	MDIF Stochastic Data Diff. $q-\theta$	MDIF Stochastic Data t value $\dfrac{q-\theta}{\sigma_q/\sqrt{n-1}}$	MDIF Deterministic Data Diff. $q-\theta$	MDIF Deterministic Data t value $\dfrac{q-\theta}{\sigma_q/\sqrt{n-1}}$
Self-feedback for X	β_x	**−.50**	−.01	−99.50	0	.00
Self-feedback for Y	β_y	**−.50**	−.13	<−100	0	.00
Coupling from X	γ_x	**.25**	−.03	−29.85	0	.00
Coupling from Y	γ_y	**−.25**	.06	59.70	0	.00
Standard deviation of X initial condition	ϕ_{x0}	**5.00**	—	—	—	—
Standard deviation of X additive component	ϕ_{xs}	**2.50**	−1.44	−13.78	−6.25	<−100
Standard deviation of Y initial condition	ϕ_{y0}	**5.00**	—	—	—	—
Standard deviation of Y additive component	ϕ_{ys}	**2.50**	1.38	11.54	.18	1.95
Mean of X initial condition	μ_{x0}	**5.00**	—	—	—	—
Mean of X additive component	μ_{xs}	**47.50**	.04	.70	.00	.00
Mean of Y initial condition	μ_{y0}	**5.00**	—	—	—	—
Mean of Y additive component	μ_{ys}	**32.50**	2.31	39.63	.00	.00
Correlation between X level and X slope	$\rho_{x0,xs}$	**.00**	—	—	—	—
Correlation between X level and Y level	$\rho_{x0,y0}$	**.00**	—	—	—	—
Correlation between X level and Y slope	$\rho_{x0,ys}$	**.00**	—	—	—	—
Correlation between X slope and Y level	$\rho_{xs,y0}$	**.00**	—	—	—	—
Correlation between X slope and Y slope	$\rho_{xs,ys}$	**.00**	—	—	—	—
Correlation between Y level and Y slope	$\rho_{y0,xs}$	**.00**	—	—	—	—
Standard deviation of error term for X	ψ_x	**5.00**	8.71	68.78	6.31	73.86
Standard deviation of error term for Y	ψ_y	**5.00**	1.96	37.50	.00	.00

Note: Population values are boldfaced; — denotes that parameters could not be estimated by MDIF analysis; Diff. denotes a difference between a population parameter (θ) and its estimate (q); t value denotes a ratio of a difference value and a bootstrap standard error (i.e., $q-\theta$ / $(\sigma_q/\sqrt{n-1})$).

measurement errors. We use the term *stochastic data* to refer to the first set and the term *deterministic* data for the second data type. As seen in the table, the traditional approach was able to recover dynamic parameters as long as all subjects provided all data points in the process. Namely, all subjects provided 19 difference scores in the process over the span of 20 occasions. However, the precision of parameter estimates was not as good as that of the bivariate dual-change score SEM except when population coupling parameters were set to zero in the simulation.

Results for Incomplete Data Analyses

The odd-number occasion paradigm involved 50% reduction of data density compared with the complete data structure. The five occasion incomplete data scheme lost 75% of data density. Four consecutive occasion, three consecutive occasion, and two consecutive occasion incomplete data sets were degraded as 20%, 15%, and 10% retention rate over the complete data structure. Finally, the completely cross-sectional single occasion data maintain only 5% of original data density.

When the MDIF was fitted to incomplete simulation data, we were no longer able to recover the characteristics of bivariate dynamics. Table 8.6 summarizes results of the multilevel regression approach to incomplete data with measurement errors and Table 8.7 summarizes results of the multilevel regression approach to incomplete data without measurement errors. The only case in which the MDIF model recovered dynamic parameters was when the data were generated without measurement errors and all 20 occasions were included in the simulation data. Whether the missing data were generated with or without measurement errors in the dynamic process makes no difference. Clearly, the MDIF failed to recover the dynamic characteristics (i.e., linear change parameters, self-feedback parameters, and coupling parameters in all incomplete data paradigms) and the density of data structure did not matter because neither the least sparse data (the odd-number occasion paradigm) nor the most sparse data (the two occasion data paradigm) led to accurate estimation of population parameters.

Table 8.8 summarizes the results of parameter estimation of DSEM applied to these alternative incomplete data sets. Analyses of highly dense data sets (10 repeated measures) and moderately dense data sets (4 or 5 repeated measures) resulted in consistently accurate estimation of the population parameters. Especially dynamic parameters (i.e., self-feedback parameters [β] and coupling parameters [γ]) are accurately recovered even if the data were inflicted with 50% or more damage. The initial condition parameters (μ_{x0}, μ_{y0}, ϕ_{x0}, ϕ_{y0}) and the constant change parameters (μ_{xs}, μ_{ys}, ϕ_{xs}, ϕ_{ys}) were accurately recovered as well.

When we analyzed three-occasion and two-occasion data sets, we found surprisingly consistent results for DSEM. Even if more than 85% of data points were eliminated, we were able to capture approximate dynamical structures of self-feedback and coupling parameters as well as initial conditions. However, we note that, as expected, the correlations among the initial conditions and latent linear slopes are no longer orthogonal.

With regard to analyses of a cross-sectional data structure where 95% of data points are lost, we were no longer able to estimate uniqueness in DSEM. Because all points are completely randomly extracted for each subject, a general trend across Occasion 1 and Occasion 20 roughly resembles the complete data structure. Hence, estimates of dynamic parameters were not gravely off the population values. However, stochastic parameters including standard deviations of initial conditions, constant slopes, uniqueness, and all factor correlations were inaccurately estimated.

There were several cases that indicate that parameter estimates were numerically imprecise. When we extracted only middle parts or only the terminal parts of the original data, the DSEM did not recover the dynamic parameters or the level and slope parameters. In addition, the bootstrap standard errors were large, indicating that these parameter estimates were highly unstable.

When we extracted only five occasions equally spaced, we were not able to recover latent means and we observed large bootstrap standard errors. By systematically skipping a fair amount of occasions, overall shapes of growth trajectories were inevitably distorted. Understandably, means of slope scores were deviated from the population means. However, the dynamic parameters (β and γ) were close to the population parameter values. Results of nonrandom level and slope selection paradigms were very similar to those of the equally spaced five-occasion data paradigm as expected because nonrandom selections were performed on the equally spaced five-occasion data.

A summary of all misfit indexes (f_θ, f_c, and f_e) are listed in Table 8.9. These indexes indicate that the dual change score SEM is both highly accurate and superior to the multilevel difference score regression (MDIF) model in identifying characteristics of population dynamics. The DSEM approach was able to accurately recover the eigen system of the dynamic model, whereas the multilevel model was not. The $f_c=0$ or $f_e=1$ means that the simulation model recovered the identical eigen system of the population dynamic model. The DSEM was able to recover the correct eigen system when fitted to a majority of the incomplete data paradigms. For the cases where the data extraction included only the middle or last part of the time sequence, however, it was unsuccessful. For the bivariate DSEM, a majority of incomplete paradigms led to that $f_c=0$ or $f_e=1$. In contrast, estimation by the MDIF approach clearly came up short in approximating the true dynamics. Given these simulation results, the dual-change score model was able to recover the dynamic eigen system even if data structures were highly degraded.

DISCUSSION

The present chapter dealt with both theoretical and practical issues of dynamic system modeling under varying degrees of data quality. We compared results of the bivariate dual-change score SEM with those of the traditional regression MDIF models that use difference scores as a dependent variable. We found that the traditional approach was only reliable when (a) all 20 data points were

TABLE 8.6

Results of Multilevel Difference Score Regression (MDIF) Models Applied to Alternative Stochastic Data Based on Alternative Missing Data Paradigms

Dynamic Parameters	Parameters in Difference Score Equation for X-variable: $\Delta X = \mu_{xx} + \beta_x X(t-1) + \gamma_x Y(t-1)$					Parameters in Difference Score Equation for Y-variable: $\Delta Y = \mu_{xy} + \beta_y Y(t-1) + \gamma_y X(t-1)$				
	μ_{xx}	β_x	γ_x	σ_{ex}	σ_{xx}	μ_{xy}	β_y	γ_y	σ_{ey}	σ_{xy}
Population values	**32.50**	**-.50**	**.250**	**25.00**	**6.25**	**47.50**	**-.50**	**-.25**	**25.00**	**6.25**
Complete data	2.31	-.01	-.03	8.71	-1.44	1.96	-.13	.06	6.68	1.38
	39.63	-99.50	-29.85	68.78	-13.78	37.50	<-100	59.70	52.75	11.54
Odd-number occasions	8.57	-0.04	-0.09	-6.28	-0.72	6.32	0.09	-0.12	-6.42	-1.21
	86.13	-39.80	-44.77	-61.87	-6.45	56.15	44.77	<-100	-67.24	-11.92
Five consecutive occasions	10.25	-0.14	0.01	38.00	-4.92	0.90	-0.26	0.15	12.49	1.30
	27.64	-23.22	1.11	11.20	-22.25	3.57	-36.96	49.75	12.80	2.62
Three consecutive occasions	8.60	-0.15	0.06	58.87	-6.25	-1.54	-0.18	0.14	23.15	-5.57
	31.12	-49.75	5.97	11.87	<-100	-6.41	-29.85	46.43	20.51	-23.38
Two consecutive occasions	0.35	0.05	-0.09	-23.89	-2.05	-1.85	0.08	-0.02	-23.69	-2.05
	3.83	24.87	-29.85	<-100	-16.72	-14.73	26.53	-19.90	<-100	-14.16

Five random occasions	4.88 **10.86**	0.09 **17.91**	−0.25 **−62.19**	3.30 **13.57**	−6.15 **<−100**	−19.14 **−31.02**	0.14 **27.86**	0.14 **27.86**	2.69 **10.22**	−6.23 **<−100**
Three random occasions	0.56 **0.85**	0.14 **19.90**	−0.25 **−41.46**	−3.26 **−8.84**	−6.08 **<−100**	−20.59 **−21.01**	0.26 **36.96**	0.08 **8.84**	−4.11 **−11.39**	−6.20 **<−100**
Two random occasions	2.15 **2.96**	0.13 **18.48**	−0.25 **−35.54**	−23.47 **−67.49**	14.20 **24.96**	−15.86 **−15.50**	0.29 **28.85**	0.02 **2.49**	−23.01 **−55.04**	10.78 **17.41**
Five equally spaced occasions	40.15 **175.21**	−0.20 **−99.50**	−0.41 **−81.59**	−4.85 **−31.13**	3.49 **16.15**	−1.22 **−7.63**	0.50 **165.83**	−0.27 **<−100**	−15.21 **−100**	−2.01 **−20.20**
First five occasions	−14.49 **<−100**	0.29 **288.55**	−0.17 **−84.57**	−9.55 **−87.98**	−6.25 **<−100**	−15.45 **<−100**	0.29 **144.27**	0.00 **0.00**	−8.66 **−61.99**	−6.21 **<−100**
Middle five occasions	−33.00 **<−100**	0.50 **248.75**	−0.24 **<−100**	−12.41 **<−100**	−6.25 **<−100**	−46.08 **<−100**	0.47 **233.82**	0.24 **119.40**	−12.16 **−100**	−6.25 **<−100**
Last five occasions	−32.55 **<−100**	0.50 **248.75**	−0.25 **<−100**	−12.60 **<−100**	−6.25 **<−100**	−47.37 **<−100**	0.50 **497.49**	0.25 **124.37**	−12.53 **−100**	−6.25 **<−100**
First and last occasions	12.84 **26.51**	0.44 **48.64**	−0.25 **−24.87**	−22.25 **−35.48**	14.16 **21.61**	−23.42 **−44.47**	0.46 **45.77**	0.24 **23.88**	−23.90 **−100**	16.17 **40.53**

Note: Population values are boldfaced; upper values in each cell are a difference between population parameter and parameter estimate $(q-\theta)$; values under the difference values is t value computed as a ratio of a difference value and a bootstrap standard error (i.e., $(q-\theta)/(\sigma_q/\sqrt{n-1})$).

TABLE 8.7
Results of Multilevel Difference Score Regression (MDIF) Models Applied to Alternative Deterministic Data Based on Alternative Missing Data Paradigms

Dynamic Parameters	Parameters in Difference Score Equation for X-variable: $\Delta X = \mu_{sx} + \beta_x X[t-1] + \gamma_x Y[t-1]$					Parameters in Difference Score Equation for Y-variable: $\Delta Y = \mu_{sy} + \beta_y Y[t-1] + \gamma_y X[t-1]$				
	μ_{sx}	β_x	γ_x	σ_{ex}	σ_{sx}	μ_{sy}	β_y	γ_y	σ_{ey}	σ_{sy}
Population values	**32.50**	**−.50**	**.250**	**.00**	**6.25**	**47.50**	**−.50**	**−.25**	**.00**	**6.25**
Complete data	.00	.00	.00	6.31	−6.25	.00	.00	.00	.00	.18
	.00	.00	.00	73.86	<−100	.00	.00	.00	.00	1.95
Odd-number occasions	5.67	−.011	0.09	−25.00	3.36	13.65	−0.11	−0.09	−25.00	3.80
	>100	<−100	90.00	<−100	23.38	>100	<−100	−90.00	<−100	23.48
Five consecutive occasions	−0.83	−0.19	0.31	0.00	6.98	0.89	−0.21	0.12	−16.62	2.54
	−4.44	−31.51	34.27	0.00	10.05	5.24	−34.82	59.70	−19.36	6.38
Three consecutive occasions	−17.58	0.00	0.34	9.46	55.57	−1.27	−0.10	0.08	−7.09	0.66
	−8.84	0.00	13.01	1.59	9.34	−1.67	−12.44	7.24	−6.24	0.24
Two consecutive occasions	1.44	0.03	−0.07	−24.04	30.77	0.07	−0.07	0.04	−23.20	30.33
	5.60	9.95	−11.61	<−100	52.33	0.31	−13.93	13.27	−38.15	40.89

Occasions										
Five random occasions	18.05	-0.15	-0.09	-24.13	3.87	4.68	-0.05	-0.02	-24.61	2.13
	10.19	-11.48	-4.71	<-100	9.63	3.27	-2.76	-2.84	<-100	5.49
Three random occasions	14.72	-0.04	-0.21	-22.74	0.33	-3.82	0.13	-0.03	-23.86	-1.09
	8.23	-2.34	-17.41	<-100	0.71	-2.15	6.81	-2.71	<-100	-2.86
Two random occasions	5.13	0.09	-0.25	-23.53	0.09	-13.13	0.31	-0.03	-23.94	-2.86
	6.44	12.79	-41.46	<-100	0.33	-12.55	44.06	-3.32	<-100	-17.14
Five equally spaced occasions	40.12	-0.20	-0.41	-4.85	3.41	-1.22	0.51	-0.27	-15.26	-2.00
	>100	-99.50	-81.59	-32.39	16.31	-8.61	>100	>100	<-100	-21.17
First five occasions	-16.55	0.20	-0.03	-25.00	-3.61	-13.22	0.20	0.03	-25.00	-3.55
	<-100	>100	-30.00	<-100	-92.10	<-100	>100	30.00	<-100	-95.47
Middle five occasions	-33.41	0.50	-0.23	-24.95	-6.25	-45.00	0.46	0.24	-24.77	-6.25
	<-100	>100	<-100	<-100	<-100	<-100	>100	>100	<-100	<-100
Last five occasions	-32.50	0.50	-0.25	-25.00	-6.25	-47.50	0.50	0.25	-25.00	-6.25
	<-100	>100	<-100	<-100	<-100	<-100	>100	>100	<-100	<-100
First and last occasions	15.47	0.39	-0.25	-23.58	3.20	-22.14	0.40	0.25	-23.84	3.56
	33.39	38.80	-22.61	<-100	12.01	-43.88	36.18	31.09	<-100	15.60

Note: Population values are boldfaced; upper values in each cell are a difference between population parameter and parameter estimate $(q-\theta)$ values under the difference value is t value computed as a ratio of a difference value and a bootstrap standard error (i.e., $(q-\theta) / (\sigma_q / \sqrt{n-1})$).

TABLE 8.8

Results of Bivariate Dual Change Score Models (DSEM) Applied to Alternative Stochastic Data Based on Alternative Missing Data Paradigms.

Dynamic Parameters	Parameters in Difference Score Equation for X-variable: $\Delta X = \mu_{sx} + \beta_x X[t-1] + \gamma_x Y[t-1]$					Parameters in Difference Score Equation for Y-variable: $\Delta Y = \mu_{sy} + \beta_y Y[t-1] + \gamma_y X[t-1]$				
	μ_{sx}	β_x	γ_x	σ_{ex}	σ_{sx}	μ_{sy}	β_y	γ_y	σ_{ey}	σ_{sy}
Population values	**32.50**	**-.50**	**.250**	**25.00**	**6.25**	**47.50**	**-.50**	**-.25**	**25.00**	**6.25**
Complete data	.06	.00	.00	-.01	.02	.04	.00	.00	-.01	-.03
	1.11	.00	.00	-1.24	.00	.70	.00	.00	-3.32	-1.66
Odd-number occasions	-.16	.00	.01	.07	-.03	-.13	.00	.00	-.17	.01
	-1.77	.00	4.97	.98	-1.49	-1.41	.00	.00	-2.14	.50
Five consecutive occasions	.13	.00	.00	-.03	.00	-.25	.01	.00	-.01	-.10
	.78	.00	.00	-1.49	.00	-1.55	3.32	.00	-.47	-3.55
Three consecutive occasions	-.10	.00	.00	-.07	.02	.08	.00	.00	-.03	-.04
	-.57	.00	.00	-2.79	.57	.41	.00	.00	-1.19	-1.33
Two consecutive occasions	-.06	.00	.01	-.03	-.01	.33	-.01	.00	-.09	.02
	-.27	.00	.83	-.85	.26	1.69	-1.99	.00	-2.24	.50

Five random occasions	**-.08**	**.00**	**.00**	**-.05**	**-.01**	**.10**	**.00**	**.00**	**-.03**	**-.08**
	-.45	.00	.00	-2.16	-.41	.56	.00	.00	-1.19	-2.57
Two random occasions	**.32**	**.00**	**-.01**	**-.04**	**-.06**	**.39**	**.00**	**.00**	**-.07**	**.05**
	1.40	.00	-1.99	-1.11	-1.76	1.52	.00	.00	-2.18	1.21
Five equally spaced occasions	**-8.28**	**.02**	**.11**	**-.63**	**.35**	**6.42**	**-.06**	**-.06**	**-.60**	**.35**
	-3.61	1.81	3.53	-26.45	4.10	3.56	-3.32	-2.98	-2.53	3.32
First five occasions	**.07**	**.00**	**.00**	**.00**	**-.05**	**.00**	**.00**	**.00**	**.00**	**-.04**
	1.01	.00	.00	.00	-1.78	.00	.00	.00	.00	-1.42
Middle five occasions	**-14.42**	**.14**	**.03**	**-.04**	**-.19**	**17.02**	**.06**	**-.22**	**-.08**	**.56**
	-5.04	4.80	1.99	-2.21	-2.01	7.48	4.26	-8.42	-4.19	6.33
Last five occasions	**-15.97**	**.11**	**.13**	**-.03**	**.44**	**-4.19**	**.28**	**-.11**	**-.06**	**.06**
	-8.22	3.77	2.75	-1.49	2.33	-1.30	7.74	-2.96	-3.14	.45
First and last occasions	**-5.60**	**-.02**	**.15**	**.89**	**-.72**	**.46**	**-.02**	**.00**	**.92**	**-.93**
	-63.32	-1.66	6.78	13.84	-7.70	3.91	-1.24	.00	17.95	-14.92
Nonrandom level selection	**-9.28**	**.02**	**.15**	**.02**	**.44**	**9.63**	**-.05**	**-.08**	**-2.15**	**2.49**
	-4.21	1.66	4.66	.87	4.29	3.04	-2.37	-3.06	-15.73	112.61
Nonrandom slope selection	**-2.63**	**-.03**	**.09**	**-.03**	**.27**	**-3.20**	**.09**	**-.02**	**-2.84**	**.44**
	-2.05	-4.26	5.27	-1.24	5.72	-2.22	5.60	-2.21	-35.32	5.61
First three occasions	**-.11**	**.05**	**-.03**	**-.07**	**.27**	**.04**	**.00**	**.00**	**.04**	**2.41**
	-1.30	1.46	-1.24	-1.70	3.24	.48	.00	.00	1.59	64.81
Random one occasion	**-5.75**	**.26**	**-.12**	**3.53**	**2.52**	**-.73**	**-.30**	**.17**	**9.06**	**5.92**
	-26.86	4.79	-1.87	7.89	9.36	-4.43	-1.66	9.40	13.68	13.54

Note: Population values are boldfaced; upper values in each cell are a difference between population parameter and parameter estimate $(q-\theta)$; values under the difference value is t value computed as a ratio of a difference value and a bootstrap standard error (i.e., $(q-\theta) / (\sigma_q / \sqrt{n-1})$).

231

Table 8.9

Summary of Misfit Indexes for the Alternative Data-Extraction Structures by the
Dynamic Modeling Method

Data-Extraction Paradigms	Multilevel Model Fitted to Stochastic Data			Multilevel Models Fitted to Deterministic data			Dual-Change Score Model		
	f_c	f_θ	f_e	f_c	f_θ	f_e	f_c	f_θ	f_e
All occasions	.032	3.033	.984	.000	.000	1.000	.000	.072	1.000
Odd-number occasions	.005	10.650	.998	.117	14.782	.943	.000	.208	1.000
Five consecutive occasions	.091	10.295	.956	.192	1.293	.909	.000	.280	1.000
Three consecutive occasions	.024	8.741	.988	.027	17.630	.987	.000	.130	1.000
Two consecutive occasions	.038	1.887	.981	.026	1.446	.987	.000	.338	1.000
Five random occasions	.109	19.755	.947	.020	18.648	.990	.000	.132	1.000
Three random occasions	.440	20.601	.803	.040	15.210	.980	.000	.398	1.000
Two random occasions	.492	16.010	.782	.472	14.103	.790	.000	.503	1.000
Five equally spaced occasions	1.035	40.175	.596	1.063	40.145	.588	.011	10.481	.995
First five occasions	.600	21.186	.741	.212	21.184	.899	.000	.071	1.000
Middle five occasions	1.906	56.683	.386	1.875	56.052	.392	.123	22.307	.940
Last five occasions	2.000	57.481	.368	2.000	57.560	.368	.117	16.518	.943
First and last occasions	1.690	26.719	.430	1.370	27.017	.504	.002	5.616	.999

Note: f_c is a complex plane distance index computed as a deviation of simulation eigenvalues from the population eigenvalues (i.e., $f_c = \sqrt{a^2 + b^2}$), where a is the real part and b is the imaginary part of the sum of weighted squared differences between the true eigenvalue and the sample eigenvalue (i.e., $f_\lambda = \sum_i (l_i - \lambda_i)^2/\lambda_i^2$); f_θ is the sum of squared deviation of dynamic parameters from their population dynamic parameters (i.e., $f_\theta = \sum_i (q_i - \theta_i)^2$); f_e is a normed measure of fit for the dynamic parameters (i.e., $f_e = exp(-.5 f_c)$).

available, (b) there were no coupling interaction between x and y variables, and (c) an error term was set to 0 on all occasions. The traditional regression model failed to recover population dynamic parameters when (a) the data were incomplete, (b) coupling parameters were introduced, and (c) residuals were introduced in the time series.

The bivariate dual-change score SEM outperformed the traditional regression model in reproducing characteristics of the population dynamic system. The dual-change score SEM enabled us to recover population parameters under a majority of incomplete data paradigms. Based on Monte Carlo simulation with incomplete data, we found that one does not need to collect hundreds of data points to extract dynamic characteristics. It seems that when data-extraction paradigms allow the overall trajectories proximate to the population trajectories, our dynamic SEM enables us to recover population parameters accurately. Thus, we found that no more than five repeated measures were sufficient to recover the population parameters given that the overall trajectories showed resemblance to the population trajectories. Surprisingly, results based on only two or three consecutive measurements could recover the overall dynamic features as well as could more dense data paradigms.

Traditional cross-sectional data schemes failed to yield accurate estimates of several parameters. However, even with cross-sectional data, the DSEM was able to roughly recover the dynamic parameters (i.e., self-feedback and coupling parameters) as long as the cross-sectional data were drawn from the full set completely at random (Little & Rubin, 1987). Stochastic terms (variance and covariance) were not accurately recovered as the density of data deteriorates. Hence, cross-sectional design should not be used as replacements for long-term repeated measures designs.

When an overall trajectory was represented by only the middle or terminal parts of data, the DSEM could not accurately recover the dynamic parameters. These data-extraction paradigms failed to establish the true initial condition of the dynamics. This suggests that an initial condition (or level) needs to be established to accurately portray dynamic characteristics, and the dynamic characteristics are sensitive to initial conditions. Furthermore, these incomplete data paradigms extract only portions of data where there is little motion (i.e., shapes of the growth were flat). Not surprisingly, it is difficult to estimate dynamic parameters when data show no movement across time.

All in all, deterioration of data did not seriously worsen ability to recover the population parameter by our DSEM dynamic system. We have to emphasize that degradation of data is not systematic in a majority of missing data paradigms. We conformed to the principle of MCAR (missing completely at random) in degrading our data set.

Dynamic systems are tested and utilized in bioengineering, physical, kinetic chemical, ecological, econometric, and other computational sciences. In social sciences, researchers are gradually beginning to see the utility of the dynamic modeling. However, it has not been seen that SEM can be applied to account for attributes of dynamic systems. The traditional approach to analyze change scores has been the use of a least squares regression model with change scores as a dependent variable. However, there exists a long controversy about and argument against the use of change scores (Allison, 1990; Cronbach & Furby, 1970). According to our simulation results, a multilevel regression model failed when the data were perturbed by missing data conditions, stochastic terms, and influences of external forces. Thus, a use of the regression model with a change score as a dependent variable warrants caution.

The current simulation study was prompted by our desire to show that bivariate difference equation systems can be structured by SEM methodology and the conviction that the approach works better than the traditional regression model approach. Before we actually apply this bivariate linear difference equation model to empirical data, we are compelled to demonstrate how well our dynamic models really work. Data collected in social science experiments are frequently short-circuited; even if they are collected repeatedly, the repeated measures are in general localized and short-ranged. Therefore, we were also prompted to examine how much data are necessary to extract dynamic features if we were lucky to have repeated measures data sets.

Our simulation study convincingly illustrated that bivariate difference equation systems can be modeled by SEM. Although we reported results based on one set of population parameters, we have examined a wide variety of bivariate dynamic population parameters such as changing a sign of β or γ, decreasing or increasing magnitude of self-feedback or coupling, nullifying coupling, and so forth. In all the instances we attempted so far, simulated dynamic system features are consistently and accurately recovered with our model. Our model is thus robust and consistent. In contrast, the traditional regression model approach failed to accurately capture characteristics of the dynamic system in all incomplete data paradigms. Thus, we argue against the use of the least squares regression approaches with change scores as a dependent variable to characterize the dynamic nature of multivariate variables systems.

Our simulation analyses showed that characteristics of linear dynamic systems can be evaluated by SEM methodology. We have simply translated bivariate difference score equations into a latent variable path model. Our model, as it turns out, does not require any analytical solution or Runge–Kutta types of numerical solution for a system of differential equations. Therefore, it is highly practical. Furthermore, our model incorporates individual differences among initial conditions and constant change scores to dynamic processes, whereas a single bivariate time-series model generally fails to characterize individual differences. Therefore, our model is suitable for analyzing multiple-subject, multivariate repeated measures data that are prevalent in social science research.

There may be other more practical ways to estimate the linear dynamic parameters of our simulation. For example, the simplification of a bivariate system proposed by Coleman (1968) may be fitted using nonlinear mixed model program (SAS PROC NLMIXED). Also the techniques described by Nesselroade and Boker (1994), Boker and Nesselroade (in press), and Boker and Graham (1998) may apply to these same models as well. These alternative techniques were not studied here, but might prove useful in future work.

An extension of this simulation study is currently in progress. This phase of the study includes structuring univariate second-order dynamic models, structuring bivariate second-order dynamic systems, examining alternative systematic data-selection effects on dynamic parameters, and stochastic difference equation models.

APPENDIX

The following is pseudocodes for generating a system of time series based on the difference equation model.

Step [1]: Establish population parameters for a bivariate dynamical system

$\mu_{x0} = 5$	Mean of Initial Condition of x	$\mu_{y0} = 5$	Mean of Initial Condition of y
$\phi_{x0} = 5$	STD of Initial condition of x	$\phi_{y0} = 5$	STD of Initial condition of y
$\psi_{ex} = 5$	STD of uniqueness of x	$\psi_{ey} = 5$	STD of uniqueness of y
$\beta_x = -.5$	Self-feedback parameter of x	$\beta_y = -.5$	Self-feedback parameter of y
$\gamma_x = -.25$	Coupling parameter from y to x	$\gamma_y = .25$	Coupling parameter from x to y
$\mu_{xs} = 32.5$	Mean of constant change for x	$\mu_{ys} = 47.5$	Mean of constant change for y
$\phi_{xs} = 2.5$	STD of constant change for x	$\phi_{ys} = 2.5$	STD of constant change for y

Step [2]: For Subject 1 to Subject 100, recursively generate X and Y scores from time 1 to time 20. In this step, first generate initial conditions for variables X and Y for each subject, then generate latent true scores and perturbed observed scores at each time point.

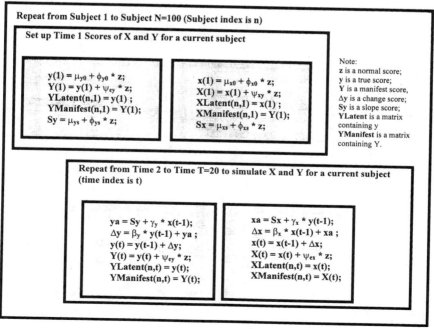

APPENDIX TABLE 8.1

Results of a Single-Level Difference Score Regression Model Applied to Alternative Deterministic Data Based on Alternative Missing Data Paradigms.

Variable	Parameters in Difference Score Equation for X-variable: $\Delta X = \mu_{sx} + \beta_x X[t-1] + \gamma_x Y[t-1]$			Parameters in Difference Score Equation for Y-variable: $\Delta Y = \mu_{sy} + \beta_y Y[t-1] + \gamma_y Y[t-1]$		
	μ_{sx}	β_x	γ_x	μ_{sy}	β_y	γ_y
Missing data paradigms	**32.500**	**−.500**	**.250**	**47.500**	**−.500**	**−.250**
Odd number	41.11	−.54	.16	54.22	−.41	−.38
occasions	2.16	.03	.08	2.27	.07	.02
Five consecutive	36.53	−.62	.35	39.34	−.50	−.15
occasions	5.00	.10	.13	6.86	.11	.04
Three consecutive	37.91	−.64	.36	43.03	−.57	−.15
occasions	2.37	.06	.14	2.51	.07	.03
Two consecutive	33.86	−.47	.18	47.22	−.55	−.21
occasions	2.17	.03	.06	2.47	.06	.03
Five random	23.10	−.26	.01	17.11	−.10	−.14
occasions	11.74	.13	.10	13.73	.09	.12
Three random	32.74	−.36	.01	24.63	−.15	−.19
occasions	8.86	.10	.08	12.79	.09	.11
Two random	38.10	−.42	.00	34.23	−.19	−.28
occasions	7.18	.07	.07	10.02	.07	.09
Five equal-spaced	74.84	−.75	−.13	51.45	−.10	−.52
occasions	5.93	.05	.16	4.23	.11	.03
First five	17.26	−.24	.13	32.67	−.23	−.25
occasions	.49	.01	.02	.65	.03	.01
Middle five	−1.10	−.00	.02	2.97	−.04	−.02
occasions	.53	.00	.01	1.12	.01	.01
Last five	−.00	.00	.00	−.00	.00	−.00
occasions	.01	.00	.00	.01	.00	.00
First and last	48.34	−.11	−.01	26.25	−.10	−.02
occasions	5.71	.11	.10	5.15	.10	.09

Note: Population values are boldfaced; upper values in each cell are parameter estimates; values under the estimates are bootstrap standard errors.

APPENDIX TABLE 8.2

Details of Simulation Results of Bivariate Dual-Change Score Models Applied to Simulation Data Based on Alternative Selection Paradigms

Models		1 Odd 50%		2 5 Consec. Occasions 25%		3 3 Consec. Occasions 15%		4 2 Consec. Occasions 10%		5 Random 25%		6 Random 10%		7 Every 5 Occasion 25%		8 First 5 Occasion 25%	
Symbol	Density True Values	Estimates	Std Error	Estimates	Std Error	Estimates	Std Error	Estimates	Std Error	Estimates	Std Error	Estimates	Std Error	Estimates	Std Error	Estimates	Std Error
β_x	-.50	-.4989	.02	-.49	.03	-.50	.04	-.51	.05	-.50	.04	-.50	.06	-.56	.18	-.50	.04
β_y	-.50	-.50	.01	-.50	.02	-.50	.02	-.50	.03	-.50	.01	-.50	.02	-.48	.11	-.50	.03
γ_x	.25	.26	.02	.25	.04	.25	.04	.25	.06	.25	.03	.24	.05	.37	.31	.25	.04
γ_y	-.25	-.25	.01	-.25	.02	-.25	.02	-.25	.02	-.25	.02	-.25	.02	-.31	.20	-.25	.03
ϕ_{x0}	5.00	5.07	.71	4.90	1.90	4.51	2.02	4.80	2.05	4.81	2.10	4.97	2.09	4.93	.80	5.00	.70
ϕ_{xs}	2.50	2.46	.20	2.40	.28	2.46	.30	2.52	.40	2.42	.31	2.55	.41	2.85	1.05	2.46	.28
ϕ_{y0}	5.00	4.83	.79	4.75	2.26	4.95	2.30	5.13	2.14	4.72	1.99	5.24	2.89	5.03	.72	4.91	.68
ϕ_{ys}	2.50	2.51	.20	2.50	.27	2.52	.35	2.51	.38	2.49	.24	2.43	.34	2.85	.85	2.45	.28
μ_{x0}	5.00	4.90	.76	4.84	2.74	5.22	2.44	4.94	2.45	4.76	2.31	4.77	2.74	5.05	.72	4.88	.72
μ_{xs}	47.50	47.37	.92	47.25	1.61	47.58	1.92	47.83	1.94	47.60	1.79	47.89	2.56	53.92	17.96	47.50	.77
μ_{y0}	5.00	4.86	.74	4.78	2.63	5.18	2.46	5.16	3.07	4.83	2.26	4.82	2.45	5.02	.71	4.97	.65

(Continued)

APPENDIX TABLE 8.2
(Continued)

Models		1 Odd 50%		2 5 Consec. Occasions 25%		3 3 Consec. Occasions 15%		4 2 Consec. Occasions 10%		5 Random 25%		6 Random 10%		7 Every 5 Occasion 25%		8 First 5 Occasion 25%	
Symbol	Density True Values	Estimates	Std Error	Estimates	Std Error	Estimates	Std Error	Estimates	Std Error	Estimates	Std Error	Estimates	Std Error	Estimates	Std Error	Estimates	Std Error
μ_{ys}	32.50	32.34	.90	32.63	1.65	32.40	1.74	32.44	2.20	32.42	1.76	32.82	2.27	24.22	22.82	32.57	.69
$\rho_{x0,xs}$	.00	-.00	.15	.08	.56	.02	.66	.14	.71	.11	.59	.10	.65	.02	.16	.03	.19
$\rho_{x0,y0}$	.00	-.03	.22	-.1148	.63	.22	.66	-.09	.70	.05	.66	-.06	.74	-.03	.22	-.00	.20
$\rho_{x0,ys}$	.00	.02	.16	-.01	.61	.00	.62	-.16	.70	.04	.64	-.05	.68	-.00	.16	-.00	.19
$\rho_{xs,y0}$	.00	.02	.15	-.03	.57	-.12	.63	.03	.75	.02	.52	.03	.68	-.00	.17	-.01	.16
$\rho_{xs,ys}$	.00	.00	.12	.02	.15	-.00	.18	-.04	.21	.00	.16	.01	.21	-.01	.00	.00	.18
$\rho_{y0,xs}$	.00	.02	.16	.01	.60	.12	.61	.14	.72	-.03	.63	-.04	.65	-.02	.18	.01	.16
Ψ_x	5.00	4.99	.11	4.99	.21	4.97	.25	4.91	.40	4.97	.25	4.94	.32	4.40	2.36	4.50	.20
Ψ_y	5.00	4.98	.13	4.97	.20	4.93	.25	4.97	.35	4.95	.23	4.96	.36	4.37	.237	5.00	.19

Note: x0 and y0 are latent initial conditions for X and Y variables; xs and ys are latent slopes for X and Y; α denotes a self-feedback parameter; γ denotes a coupling parameter; ϕ denotes a latent variable stochastic term; μ denotes a latent variable deterministic term; ρ denotes a latent variable correlation; Ψ denotes a unique stochastic term.

APPENDIX TABLE 8.3

Details of Simulation Results of Bivariate Dual-Change Score Models Applied to Simulation Data Based on Alternative Selection Paradigms

Symbol	Density True Values	9 Middle 5 Occasions 25% Estimates	Std Error	10 Last 5 Occasions 25% Estimates	Std Error	11 NR Level 43% Estimates	Std Error	12 NR Slope 43% Estimates	Std Error	13 First 3 Occasions 15% Estimates	Std Error	14 First+Last Occasions 10% Estimates	Std Error	15 Cross-Sec 3.3% Parameter Estimates	
β_x	-.50	-.44	.14	-.22	.36	-.55	.21	-.41	.16	-.50	.24	-.52	.16	-.80	.28
β_y	-.50	-.36	.29	-.39	.29	-.48	.12	-.53	.07	-.45	.34	-.52	.12	-.24	.54
γ_x	.25	.28	.15	.38	.47	.40	.32	.34	.17	.22	.24	.40	.22	.13	.64
γ_y	-.25	-.47	.26	-.36	.37	-.33	.26	-.27	.09	-.25	.33	-.25	.10	-.08	.18
ϕ_{x0}	5.00	17.59	10.51	11.68	7.27	4.78	.77	4.89	.83	4.94	.83	3.67	1.01	6.49	3.32
ϕ_{xs}	2.50	3.06	.88	2.56	1.34	2.85	1.36	2.16	.80	2.94	.78	1.57	.62	8.42	4.35
ϕ_{y0}	5.00	15.04	10.52	10.27	7.09	4.78	.74	4.78	.95	4.97	.80	3.76	.98	7.24	4.88
ϕ_{ys}	2.50	2.31	.94	2.94	1.88	2.94	1.02	2.77	.47	2.77	.83	1.78	.93	5.02	2.68
μ_{x0}	5.00	27.27	55.19	37.44	24.86	5.01	.63	5.09	.71	4.95	.65	5.10	.68	10.10	14.96
μ_{xs}	47.50	64.52	22.65	43.31	32.08	57.13	31.47	44.30	14.32	47.54	.83	47.96	1.17	46.77	1.64
μ_{y0}	5.00	43.70	57.10	65.92	34.10	5.06	.71	4.88	.74	4.99	.72	4.99	.65	16.01	24.74

(Continued)

239

APPENDIX TABLE 8.3
(Continued)

Symbol	Density True Values	9 Middle 5 Occasions 25% Estimates	Std Error	10 Last 5 Occasions 25% Estimates	Std Error	11 NR Level 43% Estimates	Std Error	12 NR Slope 43% Estimates	Std Error	13 First 3 Occasions 15% Estimates	Std Error	14 First+Last Occasions 10% Estimates	Std Error	15 Cross-Sec 3.3% Parameter Estimates	
μ_{ys}	32.50	18.08	28.47	16.53	19.33	23.22	21.91	29.87	12.77	32.39	.84	26.90	.88	26.75	2.13
$\rho_{x0,\,xs}$	.00	.08	.60	.03	.63	.00	.18	-.01	.17	-.01	.30	.01	.52	-.08	.42
$\rho_{x0,\,y0}$	.00	.03	.80	.01	.00	.02	.23	-.01	.24	-.03	.20	-.09	.41	.06	.41
$\rho_{x0,\,ys}$	.00	.35	.54	.20	.65	-.01	.16	.01	.20	-.00	.47	.02	.47	.33	.45
$\rho_{xs,\,y0}$	.00	-.22	.62	-.18	.67	.01	.18	.00	.18	.13	.33	.03	.48	.07	.37
$\rho_{xs,\,ys}$	.00	-.03	.60	.35	.60	-.04	.46	.05	.31	.00	.34	-.11	.38	.74	.30
$\rho_{y0,\,xs}$	.00	.16	.61	.24	.60	.02	.16	.02	.19	-.05	.45	-.01	.44	-.20	.37
ψ_x	5.00	4.96	.18	4.97	.20	5.02	.23	4.97	.24	4.93	.41	5.89	.64	8.53	4.45
ψ_y	5.00	4.92	.19	4.94	.19	4.99	.22	5.04	.25	4.91	.37	5.92	.51	14.06	6.59

Note: x0 and y0 are latent initial conditions for X and Y variables; xs and ys are latent slopes for X and Y variables; α denotes a self-feedback parameter; γ denotes a coupling parameter; ϕ denotes a latent variable stochastic term; μ denotes a latent variable deterministic term; ρ denotes a latent variable correlation; ψ denotes a unique stochastic term.

APPENDIX TABLE 8.4

Results of Multilevel Difference Score Regression Models Applied to Alternative Simulation Data Generated Based on Bivariate Dual-Change Score Models

	Parameters in Difference Score Equation for X-variable: $\Delta X = \mu_{sx} + \beta_x X[t-1] + \gamma_x Y[t-1]$					Parameters in Difference Score Equation for Y-variable: $\Delta Y = \mu_{sy} + \beta_y Y[t-1] + \gamma_y X[t-1]$				
	μ_{sx}	β_x	γ_x	σ_{ex}	σ_{sx}	μ_{sy}	β_y	γ_y	σ_{ey}	σ_{sy}
Population #1	**32.50**	**−.50**	**.250**	**25.0 or .00**	**6.25**	**47.50**	**−.50**	**−.25**	**25.00 or .00**	**6.25**
Stochastic Model	2.31	−.01	−.03	8.71	−1.44	1.96	−.13	.06	6.68	1.38
	39.63	−99.50	−29.85	68.78	−13.78	37.50	<−100	59.70	52.75	11.54
Deterministic Model	.00	.00	.00	6.31	−6.25	.00	.00	.00	.00	.18
	.00	.00	.00	73.86	<−100	.00	.00	.00	.00	1.95
Population #2	**−2.00**	**−.30**	**−.50**	**25.00 or .00**	**1.00**	**2.00**	**.30**	**−.50**	**25.00 or .00**	**1.00**
Stochastic Model	−.12	−.22	−.13	16.69	−.37	−.12	−.07	−.12	48.60	−1.00
	−7.02	−72.97	−64.67	>100	−8.18	−7.46	−34.82	−39.80	>100	<−100

(Continued)

APPENDIX TABLE 8.4
(Continued)

	Parameters in Difference Score Equation for X-variable: $\Delta X = \mu_{sx} + \beta_x X[t-1] + \gamma_x Y[t-1]$					Parameters in Difference Score Equation for Y-variable: $\Delta Y = \mu_{sy} + \beta_y Y[t-1] + \gamma_y X[t-1]$				
	μ_{sx}	β_x	γ_x	σ_{ex}	σ_{xx}	μ_{sy}	β_y	γ_y	σ_{ey}	σ_{sy}
Deterministic	−.01	.00	.00	.00	.03	.00	.00	.00	.00	.00
Model	−.90	.00	.00	.00	2.13	.00	.00	.00	.00	.00
Population #3	**−10.00**	**−.60**	**.00**	**25.00** or **.00**	**.25**	**−10.00**	**.600**	**.00**	**25.00** or **.00**	**.25**
Stochastic	−.01	1.20	−.00	63.98	−.25	.01	.00	−.00	65.05	−.25
Model	−.90	>100	−.00	>100	<−100	.83	.00	−.00	>100	<−100
Deterministic	.00	1.20	−.00	.00	.00	.00	.00	−.00	.00	−.01
Model	.00	>100	−.00	.00	.00	.00	.00	−.00	.00	−3.32
Population #4	**20.00**	**−.30**	**−.50**	**25.00** or **.00**	**1.00**	**30.00**	**−.50**	**.00**	**25.00** or **.00**	**1.00**
Stochastic	−4.14	−.02	.07	18.19	−1.00	5.78	−.12	−.06	5.73	−.80
Model	−56.43	−19.90	69.65	>100	<−100	99.16	<−100	−59.70	49.58	−37.90
Deterministic	−.01	.00	.00	.00	.01	−.01	.00	−.00	.00	.00
Model	−.99	.00	.00	.00	.83	−.99	.00	−.00	.00	.00

Note: Population values are boldfaced; upper values in each cell are a difference between population parameter and parameter estimate $(q-\theta)$, and values under the difference value is t value computed as a ratio of a difference value and a bootstrap standard error—that is, $(q-\theta)/(\sigma_q/\sqrt{n-1})$.

242

ACKNOWLEDGEMENT

The research was supported by grant AG-07137 from the National Institute of Aging. We thank many colleagues for their comments and suggestions, especially Dr. Steve Boker of University of Notre Dame, Dr. Michael Browne of Ohio State University, Dr. Patricia Cohen of Columbia University, and Dr. John Nesselroade and Emilio Ferrer of University of Virginia. We also thank Dr. Mike Neale of Medical College of Virginia for the free use of the Mx program and generously assisting us with this research.

REFERENCES

Alligood, K. T., Sauer, T. D., & Yorke, J. A. (1996). *Chaos: An introduction to dynamical systems.* New York: Springer-Verlag.

Allison, P. (1987). Estimation of linear models with incomplete data. In C. Clogg (Ed.), *Sociological methodology, 1987* (pp. 71–103). San Francisco: Jossey-Bass.

Allison, P. D. (1990). Change scores as dependent variables in regression analysis. In C. C. Clogg (Ed.), *Sociological methodology, 1990* (pp. 93–114). San Francisco: Jossey-Bass.

Anderson, E. (1993). Analyzing change in short-term longitudinal research using cohort-sequential designs. *Journal of Consulting and Clinical Psychology, 61*, 926–940.

Arminger, G. (1986). Linear stochastic differential equation models for panel data with unobserved variables. In N. Tuma (Ed.), *Sociological methodology, 1986* (pp. 187–212). San Francisco: Jossey-Bass.

Baltes, P. B., & Nesselroade, J. R. (1973). The development of analysis of individual differences on multiple measures. In J. R. Nesselroade & H. W. Reese (Eds.), *Life-span developmental psychology: Methodological issues* (pp. 219–251). New York: Academic.

Bell, R. Q. (1953). Convergence: An accelerated longitudinal approach. *Child Development, 24*, 145–152.

Boker, S. M., & Graham, J. (1998). A dynamical systems analysis of adolescent substance abuse. *Multivariate Behavioral Research, 33*, 479–507.

Boker, S. M., & Nesselroade, J. R. (in press, October). *Multilevel modeling of dynamical systems: Random coefficients and order parameters.* Proceedings of the Fifth International Conference on Logic and Methodology, Cologne, Germany.

Bratley, P., Fox, B. L., & Schrage, L. E. (1987). *A guide to simulation.* New York: Springer-Verlag.

Brown, C. (1988). *Ballots of tumult.* Ann Arbor: University of Michigan Press.

Brown, C. (1995). *Chaos and catastrophe theories: Nonlinear modeling in the social sciences.* Thousand Oaks, CA: Sage.

Brown, D. & Rothery, P. (1993). *Models in biology: Mathematics, statistics and computing.* New York: J. Wiley.

Burr, J. A., & Nesselroade, J. R. (1990). Change measurement. In A. von Eye (Ed.), (pp. 3–34), *New Statistical Methods in Developmental Research.* New York: Academic .

Cacciabue, P. C. (1998). *Modelling and simulation of human behaviour in system control.* New York: Springer-Verlag.

Cambel, A. B. (1993). *Applied chaos theory: A paradigm for complexity.* San Diego: Academic.

Coleman, J. S. (1964). *Introduction to mathematical sociology.* New York: The Free Press.

Coleman, J. S. (1968). The mathematical study of change. In H. M. Blalock & A. B. Blalock (Eds.), *Methodology in social research* (pp. 428–475). New York: McGraw-Hill.

Collins, L., & Horn, J. L. (1991). Best methods for the analysis of change. Washington, DC: American Psychological Association.

Cronbach, L. J., & Furby, L. (1970). How we should measure "change": Or should we? *Psychological Bulletin, 74*, 68–80.

DeWolf, D. G., & Wiberg, D. M. (1993). An ordinary differential equation technique for continuous-time parameter estimation. *IEEE Transactions on Automatic Control, 38*, 514–528.

Diggle, P. J., Liang, K. Y., & Zeger, S. L. (1994). *Analysis of longitudinal data*. New York: Oxford University Press.

Foerster, F. (1995). On the problem of initial-value-dependencies and measurement of change. *Journal of Psychophysiology, 9*, 324–341.

Fox, L. (1963). *Numerical solution of ordinary and partial differential equations*. Cambridge, MA: Addison-Wesley.

Gamerman, D. (1998). *Markov Chain Monte Carlo: Stochastic simulation for Bayesian inference*. New York: Chapman & Hall.

Gilbert, N. N., & Troitzsch, K. G. (1999). *Simulation for the social scientist*. Philadelphia, PA: Open University Press.

Goldberg, S. (1986). *Introduction to difference equation*. New York: Dover.

Hamagami, F. (1997). A review of the Mx computer program for structural equation modeling. *Structural Equation Modeling, 4*(2), 157–175.

Helms, R. (1992). Intentionally incomplete longitudinal designs: 1. Methodology and comparison of some full span designs. *Statistics in Medicine, 11*, 1189–1913.

Hertzberg, T., & Asbjornsen, O. A. (1977). *Parameter estimation in nonlinear differential equations: Computer applications in the analysis of data and plants*. Princeton, NJ: Science Press.

Huckfeldt, R. R., Kohfeld, C. W., & Likens, T. W. (1982). *Dynamic modeling: An introduction*. Thousand Oaks, CA: Sage.

Jones, K. (1991). *Longitudinal data with serial correlation: A state-space approach*. London: Chapman & Hall.

Jones, R. H., & Ackerson, L. M. (1990). Serial correlation in unequally spaced longitudinal data. *Biometrika, 77*(4), 721–731.

Jones, R. H., & Boadi-Boateng, F. (1991). Unequally spaced longitudinal data with AR(1) serial correlation. *Biometrics, 47*, 161–175.

Kamenski, D. I., & Dimitrov, S. D. (1993). Parameter estimation in differential equations by application of rational functions. *Computers and Chemical Engineering, 17*(7), 643–651.

Keen, R. E., & Spain, J. D. (1994). *Computer simulation in biology: A basic introduction*. New York: J Wiley.

Kessler, R. C. (1977). The use of change scores as criteria in longitudinal survey research, *Quality & Quantity, 11*, 43–66.

Kessler, R. C., & Greenberg, D. F. (1981). *Linear panel analysis: Models of quantitative change*. New York: Academic.

Kiiveri, H. T. (1987). An incomplete data approach to the analysis of covariance structures. *Psychometrika, 52*, 539–554.

Lange, K., Westlake, J., & Spence, M. A. (1976). Extensions to pedigree analysis: III. Variance components by the scoring method. *Annals of Human Genetics, 39*, 485–491.

Law, A. M., & Kelton, D. W. (1999). *Simulation modeling and analysis*. Boston: McGraw-Hill.

Lindfield, G., & Penny, J. (1995). *Numerical methods using MATLAB*. New York: Ellis Horwood.

Lindsey, J. K. (1993). *Models for repeated measurements*. New York: Oxford University Press.

Little, R., & Rubin, D. (1987). *Statistical analysis with missing data*. New York: Wiley.

McArdle, J. J. (1994). Structural factor analysis experiments with incomplete data. *Multivariate Behavioral Research, 29*, 409–454.

McArdle, J. J., & Aber, M. (1990). Patterns of change within latent variable structural equation models. In A. Von Eye (Ed.), *Statistical methods in longitudinal research: Vol. 1. Principles and structuring change* (pp. 151–224). New York: Academic.

McArdle, J. J., & Anderson, E. (1990). Latent variable growth models for research on aging. In J. E. Birren & K. W. Schaie (Eds.), *The handbook of the psychology of aging* (Vol. 2, pp. 21–43). New York: Plenum.

McArdle, J. J., & Epstein, D. B. (1987). Latent growth curves within developmental structural equation models. *Child Development, 58,* 110–133.

McArdle, J. J., & Hamagami, F. (1991). Modeling incomplete longitudinal data using latent growth structural equation models. In L. Collins & J. L. Horn (Eds.), *Best methods for the analysis of change* (pp. 276–304). Washington, DC: American Psychological Association.

McArdle, J. J., & Hamagami, F. (1992). Modeling incomplete longitudinal data using latent growth structural models. *Experimental Aging Research, 18,* 145–166.

McArdle, J. J., & Hamagami, F. (1999). Longitudinal dynamic analyses using latent difference score structural equation models. Under review by *Psychological Methods.*

McArdle, J. J., & Nesselroade, J. R. (1994). Structuring data to study development and change. In S. H. Cohen & H. W. Reese (Eds.), *Life-span developmental psychology: Methodological innovations* (pp. 223–267). Mahwah, NJ: Lawrence Erlbaum Associates.

McArdle, J. J., & Woodcock, R. W. (1997). Expanding test–retest designs to include developmental time-lag components. *Psychological Methodology, 2,* 403–435.

McDonald, R. P., & Marsh, H. W. (1990). Choosing a multivariate model: Noncentrality and goodness of fit. *Psychological Bulletin, 107,* 247–255.

Meredith, W., & Tisak, J. (1990). Latent curve analysis. *Psychometrika, 55,* 107–122.

Mooney, C. Z. (1997). *Monte Carlo simulation.* Thousand Oaks, CA: Sage.

Neal, M. C. (1995). *Mx: Statistical modeling* (3rd ed.). *Box 710 MCV,* Richmond, VA: Department of Psychiatry.

Nesselroade, J. R. (1991). Interindividual differences in intraindividual changes. In J. L. Horn & L. Collins (Eds.), *Best methods for studying change* (pp. 92–105). Washington, DC: American Psychological Association.

Nesselroade, J. R., & Baltes, P. B. (1979). *Longitudinal research in the study of behavior and development.* New York: Academic.

Nesselroade, J. R., & Boker, S. M. (1994). Assessing constancy and change. In T. F. Heatherton & J. L. Weinberger (Eds.), *Can personality change?* (pp. 121–147). Washington, DC: American Psychological Association.

Newell, K. M. & Molenaar, P. C. M. (Eds.) (1998). *Applications of nonlinear dynamics to developmental process modeling.* Mahwah, NJ: Lawrence Erlbaum Associates.

Nunez-Anton, V., & Woodworth, G. G. (1994). Analysis of longitudinal data with unequally spaced observations and time-dependent correlated errors. *Biometrics, 50,* 445–456.

Pooch, U. W., & Wall, J. A. (1998). Discrete event simulation: A practical approach. Boca Raton, FL: CRC.

Raykov, T. (1993). A structural equation model for measuring change and discerning patterns of growth and decline. *Applied Psychological Measurement, 17,* 53–71.

Raykov, T. (1999). Are simple change scores obsolete? An approach to studying correlates and predictors of change. *Applied Psychological Measurement, 23,* 120–126.

Rogosa, D., Brandt, D., & Zimowski, M. (1982). A growth curve approach to the measurement of change. *Psychological Bulletin, 114,* 726–748.

Rosner, B., & Nunoz, A. (1988). Autoregressive modelling for the analysis of longitudinal data with unequally spaced examinations. *Statistics in Medicine, 9,* 59–71.

Ross, S. M. (1996). *Simulation.* San Diego: Academic Press.

Rubinstein, R. Y. (1981). *Simulation and the Monte Carlo Method.* New York: J Wiley.

Schafer, J. L. (1997). *Analysis of incomplete multivariate data.* Boca Raton, FL: Chapman & Hall/CRC.

Scheinerman, E. R. (1996). *Invitation to dynamical systems.* Upper Saddle River, NJ: Prentice-Hall.

Tuma, N., & Hannan, M. (1984). *Social dynamics.* New York: Academic.

Vallicher, R. R., & Nowak, A. (Eds.) (1994). *Dynamical systems in social psychology*. San Diego: Academic.

van den Bosch, P. P., & van der Klauw, A. C. (1994). *Modeling, identification and simulation of dynamical systems*. Boca Raton, FL: CRC Press.

Wohlwill, J. F. (1973). *The study of behavioral development*. New York: Academic.

Wright, S. (1934). The method of path coefficients. *Annals of Mathematical Statistics, 5,* 161–215.

Zeigler, B. P., Kim, T. G., & Praehofer, H. (2000). *Theory of modeling and simulation*. San Diego: Academic.

9

Specification Searches in Structural Equation Modeling With a Genetic Algorithm

George A. Marcoulides
Zvi Drezner
California State University at Fullerton

There is much current research in the machine learning and statistics communities on algorithms for discovering knowledge and structure in data. Although many scholars (e.g., Selvin & Stuart, 1966) in the statistics community in the 1960s and 1970s considered such data-exploration activities as fishing or data dredging, Tukey (1977) argued that statistical theory needed to adapt to the scientific method. More than two decades hence, it appears that the statistics community has adopted Tukey's perspectives and acknowledged that model search is a critical and unavoidable step in the model-fitting process (Glymour, Madigan, Pregibon, & Smyth, 1997).

Most currently used model-fitting processes attempt to optimize some fit function with respect to a set of specified free and constrained parameters for a given collection of data. If the specified model does not fit, then the model is modified in an effort to improve the fit. In the structural equation modeling (SEM) literature, Bentler (1995), Glymour, Schienes, Spirtes, and Kelly (1987), Jöreskog and Sörbom (1990), Spirtes, Scheines, and Glymour (1990), and Marcoulides, Drezner, and Schumacker (1998) are just a few examples of the researchers who have introduced automated modification search procedures to improve model fit. It should be obvious that the starting point of SEM is a very demanding one, ideally requiring that the complete details of a proposed model be specified before being fitted and tested with data. Unfortunately, in many substantive areas, this may be too strong a requirement because theories are often poorly developed or even nonexistent. Because of these potential limitations, Jöreskog and Sörbom (1993) distinguished among three situations concerning model fitting and testing in SEM. The three situations include: (a) the strictly confirmatory situation in which a single formulated model is either accepted or rejected, (b) the alternative models or competing models situation in which several models are formulated and one of them is selected, and (c) the model-generating situation in which an initial model is specified and if it does not fit the data it is modified and repeatedly tested until some fit is obtained.

The strictly confirmatory situation is rare in practice because most researchers are simply not willing to reject a proposed model without at least suggesting some alternative models. The alternative or competing model situation is also not very popular because researchers usually prefer not to specify alternative models beforehand (Raykov & Marcoulides, 2000). As it turns out, model generating is the most common and preferred situation encountered in practice. In fact, most researchers feel that when

> extensive resources have been spent on data collection and all possible efforts have been laid down in formulating a model, but the data analysis indicates that the model does not fit . . . rather than accept this fact and leave it at that, it makes more sense to modify the model so as to fit the data better. (Sörbom, 1989, p. 384)

As a consequence, model-modification searches are common practice in SEM applications, and most available SEM computer programs provide researchers with options to try and improve model fit.

The modification of an initially specified model to improve fit has been termed a *specification search* (Long, 1983). A specification search is conducted with the intent to detect and correct specification errors between a proposed model and the true model characterizing the population and variables under study. Despite that the SEM literature has demonstrated that specification errors "can have serious consequences" and that one should "attempt and correct those errors," it has not defined an optimal procedure or a single strategy for conducting specification searches (MacCallum, 1986, p. 109). The most common approach for conducting specification searches in SEM is to change parameter restrictions (e.g., free up or constrain) in the proposed model one at a time and examine one of the many tests that have been developed (e.g., Lagrange Multiplier tests and Modification indices) to evaluate hypotheses concerning whether a restriction is statistically inconsistent with the data (Bentler, 1986; Sörbom, 1989).

A more recent specification search approach involves using a Tabu search procedure (Marcoulides, Drezner, & Schumacker, 1998). The Tabu search procedure builds on Bentler and Chou's (1990) recommendation to use the "all possible subset selection of parameters" and MacCallum's (1986) suggestion to continue the specification search even after a model with a nonsignificant chi-square has been obtained. The Tabu procedure is a simple and effective heuristic local search that proceeds by examining a neighborhood of the current solution. Unlike traditional search procedures (e.g., steepest descent), where the search terminates when there is no further improvement in the neighborhood with respect to the fit function, the Tabu procedure allows the search to exploit inferior solutions. This flexibility helps the search in getting out of local optimality when taking uphill moves. In addition, to avoid cycling, Tabu search imposes a sort of off-limits status (i.e., a *tabu* status) to those attributes recently involved in the choice of the new solution.

Although the Tabu search procedure has been shown to be very effective in SEM specification searches (Drezner, Marcoulides, & Salhi, 1999; Marcoulides, Drezner, & Schumacker, 1998), its success as a local heuristic often depends on the choice of the Tabu size and the definition of the neighborhood (Salhi, 1998). In contrast, adaptive search procedures have proved to be quite effective in such large-scale optimization problems (Salhi, 1998). A genetic algorithm is one type of adaptive heuristic search procedure that is carried out on a population of points (i.e., several solutions are considered simultaneously). Because of this, genetic algorithms are more robust than existing heuristic search methods. A genetic algorithm performs a sort of multidimensional search by maintaining a population of potential solutions and encourages information and exchange between solutions. Thus, the population undergoes a simulated evolution in which the relatively good solutions reproduce at each generation while the relatively bad solutions die. Another characteristic of a genetic algorithm that makes it somewhat different than other heuristic search procedures is that model parameters are not manipulated, but rather a coding of the parameter set is directly manipulated. Finally, and perhaps most important, a genetic algorithm generates information about a population of candidate solutions over any number of selected iterations.

The purpose of this chapter is to introduce a genetic algorithm as an alternative specification search approach for use in SEM. The chapter illustrates how a genetic algorithm can be used to discover the correct population model. The chapter is divided into several sections. The next two sections present a general overview and terminology needed to understand genetic algorithms. In the third section, an implementation of a genetic algorithm is illustrated using a simple function. Subsequently, a genetic algorithm is presented for conducting specification searches in SEM using a small example model. The final section of the chapter discusses the use of genetic algorithms and their implications for model selection in structural equation modeling (SEM).

OVERVIEW OF GENETIC ALGORITHMS

Genetic algorithms are adaptive heuristic search procedures that are capable of dealing with large-scale optimization problems (for a complete discussion, see Salhi, 1998). Genetic algorithms (GA) were first introduced by Holland (1975) as a way to emulate the processes observed in biological evolution to solve game theory and pattern-recognition problems. The main idea behind GA is that a Darwinian survival of the fittest strategy can be modeled for solving optimization problems. Based on this strategy, a population of chromosomes evolves over a number of different generations with only the best surviving from one generation to the next. Thus, evaluation of an optimization problem takes place on chromosomes (rather than model parameters), and there are chromosomal encoding and decoding processes that relate to the problem under study in a biologically evolutionary process.

In terms of specific optimization processes, the goal of a GA is to find the optimum of a given function F over a given search space S. For example, the search space S may be of cardinality 2^N (such as that for the number of possible equations in a multiple regression analysis with $N=26$ predictor variables would be equal to 67,108,864). A point of the search space S is then described by a vector of N bits, and F is a function able to compute a real value for each of the 2^N vectors. In the initialization step, a set of points in the search space (commonly referred to as a *starting population of individuals*) is selected (either at random or user-specified). Subsequently, a GA iteration occurs in four sequential steps (evaluation, selection, reproduction, and replacement) until a stopping criterion is met. The four sequential steps are depicted in Fig. 9.1 and described as follows (in a later section, these steps are illustrated and expanded using an example SEM model):

1. Evaluation: The function F is computed so that a starting population of individuals can be ordered from best to worst.
2. Selection: Pairs of individuals (quite often called *parents*) are selected (although an individual can appear in any number of pairs).
3. Reproduction: Offspring are produced by the pairs of individuals (i.e., by the parents).
4. Replacement: A new population of individuals is generated by replacing some old members of the population with new ones.

Genetic algorithms use a vocabulary borrowed from natural genetics. Some other useful terminology includes the following:

1. Chromosome: A string of binary codes representing a solution to an objective function. For example, 0101100011 could be used to represent a possible solution to an objective function. It is important to note that there are a number of possible chromosome coding schemes that can be used to set up a genetic algorithm. Besides the binary, other popular coding schemes include the decimal, character, and integer number representation (Reeves, 1993).
2. Genes: A binary coding representation of a chromosome (i.e., the 0 or 1).
3. Population: A set of chromosomes used at each iteration of the algorithm.
4. Operators: Manipulations that occur to the chromosomes (these include crossover, mutation, and reproduction).

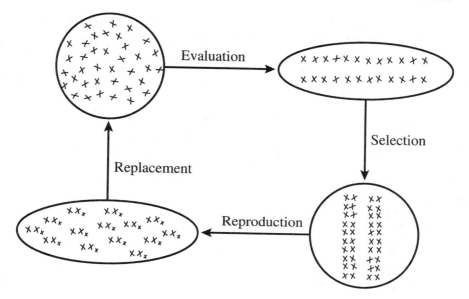

FIG. 9.1.   The basic steps of a genetic algorithm.

5. Crossover: A manipulation that occurs when two individuals (parents) exchange parts of their corresponding chromosomes to create a new chromosome.
6. Mutation: A manipulation that occurs when the gene of an individual is changed to form a new chromosome.
7. Reproduction: A manipulation that occurs when two individuals (parents) join to generate a new chromosome.
8. Neighbor: Two chromosomes are considered neighbors if the string of binary codes representing each chromosome differs by one gene. For example, the two chromosomes 111111 and 111110 are neighbors.

AN EXAMPLE OPTIMIZATION OF A SIMPLE FUNCTION

In this section, we discuss the basic features of a GA for the optimization of a simple function. The function is defined as

$$f = x_1^2 + x_2^2 + x_3^2 + x_4^2 + x_5^2 - x_1 x_2 - x_2 x_3 - x_3 x_4 - x_4 x_5,$$

with any value of x being equal to either 0 or 1. The problem is to maximize the function f.

It is clear that the prior function has only $2^5 = 32$ possible solutions with the values of the objective function varying from $f = 0$ to $f = 3$. To construct a GA that maximizes the function f, the following major components of an algorithm are needed.

Initial Population

Using a binary vector as a chromosome to represent values of the variables x_i, the initial population of size four is selected and involves randomly generated members of the possible solutions to the function f. Assuming that the following four chromosomes were genererated provides:

1. 01001 $f = 2$
2. 11011 $f = 2$
3. 01100 $f = 1$
4. 11111 $f = 1$

Genetic Operators

During the search operations of the genetic algorithm, several genetic operators are used. As mentioned earlier, genetic operators (crossover, mutation, and reproduction) are manipulations that occur to the chromosomes. To illustrate the crossover operator for Chromosomes 1 and 2, assume that the crossover point was to occur after the third gene:

$$010 \mid 01$$
$$110 \mid 11 .$$

The resulting offspring are

$$010 \mid 11$$
$$110 \mid 01 .$$

These offspring both evaluate to $f = 2$. Because the offspring are better than Chromosomes 3 and 4 in the initial population, the old chromosomes are replaced in the population with the new ones.

To illustrate mutation (i.e., the altering of one or more genes in a chromosome), assume that the second gene of Chromosome 2 was selected for mutation. Because the second gene in this chromosome is a 1, it would be flipped to a 0. Hence, the chromosome after this mutation would become equal to

$$10011.$$

This particular mutation leads to $f = 2$, and so it is also replaced in the population.

The processes of crossover and mutation continue for several cycles until finally the following best chromosome is generated

10101,

which corresponds to the optimal value of $f=3$. Table 9.1 provides the chromosomes for the 32 possible solutions to the example function, together with the value of the function for each possible neighbor based on the genetic operators. For example, Chromosome 1 evaluates to $f=0$ and has Chromosomes 17, 9, 5, 3, and 2 as neighbors. Chromosome 17 evaluates to $f=1$, whereas Chromosome 22 evaluates to $f=3$ (the optimal value), so no further improvement would be needed beyond this point in the search cycle.

IMPLEMENTING A GENETIC ALGORITHM IN STRUCTURAL EQUATION MODELING

There are a number of special issues that must be considered before a GA procedure can be set up to conduct a specification search in SEM. These issues include:

1. Choosing a criterion for the selection of a model,
2. Generating an initial (starting) population,
3. Defining the population size,
4. Selecting pairs of individuals (parents),
5. Deciding whether to improve the offspring, and
6. Establishing a stopping criterion.

Each of the aforementioned issues is described next, followed by a listing of GA search procedure steps for conducting specification searches in SEM.

Criterion for the Selection of a Model

There are many criteria that have been proposed in the SEM literature for evaluating the goodness-of-fit of a specified model (for an overview, see Marcoulides & Hershberger, 1997; Marsh, Balla, & Hau, 1996; Raykov & Marcoulides, 2000). Most criteria define goodness-of-fit in terms of the discrepancy between the observed and the model implied covariance matrices, although some combine this criterion with a parsimony criterion (Marcoulides & Hershberger, 1997). This parsimony principle has been reflected in many descriptive fit indices particularly the parsimony-related ones (e.g., Bollen, 1989; Marcoulides & Hershberger, 1997; Mulaik et al., 1989; Raykov & Marcoulides, 1999). In general, those among the fit indices that follow the parsimony principle introduce penalties for model compexity, yielding less favorable values for models having more

TABLE 9.1

All Possible Solutions for the Example Optimization of Simple Function

#	Genes	f	Neighbors (N)					Max f	N	Stop?	Max f	N	Stop?	Max f	N	Stop?	Max f	N	Stop?	Final f	Opt.?
1	00000	0	17	9	5	3	2	1	17	no	2	21	no	3	22	no	2	6	yes	3	*
2	00001	1	18	10	6	4	1	2	18	no	3	22	no	2	6	yes	—	—	—	3	*
3	00010	1	19	11	7	1	4	2	19	no	2	27	yes	—	—	—	—	—	—	2	
4	00011	1	20	12	8	2	3	2	20	no	2	28	no	2	6	yes	—	—	—	2	
5	00100	1	21	13	1	7	6	2	21	no	3	22	yes	—	—	—	—	—	—	3	*
6	00101	2	22	14	2	8	5	3	22	no	2	6	no	2	6	yes	—	—	—	3	*
7	00110	1	23	15	3	5	8	2	23	no	2	19	yes	—	—	—	—	—	—	2	
8	00111	1	24	16	4	6	7	2	24	no	3	22	yes	—	—	—	—	—	—	3	*
9	01000	1	25	1	13	11	10	2	11	no	2	27	yes	—	—	—	—	—	—	2	
10	01001	2	26	2	14	12	9	2	26	yes	—	—	—	—	—	—	—	—	—	2	
11	01010	2	27	3	15	9	12	2	27	yes	—	—	—	—	—	—	—	—	—	2	
12	01011	2	28	4	16	10	11	2	28	yes	—	—	—	—	—	—	—	—	—	2	
13	01100	1	29	5	9	15	14	2	14	no	2	30	yes	—	—	—	—	—	—	2	

254

14	01101	2	30	6	10	16	13	2	30	yes	—	—	—	—	—	—	—	—	2	—	2
15	01110	1	31	7	11	13	16	2	11	no	2	27	yes	—	—	—	—	—	2	—	2
16	01111	1	32	8	12	14	15	2	12	no	2	28	yes	—	—	—	—	—	2	—	2
17	10000	1	1	25	21	19	18	2	21	no	3	22	no	2	6	yes	—	—	—	3	*
18	10001	2	2	26	22	20	17	3	22	no	2	6	yes	—	—	—	—	—	—	3	*
19	10010	2	3	27	23	17	20	2	27	yes	—	—	—	—	—	—	—	—	—	2	
20	10011	2	4	28	24	18	19	2	28	yes	—	—	yes	—	—	—	—	—	—	2	*
21	10100	2	5	29	17	23	22	3	22	no	2	6	—	—	—	—	—	—	—	3	*
22	10101	3	6	30	18	24	21	2	6	yes	—	—	yes	—	—	—	—	—	—	3	
23	10110	2	7	31	19	21	24	2	19	yes	2	6	yes	—	—	—	—	—	—	2	*
24	10111	2	8	32	20	22	23	3	22	no	2	11	—	—	—	—	—	—	—	3	
25	11000	1	9	17	29	27	26	2	27	no	—	—	—	—	—	—	—	—	—	2	
26	11001	2	10	18	30	28	25	2	10	yes	—	—	—	—	—	—	—	—	—	2	
27	11010	2	11	19	31	25	28	2	11	yes	—	—	—	—	—	—	—	—	—	2	
28	11011	2	12	20	32	26	27	2	12	yes	—	—	—	—	—	—	—	—	—	2	
29	11100	1	13	21	25	31	30	3	21	no	3	22	no	—	—	—	—	—	—	3	*
30	11101	2	14	22	26	32	29	2	22	no	2	6	yes	2	6	yes	—	—	—	3	*
31	11110	1	15	23	27	29	32	2	23	no	2	19	yes	—	—	—	—	—	—	2	
32	11111	1	16	24	28	30	31	2	24	no	3	22	no	2	6	yes	—	—	—	3	*

255

parameters or fewer degrees of freedom (Raykov & Marcoulides, 1999). Accordingly, for two models with comparable overall fit indices, the preferred model is the one that has fewer free parameters (i.e., more degrees of freedom; Mulaik, 1998). Given the plethora of fit indices available in the SEM literature and because there is no best index, we chose to rely on one of the most popular fit as the criterion for the selection of a model in our GA search: the so-called *noncentrality parameter* (*NCP*; Bentler, P. M., personal communication, April 23, 1998). The NCP (where NCP $= \chi^2 -$ df) basically serves as a measure of the discrepancy between the observed covariance and model implied covariance matrices. It is regarded by some researchers as "a natural measure of badness-of-fit of a covariance structure model" (Steiger, 1990, p. 177). Obviously this criterion could easily be replaced by any other available fit index presented in the literature (e.g., χ^2/df, Normed Fit Index [NFI], or Root Mean Square Error of Approximation [RMSEA]; Bentler & Bonett, 1980; Jöreskog & Sörbom, 1993; Steiger, 1989, 1998).

Generating an Initial Population

In accordance with the confirmatory nature of SEM, a researcher provides an initial starting model (i.e., a user-specified theoretical model) that serves as a starting population member for the genetic algorithm. If a number of alternative models can initially be specified, these models should also be included in the initial (starting) population. Once the user-specified model or models are provided, other members of the initial population can be randomly generated. Interestingly, even an exploratory approach can be implemented by starting with a randomly generated initial model or an initial model where all parameters are constrained to zero (or all parameters are set free—a null model).

Selecting the Population Size

A number of interrelated issues must be considered when selecting the appropriate population size to use in a GA procedure. In general, increasing the population size will usually lead to better solutions as long as the number of generations is also increased appropriately. In other words, a large population size basically increases the chance of finding good solutions (or even the optimal solution) in the initial population. Of course, larger population sizes decrease the likelihood that particular pairs of individuals (parents) get selected to produce offspring that perhaps lead to the optimal solution. As such, selecting large population sizes should always be accompanied by an increase in the number of generations so that pairs of individuals have roughly the same likelihood of being selected throughout the procedure. The number of generations is roughly proportional to the square of the population size, and large population sizes require more computer time to generate the initial population.

Selecting a Pair of Individuals

A pair of individuals (parents) is always selected randomly for reproduction. The GA can then be set to either select many pairs of individuals for each generation and produce many offspring every generation or generate many offspring from one pair of parents and select the best offspring for inclusion in the population.

The Issue of Improving or Not Improving Offspring

Another important decision that must be made when implementing a GA procedure in SEM is whether to apply a descent algorithm (or any other local search algorithm) on the offspring. In simple terms, applying a descent algorithm on the offspring involves checking all possible gene changes until no better solution can be found by changing a single gene. The GA presented in this chapter applies a simple steepest-descent algorithm on offspring (but it could easily be adapted to other search procedures; see Drezner et al., 1999; Marcoulides et al., 1998; Marcoulides & Drezner, 1999). Thus, using a descent algorithm, all neighbors of a chromosome are checked to find whether there is one with an improved value of the objective function. For example, the chromosome 00000 considered as part of the maximization problem presented earlier has five neighbors:

10000
01000
00100
00010
00001

If any of these neighbors has an improved value of the objective function, the search proceeds only with that neighbor, and the five genes of this chromosome are examined. This process continues until no other neighbors can be found that improve the value of the objective function. As such, although applying the descent algorithm greatly improves the performance of the GA, with large models it can be computationally demanding and time-consuming. For example, each row presented in Table 9.1 represents an application of the descent algorithm procedure.

Stopping Criterion

There are several ways that one can control the number of generations over which a genetic algorithm iterates (i.e., the stopping criterion). One can simply run the algorithm with a fixed, prespecified number of generations or run the algorithm until a given number of generations does not change the population. Alternatively, one can even stop the algorithm after a given time period and accept the best solution in the final population as the preferred solution or report all the members of the population for consideration. The GA discussed in this chapter was forced to run until 50 generations did not change the population.

The GA Search Procedure Steps

The genetic algorithm consists of the following sequential steps:

1. An initial (starting) population is generated.
2. A pair of individuals (parents) is randomly selected.
3. The parents are merged to produce offspring.
4. The offspring are improved by a steepest-descent (or another) algorithm.
5. If the offspring's objective function is better than (or equal to) the worst population member, the worst population member is replaced by the offspring as long as it is not identical to an existing population member.
6. A mutation that is not related to the process of generating an offspring is executed. This means that a population member is randomly selected and one of its genes is randomly selected and changed. If the mutation results in a better population member, it is accepted as long as it is not identical to an existing population member. If not, the mutation is ignored. The algorithm returns to Step 2 for another iteration.

AN EXAMPLE SEM ANALYSIS

Model Definition and Chromosomal Coding

The approach used in this chapter to demonstrate the GA procedure for conducting specifications searches in SEM is similar to that implemented by numerous other researchers (e.g, Costner & Schoenberg, 1973; Herting & Costner, 1985; MacCallum, 1986; Marcoulides et al., 1998; Spirtes et al., 1990; Saris, dePijper & Zegwaart, 1979; Saris, Sattora, & Sörbom, 1987): (a) utilize data for which there is a known correct model, (b) initially fit a mispecified model to the data, and (c) determine whether a specification search leads to the correct model.

A simple confirmatory factor analytic model based on five observed variables with two common factors is used for illustrative purposes, but it should be obvious that the procedure can be adapted to any type of SEM model encountered. The example factor loading matrix has the following structure:

$$\begin{bmatrix} .87 & 0 \\ .82 & 0 \\ .81 & 0 \\ 0 & .77 \\ 0 & .78 \end{bmatrix}.$$

For this model, variances of the factors are 1.0 and covariance among the two factors is set at $\sigma_{21}=0.3$. Using the previous true model, the following population covariance matrix is generated:

$$
\begin{bmatrix}
1 & & & & \\
.71340 & 1 & & & \\
.70470 & .66420 & 1 & & \\
.20097 & .18942 & .18711 & 1 & \\
.20358 & .19188 & .18954 & .60060 & 1
\end{bmatrix}.
$$

Although any number of possible specification errors can be made in this true model, for illustrative purposes, we misspecified the two factor loading matrices presented next:

$$
\begin{bmatrix}
x & 0 \\
x & 0 \\
0 & x \\
0 & x \\
0 & x
\end{bmatrix}
$$

and generated a covariance matrix for a sample of size $n=5,000$ drawn from the known population model.

Accordingly, the model is defined by the following equation:

$$x = \Lambda\xi+\delta,$$

or simply

$$
\begin{bmatrix}
x_1 \\
x_2 \\
x_3 \\
x_4 \\
x_5
\end{bmatrix}
=
\begin{bmatrix}
\lambda_{11} & 0 \\
\lambda_{21} & 0 \\
0 & \lambda_{32} \\
0 & \lambda_{42} \\
0 & \lambda_{52}
\end{bmatrix}
\begin{bmatrix}
\xi_1 \\
\xi_2
\end{bmatrix}
+
\begin{bmatrix}
\delta_1 \\
\delta_2 \\
\delta_3 \\
\delta_4 \\
\delta_5
\end{bmatrix},
$$

where x is the vector of observed data on the variables of interest, ξ is the vector of latent variables, Λ is the factor loading matrix, and δ is the error terms vector. From the prior equation and with the usual assumptions of $E(\xi)=0$, $E(\delta)=0$, and δ uncorrelated with ξ, it follows that the covariance matrix of x implied by a model M has the form

$$\Sigma = \Lambda\Phi\Lambda'+\Theta,$$

where Θ is a diagonal matrix containing the error variances and Φ is the correlation matrix of the latent variables.

To set up the GA, one must consider the special structure of the previous matrices and set up a chromosomal coding scheme of the parameter set that can be manipulated. Looking at the covariance matrix of x, it is clear that the factor loading matrix Λ has potentially 10 elements, the Φ matrix has only 1 element, and the Θ matrix has 5 elements. Using a binary vector as a chromosome to represent these three matrices leads to the following chromosomal coding scheme:

$$\Lambda \quad \Phi \quad \Theta$$
$$1100000111\,|\,1\,|\,11111.$$

The prior chromosome therefore has 16 genes. Each gene is ordered according to the proposed structure for the first column in Λ, the second column in Λ, the covariance between the two factors in Φ, and the five error terms in Θ. A value of 0 in the chromosome means that the particular element is fixed, and a 1 means that the particular element is free. It is important to emphasize again that model parameters are never directly manipulated in a GA, only that the chromosomal codings are manipulated. Of course, it should be obvious that with more complicated models the length of the chromosome also increases. For example, looking at the model presented in Fig. 9.2 and defined by the equations

$$\eta = B\eta + \zeta,$$
$$y = \Lambda\eta + \epsilon,$$

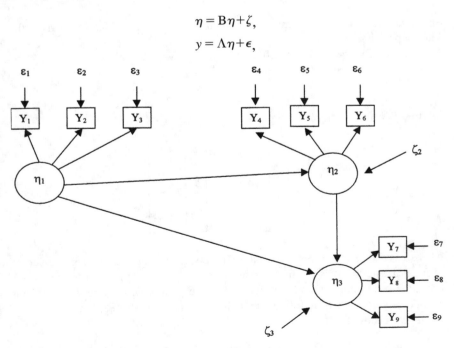

FIG. 9.2.   Example structural model.

the factor loading matrix alone has a chromosomal code of 11100000000011100000000000111.

Generating the Initial Population

Returning to the example confirmatory factor analysis model presented earlier, the next step is to generate the initial population. Before this is done, however, and to be able to trace and report the complete GA procedure introduced in this chapter, an important assumption is made concerning the matrix Θ. In particular, it is assumed that the five elements of the matrix in Θ (i.e., the error terms) will always be free (and therefore remain at a value of 1 in the chromosomal coding). Based on this assumption, the chromosome for the previous model can be written with only 11 genes as[1]

$$\Lambda \qquad \Phi$$
$$1100000111|1,$$

whose results are much easier to track and report.

Now suppose that in addition to the previously misspecified model, three other models were randomly generated to form the following four initial population members evaluated to their corresponding estimated NCP:

1. 11000001111   NCP=46.47 (50.47 − 4)
2. 10100111010   NCP=57.53 (61.53 − 4)
3. 11111001101   NCP=49.40 (51.40 − 2)
4. 00010110111   NCP=107.25 (111.25 − 4)

Tracing the GA Search Procedure[2]

Using this initial population, consider a crossover operation that combines Chromosomes 1 and 2. The crossover point is after Gene 5. This leads to the following result:

$$11000111010 \qquad NCP=57.77(61.77-4),$$

---

[1]It is important to note that the only reason this assumption is introduced is to make the chapter presentation of the GA easy to follow.

[2] The GA search procedure persented herein was programmed in FORTRAN and implemented alongside the LISREL8 program (Jöreskog & Sörbom, 1993). However, because the GA does not compute parameter estimates and fit statistics but uses the values generated by LISREL8, any other SEM program could also be used. In summary, each evaluation of the objective function for the GA is performed by iteratively creating and running an input file for LISREL8 until the stopping criterion is met.

which ends up being a better chromosome than Chromosome 4 in the initial population generated and so is replaced to yield the following new population (sorted):

1. 11000001111   NCP=46.47 (50.47−4)
2. 11111001101   NCP=49.40 (51.40−2)
3. 10100111010   NCP=57.53 (61.53−4)
4. 11000111010   NCP=57.77 (61.77−4)

To illustrate mutation (for further details, see section on Improving Offspring Using a Descent Algorithm), assume that Chromosome 2 is selected and that the mutated gene is Gene 4. The chromosome after this mutation is equal to:

$$11101001101 \qquad NCP=48.40 \ (51.40−3).$$

Because this leads to a smaller NCP value, the mutation is accepted and the chromosome is replaced in the population. This leads to the following new population (sorted):

1. 11000001111   NCP=46.47 (50.47−4)
2. 11101001101   NCP=48.40 (51.40−3)
3. 10100111010   NCP=57.53 (61.53−4)
4. 11000111010   NCP=57.77 (61.77−4)

It is important to note that if Chromosomes 4 and 1 were to be selected for a merge, the merge would not be accepted because the resulting chromosome is identical to Parent 1. Similarly, if Chromosome 3 were randomly selected for a mutation on Gene 11, because the generated chromosome

$$10100111011 \qquad NCP=58.51(61.51−3)$$

is worse than the original member, it is also not accepted. Thus, the population remains the same. At the next iteration, Chromosomes 4 and 2 are merged to yield

$$11000001101 \qquad NCP=54.36 \ (59.36−5).$$

Because this new offspring is better than the worst population member, it is replaced in the population, which leads to the following population (sorted):

1. 11000001111   NCP=46.47 (50.47−4)
2. 11101001101   NCP=48.40 (51.40−3)
3. 11000001101   NCP=54.36 (59.36−5)
4. 10100111010   NCP=57.53 (61.53−4)

Chromosome 4 is selected next for mutation and Gene 6 is randomly selected to produce a new chromosome

$$10100011010 \qquad NCP=118.96 \ (123.96-5).$$

However, because it is worse than the previous Chromosome 4 (which incidentally is the worst chromosome of the population), it is rejected. Thus, the population remains unchanged. Chromosomes 4 and 1 are then merged to produce the chromosome

$$10100001111 \qquad NCP=70.34 \ (74.34-4),$$

which is also not better than the worst population member. Chromosome 3 and Gene 3 are then randomly selected for mutation to produce the chromosome

$$11100001101 \qquad NCP=55.36 \ (59.36-4),$$

which is not better than the original population member.
   Chromosomes 2 and 1 are then merged to produce

$$11101001111 \qquad NCP=1.24 \ (3.24-2),$$

which is better than the worst population member and thus replaces population member 4 yielding the following population (sorted):

1. 11101001111 $NCP=1.24 \ (3.24-2)$
2. 11000001111 $NCP=46.47 \ (50.47-4)$
3. 11101001101 $NCP=48.40 \ (51.40-3)$
4. 11000001101 $NCP=54.36 \ (59.36-5)$

Chromosome 2 is then selected and Gene 3 is randomly picked for mutation to produce the much better chromosome

$$11100001111 \qquad NCP=0.79 \ (3.79-3),$$

which is also replaced in the following population

1. 11100001111 $NCP=0.79 \ (3.79-3)$
2. 11101001111 $NCP=1.24 \ (3.24-2)$
3. 11101001101 $NCP=48.40 \ (51.40-3)$
4. 11000001101 $NCP=54.36 \ (59.36-5)$

A merge between Chromosomes 2 and 3 results in a chromosome that is identical to Chromosome 3, and thus the population remains unchanged. Chromosome 3 is then selected and Gene 4 is randomly picked for mutation to produce

$$11111001101 \qquad NCP=49.40 \ (51.40-2),$$

which, because it is worse than the original member, is rejected. Chromosome 1 is then merged with Chromosome 3 to produce

$$11100001101 \qquad NCP = 55.36 \ (59.36 - 4),$$

which is also not better than the worst population member, and thus the population remains unchanged.

At the next iteration, Chromosome 1 is selected and Gene 8 is randomly picked for mutation to produce

$$11100000111 \qquad NCP = 0.00 \ (3.87 - 4),$$

which is replaced in the following population:

1. 11100000111   NCP=0.00 (3.87–4)
2. 11101001111   NCP=1.24 (3.24–2)
3. 11101001101   NCP=48.40 (51.40–3)
4. 11000001101   NCP=54.36 (59.36–5)

The processes of crossover and mutation continue for 50 more cycles until finally Chromosome 1 is accepted as the best solution.

Improving Offspring Using a Descent Algorithm

As discussed in a previous section, using a descent algorithm on each offspring improves the performance of the genetic algorithm because it checks all possible mutations of a chromosome. For example, consider the initial population created earlier as

1. 11000001111   NCP=46.47 (50.47−4)
2. 10100111010   NCP=57.53 (61.53−4)
3. 11111001101   NCP=49.40 (51.40−2)
4. 00010110111   NCP=107.25 (111.25−4)

All possible mutations of the chromosomes are as follows:

For Chromosome 1

1. 01000001111   NCP=115.14 (120.14−5)
2. 10000001111   NCP=108.11 (113.11−5)
3. 11100001111   NCP=0.79 (3.79−3)
4. 11010001111   NCP=42.34 (45.34−3)

  5. 11001001111   NCP=31.77 (34.77−3)
  6. 11000101111   NCP=47.47 (50.47−3)
  7. 11000011111   NCP=47.47 (50.47−3)
  8. 11000000111   NCP=56.89 (61.89−5)
  9. 11000001011   NCP=56.77 (61.77−5)
 10. 11000001101   NCP=54.36 (59.36−5)
 11. 11000001110   NCP=66.73 (72.73−6)

For Chromosome 2

  1. 00100111010   NCP=57.29 (62.29−5)
  2. 11100111010   NCP=58.37 (61.37−4)
  3. 10000111010   NCP=57.29 (62.29−5)
  4. 10110111010   NCP=53.96 (56.96−3)
  5. 10101111010   NCP=58.37 (61.37−3)
  6. 10100011010   NCP=118.96 (123.96−5)
  7. 10100101010   NCP=128.98 (133.98−5)
  8. 10100110010   NCP=106.11 (111.11−5)
  9. 10100111110   NCP=47.65 (50.65−3)
 10. 10100111000   NCP=63.00 (68.00−5)
 11. 10100111011   NCP=58.51 (61.51−3)

For Chromosome 3

  1. 01111001101   NCP=109.20 (112.20−3)
  2. 10111001101   NCP=96.39 (99.39−3)
  3. 11011001101   NCP=48.40 (51.40−3)
  4. 11101001101   NCP=48.40 (51.40−3)
  5. 11110001101   NCP=56.36 (59.36−3)
  6. 11111101101   NCP=50.05 (51.05−1)
  7. 11111011101   NCP=39.07 (40.07−1)
  8. 11111000101   NCP=48.61 (51.61−3)
  9. 11111001001   NCP=48.61 (51.61−3)
 10. 11111001111   NCP=2.18 (3.18−1)
 11. 11111001100   NCP=48.40 (51.40−3)

For Chromosome 4

  1. 10010110111   NCP=104.79 (107.79−3)
  2. 01010110111   NCP=91.02 (94.02−3)
  3. 00110110111   NCP=48.40 (51.40−3)
  4. 00000110111   NCP=106.25 (111.25−5)
  5. 00011110111   NCP=58.89 (61.89−3)
  6. 00010010111   NCP=124.27 (129.27−5)
  7. 00010100111   NCP=117.48 (121.48−5)

8.	00010111111	NCP=48.61 (51.61−3)
9.	00010110011	NCP=106.25 (111.25−5)
10.	00010110101	NCP=111.96 (116.96−5)
11.	00010110110	NCP=106.25 (111.25−5)

As illustrated earlier, the best mutation for each chromosome is selected and the process continues until no better mutation is found.

CONCLUSION

This chapter introduced a GA procedure for conducting specification searches in SEM. Using data with known structure, the performance of an adaptive GA procedure was illustrated. Although GAs have been used extensively for solving other types of large-scale optimization problems, their application to the SEM literature is new and a great deal of research remains to be done. There is no doubt that model specification searches in SEM are extremely difficult especially whenever the number of possible alternative models is high. Thus, there is a definite usefulness to any automated procedure that can make such a chaotic situation somewhat more manageable. We believe that GA specification searches will quickly prove to be quite helpful for improving models that are not fundamentally misspecified, but are incorrect only to the extent that they have some missing paths or parameters that are involved in unnecessarily restrictive constraints. Nevertheless, despite the fact that GA specification searches will generally find the best models according to a given fit criteria, all final generated models need to be cross-validated before any real validity can be claimed. In the case that equivalent models are encountered, GA specification searches will lead one to a list of population models, but it is the responsibility of the researcher to decide which model to accept as the best model. To date, no automated specification search can make such a decision. Therefore, as long as researchers keep in mind that the best use of automatic search procedures is to narrow attention to models on a recommendation list (a sort of top-10 list), the procedure will not be abused in empirical applications.

REFERENCES

Bentler, P. M. (1986). *Lagrange multiplier and Wald tests for EQS and EQS/PC*. Los Angeles, CA: BMDP Statistical Software.

Bentler, P. M. (1995). *EQS structural equation program manual*. Encino, CA: Multivariate Software Inc.

Bentler, P. M., & Bonett, D. G. (1980). Significance tests and goodness of fit in the analysis of covariance structures. *Psychological Bulletin, 88*, 588–606.

Bentler, P. M., & Chou, C.-P. (1990). Model search with TETRAD II and EQS. *Sociological Methods and Research, 19*(1), 67–79.

Bollen, K. A. (1989). *Structural equations with latent variables*. New York: Wiley.

Costner, H. L., & Schoenberg, R. (1973). Diagnosing indicator ills in multiple indicator models. In A. S. Goldberger & O. D. Duncan (Eds.), *Structural equation models in the social sciences* (pp. 167–199). New York: Seminar.

Drezner, Z., Marcoulides, G. A., & Salhi, S. (1999). Tabu search model selection in multiple regression models. *Communications in Statistics, 28*(2), 349–367.

Glymour, C., Madigan, D., Pregibon, D., & Smyth, P. (1987). Statistical themes and lessons for data mining. *Data Mining and Knowledge Discovery, 1*, 11–28.

Glymour, C., Schienes, R., Spirtes, P., & Kelly, K. (1987). *Discovering causal structure: Artificial intelligence, philosophy of science, and statistical modelling*. San Diego, CA: Academic.

Herting, J. R., & Costner, H.L. (1985). Respecification in multiple indicator models. In H.M. Blalock, Jr. (Ed.), *Causal models in the social sciences (2nd ed.)*. (pp. 321–393) Hawthorne, NY: Aldine.

Holland, J. H. (1975). *Adaptation in natural and artificial systems*. Ann Arbor: University Michigan Press.

Jöreskog, K. G., & Sörbom, D. (1990). Model search with TETRAD II and LISREL. *Sociological Methods and Research, 19*(1), 93–106.

Jöreskog, K. G., & Sörbom, D. (1993). *LISREL 8 user's reference guide*. Chicago, IL: Scientific Software International.

Long, J.S. (1983). *Covariance structure models: An introduction to LISREL*. Beverly Hills, CA: Sage.

MacCallum, R. (1986). Specification searches in covariance structure modeling. *Psychological Bulletin, 100*(1), 107–120.

Marcoulides, G. A., Drezner, Z., & Schumacker, R.E. (1998). Model specification searches in structural equation modeling using Tabu search. *Structural Equation Modeling, 5*(4), 365–376.

Marcoulides, G. A., & Drezner, Z. (1999). Using simulated annealing for model selection in multiple regression analysis. *Multiple Linear Regression Viewpoints, 25*(2), 1–4.

Marcoulides, G.A., & Hershberger, S. L. (1997). *Multivariate statistical methods: A first course*. Mahwah, NJ: Lawrence Erlbaum Associates.

Marsh, H. W., Balla, J. R., & Hau, K. (1996). An evaluation of incremental fit indices: A clarification of mathematical and empirical properties. In G.A. Marcoulides & R.E. Schumacker (Eds.), *Advanced structural equation modeling: Issues and techniques*. (pp. 315–353). Mahwah, NJ: Lawrence Erlbaum Associates.

Mulaik, S. A. (1998). Parsimony and model evaluation. *Journal of Experimental Education, 66*, 266–269.

Mulaik, S. A., James, L. R., Van Alstine, J., Bennett, N., Lind, S., & Stillwell, C.D. (1989). An evaluation of goodness of fit indices for structural equation models. *Psychological Buletin, 105*, 430–445.

Raykov, T., & Marcoulides, G. A. (1999). On desirability of parsimony in structural equation modeling selection. *Structural Equation Modeling, 6*(3), 292–300.

Raykov, T., & Marcoulides, G.A. (2000). *A first course in structural equation modeling*. Mahwah, NJ: Lawrence Erlbaum Associates.

Reeves, C. R. (1993). *Modern heuristic techniques for combinatorial problems*. Oxford, England: Blackwell.

Salhi, S. (1998). Heuristic search methods. In G. A. Marcoulides (Ed.), *Modern methods for business research*. (pp. 147–175). Mahwah, NJ: Lawrence Erlbaum Associates.

Saris, W. E., dePijper, W. M., & Zegwaart, P. (1979). Detection of specification errors in linear structural equation models. In K.F. Schuessler (Ed.), *Sociological methodology*. (pp. 151–171). San Francisco, CA: Jossey-Bass.

Saris, W. E., Sattora, A., & Sörbom, D. (1987). The detection and correction of specification errors in structural equation models. In C. Clogg (Ed.), *Sociological methodology*. (pp. 105–129). San Francisco, CA: Jossey-Bass.

Selvin, H., & Stuart, A. (1966). Data dredging procedures in survey analysis. *The American Statistician, 20*(3), 20–23.

Sörbom, D. (1989). Model modification. *Psychometrika, 54*(3), 371–384.

Spirtes, P., Scheines, R., & Glymour, C. (1990). Simulation studies of the reliability of computer-aided model specification using the TETRAD II, EQS, and LISREL programs. *Sociological Methods and Research, 19*(1), 3–66.

Steiger, J.H. (1989). *Ez-path: A supplementary module for SYSTAT and SYGRAPH*. Evanston, IL: SYSTAT.

Steiger, J. H. (1990). Structural model evaluation and modification: An interval estimation approach. *Multivariate Behavioral Research, 25*, 173–180.

Steiger, J. H. (1998). A note on multisample extensions of the RMSEA fit index. *Structural Equation Modeling, 5*(4), 411–419.

Tukey, J. W. (1977). *Exploratory data analysis*. Reading, MA: Addison-Wesley.

10

Item Parceling Issues in Structural Equation Modeling

Deborah L. Bandalos
Sara J. Finney
University of Nebraska–Lincoln

The use of item parcels in structural equation modeling (SEM) has become quite common in recent years. The practice of parceling involves summing or averaging together two or more items and using the resulting sum or average as the basic unit of analysis in SEM. This practice appears to have originated with the work of Cattell (1956; 1974) and has become increasingly popular in applied research areas such as education, psychology, and marketing. We conducted a review of the use of parceling by examining issues of the following journals from 1989 to the present: *Journal of Educational Measurement, Journal of Educational Psychology, Applied Psychological Measurement, American Educational Research Journal, Educational and Psychological Measurement, Structural Equation Modeling*, and *Journal of Marketing Research*. We found that, of 317 applied SEM or CFA studies, 62 (19.6%) employed some type of parceling procedure. More specifically, we found the following percentages within each journal: *Journal of Educational Measurement*, 60%; *Journal of Educational Psychology*, 23%; *Applied Psychological Measurement*, 25%; *American Educational Research Journal*, 33%; *Educational and Psychological Measurement*, 18%; *Structural Equation Modeling*, 13%; and *Journal of Marketing Research*, 9%.

The use of parcels has been advocated on several grounds. Parcels are said to be more reliable than individual items and to have more definitive rotational results

(Cattell & Burdsal, 1975; Kishton & Widaman, 1994). Increased reliability was cited most frequently as a reason for parceling in our review of the literature (29%). Another commonly offered advantage for the use of item parceling is that parcels have distributions that are more continuous and normally distributed than those of individual items, and thus conform more closely to the assumptions of common normal theory-based estimation methods such as maximum likelihood (ML). In our review of the literature, approximately 8% of the studies employing parceling cited this as a reason for doing so. A typical example of this rationale is found in Bridgeman and Rock (1993): "In order to better approximate the linear factor model assumption of multivariate normality, item parcels rather than individual items were analyzed" (p. 317). In the area of education, item distributions that lack normality and continuity often manifest themselves in the presence of so-called *difficulty factors*. References to problems with difficulty factors are commonly found in factor analyses of dichotomously scored items, such as those typically found on achievement and aptitude tests (e.g., Cook, Dorans, & Eignor, 1988). In the area of organizational research, Bagozzi and his colleagues (Bagozzi & Edwards, 1998; Bagozzi & Heatherton, 1994) have suggested that the use of parceling (referred to in their papers as a *partial disaggregation model*) results in the estimation of fewer model parameters because factor loadings and measurement error variances need only be estimated for each parcel rather than for each item. Because of this, it is commonly argued that the use of parcels may be beneficial in studies involving small samples because it will result in a more optimal variable to sample size ratio and thus more stable parameter estimates. In our review of the literature, 22.6% of the studies that used parceling referred to improving the variable to sample size ratio, 21% used parceling due to small sample sizes, and 29% stated that they used parceling to obtain more stable parameter estimates. For example, Gottfried, Fleming, and Gottfried (1994) stated, "To reduce further the number of variables and hence keep the models' degrees of freedom reasonable, variables were combined by averaging to create two indicators per factor" (p. 107). Similarly, Vandenberg and Scarpello (1991) provided the following reasoning:

> Creating subscales is the procedure recommended when item-to-subject ratios are too low to obtain stable factor solutions (Marsh & Hocevar, 1988). That is, if all 44 of the original items had been used, the ratio would have been less than 3 subjects per item. This is far below the ideal ratio of 10:1 (Nunnally, 1978) and even below the acceptable lower-bound limit of a 5:1 ratio. By creating subscales (three for each measure for a total of 12), an 8.3:1 ratio was maintained. (p. 206).

However, the assumption that smaller parameter to sample size ratios will necessarily result in greater stability of parameter estimates has been called into question by recent studies (e.g., MacCallum, Widaman, Zhang, & Hong, 1999; Marsh, Hau, Balla, & Grayson, 1998).

In our review of the literature, we encountered several other reasons for item parceling. These included arguments that parceling reduces the influence of idiosyncratic features of the items and simplifies the interpretation of model parameters. For example, Chapman and Tunmer (1995) stated,

> The main reasons for our adoption of this procedure in the present experiment are that each variable should be more reliable and should have a smaller unique component, and idiosyncratic wording of individual items should have less effect on factor loadings (Marsh & O'Neil, 1984). (p. 160)

Finally, some authors argued for the use of parceling on the grounds that parceled solutions will typically result in better model fit than solutions at the item level (e.g., Thompson & Melancon, 1996). As is argued in this chapter, however, this seeming improvement in fit may actually mask important model misspecifications.

Despite the apparent advantages alluded to earlier, the use of item parceling is not without controversy. Perhaps most important, the use of parceling depends on the unidimensionality of the items being combined (Bandalos, in review; Cattell, 1956, 1974; Hall et al., 1999), an assumption that is rarely tested. Of the articles that used parceling in our review of the literature, only 32.3% described the dimensionality of the items either by referencing previous studies of dimensionality or conducting an exploratory or confirmatory factor analysis on the items. The remaining articles, whether using newly or previously created scales, made no specific mention of dimensionality. Therefore, it cannot be assumed that when item parceling is practiced it is conducted within a set of unidimensional items. This is problematic in that, when this assumption is not met the use of parcels can obscure rather than clarify the factor structure of the data (West, Finch, & Curran, 1995). Another disadvantage of parceling is that it can result in biased estimates of other model parameters in some situations (Bandalos, in review; Hall et al., 1999). Finally, the use of item parcels will not yield as stringent a test of SEM models as would analyses based on the individual items because not as many free parameters are being tested as in models based on individual items.

PREVIOUS RESEARCH ON ITEM PARCELING

Despite the widespread use of parceling and the questions regarding its use, few studies have investigated whether, and under what conditions, parceling may be a defensible strategy. Of those studies that have been done, most have utilized actual data sets for which the true factor structure is not known (Bagozzi & Heatherton, 1994; Bagozzi & Edwards, 1998; Gribbons & Hocevar, 1998; Michael & Bachelor, 1988; Takahashi & Nasser, 1996; Thompson & Melancon, 1996). Because of this, it is not possible to determine from these studies how the use of parceling impacts recovery of a true factor structure or the accuracy of parameter estimates. The effects of parceling have therefore been assessed in these studies by comparing parcel- and item-based solutions.

For example, Michael and Bachelor (1988) used an existing data set consisting of 90 items to conduct exploratory factor analyses (EFA) on both item-level and parceled data. Although the factor solutions produced by the item- and parcel-level analyses were not completely consistent, these authors concluded that "if the scales of the measures are quite homogenous" (p. 102), the outcomes of these two analyses are likely to be similar. In a similar study, Takahashi and Nasser (1996), using an existing data set, formed parcels of 2, 3, 4, and 5 items. They found that the ad hoc fit indexes (GFI, NNFI, CFI, and ECVI) and the chi-square values for a CFA model improved as the number of items per parcel increased (and the number of parcels decreased). Thompson and Melancon (1996) used an existing data set consisting of 76 items to illustrate how items could be parceled together to ameliorate situations in which item level distributions are nonnormal. Items were parceled together "with the view of maximizing normality" (p. 9) presumably by parceling together items with positively and negatively skewed distributions, as suggested by Gorsuch (1983). Their results demonstrate that the parcel distributions were indeed more normally distributed than the item distributions and that the fit of maximum likelihood CFA solutions improved as the number of parcels decreased (and the number of items per parcel increased).

Bagozzi and his colleagues (Bagozzi & Heatherton, 1994; Bagozzi & Edwards, 1998) include the parceling approach as one level in a hierarchical series of item aggregation strategies that ranges from item-level analyses through parcel-, subscale-, and total scale-based analyses. These researchers argued that item level or totally disaggregated models are "unlikely to be applied successfully" (Bagozzi & Heatherton, 1994, p. 43) when the number of items is greater than four or five. However, these authors stated that the totally disaggregated model may be useful for scale development and refinement. They also argued that the parcel-level or partially disaggregated model will result in less measurement error than the item-level model and may be preferred for that reason. Nonetheless, they pointed out that parcels may provide misleading results if not constructed carefully, and provided the following guidelines for parceling items together: (a) items must be valid individual measures of the construct of interest, (b) items must be at the same level of specificity both within and across parcels (i.e., items and scales or subscales should not be parceled together), and (c) items within a parcel must be unidimensional.

In their 1994 study, Bagozzi and Heatherton, using a real data set, demonstrated the use of models at various levels of aggregation in estimating a second-order factor structure. In this study, the item-level model did not fit the data, whereas both the parcel and subscale-level models fit satisfactorily. The item-level model apparently resulted in large modification indexes for covariances among various measurement error variances. The authors interpreted this as possible evidence of method effects; more generally, it could be interpreted as evidence of an unmodeled secondary factor of some kind. As is seen in later sections, this type of influence can be effectively masked through the use of parceling. Bagozzi and Edwards (1998) used data from several scales to demonstrate similarities and differences among models at different levels of aggregation. Although the models using parcel- and item-level data resulted in approximately equal factor correlations, the two models differed with respect to the results obtained for multiple group analyses investigating the invariance of factor structures across groups of males and females. Finally, Gribbons and Hocevar (1998) conducted several CFA studies at different levels of aggregation on an 80-item self-concept scale. They found that, although the parcel- and subscale-level analyses differed little in goodness-of-fit, both were superior to the item-level results in this regard. They recommended that method effects be modeled when using item-level analyses and that large sample sizes be used to ensure stability of the estimates of these effects.

We are aware of four studies in which the effects of item parceling were investigated either experimentally or analyticallly. Marsh, Hau, Balla, and Grayson (1998), using simulated data, found that CFA solutions based on two (six-item), three (four-item), four (three-item), or six (two-item) parcels resulted in greater numbers of proper solutions than analyses based on the two, three, four, or six individual items. However, solutions based on the 12 individual items resulted in proper solutions for all samples. The chi-square/df ratio increased with the number of parcels used and was highest for solutions based on the individual items. The results with regard to proper solutions are consistent with those of Yuan, Bentler, and Kano (1997), who showed that CFA solutions based on parcels had greater power and smaller mean squared error that those based on individual items when the numbers of items used was equivalent to the number of parcels.

Recent simulation studies by Bandalos (in review) and Hall, Snell, and Singer Foust (1999) are of interest because they allow for the comparison of factor structures and parameter estimates obtained from parcel-based solutions to known population values. These studies are discussed in some detail because they illustrate several important issues that come into play when item parceling is used. Two investigations were included in the Bandalos (in review) study. In the first, coarsely categorized data with non-normal item distributions were simulated to study the efficacy of item parceling in ameliorating problems associated with such data. Results indicate that, when item distributions were non-normally distributed, the use of item parceling resulted in rejection rates that were much closer to the nominal .05 level than did use of individual items.

The second investigation of the Bandalos (in review) study was concerned with whether the use of item parceling could obscure a true multifactor solution. In this study, data were simulated to fit a complex three-factor structure in which half of the items with primary loadings on each of two main factors had additional loadings on a secondary factor (see Fig. 10.1). Primary loadings were set at .7, secondary loadings at .4, and measurement error variances at .3 for all items. A misspecified two-factor structure, in which the secondary factor was omitted, was then fit to both parceled and unparceled data. Items were parceled in two

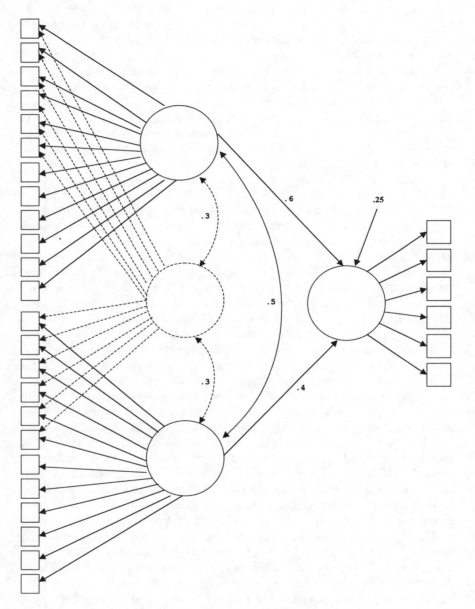

FIG.10.1.   Model from Study 2 of Bandalos (in review).

ways. In the within parceling condition, items with secondary loadings were placed in the same parcel, whereas in the across parceling condition, items with secondary loadings were placed in different parcels. Although both parceling strategies resulted in lower rejection rates than use of the individual items, use of the across parceling strategy resulted in substantially lower rejection rates than the within parceling strategy. Because the model was misspecified, however, a failure to reject the model represents a Type II error. Thus, parceling items with a shared secondary influence into different parcels resulted in the greatest number of Type II errors for this scenario. With regard to parameter estimate bias, substantial positive bias was found for the correlation between the two primary factors for both the within and across parceling strategies, with the latter approach resulting in slightly lower levels of bias. Parameter estimates for both of the paths from the two exogenous factors to the endogenous factor were negatively biased. However, this bias was not as severe as that observed in the factor correlation. Use of the individual items resulted in greater levels of bias than did either parceling strategy.

In the study by Hall et al. (1999), both simulated and empirical data sets were used to demonstrate the effects of parceling on parameter estimates and goodness-of-fit. In the simulated data, six items were generated to have primary loadings on one factor. In addition, two of these items had secondary loadings on another factor. The model also contained an endogenous factor (see Fig. 10.2). The relationship of the secondary factor to the endogenous factor was manipulated to determine the effect of parceling on this relationship. Parcels were formed in two ways: Items sharing the secondary loading were parceled into either the same parcel (isolated uniqueness strategy) or different parcels (distributed uniqueness strategy). These strategies correspond to the within and across parceling strategies, respectively, from the Bandalos (in review) study. Models were then analyzed in which all parcels were forced to load on only the primary factor; the secondary factor was omitted. Thus, the models analyzed were misspecified.

Results show that the goodness-of-fit for the parcels based on the distributed uniqueness strategy was not as good as that for the isolated uniqueness strategy when the secondary factor did not influence any other factor in the model. However, when the secondary factor also influenced an endogenous factor, the fit for the model based on distributed uniqueness parcels was superior to that for the model using the isolated uniqueness strategy. In the latter case, the estimate of the path from the primary to the endogenous factor was biased for both parceling strategies, although more bias was found for the distributed uniqueness strategy.

Hall et al. (1999) explained these results in terms of the treatment of the variance resulting from the secondary factor. When the two items that were influenced by the secondary factor were put into separate parcels, the influence of the secondary factor became common to two of the parcels. This source of variation thus became shared variance and was reflected in higher loadings for those parcels. Basically, then, this strategy allowed for the variance associated with the secondary factor to be absorbed into the primary factor. However, when the sec-

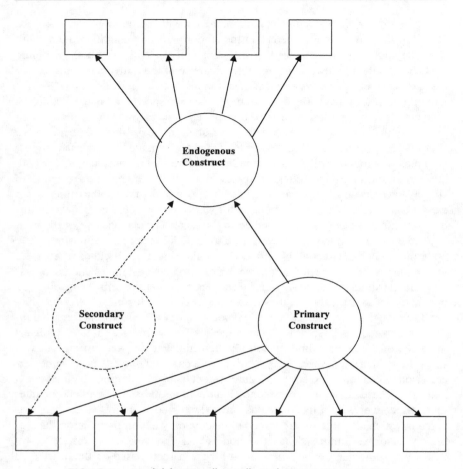

FIG.10.2.   Model from Hall, Snell, and Singer Foust (1999).

ondary factor was not related to an additional endogenous factor in the model, the
path from the primary factor to the endogenous factor was attenuated because the
proportion of variance shared by the new primary factor with the endogenous factor was smaller. This resulted in a poorer fit for this model as compared with the
isolated uniqueness model. When the isolated uniqueness strategy was used, the
variance associated with the secondary factor was isolated into one parcel. Thus,
the variance due to the secondary factor was absorbed into the error term for the
parcel with which it was associated instead of into the primary factor. This strategy resulted in a better model fit because the path from the primary factor to the
endogenous factor was not biased.

The relative goodness-of-fit of the distributed and isolated uniqueness strategies was reversed for the situation in which the secondary factor influenced the

endogenous as well as the primary exogenous factor. In this case, the fit of the model using the distributed uniqueness strategy was better than that for the isolated uniqueness strategy. In the distributed uniqueness strategy, the shared variance associated with the secondary factor was absorbed into the primary factor. Thus, the secondary factor was still able to have an influence on the endogenous factor somewhat indirectly, although this resulted in an upward bias of the path from the primary to the endogenous factor. However, because the variance associated with the secondary factor was isolated in the error term in the isolated uniqueness strategy, it was unable to have any influence on the endogenous factor, resulting in a greater lack of fit.

These results are consistent with those of the Bandalos (in review) study, in which an endogenous factor was influenced by two primary factors. However, in the Bandalos study, the omitted secondary factor did not influence the endogenous factor. Under this scenario, when using the across or distributed strategy, the effects of the secondary factor were absorbed into both primary factors. This resulted in more shared variance between these two factors and inflated the estimate of the factor correlation. However, the estimates of the paths from the two exogenous to the endogenous factor were negatively biased because the extra variance that was absorbed into the exogenous factors was not shared with the endogenous factor.

Based on the results of their study, Hall et al. (1999) made several recommendations for practice. First, item parceling should be used only when items are unidimensional. Use of the isolated uniqueness parceling strategy can increase the unidimensionality of a factor by forcing the influence of a secondary factor into the error term. It should be noted, however, that the model in this case is actually misspecified and will mask the true factor structure of the items. Because of this, Hall et al. suggested that this strategy works best when the secondary factor has a relatively weak influence on the items. In practice, however, it may be difficult to identify the secondary factor to accomplish this type of parceling, as well as to determine how strong its influence is. Use of the distributed parceling strategy, because it results in the variance associated with the secondary factor being treated as shared primary factor variance, can also mask a true multifactor structure. Thus, it appears that the defensibility of either the isolated or distributed uniqueness strategies depends on whether the researcher is comfortable with treating the secondary factor (or factors) as ignorable.

THEORETICAL FRAMEWORK

A recent article by MacCallum et al. (1999) provided a theoretical framework for the results found in the studies by Hall et al. (1999) and Bandalos (in review). This section and the next summarize their framework and relate it to these two studies. Although the purpose of the study was to investigate the relationship between the variable to factor ratio, level of communality, and sample size in the context of exploratory factor analysis (EFA), this study provides a general framework that underlies both exploratory and confirmatory factor analyses. The discussion hinges on the manner in which sampling error affects parameter estimation in these procedures. Using a framework adapted from an earlier article by MacCallum and Tucker (1991), MacCallum et al. showed that there are two sources of sampling error that come into play when a sample covariance matrix is used as an estimator of the population parameters of a factor analysis model. Using the notation of MacCallum et al., the population covariance matrix Σ_{yy} can be expressed in terms of matrixes of common and unique factor scores and their loadings as:

$$\Sigma_{yy} = \Omega\Sigma_{xx}\Omega', \tag{1}$$

where Ω is a matrix of loadings for common and unique factors ($\Omega = [\Lambda, \Theta]$ and Σ_{xx} is partitioned as

$$\Sigma_{xx} = \begin{bmatrix} \Sigma_{CC} & \Sigma_{CU} \\ \Sigma_{UC} & \Sigma_{UU} \end{bmatrix}. \tag{2}$$

Here Σ_{cc} is a population covariance matrix for the common factors, Σ_{uu} is a population covariance matrix of the unique factors, Σ_{cu} is the population covariance matrix of common and unique factors, and Σ_{uc} is the transpose of Σ_{cu}. If factors are standardized in the population, these matrixes would contain correlations instead of covariances. Further, unique factors are usually taken to be uncorrelated with each other and with the common factors. Thus, matrixes Σ_{cu} and Σ_{uc} must contain all zeros, and matrix Σ_{uu} is an identity matrix. Matrix Σ_{xx} then becomes

$$\Sigma_{xx} = \begin{bmatrix} \Phi & 0 \\ 0 & I \end{bmatrix}. \tag{3}$$

Substituting from Eq. (3) into Eq. (1), we obtain the familiar result

$$\Sigma_{yy} = \Lambda\Phi\Lambda' + \Theta^2. \tag{4}$$

In the sample, the model specified in Eq. (1) will not hold exactly. The factor loadings in Ω represent fixed values for each individual in the population and thus will have the same values in the sample and population (although the sample estimates of these may differ across samples due to estimation error). However, the matrix of covariances among the factors will depend on the sample analyzed. The sample matrix of covariances among the common and unique factors is:

$$C_{xx} = \begin{bmatrix} C_{cc} & C_{cu} \\ C_{uc} & C_{uu} \end{bmatrix}. \tag{5}$$

In particular, even when the assumption of zero correlations among the unique factors and among the unique and common factors holds in the population, these elements will typically deviate from zero in the sample simply because of random sampling fluctuations. The matrixes C_{cu} and C_{uc} will thus not be zero, and the matrix C_{uu} will not be diagonal. The decomposition of the sample covariance matrix C_{yy} resulting from Eqs.(1) and (5) will be:

$$C_{yy} = \Lambda C_{cc} \Lambda' + \Lambda C_{cu} \Theta' + \Theta C_{uc} \Lambda' + \Theta C_{uu} \Theta'. \tag{6}$$

The nonzero elements in C_{cu}, C_{uc}, and C_{uu} will result in a lack of fit of the model implied by Eq. (1) to the sample covariance matrix. This, then, is one source of sampling error that will affect both EFA and CFA solutions.

The second way in which sampling error affects the fit of the model in the sample can be seen from Eq. (6). Note that the unique loadings in Θ essentially serve as weights for the matrixes C_{cu}, C_{uc}, and C_{uu}. When common factor loadings or communalities are high, these unique loadings will be low, and the elements in C_{cu}, C_{uc}, and C_{uu} will not have as great an impact on the solution for C_{yy}. However, with lower communalities, the weights in Θ will be larger, and the elements of C_{cu}, C_{uc}, and C_{uu} will be weighted more heavily. Thus, it can be seen that, when communalities are high, a smaller sample size may be sufficient to obtain accurate results. The finding that, with more reliable or highly determined variables, one may not need as large a sample size is consistent with previous research (e.g., Bandalos, 1993; Velicer & Fava, 1998). This suggests that parceling items to reduce the variable to factor ratio may not be necessary for obtaining more accurate or stable solutions.

RELEVANCE TO ITEM PARCELING

In the context of item parceling, the framework provided by MacCallum et al. (1999) is relevant because it provides an explanation for the improvement in model fit associated with parceled solutions. With regard to the first sampling effect described by MacCallum et al., one result of parceling is to reduce the size of the matrixes C_{uu}, C_{cu}, and C_{uc} with a consequent reduction in the contribution from error resulting from unmodeled associations in these matrixes. This produces a better fit of the sample matrix C_{yy} to the model implied by Eq. (4) and is one reason that parceled solutions provide a better fit of the model to the data. In addition, as shown by Bandalos (in review) and Hall et al. (1999), parceling can be done in such a way that items with correlated uniquenesses, or nonzero diagonal elements in C_{uu}, are parceled together. When these parcels are then treated as indicators of the same factor, the correlated uniqueness is reformulated as shared common variance and becomes part of the modeled variance in the diagonal of C_{cc} rather than of unmodeled associations in the off-diagonal elements of

C_{uu}. However, parameter estimates of structural paths from the factor into which the shared variance is incorporated to other endogenous variables in the model may be biased when this type of parceling is used. These effects are illustrated in the studies by Bandalos and Hall et al., as described earlier.

With regard to the second sampling effect of MacCallum et al., the size of the elements of Θ affect the fit of the model through their use as weighting elements for the matrixes C_{cu}, C_{uc}, and C_{uu}, as seen in Eq. (6). One effect of parceling is to reduce the size of the elements of Θ. This is because parcels, being based on several items, are more reliable indicators of a construct than are individual items, and have less error variance. A second reason that parceling improves model-data fit is thus due to the reduction in the impact of the matrixes C_{cu}, C_{uc}, and C_{uu} on the solution. Another consequence of the reduction in error variance is greater efficiency of parceled solutions relative to solutions based on individual items. This effect is reflected in the finding by Marsh et al. (1998) that parceled solutions result in a greater number of proper solutions than solutions based on the same number of items. Similarly, Yuan et al. (1997) have shown that solutions based on parcels have more power and yield more efficient estimates of model parameters than do solutions based on the same number of items. These effects can be understood in the context of the higher levels of communality associated with item parcels, which results in greater stability and power.

The use of parceling can thus be seen to reduce the lack of fit of C_{yy} to the model implied by Eq. (4) in three complementary ways: by reducing the size of the matrixes C_{uu}, C_{cu}, and C_{uc}; by reducing the contribution of these elements to the sample matrix C_{yy}; and by reformulating variance due to cross-loadings. The first two effects occur to some degree for any type of parceling regardless of how items are parceled together or whether secondary factors are involved. Note that these sources of error reduction function independently of each other. When all effects are strong, a substantial improvement in fit would be expected over the corresponding item-level solution.

These results also have a bearing on the argument that the use of parceling is necessary in applications with a large number of variables relative to the sample size. The framework provided by MacCallum et al. (1999) demonstrates the mediating effect of the level of communality on the variable to sample size ratio. As sample size increases, the covariances in C_{cu}, C_{uc}, and C_{uu} tend toward their population values of zero, resulting in less error in fitting C_{yy} to Eq. (4). However, this effect is mediated by the size of the communalities: When communalities are high, the nonzero elements of C_{cu}, C_{uc}, and C_{uu} receive less weight in the solution, as described previously. In such situations, the impact of sample size in reducing the error associated with these nonzero covariances is less pronounced. In situations such as these, the emphasis on the need for item parceling may be exaggerated. With smaller communalities, these elements are weighted more heavily into the solution, and sample size plays a greater role in reducing this source of error. In these cases, the use of item parceling results in a greater reduction in error.

Finally, it would be expected that the use of item parcels rather than individual items would result in the largest improvement in model fit for situations in which the influence of secondary factors is fairly strong and the communalities of the items are fairly low. In the study by Hall et al. (1999), communalities are quite high (.89), and the influence of the secondary factor was fairly strong with the two loadings set at .4 and .5. Similarly, in the Bandalos (in review) study, communalities were .7 and secondary loadings were set at .4. Even in these situations, however, the influence of the parceling strategies on model fit was substantial.

RECOMMENDATIONS REGARDING THE USE OF ITEM PARCELING

Having established the necessary background, we use this section to consider in more depth the validity of arguments for item parceling and establish what we consider to be defensible as well as undesirable applications of this practice. We note here that the advantages cited for parceling differ across studies using achievement or aptitude scales and those using attitude or personality measures.

In the area of achievement and aptitude measurement, items are nearly always scored in a binary right/wrong format (although the increasing use of performance assessments has resulted in some changes in this traditional format). Items responses are thus, by definition, not normally distributed or continuous. Because traditional approaches to SEM assume the use of continuous, normally distributed data, methods of improving the normality and continuity of variable distributions is of major concern to researchers in these areas. This concern predates the use of SEM and was discussed in the literature as early as 1941 (Ferguson, 1941) in the context of so-called *difficulty factors,* which were found to arise in the factor analysis of binary data. As explained by McDonald and Ahlawat (1974), difficulty factors result from the fact that the regression of assumed continuous latent factors on binary items is nonlinear and is thus misspecified under a traditional linear factor analysis model. Carroll (1983) also pointed out that factor analyses of binary-scored achievement test items are affected by differences in guessing across items. Item parceling is one method that has been commonly used to circumvent these problems in factor analysis as well as in SEM. Cook, Dorans, and Eignor (1988) presented one application in the CFA area. These authors described the use of parcels as a way to linearize the nonlinear factor/item relationship and recommended that parcels be created that have approximately equal means (or difficulty levels) and variances. These are referred to as *parallel parcels* and are widely used in CFAs of cognitive test data. In our analysis, the applications of parceling in situations such as these are among the more defensible in the CFA literature. We base this judgement on the fact that the instruments in these studies have typically been investigated extensively and the factor structures are well known to the researchers and the parceling is carried out within clearly unidimensional factors. In our opinion, this constitutes a necessary (although not a sufficient) condition for parceling. However, it should be noted that recent developments in nonlinear factor analysis may negate the need to parcel binary items as they allow for the express modeling of the nonlinear item/factor relationship (see e.g., Mislevy, 1986; Muthén & Muthén, 1998).

Another situation involving cognitive test data in which parceling is typically used is that in which sets of questions refer to the same stimulus material. A common example of this is the inclusion of a reading passage that is followed by a set of reading comprehension items based on that passage. In situations such as these, it can be argued that the items violate the assumption of conditional independence, in which the construct being measured by the test is assumed to account for all of the covariation among the items. Wainer and Kiely (1987) introduced the concept of *testlets* to describe these situations as well as other sets of locally dependent items such as those developed for use in computerized adaptive tests (CATs). Items within a testlet are aggregated as bundles or parcels for purposes of analysis. The use of testlets represents a situation in which we feel that the use of parceling may be defended on theoretical grounds. This is because the reason for the dependence among items that necessitates the parceling approach is explicitly defined in these situations, and the unidimensionality of the items used to form a parcel is typically well-established.

In contrast, we are unconvinced by many of the arguments advanced by researchers in the areas of personality and attitude measurement for the use of item parceling. A common reason cited by advocates of item parceling in these areas is that parceled solutions result in a better fit of the model to the data as compared with item-based solutions (Bagozzi & Edwards, 1998; Bagozzi & Heatherton, 1994; Michael & Bachelor, 1988; Takahashi & Nasser, 1996; Thompson & Melancon, 1996). In our view, the fact that parceled solutions improve the fit of the model does not constitute a convincing argument for the use of this practice. We base this view on the explanation provided earlier in this chapter of the manner in which this improvement in fit is achieved. It can be recalled that the use of item parceling was shown to improve fit in two complementary ways: through a reduction in the size of the matrixes C_{uu}, C_{cu}, and C_{uc} and through the reduction in the elements of Θ that serve as weights for these matrixes. Certain types of parceling may further improve fit by reconfiguring the correlated uniquenesses in C_{uu} as shared variance. Because in most applications the model to which the elements of C_{yy} are fit typically does not allow for uncorrelated uniquenesses, this reconfiguration results in an improvement in model-data fit. In our view, the crucial point with regard to these improvements in fit is that they are obtained by limiting the influence of the nonzero off-diagonal elements of C_{uu}, C_{cu}, and C_{uc} rather than by either eliminating or modeling them explicitly. Thus, although the use of item parceling may minimize the influence of these sources of lack of fit, it does nothing to either remove or explain them.

Although it may be the case that these unmodeled sources of variance are the result of random sampling error or sampling bias, they may also have resulted from unmodeled factors. In the latter case, the improvement in fit realized through the use of item parceling is obtained at the expense of masking some type of misspecification of the model.

In any applied study, it is not possible to know whether the model has been correctly specified. Lack of fit may occur because of sampling error, model misspecification, or a combination of these. In practice, however, researchers are unlikely to be able to determine with certainty which of these is operating. Although goodness-of-fit indexes may be used to assess the fit of the model to the data, adequate and even good model fit can be obtained for models that are misspecified. This appears to be particularly true for models that use item parceling. Thus, goodness-of-fit indexes supply no assurance that one's model is correctly specified. Because the use of item parceling can mask model misspecification in various ways, the fit of a parcel-based model is superior to that of the item-based solution. However, it is not clear to us what the value of this improvement in fit is if it is obtained for a misspecified model. Many of those who advocate the uncritical use of item parceling appear to justify this practice on the basis that it improves the fit of the model over that of the item-based solution. This seems to suggest that the primary aim of model testing is to obtain a good fit. However, we would argue that the primary value of model testing is in obtaining information that may be useful in understanding how and why the variables being modeled are related. This type of information is crucial to studies in which the purpose relates to scale development, refinement, or testing. Researchers may argue that their use of parceling was justified because their model's lack of fit was due to sampling error, not model misspecification. However, the use of parceling seems to preclude the possibility of an informed decision on this issue because misspecification may easily have been masked by the use of parceling. We feel that a more defensible strategy would be to model at the item level to illuminate possible sources of misspecification. If misspecification seems likely, the researcher can then determine whether it is ignorable or should be modeled.

Other arguments advanced in defense of item parceling relate to the fact that the items on the scales may not have been well constructed. For example, the assertion that parceling is useful in reducing the idiosyncrasies introduced by individual items seems to beg the question of why the items are eliciting such idiosyncratic responses. It is expected that different items on a scale will elicit somewhat different responses: That is the purpose of including multiple items. However, if responses were so idiosyncratic as to result in large amounts of unique variance, we would begin to wonder if they were actually measuring the same construct as the other items. Similarly, the argument that item parceling be used to reduce the number of error covariances required to obtain a good fit of the model leads us to ask what is driving these covariances. As discussed earlier such covariances may be due to random sampling error. However, they may also be due to nuisance factors, method factors, or some possibly substantively or theoretically interesting factor that has not been modeled. (Although we speak in terms of only one such factor for the sake of simplicity, there is no reason that such factors would be limited to one. Many such factors may exist.) A related source of lack of fit in CFA models pertains to double loading items or items influenced by modeled factors other than those they were intended to measure. Because in typical CFA applications items are constrained to load only on the factors they were designed to measure, such double loadings are not modeled and will result in model lack of fit. Depending on whether the factors associated with the double loadings are intercorrelated, this lack of fit could be manifested in bias of the item loadings, uniquenesses, and/or in correlated uniquenesses, as well as in a failure to account for the variance of the double loading indicators. As shown by Bandalos (in review), parceling these items together with other such items can mask lack of fit due to such double loading items.

Because the use of item parceling can hide sources of model misfit such as those described, we feel that a more informative approach to the problem of lack of fit would be to attempt to identify, if possible, the nature of the mechanism behind it. We realize that identification may not be possible and that if secondary factors or double loading items are identified, they may be legitimately regarded as unimportant and ignorable. It is also possible that such effects may be sample specific, resulting from random sampling error or sampling bias. We are not advocating that ever minor factor be identified and modeled, but simply that an attempt be made to do so before resorting to parceling as an easy fix to such problems. This approach seems to be in the best interest of creating well-defined and interpretable scales. It is our impression that researchers too often use item parceling as a way to disguise faulty measurement rather than expending the time and effort necessary to improve their scales.

Another way in which item parceling improves the fit of the model is by increasing the reliability of indicators. Because item parcels are based on multiple items, they necessarily have greater reliability than do individual items. However, the extent to which this improvement in fit is realized depends on the reliability of the original items. It is obvious that this improvement in fit is most marked for items with low communalities. The influence from this source of improvement in fit for items with fairly high communalities may be negligible. In the context of scale development and refinement, our preference would be for researchers to devote more resources to developing more reliable items before resorting to the use of item parceling to compensate for low item communalities.

Related arguments have been advanced that relate to the stability of solutions in the presence of small samples, large numbers of items, or both. These arguments assert that the use of parceling results in less sampling error and thus more stable parameter estimates due to reductions in the variable to sample size ratio. As noted in the discussion of the MacCallum et al. (1999) study, such an increase in stability is most marked for situations in which items communalities are low. In such situations, it is generally true that the use of item parceling results in better fitting and more stable solutions, although the extent of the improvement depends on the sample size, level of communality of the variables, and number of variables. However, if the purpose of the study is instrument development, as alluded to before, we suggest that the presence of low item communalities may serve as an indicator of problems with the items. These may be the result of such things as poorly worded or ambiguous items or a lack of homogeneity among the items. In our view, such problems may represent fundamental weaknesses in the items that should be investigated and, if possible, remedied before resorting to parceling as a solution. Although the use of item parceling masks low communalities among the items, it does not change the fact that the items may be poor measures of the construct under investigation. We are cognizant that low communalities can result from a lack of variance associated with the use of binary response formats or response scales based on a limited number of options. We suggest that, when possible, response formats be designed to include the largest number of response options among which respondents can reasonably be expected to differentiate. However, in some situations, most notably the assessment of achievement and aptitudes, this may not be possible.

Another set of reasons that have been offered for item parceling have to do with the lack of normality and continuity of item distributions. Although these problems are most likely to occur in achievement and aptitude measurement, they are certainly not restricted to those areas. When possible, we recommend that instrument developers use a sufficient number of scale points, which may ameliorate problems with non-normality and lack of continuity to some degree. This suggestion was made earlier in the context of low item communalities resulting from a lack of item-level variance. When it is not possible to increase the number of scale points, item parcels yield distributions that are more normally distributed and continuous in nature than the item distributions. Parceling together items with opposite levels of skew and kurtosis yields the best results with regard to normality of the resulting distributions. This is the motivation behind the creation of the parallel parcels used by researchers such as Cook, Dorans, and Eignor (1988). Although the use of item parceling results in more normally distributed and continuous item distributions, we caution researches against the uninformed use of this practice. The use of item parceling can result in distortions of the factor structure among the items as well as parameter estimate bias in factor correlations and structural paths in the model. In situations such as these, we feel the use of item parceling is defensible only if the factor structure of the items is well established and if the researcher is willing to assume that any secondary factors that may be masked through the use of parceling are ignorable.

Finally, in our review of the literature, many researchers (22.6%) referred to the greater parsimony achieved through the use of item parceling. We find this use of the term *parsimony* to be somewhat at variance with recent conceptualizations by such theorists as Mulaik (e.g., Mulaik, et al., 1989). In describing the principle of parsimony, Mulaik et al. referred to the Kantian view that

> ... the principle is not to be applied uncritically, for against it one could cite another regulative principle, that the varieties of things are not to be rashly diminished if we are to capture the individuality and distinctness of things in experience. (p. 437)

We feel that the use of item parceling too often results in a failure to capture distinctive effects that may be of interest. Mulaik et al. went on to describe the manner in which parsimony is related to the degree to which a model is fasifiable. In this context, they explained how "... each degree of freedom in the test of a structural equation model corresponds to an independent condition by which the model can be disconfirmed" (p. 437). When item parcels are used in lieu of items, fewer, rather than more, degrees of freedom are obtained. For example, a one-factor CFA model based on 12 items has 54 degrees of freedom. The same model based on six 2-item parcels will have 9 degrees of freedom. It is obvious that the model based on items is subjected to more possibly disconfirming tests than the model based on parcels. Thus, although parcel-based models may be more parsimonious in the somewhat superficial sense of reducing the number of entities to be modeled, they do not satisfy the more important principle of greater fasifiability.

Based on the prior discussion, the crucial factor in a researcher's decision to use item parceling appears to be the degree to which he or she is willing to make the assumption that the use of item parceling has not masked any substantively and/or theoretically important sources of lack of fit. These sources of lack of fit typically, in CFA applications, involve some sort of unmodeled minor or secondary factor, which results in covariances among the uniquenessess or may result from items that load on more than one factor. To make the judgment that these sources of lack of fit are unimportant and thus ignorable, researchers must have some information regarding the mechanism driving them. Because such judgments are concerned with the relationship among items, this information can only be obtained at the item level. Therefore, we feel that the use of item parceling for situations in which the purpose of the study is to develop or test a scale may be, at best, uninformative and, at worst, deceptive.

Model misspecifications such as those described herein can occur for several reasons. In longitudinal studies, unique variances for the same items measured at different points in time are often hypothesized, or found empirically, to be correlated. One reason this may occur is the presence of practice or memory effects. It is also possible that characteristics of the items or the respondents that are unrelated to the construct or factor being measured may be consistent across time points. In cross-sectional studies, correlated uniquenesses could occur as a result of method effects or response sets. The presence of method factors related to positively and negatively worded items (cf. Benson & Hocevar, 1985; Marsh, 1996) is perhaps the most commonly discussed source. Other such effects may have to do with similarities in wording among two or more items or even the contiguous positioning of items on a page. Another possibility is that items could have causal effects on each other. This could be related to memory or practice effects or to the sensitizing effects of earlier on later items. Items may also share common variance with modeled latent factors other than those they are hypothesized to measure. Such shared variance typically manifests itself as a double loading and, when left unmodeled, may result in biased loadings and uniquenesses as well as correlated uniquenesses depending on whether the factors involved are correlated.

There are several ways in which researchers could attempt to identify the types of secondary influences discussed earlier. An analysis of item content may reveal content or wording similarities among items that could result in shared variance. The presence of method effects, such as those sometimes found for positively and negatively oriented items on personality and attitude scales, are another possible source of shared variance. Similarly, difficulty factors in binary data can have this effect. If effects such as these are not apparent, another possibility is to make use of the modification indexes. (MIs; also called Lagrange Multiplier or [LM] tests) provided by SEM programs. Large MIs for correlated uniquenesses suggest the items have some unmodeled source of shared variance: The problem in this case would be in determining what this is and whether it is ignorable. Large MIs for unmodeled item loadings suggest shared variance between an item and a factor other than that on which it was hypothesized to load. Finally, Hall et al. (1999) suggested that a sensitivity analysis could be conducted in which items are parceled in different ways. If the method of parceling has no effect on parameter estimates, it may be safe to assume that any unmodeled sources of variance are at least not associated with other variables in the model.

If secondary influences can be identified, the researcher has several choices. One would be to model them explicitly. An example of this is provided by a study by Marsh (1996), in which factors reflecting the effects of positively and negatively worded items were modeled. We recommend this option for situations in which secondary factors can be identified and measured, and in particular for situations in which it is possible that the secondary factor may have effects on other variables or factors in the model. This approach has the advantage of providing an explicit rationale for the presence of the secondary factor, and is thus more theoretically pleasing. Explicit modeling of such a factor may also result in the removal of bias in other model parameters that could result from a failure to take this factor into account. A second option would be to use a parceling strategy that would force the influence of the secondary factor into the uniqueness term. This could be done by parceling together items that share the same secondary influence, as suggested by Hall et al. (1999). Use of this strategy would depend on both the researcher's ability to identify such items and willingness to ignore the mechanism driving the shared variance. It should be noted, however, that this strategy can result in biased estimates of structural parameters if the secondary factor is related to other constructs in the model. Unmodeled variance associated with double loading items could be modeled explicitly or such items could be modified or eliminated in future revisions of the scale.

Based on the prior arguments, our position on the use of item parceling is as follows. We are unable to support the use of item parceling in studies involving scale development, refinement, or testing. This would preclude the use of parceling in most applications of CFA reviewed for this chapter. We base this position on the reasons given earlier as well as the simple fact that, in such studies, it is the structure of the relationships among items, rather than of item parcels, that is of interest. Given the possibilities for distortion of the factors structure that are inherent in parcels, it seems unlikely that analysis at the parcel level will result in information that is useful in understanding relationships among the items.

In many applications, the focus is on the relationships among several latent factors in the model. Although measurement models for the latent factors may be included in the overall model, interest in such studies is typically centered on the structural rather than the measurement parameters. In situations such as these, we find the use of item parcels more defensible, contingent on the following conditions. These are that unidimensional factor structures of the latent constructs have been well established in other studies and parcels are formed within these factors. A third condition is that the researchers are willing to assume that any secondary influences on the items being parceled are unrelated to other variables or factors in the model. Failure to meet this assumption may result in biased estimates of structural parameters involving the parceled items.

WAYS OF FORMING PARCELS

Aside from the work of Hall et al. (1999), few recent researchers have studied the issue of how items might best be formed into parcels. However, animated arguments concerning this issue can be found in the factor analytic literature of the 1960s and 1970s. In particular, Comrey (1970) preferred the development of parcels based on items with similar content. Cattell (1974), however, argued forcefully against this approach, referring to it as "this 'face validity' whore in the family of psychometric validities" (p. 109). Cattell proposed the technique of radial item parceling and demonstrated its use in several articles (Cattell, 1956, 1974; Cattell & Burdsal, 1975). Essentially, the radial parceling technique is carried out by conducting an initial factor analysis and then combining the pair of items whose loadings have the highest coefficient of congruence. The pair of items with the next highest level of congruence is then combined, and so on, until all items have been formed into parceled pairs. If four-item pairs are desired, the process is repeated on the two-item pairs. This process can be extended to obtain parcels consisting of any number of items that is a multiple of 2. Cattell argued for the use of item parcels rather than individual items in factor analysis because of their greater reliability, which results in a greater probability of reaching simple structure and greater structural consistency across samples (Cattell, 1974; Cattell & Burdsal, 1975). Cattell (1974) also argued that the solutions obtained from item- and parcel-level factoring are essentially the same. However, for the comparisons between item- and parcel-level solutions presented in his article, the coefficients of congruence between the two solutions ranged from .11 to .63 In our view, this is not convincing evidence of the similarity of the solutions.

Barrett and Kline (1981) conducted an independent investigation of the radial parceling technique. One interesting result of this study, which was also found in Cattell (1974), was that items from different factors were often parceled together. Cattell suggested that this happens because, with real data, factor structures do not reflect perfect simple structure. A similar point has been made more recently in the SEM literature by Browne and Cudeck (1992) among others. Although we agree with this view, we would add that the lack of simple structure may reflect substantively meaningless nuisance factors or may be identifying a more complex, but theoretically meaningful, structure.

Kishton and Widaman (1994) proposed two alternative methods for parceling items and illustrated their use with an empirical data set. In the first of these, it was assumed that items to be parceled together represented the same unidimensional construct. These items are assigned randomly to parcels, and the internal consistency and dimensionality of each parcel are assessed. Parcels meeting some prespecified criteria in these areas are then considered acceptable for use in further analyses. The second method assumes that the construct being measured is multidimensional and that a "single, broad construct spanning the multiple dimensions" (p. 762) may be of interest. In this method, items from the different dimensions are randomly assigned to different parcels so that each parcel contains the same number of items from each dimension. These parcels are then used as indicators of the multidimensional construct. Kishton and Widaman used these two methods to form parcels and concluded that both were 'quite effective.' This evaluation was based on the fact that both solutions were found to provide acceptable fits to the data. We have already expressed our opinion on this basis for advocating item parceling. Given the framework established by MacCallum et al. (1999) and described earlier in this chapter, it can be seen that the second of these two approaches results in factors that reflect the shared variance of the different dimensions, as well as any unique variance an item may share with that of other items in its parcel. It is not clear to us what is gained through this procedure over simply using subscale scores from each dimension as indicators of the construct. If the purpose of the parceling is to obtain indicators with higher reliability, the latter procedure is superior. Clearly, however, any differential predictability the original dimensions may have had is lost in the parceled solution when this type of strategy is used.

Several of the studies we reviewed used strategies similar to Cattell's radial parceling (e.g., combining items with the highest correlations or with similar factor loadings; 8%) or used Kishton and Widaman's (1994) method of random assignment of items within a dimension (13%). However, the most commonly used method of forming parcels was to systematically group together items that were arranged contiguously on the scale (i.e., Items 1–3, Items 4–6, etc.) within a dimension or factor (29%). Odd/even splits of items were also used (3%). Some researchers used parceling methods that combined positively and negatively oriented items in an attempt to circumvent possible method effects (6.5%).

Of the studies involving achievement or aptitude scales, 50% combined items in such a way as to produce parcels with approximately equal difficulty levels. Another common method used in this area was to parcel together items based on the same stimulus, such as a series of questions based on the same reading passage (20%). This is the testlet approach described by Wainer and Kiely (1987). Random assignment of items to parcels within a dimension was used in 20% of these studies.

We have already expressed our views on the use of item parcels. We hope that researchers carefully consider the advantages and disadvantages of this approach when considering the use of parceling. For situations in which the researcher feels that this approach would be efficacious, we offer the following advice with regard to forming item parcels. Because the relative efficacy of the approaches described earlier has not been studied systematically, we are currently able to offer only tentative recommendations in this area. However, one general principal does seem clear: Items should be combined only within well-documented unidimensional domains. We previously discussed how the formation of parcels based on multidimensional items can result in distortions of the factor structure and biased parameter estimates, as well as a loss of information regarding the possible differential effects of the dimensions on other variables in the model. Given this caveat, it seems to us that the method used for parceling items should depend on the researcher's purpose in forming parcels. If the researchers is concerned about non-normality or possible dependencies among items based on the same stimulus, the parceling strategy should be designed to alleviate these problems. If the purpose of parceling is to obtain indicators with higher communalities, we would recommend combining items with the highest levels of congruence within dimensions. This could be based on coefficients of congruence, as suggested by Cattell (1956, 1974). This approach seems most likely to retain the item-level factor structure. At the risk of appearing tedious, we would again point out that any of these parceling procedures may obscure rather than clarify the factor structure and/or result in bias in other parameter estimates.

In our survey of the use of parceling in applied studies, it became apparent that practitioners often do not provide sufficient detail with regard to their use of this practice. In some cases, authors did not even explicitly state that parceling was being used. In a number of cases (13%), no information was provided with regard to how parcels were formed, and 47% of the articles that used parceling did not provide any indication of why parcels were used in lieu of items. Also several articles (27%) simply noted that parceling was completed within content areas, but did not explain exactly how the items were assigned to parcels. In many studies, it was extremely difficult to determine how many items were on the original scale, how many items were in each parcel, and how many parcels were formed.

Because this type of information could have a bearing on the interpretation of study results, we make several recommendations with regard to the reporting of results for studies that use item parceling. First, an explanation should be provided regarding why it was deemed necessary to form parcels instead of using item-level data. We also feel that a clear treatment of both the advantages and disadvantages of parceling would provide the most informative basis for the interpretation of results. Second, the dimensionality of the items should be clearly documented with references to studies in which this has been established. Third, the number of items contributing to each factor and the total number of items on the original scale should be noted, along with the number of parcels and items within each parcel. Fourth, the manner in which parceling was accomplished should be completely described to enable readers to more carefully evaluate and, if desired, replicate the study. Finally, if the purpose of parceling is to obtain more normally distributed indicators, the distributions of the items prior to parceling and the distribution of the parcels should be noted.

CONCLUSIONS

Although the applied studies we reviewed cited various sources in defense of the practice of parceling, the work of Marsh (Marsh, 1987, 1988, 1990a, 1990b, 1990c, 1992a, 1992b, 1993; Marsh & Hocevar, 1985; Marsh & Hocevar, 1988; Marsh & O'Neill, 1984) was cited most often (69.6% of the studies using parceling that cited a reference for doing so cited one of these articles). However, we find it interesting to note that, although the earliest article by Marsh and his colleagues (Marsh & O'Neill, 1984) included statements regarding both the advantages and disadvantages of item parceling, the arguments advanced in the latter category were all but ignored in the applied studies we reviewed. Specifically, those citing Marsh refer to the advantages of parsimony, including more normally distributed indictors, less idiosyncratic indicator variance, more reliable indicators, less unique variance, ability to use a smaller sample size, and reductions in computer resources. However, Marsh and O'Neill also listed the following disadvantages of parceling: Information about the individual items will be lost, items being parceled must be reasonably unidimensional, and parameter estimates and factor scores derived from parceled analyses will be dependent on the particular items parceled together. To these we would add the very real possibilities of obscuring the true factor structure of the items and obtaining biased estimates for other model parameters. Such effects have been demonstrated in recent studies by Bandalos (in review) and Hall et al. (1999). In only one study that we reviewed (Mitchell, 1993) were disadvantages of parceling cited as well as advantages. It is difficult to know whether Mitchell is the only researcher other than Marsh who is aware of the disadvantages of parceling or the only one who sees the importance in explicitly stating them. Whatever the case, we find the widespread, uncritical use of item parceling, in Breckler's (1990) words, "cause for concern." In many cases, it appears to us that the use of item parceling is motivated by the improvement in fit that can be obtained through the use of this practice. However, such increases in fit are largely artifactual and are likely to be obtained at the expense of masking model misspecification of some kind. We therefore feel that if the purpose of one's study is to better understand the relationships among items, analysis at the parcel level is unlikely to be useful.

Primary arguments for the use of item parceling are that it will result in indicators with greater reliability and in more stable parameter estimates. Although these arguments are true to some degree, the results of MacCallum et al. (1999) as well as our own unpublished simulation work indicate that these benefits will be most evident for situations in which the communalities of the variables are low and the sample size small. In situations such as these, any results, whether based on items or parcels, are likely to be untrustworthy. In situations with more moderate communalities and/or sample sizes, the benefits of item parceling are less pronounced. In such cases, we feel that the risk of masking model misspecifications and/or of obtaining biased parameter estimates will in most cases outweigh the increases in reliability and stability that will be obtained.

Improvements in parsimony were the second most frequently cited reason for the use of parceling. However, as discussed earlier, we feel that this argument for parsimony is not in keeping with recent conceptuatlizations. In particular, arguments that the use of parceling results in more parsimonious solutions are true only in the sense that parceling yields fewer parameters to be estimated. However, the use of item parcels also results in fewer degrees of freedom, and thus fewer ways in which the model can be tested.

The previous remarks apply to the use of parceling in both CFA and full structural modeling applications. However, we particularly caution against the use of item parceling in studies involving scale development, refinement, and testing. In these applications, we feel that the information obtained from modeling at the item level is crucial in determining whether and to what degree unmodeled shared variance is present. Such shared variance could be the result of such things as methods effects, practice or memory effects, similarities in wording, or response sets. We feel that information about such effects can be extremely valuable in the scale development process and should be carefully considered by the researcher. Unmodeled shared variance could also be the result of nuisance factors. If so, the researchers may choose to ignore this source of variance. However, the crucial point, in our view, is that it is not possible to make any determination about the source of such variance in the absence of information obtained at the item level. Because the use of item parceling can obscure the presence of unmodeled variance, analysis at the parcel level cannot provide information with regard to its source. Therefore, to paraphrase Cattell (1974), we have no use for this parceling whore in the family of scale development procedures. Given this, we find it distressing that, of the 62 studies using item parceling we found in our review of the literature, 82.3% were CFA applications involving some type of scale development process.

Given the prior discussion, we offer the following recommendations regarding the use of item parceling. We have already given our view on the use of parceling in scale development studies. In other contexts, such as the inclusion of parcel-based measurement models in studies of the relationships among latent constructs, we recommend that parceling only be conducted on scales for which unidimensionality has been clearly established in previous research. Parcels should then be formed within each unidimensional factor. Researchers using parcels should also be reasonably sure that any secondary factors that may influence the dimensionality of the items being parceled are ignorable and do not affect other constructs in the model. We would also urge researchers to provide full explanations of the parceling process in their manuscripts. These should include explanations of why parceling was deemed appropriate, how the unidimensionality of the items being parceled was established, and the procedure used to parcel items. Researchers should also report the numbers of both items and parcels and the number of items in each parcel. If parceling has been used to obtain indicators that are more normally distributed, the distributional characteristics of the items as well as the parcels should be reported. Finally, researchers should clearly point out both the advantages and disadvantages of item parceling.

Is the use of item parceling in SEM studies cause for concern? Although the use of this practice may be efficacious in some situations, we feel that uninformed and uncritical use of parceling may have resulted in poorer, rather than greater, understanding of the relationships among sets of items. We hope that the discussion provided in this chapter results in a more critical view of this procedure among SEM practitioners.

ACKNOWLEDGEMENT

The authors would like to acknowledge the members of the structural equation modeling listserve (SEMNET) for valuable discussions that served to stimulate our thinking on topics for this chapter. In particular, the contributions from Stanley Mulaik and Steve Gregorich were extremely useful. However, the opinions stated in this chapter are those of the authors and should be attributed only to them.

REFERENCES

Bandalos, D. L. (1993). Factors influencing cross-validation of confirmatory factor analysis models. *Multivariate Behavioral Research, 28*(3), 351–374.

Bandalos, D. L. (in review). The effects of item parceling in structural equation modeling: A Monte Carlo study. *Structural Equation Modeling.*

Bagozzi, R. P., & Edwards, J. R. (1998). A general approach for representing constructs in organizational research. *Organizational Research Methods, 1*(1), 45–87.

Bagozzi, R. P., & Heatherton, T. F. (1994). A general approach to representing multifaceted personality constructs: Application to state self-esteem. *Structural Equation Modeling, 1*(1), 35–67.

Barrett, P. T., & Kline, P. (1981). Radial parcel factor analysis. *Personality and Individual Differences, 2*, 311–318.

Benson, J., & Hocevar, D. (1985). The impact of item, phrasing on the validity of attitude scales for elementary school children. *Journal of Educational Measurement, 22*, 231–240.

Breckler, S. J. (1990). Applications of covariance structure modeling in psychology: Cause for concern? *Psychological Bulletin, 107*(2), 260–273.

Bridgeman, B., & Rock, D. A. (1993). Relationships among multiple-choice and open-ended analytical questions. *Journal of Educational Measurement, 30*, 313–329.

Browne, M. W., & Cudeck, R. (1992). Alternative ways of assessing model fit. *Sociological Methods and Research, 21*(2), 230–258.

Carroll, J. B. (1983). The difficulty of a test and its factor composition revisited. In S. Messick & H. Wainer (Eds.), *Principles of modern psychological measurement: A festschrift for Frederic M. Lord.* (pp. 257–282). Hillsdale, NJ: Lawrence Erlbaum Associates.

Cattell, R. B. (1956). Validation and intensification of the sixteen personality factor questionnaire. *Journal of Clinical Psychology, 12*, 205–214.

Cattell, R. B. (1974). Radial item parcel factoring vs. item factoring in defining personality structure in questionnaires: Theory and experimental checks. *Australian Journal of Psychology, 26*(2), 103–119.

Cattell, R. J., & Burdsal, C. A., Jr. (1975). The radial parceling double factoring design: A solution to the item-vs.-parcel controversy. *Multivariate Behavioral Research, 10*, 165–179.

Chapman, J. W., & Tunmer, W.E. (1995). Development of young children's reading self-concepts: An examination of emerging subcomponents and their relationship with reading achievement. *Journal of Education Psychology, 87*(1), 154–167.

Comrey, A. L. (1970). *Manual for the Comrey Personality Scales.* San Diego: Educational and Industrial Testing Service.

Cook, L. L., Dorans, N. J., & Eignor, D. R. (1988). An assessment of the dimensionality of three SAT-Verbal test editions. *Journal of Educational Statistics, 13*(1), 19–43.

Ferguson, G. A. (1941). The factorial interpretation of test difficulty. *Psychometrika, 6*, 323–329.

Gorsuch, R. L. (1983). *Factor analysis* (2nd ed.). Hillsdale, NJ: Lawrence Erlbaum Associates.

Gottfried, A. E., Fleming, J. S., & Gottfried, A. W. (1994). Role of parental motivational practices in children's academic intrinsic motivation and achievement. *Journal of Educational Psychology, 86*, 104–113.

Gribbons, B. C., & Hocevar, D. (1998). Levels of aggregation in higher level confirmatory factor analysis: Application for self-concept. *Structural Equation Modeling, 5*(4), 377–390.

Hall, R. J., Snell, A. F., & Singer Foust, M. (1999). Item parceling strategies in SEM: Investigating the subtle effects of unmodeled secondary constructs. *Organizational Research Methods, 2*(3), 233–256.

Kishton, J. M., & Widaman, K. F. (1994). Unidimensional versus domain representative parceling of questionnaire items: An empirical example. *Educational and Psychological Measurement, 54*(3), 757–765.

MacCallum, R. C., & Tucker, L. R. (1991). Representing sources of error in the common factor model: Implications for theory and practice. *Psychological Bulletin, 109*, 502–511.

MacCallum, R. C., Widaman, K. F., Zhang, S., & Hong, S. (1999). Sample size in factor analysis. *Psychological Methods, 4*(1), 84–99.

Marsh, H. W. (1987). The hierarchical structure of self-concept and the application of hierarchical confirmatory factor analysis. *Journal of Educational Measurement, 24*, 17–39.

Marsh, H. W. (1988). *Self description questionnaire: A theoretical and empirical basis for the measurement of multiple dimensions of preadolescent self-concept: A test manual and a research monograph.* San Antonio, TX: Psychological Corporation.

Marsh, H. W. (1990a). *Self description questionnaire II: A theoretical and empirical basis for the measurement of multiple dimensions of preadolescent self-concept: A test manual and a research monograph.* San Antonio, TX: Psychological Corporation.

Marsh, H. W. (1990b). The causal ordering of academic self-concept and academic achievement: A multiwave, longitudinal panel analysis. *Journal of Educational Psychology, 82,* 646–656.

Marsh, H. W. (1990c). The structure of academic self-concept: The Marsh/Shavelson model. *Journal of Educational Psychology, 82,* 623–636.

Marsh, H. W. (1992a). *Self-description questionnaire-II manual.* Campbellton, Australia: University of Western Sydney, Macarthur.

Marsh, H. W. (1992b). *Self description questionnaire (SDQ) II: A theoretical and empirical basis for the measurement of multiple dimensions of adolescent self-concept: An interim test manual and a research monograph.* Campbelltown, Australia: University of Western Sydney, Macarthur.

Marsh, H. W. (1993). Academic self-concept: Theory measurement and research. In J. Suls (Ed.), *Psychological perspectives on the self* (Vol. 4, pp. 59–98). Hillsdale, NJ: Lawrence Erlbaum Associates.

Marsh, H. W. (1996). Positive and negative global self-esteem: A substantively meaningful distinction or artifactors? *Journal of Personality and Social Psychology, 70*(4), 810–819.

Marsh, H. W., Hau, K.-T., Balla, J. R., & Grayson, D. (1998). Is more ever too much? The number of indicators per factor in confirmatory factor analysis. *Multivariate Behavioral Research, 33*(2), 181–220.

Marsh, H. W., & Hocevar, D. (1985). Application of confirmatory factor analysis to the study of self-concept: First and higher order factor models and their invariance across groups. *Psychological Bulletin, 97,* 562–582.

Marsh, H. W., & Hocevar, D. (1998). A new, more powerful approach to multitrait-multimethod analyses: Application of second-order confirmatory factor analysis. *Journal of Applied Psychology, 73,* 107–117.

Marsh, H. W., & O'Neill, R. (1984). Self description questionnaire III: The construct validity of multidimensional self-concept ratings by late adolescents. *Journal of Educational Measurements, 21*(2), 153–174.

McDonald, R. P., & Ahlawat, K. S. (1974). Difficulty factors in binary data. *British Journal of Mathematical and Statistical Psychology, 27,* 82–99.

Michael, W. B., & Bachelor, P. (1988). A comparison of the orthogonal and the oblique factor structures of correlation matrixes of individual items and of composites of items (subtests) derived from a standardized affective measure. *Educational and Psychological Measurement, 48,* 93–103.

Mislevy, R. J. (1986). Recent developments in the factor analysis of categorical variables. *Journal of Educational Statistics, 11*(1), 3–31.

Mitchell, M. (1993). Situational interest: Its multifaceted structure in the secondary school mathematics classroom. *Journal of Educational Psychology, 85*(3), 424–436.

Mulaik, S. A., James, L. R., Van Alstine, J., Bennett, N., Lind, S., & Stilwell, C. D. (1989). Evaluation of goodness-of-fit indices for structural equation models. *Psychological Bulletin, 105*(3), 430–445.

Muthén, L. K., & Muthén, B. O. (1998). *Mplus user's guide.* Los Angeles: Author.

Nunnally, J. C. (1978). *Psychometric theory* (2nd ed.). New York: McGraw-Hill.

Takahashi, T., & Nasser, F. (1996). *The impact of using item parcels on ad hoc goodness of fit indices in confirmatory factor analysis: An empirical example.* ERIC Document # Ed-398-279.

Thompson, B., & Melancon, J. G. (1996). Using item "Testlest"/"Parcels" in confirmatory factor analysis: An example using the PPSDQ-78. ERIC Document # ED-404-349.

Wainer, H., & Kiely, G.L. (1987). Item clusters and computerized adaptive testing: A case for testlets. *Journal of Educational Measurements, 24*(3), 185–201.

West, S. G., Finch, J. F., & Curran, P. J. (1995). Structural equation models with nonnormal variables: Problems and remedies. In R. H. Hoyle (Ed.), *Structural equation modeling: Concepts, issues, and applications* (chapter 4, pp. 56–75). Thousand Oaks, CA: Sage.

Vandenberg, R. J., & Scarpello, V. (1991). Multitrait-multimethod validation of the satisfaction with my supervisor scale. *Educational and Psychological Measurement, 52,* 203–212.

Velicer, W. F., & Fava, J. L. (1998). Effects of variable and subject sampling on factor pattern recovery. *Psychological Methods, 3,* 231–251.

Yuan, K.- H., Bentler, P. M., & Kano, Y. (1997). On averaging variables in a confirmatory factor analysis model. *Behaviormetrika, 24*(1), 71–83.

11

The Problem of Equivalent Structural Equation Models: An Individual Residual Perspective

Tenko Raykov
Fordham University

Spiridon Penev
University of New South Wales, Sydney

Structural equation models are currently widely used in the behavioral, social, and educational sciences. They permit the modeling of complex multivariate phenomena, whereby measurement errors are accounted for both in the dependent and explanatory variables. Application of these models for testing behavioral and social theories has been on the increase for a considerable period of time. A large body of literature on evaluation of model fit has accumulated over the past two decades (e.g., Bollen, 1989; Browne & Cudeck, 1993). However, essentially all of it has been concerned with indexes of overall goodness-of-fit. Thereby, little attention has been paid to the assessment of model fit at the individual subject level.

The problem of equivalent structural equation models has drawn substantial methodological interest over the last 10 years or so, although insightful discussions of it can already be found in the literature of the 1960s and 1970s (e.g., Bollen, 1989; Breckler, 1990; Hayduk, 1996; Hershberger, 1994; Jöreskog & Sörböm, 1996; Lee & Hershberger, 1991; Luijben, 1991; MacCallum, Wegener, Uchino, & Fabrigar, 1993; Raykov, 1997; Raykov & Penev, 1999; Raykov & Marcoulides, in press; Stelzl, 1986; Williams, Bozdogan, & Aiman-Smith, 1996). Equivalent models cannot be differentiated between using overall fit measures because the models are typically associated with identical goodness-of-fit indexes, such as chi-square values and descriptive fit indexes, degrees of freedom and p values, as well as identical residual covariance matrices. For essential any structural equation model there exist potentially many models equivalent to it. They represent equally plausible means to description of the data as the initial model, yet generally lead to different, incompatible, or contradictory substantive explanations of the studied phenomenon. Some equivalent models can be obtained using specifically developed rules by Stelzl (1986), Lee and Hershberger (1990), or Hershberger (1994), unlike other equivalent models that contain parameter restrictions (e.g., Raykov & Penev, 1999). Thus, the problem of equivalent models represents a serious threat to behavioral and social theory development and construct validation using the SEM methodology. Therefore, unless the problem is dealt with, an originally considered model—regardless of how well it fits the data—remains only one possible means of its description and explanation (e.g., Breckler, 1990; MacCallum et al., 1993).

The present chapter has a twofold goal. First, a general approach to the construction of individual case residuals in structural equation models is discussed. The method is based on projection from the raw data space on a model-generated subspace and generalizes the observational (Bartlett-based) residuals by Bollen and Arminger (1991). Second, this approach is used to examine similarities and possible differences between some equivalent models with respect to subject level fit.

The intention of this chapter is to respond to the lack of wider research attention in SEM that evaluation of fit at the individual case level has received so far, as opposed to overall fit to the empirical covariance matrix, as well as to address issues pertaining to potential applicability of individual residuals in the difficult process of selection between equivalent models. A reason for this lack of attention may well be the inherent difficulty of estimating subject residuals. It stems from the fact that, although many structural equation models regress observed on latent variables and the latter possibly on other unobserved variables, unlike the case in regression analysis, no exact measurements of the (explanatory) latent variables are available. Nonetheless, it is both important and informative to develop and utilize such individual residuals of structural equation models, which conceptually resemble the widely employed residuals within the framework of the general linear model (e.g., Neter, Kutner, Nachsheim, & Wasserman, 1996). These individual residuals may be particularly beneficial for a deeper understanding of model fit and equivalent models. Unfortunately, to our knowledge, only a few publications in the behavioral and social science literature have dealt with estimation of subject level residuals in SEM or closely related topics (e.g., Hopper & Mathews, 1983; Bollen & Arminger, 1991; Neale, 1997; cf. Lange, Westlake, & Spence, 1976; Reise & Widaman, 1999). The present chapter aims at contributing to this discussion by generalizing work of Bollen and Arminger and addressing issues pertaining to applicability of individual case residuals as a potentially useful adjunct to substantive considerations when dealing with equivalent models (McDonald, 1997; McDonald, 1998).

NOTATION, DEFINITIONS,
AND BACKGROUND

This chapter utilizes notation commonly employed in the SEM literature (e.g., Bollen, 1989). In it, $y = (y_1, y_2, ..., y_p)'$ is the vector of observed data on p manifest variables of interest $(p > 1)$, γ denotes the vector of all parameter of a structural equation model M under consideration, Ω is its parameters space containing all possible values of γ, and $\Sigma(\gamma)$ is the covariance matrix implied by M at γ. (Underlining denotes vector and priming stands for transposition in this chapter. As usual in social and behavioral research, we assume throughout that all considered covariance matrices, in particular error covariance matrices, are positive definite and hence variable variances are positive.) Repeated use of some linear algebra notions is also made, particularly the concepts of column space and projection on a subspace, which are discussed next (e.g., Graybill, 1983).

Spaces

Instrumental for the following discussion are matrices of factor loadings or closely related quantities of structural equation models. Like essentially all matrices currently used in behavioral and social research, those of concern will contain only real numbers as elements and have at least one nonzero entry. If the q columns of a matrix A of size $p \times q$ are designated by $a_1, a_2, ..., a_q$, then the rank of A, denoted rk(A), is the number of its linearly independent columns. If $p > q$ and rk(A) $= q$, A is called a full-rank matrix. The column space of A is defined as the set R(A) of all possible linear combinations of $a_1, a_2, ..., a_q$—that is, all vectors in R^p (the set of all p-tuples of real numbers) that are representable as $\alpha_1 a_1 + \alpha_2 a_2 + ... + \alpha_q a_q$, where $\alpha_1, \alpha_2, ..., \alpha_q$ are real numbers. Alternatively, the null space of A, denoted N(A), is defined as the set of all vectors x in R^p that are orthogonal to R(A). That is, N(A) comprises all vectors x for which $x'A = 0$ holds. If two equal-size matrices A and B have the same null spaces [i.e., N(A) $=$ N(B)], then their column spaces are identical too—that is, R(A) $=$ R(B) holds as well (e.g., Graybill, 1983).

Projections

A fundamental role in the remainder of this chapter is played by projections from the space of observed data, R^p, on a model-generated lower dimensional subspace. Let y be an individual data vector from R^p, and let A be a matrix of size $p \times q$ with $p > q$. The projection of y on the column space of A using a weight matrix Θ that is positively definite and symmetric is defined as

$$u^\Theta = A(A'\Theta^{-1}A)^- A'\Theta^{-1}y, \tag{1}$$

regardless of the rank of A, where $(A'\Theta^{-1}A)^-$ is a generalized inverse of $A'\Theta^{-1}A$ (e.g., Christensen, 1989). This generalized inverse is defined by the characteristic property

$$A'\Theta^{-1}A(A'\Theta^{-1}A)^-A'\Theta^{-1}A = A'\Theta^{-1}A \qquad (2)$$

and always exists (e.g., Rao, 1973). Because the matrix $A'\Theta^{-1}A$ is obviously symmetric (Θ being symmetric), it is possible to construct such a generalized inverse of it, which is also symmetric and in addition fulfills the relation

$$(A'\Theta^{-1}A)^-A'\Theta^{-1}A(A'\Theta^{-1}A)^- = (A'\Theta^{-1}A)^-. \qquad (3)$$

This can be achieved using the spectral decomposition of A (e.g,. Christensen, 1989). This generalized inverse is the so-called *Moore–Penrose inverse*, which always exists and is unique, and is used throughout this chapter (it is easily obtained with SAS/IML procedure GINV; see also Appendix 2). Thus, irrespective of the number of linearly independent columns of the considered matrix A, the result of the projection u^Θ defined by Eq. (1) is unique and always exists (e.g., Rao, 1973). The matrix that produces the projection by postmultiplication with y is called *projection matrix*. For the case in Eq. (1), the projection matrix is $A(A'\Theta^{-1}A)^-A'\Theta^{-1}$.

For the purpose of this chapter, the attractive feature of the projection outcome is that u^Θ represents the closest to y point from the column space of A, in the distance $d_\Theta(.,.)$ defined (induced) by the matrix Θ as

$$d_\Theta(x, z) = (x - z)'\Theta^{-1}(x - z), \qquad (4)$$

where x and z are points from R^p. In the special case $\Theta = I_p$, the identity matrix of size p, Eq. (1) defines the orthogonal (Euclidean) projection on R(A), which is used in the method of ordinary least squares. The difference between the original data point and its projection then represents the well-known residual in conventional regression models (with error covariance matrix I_p). When the error covariance matrix Θ is not the identity matrix within the general linear model framework, Eq. (1) defines an oblique projection on R(A), which is used in the method of weighted least squares. The difference between the raw data point and its projection then represents the residual in these more general regression models. This chapter uses this general projection idea to obtain individual residuals also in the SEM context.

Linear Structural Relationship Models

This chapter is concerned with linear structural relationship (LISREL) models. They are covered by the comprehensive Submodel 3B of the general structural equation model underlying the widely circulated SEM program *LISREL*

(Jöreskog & Sörböm, 1996). This general model, in different yet equivalent notational forms, underlies also most other available SEM programs, such as *EQS, AMOS, SEPATH, Mx, RAMONA* (Arbuckle, 1997; Bentler, 1995; Browne & Mels, 1994; Neale, 1997; Steiger, 1999). Accordingly, a LISREL model is one that is defined by the pair of equations:

$$\eta = B\eta + \zeta \text{ and} \tag{5}$$

$$y = \Lambda\eta + \varepsilon, \tag{6}$$

where η is the $q \times 1$ vector of latent variables (factors), B the $q \times q$ matrix of structural regression coefficients relating the latent variables among themselves, Λ is the $p \times q$ factor loading matrix, ζ is the $q \times 1$ structural regression residual vector with covariance matrix denoted Ψ, and ε is the $p \times 1$ error terms vector with covariance matrix Θ. In addition, a standard assumption (Jöreskog & Sörböm, 1996) is that of invertibility of the matrix I_q-B, which is similarly made in the present chapter. Throughout the reminder, we also assume that the considered LISREL models are identified and that as usual error means vanish and errors are uncorrelated with factors.

Equations (6) and (5) define the relationships between the observed and latent variables and among the latent variables, respectively. In the standard nomenclature, they are correspondingly referred to as *measurement model* and *structural model* of the model in question (e.g., Bollen, 1989). To avoid the tautological repetition of *model*, we call Eq. (6) *measurement part* and Eq. (5) *structural part* of the considered model. We emphasize that Eqs. (5) and (6) define the most general LISREL model that encompasses the so-called *general LISREL model*. The latter uses a different (but not necessary) notation for the latent independent variables and their indicators (Jöreskog & Sörböm, 1996). Currently, the LISREL model in Eqs. (5) and (6) covers essentially all models used in routine application of the SEM methodology in the social, behavioral and educational sciences.

For the aims of this chapter, as indicated earlier, we deal with LISREL models having more observed variables than factors (i.e., models with $p > q$). This requirement is not considered here to be limiting substantially the generality of the following discussion. This is because structural equation models, like factor analysis models used in behavioral and social research, are often based on less latent than manifest variables. That the condition $p > q$ holds is necessitated by the projection approach underlying this discussion. For its method to be applicable, it is essential to be able to project from a higher dimensional subspace generated by the observed variables (viz. R^p) on a lower dimensional subspace generated by the fewer factors of an entertained model. Under these circumstances, the approach followed in the sequel allows estimation of individual case residuals. (We note as an aside that the same assumption, $p > q$, is needed for the observational residuals of Bollen & Arminger, 1991, to exist.) The class of LISREL models with more manifest variables than latent factors, which is of concerns to this chapter, covers a great deal of current SEM utilizations in the social and behavioral sciences.[1]

Solving Eq. (5) in terms of η and substituting the result into Eq. (6), one obtains what can be referred to as a reduced form of the considered LISREL model:

$$y = \Lambda(I_q - B)^{-1}\zeta + \varepsilon = A\zeta + \varepsilon, \tag{7}$$

where

$$A = \Lambda(I_q - B)^{-1}. \tag{8}$$

Evidently, $A = \Lambda$ if $B = 0$, as is the case in confirmation factor analysis models; alternatively, if $B \neq 0$, then, according to Eq. (7), a structural equation model with explanatory relationships between its latent variables is rewritten as a factor analysis model for their indicators (cf. Bollen & Arminger, 1991). In terms of either the original or reduced forms of a LISREL model—that is, Eqs. (5) and (6), or (7), respectively—its implied covariance matrix is:

$$\Sigma(\gamma) = A\Psi A' + \Theta = \Lambda(I_q - B)^{-1}\Psi(I_q - B')^{-1}\Lambda' + \Theta = \Lambda\Phi\Lambda' + \Theta, \tag{9}$$

where Φ is the covariance matrix of the factors in η (e.g., Bollen, 1989).

Equivalent Models

Two LISREL models M_1 and M_2 with parameter spaces Ω_1 and Ω_2 are called equivalent, denoted $M_1 \sim M_2$, if they give rise to the same sets of implied covariance matrices (e.g., Stelzl, 1986; cf. Raykov & Penev, 1999). That is, $M_1 \sim M_2$ if and only if the following set identity holds:

$$\{\Sigma_1(\gamma_1) \text{ for } \gamma_1 \text{ from } \Omega_1\} = \{\Sigma_2(\gamma_2) \text{ for } \gamma_2 \text{ from } \Omega_2\},$$

where $\Sigma_1(\gamma_1)$ and $\Sigma_2(\gamma_2)$ are the implied covariance matrices by M_1 and M_2, respectively, and $\{.\}$ denotes set defined within brackets. Thus, for two equivalent LISREL models, the implied covariance matrices are identical at appropriately chosen points γ_1 and γ_2 in their parameter spaces (e.g., Raykov & Penev, 1999). In other words, if the equivalent models M_1 and M_2 (with possibly different numbers of latent factors q_1 and q_2) are defined as

$$y = \Lambda_1\eta_1 + \varepsilon_1 = \Lambda_1(I_{q_1} - B_1)^{-1}\zeta_1 + \varepsilon_1 = A_1\zeta_1 + \varepsilon_1 \text{ and} \tag{10}$$

$$y = \Lambda_2\eta_2 + \varepsilon_2 = \Lambda_2(I_{q_2} - B_2)^{-1}\zeta_2 + \varepsilon_2 = A_2\zeta_2 + \varepsilon_2, \tag{11}$$

---

[1] The term *factor* is used in this chapter to refer to latent variables other than the observed variable error or structural regression residual terms (i.e., other than ϵs, δs, and ζs in the *LISREL* terminology; Jöreskog & Sörböm, 1996).

respectively, with Φ_1 and Φ_2 and $\Theta_{\varepsilon 1}$ and $\Theta_{\varepsilon 2}$ being their corresponding factor and error covariance matrices (see Eqns. [5] and [6]), then for their reproduced covariance matrices follows that

$$\Sigma_1(\gamma_1) = A_1\Psi_1A_1' + \Theta_{\varepsilon 1} = \Sigma_2(\gamma_2) = A_2\Psi_2A_2' + \Theta_{\varepsilon 2}$$
$$= \Lambda_1\Phi_1\Lambda_1' + \Theta_{\varepsilon 1} = \Lambda_2\Phi_2\Lambda_2' + \Theta_{\varepsilon 2} = \Sigma, \text{ say.} \qquad (12)$$

We emphasize that Σ is common to the whole set of models equivalent to a given one, not only to a particular pair of equivalent models from that set.

Classes of Equivalent LISREL Models

Equation (12) states the identity of the implied covariance matrices by two equivalent models, $M_1 \sim M_2$, and relates a number of constituent matrices containing model parameters. Differences and similarities between same (role-playing) matrices across the models allow one to make useful distinctions among several classes of equivalent models that necessarily differ in at least one of these matrices.

First, many equivalent models are associated with identical factor loading matrices, $\Lambda_1 = \Lambda_2$ (see Eq. [5]). For example, such are models obtained from an initial one using the replacement rule by Lee and Hershberger (1990) or Stelzl's (1986) rules subsumed under it. This is because all changes introduced by the replacement rule in an original model are confined to its structural part (e.g., MacCallum et al., 1993). Because these models are identical in their measurement parts and factor loading matrices, the spaces generated by their columns are obviously identical as well [i.e., $R(\Lambda_1) = R(\Lambda_2)$]. However, not all equivalent models to a given one have necessarily the same factor loading matrices. For example, models resulting from an application of the inverse indicator rule by Hershberger (1994) differ in their measurement parts and have distinct factor loading matrices. Furthermore, equivalent models can have different factor loading matrices that possess identical column spaces. For example, Models A1 and A2 in Raykov and Penev (1999, Fig. 8) have different numbers of latent variables and hence different factor loading matrices, $\Lambda_1 \neq \Lambda_2$. However, as can be shown directly, their column spaces are identical [i.e., $R(\Lambda_1) = R(\Lambda_2)$].

Second, many equivalent models have identical error covariance matrices, $\Theta_{\varepsilon 1} = \Theta_{\varepsilon 2}$. Such models are those resulting from applications of the replacement rule or Stelzl's rules. Alternatively, not all equivalent models have identical error covariance matrices. For example, Models M1 and M2 in Raykov and Penev (1999, Fig. 7; see Fig. 11.1) are identical in their error variances yet different in error covariances. Indeed, in M1, the latent variables are related and the error covariances are all zero, whereas in M2, the latent factors are unrelated yet most of the error covariances are free (as opposed to fixed to 0) model parameters, although constrained for equality, indicating possible uncaptured sources of common latent variance for the pertinent observed variables.

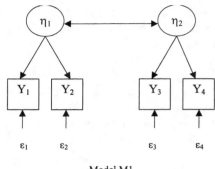

Model M1

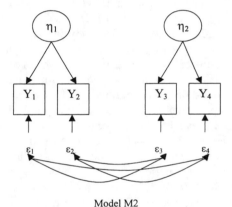

Model M2

FIG. 11.1 Models M1 and M2 (Raykov & Penev, 1999, Fig. 7; all
four error covariances are constrained for equality; the pairs of test
per factor are tau-equivalent).

In short, two or more equivalent models may be identical or differ from one
another in their (a) factor loading matrices, (b) factor loading matrices' column
spaces, (c) error covariance matrices, and/or (d) their structural parts (Eq. [6]).

A DEFINITION OF INDIVIDUAL
CASE RESIDUALS

For each studied subject, with data vector $y_i = (y_{i1}, y_{i2}, ..., y_{ip})'$, a generalization
of the observational (Bartlett-based) residuals of Bollen and Arminger (1991) to
the case of arbitrary-rank factor loading matrix of a LISREL model M with more
observed than latent variables is obtained using the earlier discussed projection method ($i = 1, ..., N$; N denotes sample size in this chapter). The resulting
individual residuals are defined as the difference between the subject's raw data

point and its projection on the column space of the factor loading matrix A in the reduced form of M—that is, as

$$r_i^\Theta = y_i - u_i^\Theta = [I_p - A(A'\Theta^{-1}A)^-A'\Theta^{-1}]y_i \qquad (13)$$

(see Eqns. [1] and [7]; $i = 1, \ldots, N$). That is, for each subject and a given LIS-REL model M, the individual residual in Eq. (13) is the shortest distance between his or her raw data point and the space spanned by the columns of its matrix A in the distance metric induced by the error covariance matrix of M. For ease of reference, throughout the remainder of this chapter, we call r_i^Θ in Eq. (13) *individual case residual* (for the ith subject, $i = 1, \ldots, N$, ICR).

We emphasize that the ICR is not a scalar but a p-dimensional vector. Thereby, each of its components reflects the unexplained (unaccounted for) by the model part of the individual datum on the variable in question. That is, the jth component of r_i^Θ, r_{ij}^Θ, represents that part of the datum y_{ij} of the ith subject on the jth analyzed variable, which is not accounted for by the model ($i = 1, \ldots, N$, $j = 1, \ldots, p$). The SAS program provided in Appendix 2 estimates for each subject their ICR, with one component per studied variable, once it is given the raw data set and the estimates of the Λ and Θ matrices of a fitted LISREL model (with more observed than latent variables, see Lemma 1 below).

If for the model under consideration its factor loading matrix Λ is of full rank, the matrix $A'\Theta^{-1}A$ is invertible, and hence its (unique) inverse $(A'\Theta^{-1}A)^{-1}$ substitutes the generalized inverse $(A'\Theta^{-1}A)^-$ in Eq. (13) that represents the general ICR definition due to $(A'\Theta^{-1}A)^- = (A'\Theta^{-1}A)^{-1}$ holding then. In this special case, r_i^Θ is identical to the observational (Bartlett-based) residuals of Bollen and Arminger (1991) for the reduced form of the model. Unlike their residuals, however, the ICR in Eq. (13) can be applied regardless of the rank of the factor loading matrix Λ (or corresponding matrix A, see Lemma 1 in the next subsection). That is, the ICR exist (and are unique) also when not all columns of Λ (or A) are linearly independent, whereas the Bollen and Arminger's residuals can be obtained only for full-rank factor loading matrices (or A matrices). Hence, the ICR can be used with a number of structured equation models having less-than-full-rank factor loading matrices that are not infrequently utilized by behavioral and social scientists (e.g., Grayson & Marsh, 1994), in contrast to Bollen and Arminger's observational (Bartlett-based) residuals, which cannot be employed because they do not exist due to the singularity of the critical matrix $A'\Theta^{-1}A$.

Simplified Expression

The ICR definition in Eq. (13) can be simplified using the following statement, which is proved in Appendix 1.

Lemma 1. The column spaces of a $m \times n$ matrix C and of the matrix CK, where the $n \times n$ matrix K is nonsingular, are identical (m and n are integer numbers).

Because the matrix I_q-B in the general LISREL model (Eqs. [5] and [6]) was assumed nonsingular (as is the case effectively in all structural equation models currently used in social and behavioral research practice; e.g., Jöreskog & Sörböm, 1996), so is its inverse, $(I_q$-B$)^{-1}$. Because A results when multiplying Λ from the right with $(I_q$-B$)^{-1}$ (see Eqns. [6]–[8]), A is of full rank if and only if Λ is so (e.g., Rao, 1973). Moreover, for C $=$ Λ and K $=$ $(I_q$-B$)^{-1}$, Lemma 1 implies that the column spaces of Λ and A are identical. Therefore, projecting the raw data point y on R(A) is the same as projecting that point on the identical space R(Λ) $=$ R(A), and hence the results of these two projections coincide. Thus, the ICR obtained either way are identical because they by definition are the differences between the point being projected and its projection. This demonstrates the validity of the following simplification of the ICR general definition in Eq. (13).

Proposition 1. For every structural equation model having less latent than observed variables, the individual case residuals are also obtained as:

$$r_i^\Theta = [I_p - \Lambda(\Lambda'\Theta^{-1}\Lambda)^-\Lambda'\Theta^{-1}]y_i \quad (i = 1, \ldots, N). \tag{14}$$

We stress that the ICR are defined for *any* structural equation model M with more observed variables than latent factors (and positively definite error covariance matrix, as assumed throughout this chapter). Thus, they exist and are unique regardless of the particular specification of M and irrespective of the observed variables' distribution. That is, for any structural equation model with more observed that latent variables, one can obtain subject level residuals with this projection method.

Comparison to Regression Residuals

Because latent variables are not observed or even observable, we consider the ICR in Eq. (13) or (14) as one possible approach to defining individual level residuals for structural equation models. Because unobserved variables are not measured precisely, unlike predictors are assumed in regression analysis, the present need not be the only conceivable way of defining residuals at the subject data level within the SEM framework. Another possible approach is discussed in the next section and compared with this one.

We note that the ICR cannot be considered full analogs of the widely used residuals in regression analysis (e.g., Neter et al., 1996). The reason is that the ICR are not strictly based on model-predicted individual values that are of crucial importance for the definition of the regression residuals. As mentioned, this is in turn due to the lack of (precise) measurements of the unobserved variables in SEM and hence possibility to define exact individual predictions for a LISREL model, unlike the situation in regression analysis. Nonetheless, we emphasize that the present ICR follow the same conceptual idea underlying the regression residuals, and thus provide valuable information about the relationship between subject data and fitted model(s). This is because an individual level residual in Eq. (13) or (14) is the difference between a subject's raw data point and its *closest* point, in the distance defined by the error covariance matrix, in the observed variable subspace spanned by the accounted for part of the model under consideration. In this sense, the ICR contain information about the minimal distance between any studied subject and the model. Therefore, the ICR may be used for a number of modeling-related purposes in social and behavioral research, such as (a) outliers' detection, (b) studying potentially influential points, or (c) identification of persons markedly inconsistent with a considered model, as demonstrated by Bollen and Arminger (1991) for models with full-rank factor loading matrices. Aims (a) to (c) are typically accomplished by examining those individuals with the highest distances from the model (see also Reise & Widaman, 1999).

Relationship to Other Subject Level Residuals

The present ICR differ from subject level residuals that can be obtained using the so-called *raw data maximum likelihood* (RDML) method of model fitting (Arbuckle, 1996; Neale, 1997; see also Hopper & Mathews, 1983; Lange et al., 1976; Reise & Widaman, 1999). The latter residuals are based on an alternative to the present approach, which used the likelihood ratio test statistic for a fitted mean structure model rather than a projection method. With the RDML method, raw data residuals can be defined in terms of subject data vector's contribution to the likelihood ratio test statistic, viz. as

$$c_i = (y_i - \mu(\gamma))'\Sigma(\gamma)^{-1}(\gamma_i - \mu(\gamma)), \tag{15}$$

where $\Sigma(\gamma)$ is the model-implied covariance matrix, in practice taken at the solution point for γ (fit function minimizer), and similarly $\mu(\gamma)$ is the model-implied mean vector, practically taken at that point as well.[2] For ease of reference, we call the indexes defined in Eq. (15) *RDML residuals*.

The RDML residuals have been shown to be quite useful in examining individual subject contributions to the overall chi-square fit index (e.g., Neale, 1997; Reise & Widaman, 1999). At the same time, it is noted that they are identical, for

---

[2]Equation (15) covers the case of no missing values for the ith subject ($i = 1, ..., N$). With missing values, $\Sigma(\gamma)$ in Eq. (15) is modified by deleting those of its rows and columns that correspond to the variables on which values are missing for the ith subject (for details, see Arbuckle, 1996), and the logarithm of its determinant is added to the right-hand side of Eq. (15) ($i = 1, ..., N$). This modification does not invalidate the present argument in the main text.

each studied person, across all members of a set of equivalent mean structure models. This identity follows from the fact that they are defined only in terms of (a) the raw data vector y_i ($i = 1, ..., N$), and (b) the model-implied first- and second-order moments, viz. the elements of $\Sigma(\gamma)$ and $\mu(\gamma)$ at the solution point. However, all constituents of the right-hand side of Eq. (15), mentioned in (a) and (b) are identical across all members of a considered set of equivalent mean structure models. Hence, for each subject, the RDML residuals in Eq. (15) are the same for any member of that set.

Furthermore, use of the RDML residuals is strictly justified only with multi-normal data, because they capitalize on the specific form of the likelihood ratio test statistic (see Eq. [15]). In contrast, the ICR definition in Eq. (13) or (14) does not make any assumptions regarding the observed variable distributions. Moreover, although the RDML residual confounds into a single number the discrepancies between individual data point and model across all studied variables (dimensions), the ICR keeps these discrepancies separate and thus provides a more complete picture of the distance of a personal data point to the accounted for part of a fitted model.

INDIVIDUAL RESIDUALS AND EQUIVALENT STRUCTURAL EQUATION MODELS

The following statement proved in Appendix 1 shows an important limitation of the ICR in Eq. (13) or (14) for purposes of differentiation between equivalent models in the case of full-rank factor loading matrices.

Proposition 2

Any pair of equivalent models with full-rank factor loading matrices that have identical column spaces and less latent than observed variables are associated with identical ICR for the same subjects.

Proposition 2 also implies that the observational (Bartlett-based) residuals by Bollen and Arminger (1991) cannot be used to discern among such equivalent models because, being a special case of the ICR, their residuals are identical for the same subject across the models. This model class encompasses many equivalent models resulting from one another via applications of the replacement rule or Stelzl's (1986) rules. We stress that Proposition 2 does not require identity of the error covariance matrices or the factor loading matrices in considered equivalent models—it only assumes identity of the spaces spanned by the columns of these loading matrices (and that they have full rank). Thus, Proposition 2 covers a large class of LISREL models of possible interest in behavioral and social research. As a byproduct of Proposition 2, we obtain the following relationship.

Corollary

For equivalent models $M_1 \sim M_2$ with full-rank factor loading matrices Λ_1 and Λ_2 having identical column spaces (and less latent than observed variables) and identical error covariance matrices $\Theta_{\varepsilon 1} = \Theta_{\varepsilon 2} = \Theta$ say,

$$\Lambda_1(\Lambda_1'\Theta^{-1}\Lambda_1)^{-1}\Lambda_1'\Theta^{-1} = \Lambda_2(\Lambda_2'\Theta^{-1}\Lambda_2)^{-1}\Lambda_2'\Theta^{-1} \text{ and}$$

$$A_1(A_1'\Theta^{-1}A_1)^{-1}A_1'\Theta^{-1} = A_2(A_2'\Theta^{-1}A_2)^{-1}A_2'\Theta^{-1}. \qquad (16)$$

The validity of Eq. (16) follows from the fact that each of its sides is used to define the pertinent model ICR as projections of the same data points on identical spaces, $R(A_1) = R(A_2) = R(\Lambda_1) = R(\Lambda_2)$ (see Lemma 1), employing the common error covariance matrix Θ as a weight matrix. Because these residuals are then identical due to Proposition 2, simple algebra on their definition Eqs. (13) and (14) yields Eq. (16).

Furthermore, the proof of Proposition 2 in Appendix 1 demonstrates in Eq. (A1.7) another representation of the ICR for a given structural equation model with a full-rank matrix A (and less latent than observed variables):

$$r_i^\Theta = [I_p - A(A'\Sigma^{-1}A)^{-1}A'\Sigma^{-1}]y_i \quad (i = 1, \ldots, N). \qquad (17)$$

We thereby note that in Eq. (17) the matrix Σ remains the same regardless of which member of a set of equivalent models is focused on, whereas the matrices Λ, B, Ψ, and Θ generally differ across the set (and at the same time $A\Psi A' + \Theta = \Sigma$ is unchanged; see Eq. [12] and earlier discussion on different classes of equivalent models).

EXTENDED INDIVIDUAL
CASE RESIDUALS

The preceding discussion indicates instances of lack of discernibility between equivalent models at the individual fit level using the ICR in Eq. (13) or (14). Thereby, we noted that the class of models covered by Proposition 2 is very wide (e.g., contains those models with less latent than observed variables and identical full-rank factor loading matrices, on which the popular replacement rule by Lee & Hershberger [1990] is applicable). That is, for very many models of interest in practice (e.g., MacCallum et al., 1993), between which a social or behavioral researcher is typically interested in differentiating, the ICR are not helpful because they are identical for the same subjects in all models. This result provides another illustration of the great difficulty in managing the equivalent models problem in SEM. In addition to lack of discernibility at the overall fit level, which has been well known for many years, Proposition 2 is indicating many interesting cases where equivalent models are not discernible at the subject fit level using the ICR.

Notwithstanding this finding, however, we would like to suggest that a modified definition of ICR yields in general different indices of subject fit for certain equivalent models. These are the extended individual case residuals (EICR) that result after a rescaling of the coordinate system whose axes represent the components of the individual residuals and subsequent application of the general projection approach used thus far. The rescaling is specific to a considered structural equation model M (with less latent than observed variables) and has the goal of highlighting the discrepancy between M and the analyzed raw data y. To this end, the rescaling is carried out using the error covariance matrix Θ of M (assumed positive define throughout this chapter)—that is, the coordinate axes are adjusted to account for the interrelationships between the unexplained terms of M, viz. its errors, as reflected in its error covariance matrix. That is, in the rescaled data space projected are the raw data that are then $\Theta^{-1/2}y$, where $\Theta^{-1/2}$ is the inverse of the square root of Θ ($\Theta^{-1/2}y$ represents the original individual raw data point after the rescaling of the space). By using $\Theta^{-1/2}$ rather than Θ^{-1}, this adjustment conforms to the raw data metric in which it is carried out. (The error covariance matrix contains second-order moments of the error terms, which suggests as necessary for this purpose to use the square root of the matrix.) The space on which the point $\Theta^{-1/2}y$ is projected is then correspondingly spanned by the columns of $\Theta^{-1/2}$ A—that is, $R(\Theta^{-1/2}A)$—due to the carried out rescaling, where A is the factor loading matrix of M or its reduced form (see Eqs. [5] and [7]).

If all columns of A are linearly independent (i.e., A is of full rank) after this rescaling, the orthogonal projection matrix of interest here is:

$$^{\Theta}P_A = \Theta^{-1/2}A(A'\Theta^{-1}A)^{-1}A'\Theta^{-1/2}. \tag{18}$$

The matrix $^{\Theta}P_A$ is obtained from the standard formula $X(X'X)^{-1}X'$ for orthogonal projection on $R(X)$ for a given matrix X (e.g., Christensen, 1989), whereby $\Theta^{-1/2}$ A is substituted for X according to the prior discussion. Therefore, for the ith subject raw data point, its projection on the space $R(\Theta^{-1/2}$ A) of interest is

$$v^{\Theta}_i = {}^{\Theta}P_A(\Theta^{-1/2}y_i) \tag{19}$$
$$= \Theta^{-1/2}A(A'\Theta^{-1}A)^{-1}A'\Theta^{-1/2}(\Theta^{-1/2}y_i)$$
$$= \Theta^{-1/2}A(A'\Theta^{-1}A)^{-1}A'\Theta^{-1}y_i,$$

$i = 1,...,N$. Thus, the projection result, v^{Θ}_i, has the property that it represents the unique point of $R(\Theta^{-1/2}$ A), which is closest to the raw data point $\Theta^{-1/2}y_i$ in the

Euclidean (unweighted) distance between $\Theta^{-1/2}y_i$ and $R(\Theta^{-1/2}A)$, $i = 1,\ldots,N$ (e.g., Seber, 1977).

If the columns of A are not linearly independent (i.e., A is not of full rank, and hence the ordinary inverse $[A'\Theta^{-1}A]^{-1}$ does not exist), then the projection matrix of concern here is

$$^{\Theta}P_A = \Theta^{-1/2}A(A'\Theta^{-1}A)^-A'\Theta^{-1/2}, \tag{20}$$

where $(A'\Theta^{-1}A)^-$ is a generalized inverse of $A'\Theta^{-1}A$. Again, we can take this generalized inverse to be the unique (and always existing) Moore–Penrose inverse (Christensen, 1989). This justifies use of the same symbol $^{\Theta}P_A$, regardless of the rank of A, in Eqs. (18), (19), and (20).

Thus, the proposed EICR are defined as

$$h_i^{\Theta} = (\Theta^{-1/2}y_i) - v_i^{\Theta} = \Theta^{-1/2}y_i - {}^{\Theta}P_A(\Theta^{-1/2}y_i) \tag{21}$$
$$= \Theta^{-1/2}[I_p - A(A'\Theta^{-1}A)^-A'\Theta^{-1}]y_i,$$

$i = 1,\ldots,N$). A simplified expression for the EICR is arrived at using the following auxiliary statement demonstrated in Appendix 1.

Lemma 2

If D and F are equal-size matrices with identical column spaces and K is a nonsingular matrix that is multiplication-conform with them, then the column spaces of KD and KF are also identical.

To obtain the simplified expression for the EICR, Lemma 1 ensured before that the column spaces of the matrices A and Λ are identical. Then Lemma 2 implies that the column spaces of $\Theta^{-1/2}A$ and $\Theta^{-1/2}\Lambda$ are identical too—that is, $R(\Theta^{-1/2}A) = R(\Theta^{-1/2}\Lambda)$. (Because Θ is assumed throughout positive definite, $\Theta^{-1/2}$ is nonsingular as well.) Therefore, projecting the data point $\Theta^{-1/2}y$ on $R(\Theta^{-1/2}A)$ is the same as projecting the point on the identical space $R(\Theta^{-1/2}\Lambda)$. Hence, the individual residuals obtained either way are identical because they, by definition, are the differences between the (same) point being projected and its (identical) projection. That is, the EICR are also defined as

$$h_i^{\Theta} = \Theta^{-1/2}[I_p - \Lambda(\Lambda'\Theta^{-1}\Lambda)^-\Lambda'\Theta^{-1}]y_i. \tag{22}$$

Equation (22) shows a direct relationship between the EICR and the ICR defined in Eq. (13):

$$h_i^{\Theta} = \Theta^{-1/2}r_i \quad (i = 1,\ldots,N). \tag{23}$$

Differences in Extended Individual Case Residuals for the Same Subjects

The next statement points out cases of equivalent models where the EICR in Eq. (21) or (22) can differ for the same subject across the models.

Proposition 3. A pair of equivalent models having full-rank factor loading matrices with identical column spaces (and less latent than observed variables) are in general associated with different EICR for the same subject.

The validity of the statement is implied from Proposition 2 and Eq. (23) relating the ICR in Eq. (13) to the EICR in Eq. (22). Indeed, the premises of Proposition 3 ensure that the ICR for the same subject are identical across the models due to Proposition 2. Hence, according to Eq. (23), the EICR result after identical ICR are multiplied by the model-specific error covariance matrix that may or may not be identical across the models (see discussion on different classes of equivalent models in an earlier section). Specifically, for equivalent models with full-rank factor loading matrices having identical column spaces as well as identical error covariance matrices, both their ICR and EICR are identical for each subject. Alternatively, these types of equivalent models with differing error covariance matrices, $\Theta_{\varepsilon 1} \neq \Theta_{\varepsilon 2}$, are generally associated with different EICR for the same person because, due to Eq. (23), their EICR result after premultiplying identical ICR with different matrices, $\Theta_{\varepsilon 1}$ and $\Theta_{\varepsilon 2}$, respectively. An example of such equivalent models in presented in Raykov and Penev (1999, Fig. 7) and was discussed earlier in this chapter; for completeness of this discussion, the models are reproduced in Fig. 11.1 as well.

Within the set of models with full-rank factor loading matrices having identical column spaces, this class of equivalent models associated with generally different EICR for the same subject also contains the following pairs of equivalent models. They have two latent variables measured by the same number $k \geq 2$ of tau-equivalent tests (Jöreskog, 1971) and are obtained from one another in the same way as model M2 is obtained from M1 in Fig. 11.1 (i.e., by exchanging the latent covariance in one of them with equal covariances between the corresponding indicator errors for each factor in the other model—viz., 1st and $k + 1^{st}$, 1st and $k + 2^{nd}$, ..., 1st and $2k$th indicator errors; 2nd and $k + 1^{st}$, 2nd and $k + 2^{nd}$, ..., 2nd and $2k$th indicator errors, ..., kth and $k + 1^{st}$, kth and $k + 2^{nd}$, ..., kth and $2k$th indicator errors). Further members of this class of equivalent models with generally differing ICR for the same subject are those having two of their independent latent variables measured with the same number of tau-equivalent tests and being identical in all other aspects, except obtained from one another in the same way M2 is from M1 (see Fig. 11.1).

Whereas the EICR for the same subject differ in general across equivalent models in this class, the following statement holds true and is demonstrated in Appendix 1. It shows yet another aspect in which equivalent models are associated with identical fit-related quantities beyond the overall fit indexes.

Proposition 4. For each subject, the sum of squares of the components of their extended individual case residuals h_i^Θ $(i = 1, ..., N)$ is invariant across two equivalent models M_1 and M_2, with full-rank factor loading matrices having identical column spaces (and less latent than observed variables).

Thus, the Euclidean norm (sum of squares of components) of the EICR cannot be used to differentiate between these equivalent models. Hence, the sum of these norms of all EICR across the studied group of persons (cases) cannot be used for this purpose either.

DISCUSSION AND CONCLUSION

The aim of this chapter was to discuss a general method of constructing individual case residuals for structural equation models and to address issues pertaining to their possible utility for differentiation between some equivalent models. The described individual level residuals, the ICR and EICR defined in Eqs. (13) and (22), capitalize on projection of raw data on model-specific generated spaces. These residuals exist and are unique for any structural equation model with more observed than latent variables. The ICR and EICR quantify, in the metric induced by the error covariance matrix, the distance between any subject's raw data vector to its closest point in the subspace generated by the accounted for part of the model. As such distances, the outlined individual level residuals appear to be useful in modeling-related analytic activities for which subject's data discrepancy from model-generated manifolds is of substantive importance, as demonstrated by Bollen and Arminger (1991) for a special case of the ICR in Eq. (13).

Utility of Individual Case Residuals

The described individual level residuals in this chapter represent a generalization and an extension of Bollen and Arminger's (1991) observational (Bartlett-based) residuals, and thus are more generally applicable. The present residuals can be used for (a) evaluation of subject level fit to the raw data, as opposed to indexes of overall model fit to the sample covariance matrix (and possibly means); and (b) possible formal differentiation between some equivalent models via the extended individual residuals. These beneficial features of the EICR in Eq. (22) stem from their definition as projection of subject's data point in such a way that highlights discrepancies between the sample covariance matrix and the part of the model explained by its latent factors, as reflected in its error covariance matrix. Like the ICR in Eq. (13) and the Bollen and Arminger observational (Bartlett-based) residuals, the EICR can be used in empirical research with normal or non-normal variable distributions.

As mentioned before, the described individual residuals in the preceding sections of this chapter may also be beneficial in the identification of multivariate outliers that have not been found so by earlier analyses, and of subjects that do not obey (even to an approximate degree) a considered model but may not have been found alternatively to exhibit aberrant characteristics. Further research is needed to establish in more detail the specific utility of these individual residuals in this regard. However, for purposes of outlier identification or subjects markedly violating a model of interest, it seems natural to consider as a possible criterion the magnitude of the absolute value of the standardized components of the ICR and/or the EICR (cf. Bollen & Arminger, 1991).

Relationship to Regression Residuals and Limitations of the Individual Case Residuals

The projection method underlying this chapter yields in its individual level residuals conceptual counterparts of the widely used residuals in regression analysis models. At the same time, the individual residuals discussed in this chapter do not represent strict analogs within the SEM framework of the regression residuals. This limitation follows from the fact that in SEM there are no recorded observations of the latent variables, and therefore it is not possible to determine exact model-based predictions for each subject. As also stressed throughout the chapter, the ICR and EICR are limited to LISREL models with more observed variables than latent factors due to their projection rationale, rather than existing for all possible structural equation models.

Another limitation of the ICR residuals discussed in this chapter is that LISREL models are best fitted with large samples (i.e., results obtained with them are most trustworthy then). Although the ICR and EICR definitions do not require explicitly large samples to be used, small samples are not likely to yield a trustworthy estimate of the empirical covariance matrix to begin with. Because the ICR and EICR depend critically on the particular fitted model and especially its estimates, and because with small samples the latter may be misleading, so can these individual level residuals be with these samples. Further research is needed to present a more informed opinion on this issue, yet for the same reason any factor that leads to a seriously biased estimate of the covariance matrix may adversely affect the present individual residuals as subject fit indicators. Hence, preliminary explorative work on variable distributions and in particular outliers may well enhance the utility and amount of trustworthy information contained in the present individual residuals when obtained subsequently.

Discerning Between Equivalent Models Using Individual Case Residuals

The proposed EICR in Eq. (22) were shown to potentially differ, for the same subject, across pairs of equivalent models. The class of such models contains equivalent models having full-rank factor loading matrices with identical column spaces, less latent than observed variables, and different error covariance matrices. This class does not cover models obtained from one another using the replacement rule or Stelzl's rules (1986), but consists of other important models for social and behavioral research.

Given the unquestioned complexity and difficulty of the problem of equivalent models, presently we have no information on whether there may be other classes of equivalent models for which the EICR or other related individual level residuals may differ in general or be identical for the same subjects. Similarly, we have no information as to whether there may be other classes of equivalent models for which the ICR defined in Eq. (13) are different, or identical, for the same subjects. Like the earlier raised issues pertaining to subject level fit in SEM, we do encourage further research in this area of the study of equivalent models. It is our view that (a) the differentiation between equivalent models, and in this regard the development of statistical means to aid it, is of major help to behavioral and social scientists in managing the consequential and difficult problem of equivalent models (e.g., Breckler, 1990; MacCallum et al., 1993); and (b) indexes of raw data level fit are informative for evaluation of fit of structural equation models, in addition to the overall goodness-of-fit measures such as the chi-square value and related fit indexes, including the covariance residuals.

The class of equivalent models with full-rank factor loading matrices having identical column spaces and differing error covariance matrices, for the members of which there are in general differences in the EICR, covers important models for behavioral and social research. This is because error covariances may be resulting from important omitted variables. With the EICR, the present chapter suggests a method that may help differentiate between such models, and hence appears to present a promising tool in examining some issues pertaining to model misspecification as well.

Although this chapter has shown that within a certain class of equivalent models the EICR generally differ for the same subject across the models, it is as yet unclear what an optimal way may be of utilizing such differences for purposes of selection between these models. Further research will hopefully inform the development of such ways. In this regard, it appears that the standardized EICR components mentioned before may offer a promising option. For example, if one of the considered equivalent models is associated with an inordinate number of excessive standardized EICR on a number of dimensions, unlike other models, one may consider ruling out the former model on grounds of substantial inconsistency with the analyzed data set. Such a decision, however, may be overruled by substantive considerations if they indicate that model as a viable candidate means of data description and explanation.

Individual Case Residuals and the "True" Model

The individual level residuals of this chapter, the EICR and/or ICR, do not necessarily have the potential of finding out the "true" model that has generated the analyzed data, whichever that model may be. This is because the residuals do not contain sufficient information that can help to identify that model based on only a sample of data. Similarly, the individual residuals do not contain sufficient information that may indicate for one or more equivalent models specific relationships to the true model. The discussion of individual residuals with the SEM framework in this chapter was only meant to suggest additional indexes of fit of considered models, which operate at the individual subject level and inform about model proximity to the raw data. In our view, in addition to substantive considerations, these indexes may be helpful in the process of ruling out one or more members of an appropriate set of equivalent models as a means of data description and explanation. In those cases, the behavioral or social researcher may be in a position to decrease the number of competing equivalent models as equally plausible means for this purpose. In this possibility to contribute to ruling out some equivalent models as candidate means of a studied phenomenon explanation, we see the potential of the individual residuals of Eq. (13) and particularly Eq. (23) to help researchers as an adjunct to substantive theories and considerations, or such of underlying design and/or temporal sequence features, in the complex and at times controversial process of model selection in the social and behavioral sciences.

APPENDIX 1: PROOFS OF LEMMA 1 AND LEMMA 2, AND PROPOSITIONS 2 AND 4

Proof of Lemma 1

We show that the null spaces of C and CK are identical, from which it follows that the spaces spanned by their columns are identical as well (e.g., Graybill, 1983; see also introductory section of this chapter). To prove that $N(C) = N(CK)$, we demonstrate that either null space is contained in the other. Indeed, if x is from $N(C)$, $x'C = 0$ holds by definition, then $x'CK = 0$ is true as well (i.e., x is from $N[CK]$ too). Conversely, if z is from $N(CK)$ then $z'CK = 0$ by definition. Because K was assumed nonsingular, it follows that $z'C = 0$ as well (i.e., z is from $N[C]$ too). Hence, $N(C) = N(CK)$. Therefore, $R(C) = R(CK)$.

Proof of Lemma 2

Let x be from $R(KD)$. Thus, x is a linear combination of the columns of KD (i.e., $x = KDz$, where z has as its elements the weights of that combination). Because K is nonsingular, it follows that $K^{-1}x = Dz$ (i.e., $K^{-1}x$ is a linear combination of the columns of D), or in other words $K^{-1}x$ is from $R(D)$ that here is assumed identical to $R(F)$. Thus, $K^{-1}x$ is a linear combination of the columns of F too (i.e., $K^{-1}x = Fv$), or in other words $x = KFv$. The last means that x is also from $R(KF)$. This shows that any element of $R(KD)$ is an element of $R(KF)$ as well. In the same way, one shows the reverse, viz., that any element of $R(KF)$ is also an element of $R(KD)$, which with the immediately preceding statement implies that $R(KD) = R(KF)$.

Proof of Proposition 2

Denote by Φ_1 and Φ_2 the covariance matrices of the latent factors comprised in η_1 and η_2, respectively, in the measurement parts of two corresponding equivalent LISREL models $M_1 \sim M_2$ (see Eqs. [10] and [11]). Then given the earlier assumption of positive definite covariance matrices (i.e., $\Theta_{\varepsilon 1} > 0$, $\Theta_{\varepsilon 2} > 0$, $\Phi_1 > 0$, and $\Phi_2 > 0$), it follows that $\Sigma - \Lambda_i \Phi_i \Lambda_i' = \Theta_{\varepsilon i} > 0$, $i = 1, 2$, where Σ denotes for simplicity $\Sigma(\gamma)$, the common implied covariance matrix by both equivalent models (see Eq. [12]). Now use is made of the following formula (2.9) from Rao (1973, p. 33) for inverting a complex sum of matrices:

$$(A+BDB')^{-1} = A^{-1} - A^{-1}BEB'A^{-1} + A^{-1}BE(E+D)^{-1}EB'A'^{-1}, \quad (A1.1)$$

where

$$E = (B'A^{-1}B)^{-1}.[3] \quad (A1.2)$$

When the substitution

$$A = \Sigma, B = \Lambda_i, \text{ and } D = -\Phi_i \quad (A1.3)$$

is made in (A1.1), the latter implies (for $i = 1$ and 2)

$$\Theta_{\varepsilon i}^{-1} = \Sigma^{-1} - \Sigma^{-1}\Lambda_i(\Lambda_i'\Sigma^{-1}\Lambda_i)^{-1}\Lambda_i'\Sigma^{-1} + \quad (A1.4)$$
$$+ \Sigma^{-1}\Lambda_i(\Lambda_i'\Sigma^{-1}\Lambda_i)^{-1}(\Lambda_i'\Sigma^{-1}\Lambda_i - \Phi_i)^{-1}(\Lambda_i'\Sigma^{-1}\Lambda_i)^{-1}\Lambda_i'\Sigma^{-1}.$$

Multiplying both sides of Eq. (A1.4) from the left by Λ_i' and from the right by Λ_i, we obtain after cancellations

$$\Lambda_i' \Theta_{\varepsilon i}^{-1}\Lambda_i = (\Lambda_i' \Sigma^{-1}\Lambda_i - \Phi_i)^{-1}, \quad (A1.5)$$

that is,

$$(\Lambda_i' \Theta_{\varepsilon i}^{-1}\Lambda_i) = \Lambda_i'\Sigma^{-1}\Lambda_i - \Phi_i. \quad (A1.6)$$

Then the pertinent projection matrix, after direct substitutions and simplifications, is obtained as (see Eqs. [A1.4] and [A1.6]):

$$P_i = \Lambda_i(\Lambda_i' \Theta_{\varepsilon i}^{-1}\Lambda_i)^{-1}\Lambda_i'\Theta_{\varepsilon i}^{-1} = \Lambda_i(\Lambda_i'\Sigma^{-1}\Lambda_i)^{-1}\Lambda_i'\Sigma^{-1}. \quad (A1.7)$$

---

[3] The last appearance of the matrix B in the right-hand side of Eq. (A.1.1) should be B', as in this chapter, rather than as untransposed B like in the cited formula 2.9 on p. 33 of Rao (1973) where there is a typographical error.

(Cancellation details pertaining to the derivations of Eqs. [A1.5] and [A1.7] can be obtained from the authors on request.)

Equation (A1.7) implies that, to obtain the ICR in Eq. (13) for either model, M_1 or M_2, one uses the procedure of weighted least squares (e.g., Bollen & Arminger, 1991) with the same weighting matrix, viz. Σ. Thereby, one in fact projects on the same subspace, $R(\Lambda_1) = R(\Lambda_2)$, because their identity was assumed (as a condition of Proposition 2). Thus, the results of these identical projections coincide, and hence for every subject the ICR with model M_1 is identical to his or her ICR with model M_2.

Proof of Proposition 4

From Proposition 1 and the proof of Proposition 2—particularly Eq. (A1.7)—follows that $A_1(A_1'\Sigma^{-1}A_1)^{-1}A_1'\Sigma^{-1} = A_2(A_2'\Sigma^{-1}A_2)^{-1}A_2'\Sigma^{-1} = P_\Sigma$ say. Under the premises of the present proposition, in the same way as that of deriving Eq. (A1.7), we obtain $P_\Sigma = A_1(A_1'\Theta_{\varepsilon1}^{-1}A_1)^{-1}A_1'\Theta_{\varepsilon1}^{-1} = A_2(A_2'\Theta_{\varepsilon2}^{-1}A_2)^{-1}A_2'\Theta_{\varepsilon2}^{-1}$.

Now for a specific observation vector y from R^p, let $h_1^{\Theta_{\varepsilon1}}$ and $h_2^{\Theta_{\varepsilon2}}$ be its EICR (defined in Eq. [23]) with regard to two equivalent models, M_1 and M_2, respectively. Then for the squared Euclidean norm of these residuals, we have

$$\|h_i^{\Theta_{\varepsilon i}}\|^2 = (Y - P_\Sigma Y)'\, \Theta_{\varepsilon i}^{-1}(Y - P_\Sigma Y) \tag{A1.8}$$

$$= Y'[\Theta_{\varepsilon i}^{-1} - P_\Sigma'\Theta_{\varepsilon i}^{-1} - \Theta_{\varepsilon i}^{-1}P_\Sigma + P_\Sigma'\Theta_{\varepsilon i}^{-1}P_\Sigma]Y \qquad (i = 1, 2).$$

Note that the matrix P_Σ is not symmetric, but $\Theta_{\varepsilon1}^{-1}P_\Sigma$ is symmetric (see first paragraph of this proof; i.e., $P_\Sigma'\Theta_{\varepsilon1}^{-1} = \Theta_{\varepsilon1}^{-1}P_\Sigma$). Writing out the matrix $P_\Sigma'\Theta_{\varepsilon1}^{-1}P_\Sigma$ and carrying out resulting cancellations shows that $P_\Sigma'\Theta_{\varepsilon1}^{-1}P_\Sigma = \Theta_{\varepsilon1}^{-1}P_\Sigma$. Hence, the right-hand side of Eq. (A1.8) simplifies for M_1 to

$$\|h_1^{\Theta_{\varepsilon1}}\|^2 = Y'[\Theta_{\varepsilon1}^{-1} - \Theta_{\varepsilon1}^{-1}P_\Sigma]Y. \tag{A1.9}$$

Using Eq. (A1.4) for $\Theta_{\varepsilon1}^{-1}$, Eq. (A1.9) yields after cancellations

$$\|h_1^{\Theta_{\varepsilon1}}\|^2 = Y'[\Sigma^{-1} - \Sigma^{-1}A_1(A_1'\Sigma^{-1}A_1)^{-1}A_1'\Sigma^{-1}]Y. \tag{A1.10}$$

We note that the right-hand side of Eq. (A1.10) does not depend on $\Theta_{\varepsilon1}$. In exactly the same way, we obtain for $\|h_2^{\Theta_{\varepsilon2}}\|^2$ the following expression

$$\|h_2^{\Theta_{\varepsilon2}}\|^2 = Y'[\Sigma^{-1} - \Sigma^{-1}A_2(A_2'\Sigma^{-1}A_2)^{-1}A_2'\Sigma^{-1}]Y.$$

For the case $R(A_1) = R(A_2)$ of identical spanned spaces that we are dealing with in this proposition, the last two equalities imply

$$\|h_1^{\Theta \varepsilon 1}\|^2 = \|h_2^{\Theta \varepsilon 2}\|^2 = Y'[\Sigma^{-1} - \Sigma^{-1}P_\Sigma]Y \qquad (A1.12)$$

because P_Σ is the projection matrix on identical spaces.

APPENDIX 2: SAS SOURCE CODE FOR OBTAINING THE INDIVIDUAL CASE RESIDUAL (ICR) AND EXTENDED INDIVIDUAL CASE RESIDUAL (EICR) ESTIMATES FOR MODELS M1 AND M2 (SEE FIG. 11.1)

```
DATA EICR;
INFILE 'FILE_NAME'; * GIVE NAME OF FILE WITH RAW DATA;
INPUT Y1 Y2 Y3 Y4;
PROC IML;
USE ICR VAR {Y1 Y2 Y3 Y4};
READ ALL VAR _NUM_ INTO Y_1;
Y = Y_1';
THETA1 = {.321 0 0 0, 0 .313 0 0, 0 0 .312 0, 0 0 0 0.297};
* THESE AND NEXT NUMBERS ARE THE ESTIMATES OF;
* THE ERROR COVARIANCE MATRIX OF MODELS M1 AND M2.;
* THAT ARE OBTAINED USING A SEM PROGRAM, ON 'FILE-NAME';
THETA2 = {.321 0 .109 .109, 0 .313 .109 .109, .109 .109
.312 0, .109 .109 0 .297};
LAMBDA1 = {1 0, 1 0, 0 1, 0 1}; * SEE FIGURE 1;
LAMBDA2 = LAMBDA1;
N = NROW(Y);
TH1_INV = INV (THETA1);
TH2_INV = INV (THETA2);
CALL EIGEN (VAL, VECT, TH1_INV);
VAL = SQRT (VAL);
TH1P12 = VECT*DIAG (VAL)*VECT'; * THIS IS THETA1 TO -1/2;
CALL EIGEN (VAL, VECT, TH2_INV);
VAL = SQRT (VAL);
TH2P12 = VECT*DIAG (VAL)*VECT'; * THIS IS THETA2 TO -1/2;
MATRIX1 = I(N) - LAMBDA1*INV (LAMBDA1' *TH1_INV* LAMBDA1)*
LAMBDA1'*TH1_INV;
```

MATRIX2 = I(N) – LAMBDA2*INV (LAMBDA2' *TH2_INV* LAMBDA2)*
LAMBDA2'*TH2_INV;
ICR1 = (MATRIX1* Y)'; * THESE ARE (13) FOR MODEL M1;
ICR2 = (MATRIX2* Y)'; * THESE ARE (13) FOR MODEL M2;
EICR1 = (TH1P12*MATRIX1*Y)'; * THESE ARE (23) FOR MODEL M1;
EICR2 = (TH2P12*MATRIX2*Y)'; * THESE ARE (23) FOR MODEL M2;
FILE 'EICRM1.OUT'; * GIVE NAME OF FILE OF EICR FOR M1;
DO I = 1 TO NROW (EICR1);
DO J = 1 TO N;
PUT (EICR1[I,J]) + 2 @;
END; PUT; END; CLOSEFILE 'EICRM1.OUT'; * GIVE SAME FILE NAME;
FILE 'EICRM2.OUT'; * GIVE NAME OF FILE OF EICR FOR M2;
DO I = 1 TO NROW (EICR2);
DO J = 1 TO N;
PUT (EICR2[I,J]) + 2 @;
END; PUT; END; CLOSEFILE 'EICRM2.OUT' * GIVE SAME FILE NAME;
QUIT;

Note. For other equivalent models, corresponding changes in the number of matrix rows and columns, as well as columns of the raw data file, are in general needed.

ACKNOWLEDGEMENT

This research was partly supported by a faculty fellowship grant to T. Raykov from Fordham University. We are grateful to G. A. Marcoulides, M. C. Neale, G. Qian, and S. Reise for valuable discussions on issues raised in this chapter.

REFERENCES

Arbuckle, J. L. (1996). Full information estimation in the presence of incomplete data. In G. A. Marcoulides & R. E. Schumacker (Eds.), *Advanced structural equation modeling. Issues and techniques* (pp. 243–277). Mahwah, NJ: Lawrence Erlbaum Associates.

Arbuckle, J. L. (1997). *AMOS 3. User's guide manual.* Chicago, IL: Smallwaters.

Bentler, P. M. (1995). *EQS structural equation program manual.* Encino, CA: Mutivariate Software.

Bollen, K. A. (1989). *Structural equations with latent variables.* New York: Wiley.

Bollen, K. A., & Arminger, G. (1991). Observational residuals in factor analysis and structural equation models. In P. V. Marsden (Ed.), *Sociological methodology* (pp. 235–262). San Francisco, CA: Jossey-Bass.

Breckler, S. (1990). Applications of covariance structure modeling in psychology: Cause for concern? *Psychological Bulletin, 107,* 260–273.

Browne, M. W., & Cudeck, R. (1993). Alternative ways of assessing model fit. In K. A. Bollen & J. S. Long (Eds.), *Testing structural equation models* (pp. 132–162). Beverly Hills, CA: Sage.

Browne, M. W., & Mels, G. (1994). *RAMONA PC user's guide.* Columbus, OH: Ohio State University.

Christensen, R. (1989). *Plane answers to complex questions. The theory of linear models.* New York: Springer.

Graybill, F. A. (1983). *Matrices with applications in statistics.* Belmont, CA: Wadsworth.

Grayson, D. A., & Marsh, H. W. (1994). Identification with deficient rank loading matrices in confirmatory factor analysis: Multitrait-multimethod models. *Psychometrika, 59,* 1, 121–134.

Hayduk, L. A. (1996). *LISREL issues, debates, and strategies.* Baltimore, MD: Johns Hopkins University Press.

Hershberger, S. L. (1994). The specification of equivalent models before the collection of data. In A. von Eye & C. C. Clogg (Eds.), *Latent variables analysis* (pp. 68–108). Thousand Oaks, CA: Sage.

Hopper, J. L., & Mathews, J. D. (1983). Estensions to multivariate normal models for pedigree analysis: II. Modeling the effect of shared environments in the analysis of variation in blood lead levels. *American Journal of Epidemiology, 117,* 334–335.

Jöreskog, K. G. (1971). Statistical analysis of sets of congeneric tests. *Psychometrika, 36,* 109–133.

Jöreskog, K. G., & Sörböm, D. (1988). *LISREL 7: A guide to the program and its applications.* Chicago, IL: SPSS.

Jöreskog, K. G., & Sörböm, D. (1996). *LISREL 8: User's guide.* Chicago, IL: Scientific Software.

Lange, K., Westlake, J., & Spence, M. (1976). Extensions of pedigree analysis: III. Variance components by the scoring method. *Annals of Human Genetics, 39,* 486–491.

Lee, S., & Hershberger, S. (1990). A simple rule for generating equivalent models in covariance structure modeling. *Multivariate Behavioral Research, 25,* 313–334.

Luijben, T. C. W. (1991). Equivalent models in covariance structure analysis. *Psychometrika, 56,* 653–665.

MacCallum, R. C., Wegener, D. T., Uchino, B. N., & Fabrigar, L. R. (1993). The problem of equivalent models in applications of covariance structure analysis. *Psychological Bulletin, 114,* 185–199.

McDonald, R. P. (1997). Haldane's lungs: A case study in path analysis. *Multivariate Behavioral Research, 32,* 1–38.

McDonald, R. P., & Bolt, D. M. (1998). The determinacy of variables in structural equation models. *Multivariate Behavioral Research, 33,* 385–402.

Neale, M. C. (1997). *Mx. Statistical modeling.* Richmond, VA: Department of Psychiatry, Virginia Commonwealth University.

Neter, J., Kutner, M. H., Nachsheim, C. J., & Wasserman, W. (1996). *Applied linear statistical models.* Chicago, IL: Irwin.

Rao, C. R. (1973). *Linear statistical inference and its applications.* New York: Wiley.

Raykov, T. (1997). Equivalent structural equation models and group equality constraints. *Multivariate Behavioral Research, 32,* 95–104.

Raykov, T., & Marcoulides, G. (in press). Can there be infinitely many models equivalent to a given structural equation model? *Structural Equation Modeling, 8,* 142–149.

Raykov, T., & Penev, S. (1999). On structural equation model equivalence. *Multivariate Behavioral Research, 34,* 199–244.

Reise, S. P., & Widaman, K. F. (1999). Assessing the fit of measurement models at the individual level: A comparison of item response theory and covariance structure approaches. *Psychological Methods, 4,* 3–21.

SAS Institute. (1992). *SAS/STAT user's guide.* Cary, NC: Author.

Seber, G. A. F. (1977). *Linear regression analysis.* New York: Wiley.

Steiger, J. H. (1999). *SEPATH program manual.* Tulsa, OK: StatSoft.

Stelzl, I. (1986). Changing a causal hypothesis without changing the fit: Some rules for generating equivalent path models. *Multivariate Behavioral Research, 21,* 309–331.

Williams, L. J., Bozdogan, H., & Aiman-Smith, L. (1996). Inference problems with equivalent models. In G. A. Marcoulides & R. E. Schumacker (Eds.), *Advanced structural equation modeling. Issues and techniques* (pp. 279–314). Mahwah, NJ: Lawrence Erlbaum Associates.

Author Index

F

Fabrigar, L.R., 297, 298, 303, 309, 315, *321*
Fang, K.T., 48, 51, *54*
Farrington, D.P., 191, *199*
Fava, J.L., 279, *296*
Ferguson, A., 93, 97, *126*
Ferguson, G.A., 281, *294*
Finch, J.F., 44, *54*, 271, *296*
Fisher, R.A, 90, *125*
Fleming, J.S., 270, *294*
Foerster, F., 204, 219, *244*
Formann, A.K., 10, *32*
Fornell, C., 141, *156*
Fotiu, R., 103, *125*
Fox, B.L., *243*
Fox, L., 204, 206, *244*
Francis, D., 22, 30, *33*
Furby, L., 204, 219, 234, *244*

G

Gamerman, D., 140, *156*, 204, *244*
Gardner, R.C., 35, *56*
Geisser, S., 143, *156*
Gelfand, A.E., 140, 143, *156*
Gelman, A., 140, *156*
Geman, D., 140, *156*
Geman, S., 140, *156*
Geyer, C.J., 140, *156*
Gilbert, N.N., 204, *244*
Glymour, C., 247, 258, *267*, *268*
Goldberg, S., 205, *244*
Goldstein, H., 90, 92, 95, 101, *125*, *126*, 129, *156*, *157*
Goodman, L.A., 6, 10, 11, 29, *32*
Gordon, A.S., 184, *198*
Gorsuch, R.L., 272, *294*
Gottfried, A.E., 270, *294*
Gottfried, A.W., 270, *294*
Graham, J., 234, *243*
Graybill, F.A., 299, 316, *321*
Grayson, D.A., 270, 273, 280, *295*, 305, *321*
Green, P.J., 48, *55*
Greenberg, D.F., 203, *244*
Greenberg, E., *156*
Gribbous, B.C., 271, 273, *294*
Gupta, A., 130, *155*
Gustafsson, J.E., 121, *125*

H

Hall, R.J., 271, 273, 275, 276, 277, 279, 280, 281, 287, 288, 291, *294*
Hamagami, F., 94, 95, 98, *126*, 130, *157*, 174, *200*, 204, 205, 215, 219, *244*, *245*
Hanfelt, J., 8, *33*
Hannan, M., 203, 205, 206, 220, *245*
Harmer, P., 193, *199*
Hartley, H.O., 90, *125*
Harville, D.A., 92, *125*
Hau, K., 253, *267*, 270, 273, 280, *295*
Hayduk, L.A., 297, *321*
Heatherton, T.F., 270, 271, 272, 282, *294*
Heijden, P.G.M., 10, *32*
Helms, R., 219, *244*
Henry, N.W., 6, *32*
Hershberger, S.L., 97, 253, *267*, 297, 298, 303, 309, *321*
Herting, J.R., 258, *267*
Hertzberg, T., 206, *244*
Hill, P., 99, *125*
Hirano, K., 79, *86*
Hocevar, D., 270, 271, 273, 286, 291, *294*, *295*
Hoijtink, H., *157*
Holland, J.H., 249, *267*
Holland, P.W., 60, *86*
Hollis, M., 36, *55*
Hong, S., 270, 277, 278, 279, 280, 284, 289, 292, *294*
Hopper, J.L., 298, 307, *321*
Hops, H., 183, 184, *198*, *199*
Horn, J.L., 174, *198*, 204, 205, *244*
Hox, J., 89, 93, 94, 95, 99, 103, 105, *125*
Hoyle, R., 35, *55*, 104, *125*
Hu, L., 44, *55*, 186, *199*
Huckfeldt, R.R., 203, *244*

I

Ialongo, N.S., 60, 76, *86*
Imbens, G.W., 60, 61, 70, 71, 79, *86*

J

Jaccard, J., 173, 174, 176, 179, 180, 189, 191, 192, 193, *199*
Jackson, K.M., 13, *32*
Jagpal, S., 137, 144, 151, *156*
James, L.R., 253, *267*, 286, *295*

Subject Index

A

Adaptive heuristic search procedures, *see* Heuristic search
AMOS, *see* Computer programs
Analysis of Covariance, *see* ANCOVA
Analysis of Variance, *see* ANOVA
ANCOVA, 64–66, 76–77
ANOVA, 90–92
Asymptotic standard errors, *see* Standard errors

B

Balanced groups, 103–105
Bartlett-based residuals, *see* Equivalent models
Bayesian information criterion, 7, 21–22
Bayesian models, 129–171
BIC, *see* Bayesian information criterion

C

CACE, 59–82
Categorical latent variables, 1–2, 6–7
Change score model, *see* Dynamic models
Chi-square difference test, 39
Chi-square goodness-of-fit statistics, 168–170
Chromosomal coding, *see* Genetic algorithms
Chromosomes, *see* Genetic algorithms
Clustered data, *see* Multilevel models
Compliance, 57–83
Complier average causal effect, *see* CACE
Computer programs, 5–32
    AMOS, 5, 301
    EQS, 5, 301

LISCOMP, 95
LISREL, 5, 176–192, 194–198, 301
Mplus, 5–32, 66–85, 95–105
Mx, 219–221, 301
RAMONA, 301
SAS PROC MIXED, 219–221
SAS PROC NLMIXED, 234
SEPATH, 301
Conditional distributions, 152–155
Conditional independence assumption, 3
Confirmatory latent class analysis, *see* Latent class analysis
Continuous latent variables, 1–2
Covariance component models, *see* Multilevel models
Crossover, *see* Genetic algorithms

D

Difference scores, *see* Longitudinal data analysis
Disaggregated models, *see* Item parcels
DSEM, 221–225
Dual-change score structural equation model, *see* DSEM
Dynamic models, *see* Longitudinal data analysis
Dynamic systems approaches, 205–206

E

EICR, 310–314
EM algorithm, 63–66
EQS, *see* Computer programs